ENCORE

More of

Popi's

Athenian Cuisine

Happy Cooking

Tina

with love

Topi Terp

Encore

More of
Popi's
Athenian Cuisine

By

Popi Terzi

Cover, Photography, and Food Styling
by Sunday M. Christy

Encore
More of
Popi's
Athenian Cuisine

Published by Popi Terzi
16382 Woodstock Lane
Huntington Beach, CA 92647
(714) 840-8071

Manufactured in the United States of America

ISBN 0-9743857-0-0

Printed by KNI Incorporated, Anaheim, CA

Dedicated to my grandchildren
Sierra, Tyler, Kaylie, Nicole, and Kyle
"The apples of my eye"

INTRODUCTION

Sixteen years ago, I realized my lifelong dream by publishing my first cookbook, *Athenian Cuisine*. Now, at the urging of my family, friends, and students, I am proud to introduce my second cookbook, *Encore - More of Popi's Athenian Cuisine*.

This a special collection of recipes that includes my own creations along with recipes that have been in my family for generations. This beautiful cookbook will bring you all the skills necessary to easily recreate authentic Greek dishes such as avgolemono soup, dolmathes, mousaka, souvlakia, spanakopita, baklava, koulourakia, and loukomathes, along with many other favorites.

You will find many of my recipes are low in fat and cholesterol, but high in richness and taste. Just turn the pages one by one, and your taste buds will travel a tasteful and most appealing journey through Greece.

"Kali orexi!"

Popi Terzi

CONTENTS

APPETIZERS

AVOCADO WITH SHRIMP
Avocado me Yemisi Gharithas

4 avocados
8 Tbsp mayonnaise
8 Tbsp whipping cream
3 Tbsp fresh lemon juice
1 tsp Worcestershire sauce
Salt and pepper to taste
1 Tbsp minced fresh dill
1 Tbsp minced green of the scallions
1 pound cooked medium sizes shrimp
Whole leaves of lettuce

Wash and dry avocados. Cut in half, remove pit and discard. Remove flesh from avocados, place into a bowl and mash them. Save shells. Combine the rest of the ingredients except shrimp and lettuce with avocado and mix well. Save 20 shrimp and add rest to mixture, toss well. Spoon avocado mixture into avocado shells or wide-rimmed champagne glasses and decorate each with remaining shrimp. Chill. When ready to serve, place one leaf of lettuce on each plate and place avocado shell over lettuce. Serves 8.

❧❀❧

BAKED SCALLOPS WITH FETA CHEESE
Ktenia Saghanaki

1 pound scallops
1/2 cup butter, margarine or good quality olive oil
3/4 cup minced shallots
3 large garlic cloves, minced
1/2 chopped bell pepper
1 1/2 pound sliced button mushrooms
4 cups peeled, seeded and chopped fresh ripe
        tomatoes (about 3 pounds)
3 Tbsp. chopped flat leaf parsley

1/2 cup dry white wine or Vermouth
Salt and pepper to taste
12 ounces feta-cheese, cut into small chunks

Sauté shallots, garlic, bell pepper if desired and mushrooms in butter, until soft and all liquid has evaporated. Add wine, tomatoes, parsley, salt and pepper. Simmer for 40 minutes or until mixture is thick. Spoon half the mixture into 6-8 individual shells or baking dishes, and arrange (rinse and drain well) scallops in each dish. Spoon remaining mixture over scallops. Top with feta cheese. Bake in a preheated 400 F (205 C) oven for 10-15 minutes, depending on size of scallops. Serve immediately. Serve with fresh crusty bread. Serves 6-8.

❧❀❧

BAKED SHRIMP WITH FETA CHEESE
Gharithes me Feta Saghanaki

1 pound raw shrimp
1/3 cup minced onion
1/3 cup or less good quality olive oil
2 large garlic cloves or more finely minced
1/4 cup dry white wine (optional)
4 cups peeled, seeded and chopped fresh ripe
        tomatoes or can whole tomatoes, finely
        chopped liquid included
2 Tbsp. minced flat leaf parsley
Salt and pepper to taste
6-8 ounces feta cheese, cut into small chunks

Wash shrimp in lots of cold water, then peel and devein them. Sauté onion in oil until soft. Add garlic and sauté few minutes longer; don't brown garlic. Add wine if desired, tomatoes, parsley, salt and pepper. Cover and simmer for 40 minutes or until sauce is thick. Spoon half the sauce into 2-4 small individual oven dishes and arrange shrimp in each dish. Spoon remaining sauce over shrimp, and top with feta cheese. Bake in a preheated 400 F (204C) oven for 10-15 minutes. Serve immediately. Serve with fresh crusty bread. Serves 2-4.

Note: Serve baked shrimp with feta cheese over rice pilaf and salad for a special lunch.

❧❦❧

BEAN SPREAD
Fasolia Salata

2 cups boiled and drained white beans
1 Tbsp chopped parsley
2 garlic cloves, chopped
2 Tbsp chopped onion
2 Tbsp olive oil
2 Tbsp fresh lemon juice
4 pieces dried tomatoes in oil, chopped
1/3 cup or more mayonnaise

In a food processor blend all ingredients, except mayonnaise, until very smooth. Add mayonnaise and mix well to combine about 5 seconds. Chill. Serve with toasted Greek pita bread.

❧❦❧

TYROPITA WITH HAM IN A BUNDT PAN
Tyropita me Ham stin Forma

1 cup butter or margarine at room temperature
5 large eggs
1 1/2 cups flour, sifted with
5 tsp. baking powder
3/4 cup shredded Kaseri cheese
1/2 cup shredded Cheddar cheese
1/4 cup grated Parmesan cheese
1/4 shredded Swiss cheese
1/4 tsp. pepper
8 ounces boiled ham, cut into dice
1/3 cup milk

Cream butter until light. Add eggs one at a time, beating thoroughly after each addition. Add flour alternately with milk. Fold in cheeses, pepper and ham. Pour into greased tube pan. Bake in a preheated 350 F (180 C) oven for 45 minutes or

until golden brown. Cool slightly. Remove from pan and slice. Serve warm.

❧❦❧

CHEESE AND HAM TURNOVERS WITH PUFF PASTRY
Pitakia me Tyri ke Zampon se Sfoliata

1 pkg puff pastry (thawed)
4 ounces coarsely grated Gouda cheese
4 ounces grated Parmesan cheese
4 ounces coarsely grated Swiss cheese
8 ounces best-quality boiled ham, cut into
          small cubes
2 eggs, beaten
White pepper to taste
1 egg, beaten with 1 tsp water

Combine all ingredients together and mix well. Take one piece of the puff pastry at a time. Roll out pastry dough on lightly floured surface to double the size. Cut into 33/4-inch rounds; place one tsp of the filling on middle of circle. Lightly brush edges of rounds with egg, and gently fold circle into half to make a half moon shape. Pinch edges together well to seal or seal by pressing with tines of fork. Place turnovers on baking sheets lined with parchment paper. Repeat same procedure with second piece of puff pastry and filling. Brush turnovers with egg. Let stand for 5 minutes to allow egg to dry. Bake in a preheated 450 F (200 C) oven on middle rack for 20-30 minutes or until golden brown. Serve hot.

Note: Turnovers may be frozen before or after baking, as in cheese puffs (see index for preparation).

❧❦❧

CHEESE PUFF WITH HOMEMADE PASTRY
Tyropitakia me Fillo Spitiko

For the pastry:
Use 1 recipe homemade pastry for tyropitakia (see index for recipe). Follow recipe and preparation as directed in any of the pasty A or B

For the filling:
1 extra large egg
8 ounces crumbled feta or goat cheese
2 cups lightly pressed down coarsely grated Swiss, Kaseri, Cheddar or Gouda cheese
1/8 tsp pepper
1 extra large egg, beaten with 1 Tbsp of water

Prepare pastry as directed. While dough is resting prepare filling. In a bowl beat egg add cheeses and pepper, mix well to combine. On lightly floured surface, roll out one part of dough, at a time to a 20-inch circle about and 1/8-inch thick. With a 33/4-inch round cookie cutter or smaller, cut out circles of dough. Place one half of a Tbsp of filling on middle of each of circles. Gently fold circle into half to make half-moon shape, use a spatula to lift dough if dough sticks to surface. Gently lift tyropitakia with spatula one at a time and pinch edges together with your fingers well to seal. Place tyropitakia on baking sheets lined with parchment paper. Repeat same procedure with remaining of dough and filling. Brush tyropitakia with beaten egg. Let stand for 5 minutes to allow egg to dry. Use tines of a fork to prick a small vent in each tyropitaki. Bake in a preheated 375 F (190 C) oven on middle rack for approximately 20-25 minutes or until golden brown. Serve hot. Makes about 60-70 tyropitakia.

Note: Tyropitakia may be frozen before or after baking, as in cheese puffs (see index for recipe).

❦❦❦

CHEESE PUFFS
Southakia me Tyri

1/2 cup water
1/2 cup milk plus extra for brushing
Salt and white pepper to taste
1/4 tsp Cayenne pepper
1/2 cup unsalted butter, at room temperature
1 1/2 cups all-purpose flour
1/4 tsp baking powder
6 extra large eggs, at room temperature
*1/2 cup each lightly pressed down coarsely grated
    Swiss and Kaseri cheese*
*1/2 cup lightly pressed down grated Parmesan
    cheese plus extra for sprinkling*
Large baking sheets
Parchment paper

In a 3-quart saucepan add water and milk and bring to a boil. Reduce heat and add butter, white and cayenne pepper, and bring to a boil again. Sift flour with baking powder together. Remove from heat and add flour mixture all at once and stir vigorously with a wooden spoon until mixture forms a ball, leaving pan clean. Remove from heat. Spoon pastry in bowl of a mixer fitted with a paddle. Add eggs one at a time, beating until dough is smooth and shiny. Add cheeses and beat just to combine. Spoon mixture into a pastry bag, and pipe in 1-1 1/2-inch mounds using a # 7 round tip, on a baking sheet lined with parchment paper 1-inch apart. Or drop with a teaspoon. Brush with remaining milk and sprinkle with remaining cheese. Bake in a preheated 400 F (205 C) oven on middle rack for 15 minutes or until golden brown. Reduce heat to 375 F (190 C) and bake for 3-4 minutes longer. Serve hot or at room temperature.

❦❦❦

CHEESE ROLL UPS
Mourekakia me Tyri

31/2 Tbsp butter or margarine
4 Tbsp flour
1 cup milk
2 beaten eggs plus 1 egg-yolk
8 ounces Feta cheese, crumbled
4 ounces Swiss cheese, cut into cubes
8 ounces Ricotta of Farmers cheese
2 Tbsp grated Parmesan cheese
1 Tbsp finely chopped parsley (optional) or
1 Tbsp finely chopped fresh mint
1 pound phyllo pastry (thawed)
1 1/2 cups clarified butter or margarine (see index)

In a small saucepan melt butter over medium heat. Using a wire whisk, stir in flour and blend well. Gradually stir in milk, stirring constantly until sauce is thick and smooth. Stir little of the hot sauce into the eggs. Pour egg mixture into sauce and cook over low heat for 5 minutes, stirring constantly. Remove from heat, Add cheeses, parsley if desired, mint and pepper, in the egg mixture and mix well to combine. Let cool. Take the phyllo sheets from the package, cut into three strips about 6x13-inches each strip. Take one strip at a time, covering the remaining strips with a dry cloth, then with lightly dampened towel to prevent them from drying out.

Every strip has 20x22 sheets. For each cheese roll up brush 1 sheet with hot melted butter and fold in half crosswise. Brush again with butter. Place 1 tsp. cheese mixture at a narrow end and fold sides in toward the middle to enclose filling. Brush with melted butter and roll up into a tube shape. Repeat with the remaining phyllo sheets. Place the cheese roll ups in a large buttered baking sheet and brush them with hot melted butter, again. Bake in a preheated 350 F (180 C) oven until golden, about 15-20 minutes Makes 60-65 cheese roll ups. Serve hot.

Note: Cheese roll ups may be frozen before or after baking. When ready to bake, bake in a preheated 350F (180 C) oven until ready, about 30 minutes. Serve hot

❧❀❧

CHEESE SAGHANAKI

Saghanaki me Tyri

4 slices kefalotyri cheese 1/4-inch thick
Four for dredging
2 Tbsp cognac
Clarified butter for frying
Fresh lemon juice

Dredge cheese slices with flour. In a non-stick frying pan heat 2 Tbsp butter until it bubbles. Add 2 cheese s slices at a time in the hot butter and fry until golden brown. Add 1 Tbsp. of the cognac, and some of the lemon juice. Serve immediately with fresh crusty bread and good ouzo (Greek liqueur). Serves 4-8.

Traditionally this was fried and served in individual frying pan called saghanaki.

❧❀❧

CHEESE SAGHANAKI WITH TOMATO

Saghanaki me Tyri ke Tomates

1 can (28 ounces) whole tomatoes, finely chopped or 4 large ripe tomatoes, peeled, seeded and chopped
1 (or more) large garlic clove, crushed
1/2 green bell pepper, finely chopped
Salt and pepper to taste
2 Tbsp olive oil
1/4 tsp crushed Greek oregano
1 pound Kefalotyri cheese, cut into 1/4-inch slices

1/2 cup finely ground dried breadcrumbs
1 egg, beaten with 1 tsp. water
Clarified butter or oil for frying

In a large frying pan combine chopped tomatoes and liquid, garlic, green pepper, salt, pepper, olive oil and oregano. Bring to a boil, reduce heat and simmer for 30 minutes. Cut each cheese slice into half. Dip each cheese slice into flour, then into egg, then into breadcrumbs until completely covered. Brown the cheese slices in hot butter or oil until golden. When you brown all the cheese slices, place them in the sauce and simmer for 2 minutes. Traditionally this was fried and served in individual frying pan called saghanaki. Serve with fresh crusty bread. Serves 8.

❧❀❧

CHEESE SWIRLS

Tyropitakia

8 ounces grated Pecorino-Romano or Parmesan cheese
8 ounces coarsely grated Kaseri cheese
1 pound crumbled Feta cheese
1 1/4 cups sour cream
4 large eggs, lightly beaten
White pepper to taste
1 pound fillo pastry (thawed)
1 1/2 cups melted butter or margarine

Divide Pecorino-Romano cheese into four parts, set aside. Combine cheeses, sour cream, eggs, pepper, and mix well. Divide into four parts, set aside. Take 6 fillo sheets at a time covering the remaining fillo sheets with a dry cloth, then with lightly dampened towel to prevent them from drying out. Place one fillo sheet on a 20x14-inch heavy-duty foil. Gently brush fillo with hot melted butter if desired without brushing the foil. Place one more fillo sheets on top of the first, then brush again with the hot melted butter. Sprinkle evenly with a handful of the grated Pecorino-Romano cheese. Place another fillo sheet on the cheese, brush with melted butter. Sprinkle evenly with another handful of the cheese. Repeat and continue until all the cheese and fillo is used. Take one part of the cheese egg mixture and spread evenly over the fillo sheets. Gently lift layered sheets from the wide side without the foil and roll, like a jelly roll. Wrap the roll with the foil, seal and freeze. Continue with the rest parts. Follow preparation as the first. When you are ready to use the cheese swirls, thaw for 60 minutes. With a sharp serrated knife slice rolls one at a time into 3/4-inch slices. Place slices on a well greased baking sheets and bake in a preheated 350 F (180 C) oven for 30 minutes or until golden. Serve hot. Makes 4 cheese swirls.

❧❀☙

CHEESE TRIANGLES
Trighona Tyropitakia

Follow recipe as directed in Cheese Puffs (see index for the recipe). Prepare and bake them as directed in Spinach Triangles (see index for the preparation).

❧❀☙

CHEESE AND HOT PEPPER SPREAD
Tyri me Kafteri Piperia

2 large red hot peppers or 4 small, roasted
1 pound crumbled goat cheese
1 garlic clove, crushed
1/3 cup or less olive oil
2 Tbsp fresh lemon juice

Place peppers in a baking pan lined with parchment paper, and broil in the oven or on the charcoal until skin is blistered and peppers are soft. Place in a plastic bag for 15-30 minutes. Peel them and remove seeds. Chop peppers and place in a food processor with the cheese and the garlic and process until creamy. Slowly add oil and lemon and process until thick and creamy. Transfer to a serving bowl and chill. Serve with crackers, fresh crusty bread or toasted pita bread.

❧❀☙

CHICKEN TRIANGLES
Kotopitakia

1 whole chicken breast cooked but not dried, cut into 1/4-inch diced
1/2 cup chopped onion
2 Tbsp butter or margarine

2 garlic cloves, crushed
1/2 cup finely chopped carrot
1/2 red pepper, seeded, membranes removed and finely chopped
2 medium potatoes, cut into 1/4-inch diced
Salt and pepper to taste
Pinch of cayenne pepper
1 pound fillo pastry (thawed)
1 1/2 cups clarified melted butter or margarine

In a skillet, sauté onion with butter until soft. Add garlic and sauté few minutes longer. Add the vegetables, 2 Tbsp. water, salt, pepper and cayenne. Stir. Cover, and simmer for 15 minutes. Remove from heat. Let cool. Add chicken, and stir to combine. Follow preparation as directed in Spinach triangles.

❧❀☙

CHICKEN LIVER PATE WITH COGNAC
Sikoti Kotopoulou Pate me Cognac

8 ounces chicken livers
4 Tbsp butter or margarine at room temperature
1/2 cup chopped onion
Salt and pepper to taste
Dash of Cayenne pepper
1/4 tsp of dry mustard
3 Tbsp of cognac
1/2 cup heavy cream

Carefully clean and rinse the livers. In a skillet melt the butter; add chopped onion and sauté until it is transparent (don't brown the onion). Add the chicken livers and cook slowly for 10 minutes or until they are no longer pink, stirring occasionally. Add salt, pepper and mustard. Turn the liver mixture into a blender or food processor container, add the cognac and blend until smooth. Add the heavy cream to the liver mixture and blend until smooth and creamy. Pour into a bowl, cover and chill.

❧❀☙

CHICKEN LIVE PATE
Sikoti Kotopoulou Pate

8 ounces chicken-livers
8 Tbsp butter or margarine, at room temperature
1/2 cup chopped onion
Salt and pepper to taste

Dash of cayenne pepper
1/4 tsp dry-mustard

Carefully clean and rinse livers. In a skillet melt four Tbsp of butter; add chopped onion and sauté until it is transparent. Add the chicken livers and cook slowly for 10 minutes or until they are no longer pink, stirring occasionally. Add salt, pepper and mustard. Turn the liver mixture into a blender of food processor container and blend until smooth. Add the remaining four Tbsp. of butter to the liver mixture and blend until smooth and creamy. Pour into a bowl, cover and chill. This preparation makes excellent canapés or sandwiches or spread on pieces of bread or crackers.

❧✵❧

CHICKEN OR TURKEY PUFFS
Bourekakia Kottas or Galopoulas

1 1/2 cups water
1/2 cup butter or margarine
1 1/2 cups all-purpose
Salt and white pepper to taste
5 extra large eggs
21/4 cups cooked chicken or turkey, cut into small cubes and lightly pressed down
1/2 cup finely chopped red bell pepper
3/4 cup finely chopped celery
1 large shallot, minced
1/4 tsp crushed tarragon
1/2 cup of each Kaseri and Swiss cheese, cut into small cubes
1/4 cup grated and lightly pressed down Parmesan or Kefalotyri cheese
Pinch of Cayenne pepper

In a 2-quart saucepan add water and butter and bring to a boil. Reduce heat. Add flour all at once and stir vigorously with a wooden spoon until mixture forms a ball around spoon, and leaving pan clean. Remove from heat. Transfer to a large mixing bowl. Add one egg at a time, beating thoroughly with the mixer, after each one is added. Season the mixture with salt and pepper. Continue beating until mixture is thick and smooth. Add the rest of the ingredients and mix well with a spatula to combine. On a baking sheet lined with parchment paper, drop 1 heaping Tbsp. for each puff (depending on the size you desire). Bake in a preheated 450 F (230 C) oven for 20 minutes or golden brown. Makes about 3 dozens chicken puffs.

❧✵❧

COCKTAIL MEATBALLS IN WINE SAUCE
Keftethakia me Saltsa Krasiou

1/3 cup milk
1 egg plus 1 egg yolk, lightly beaten
1 1/3 cups soft breadcrumbs (see index for recipe)
1/2 cup butter, margarine or olive oil
1/2 cup minced onion
1 pound lean ground beef
1/2 pound lean ground pork, lamb or veal
2 tsp salt
1/4 tsp pepper
1 Tbsp. minced flat leaf parsley
1 tsp. Worcestershire sauce
1 clove garlic, crushed
1 Tbsp flour
1 cups dry Vermouth
1/2 cup water

In a large mixing bowl, mix milk, eggs and breadcrumbs. Let stay 15 minutes. In a small skillet heat half the butter if desired and sauté the onion until soft. In the milk mixture add onion, ground beef, pork if desired, 1 1/2 tsp. salt, pepper, parsley, Worcestershire sauce and garlic. Mix well with your hand until thoroughly blended. Cover and chill for two hours or longer. Shape into 60-70 meatballs, each about 1-inch in diameter. Heat remaining butter in a skillet over medium heat, add meatballs a few at a time and brown on all sides. Remove the meatballs as they browned and set-aside. Drain fat from skillet into a large saucepan. Stir in flour and blend well over low heat. Add wine, water and 1/2 tsp. salt. Bring the sauce to a simmering point, and gently add meatballs. Simmer covered for 15 minutes. Serve in a chafing dish.

❧✵❧

COCKTAIL MEATBALLS
Keftethakia Meze

1/3 cup milk or wine

6

Appetizers

Clockwise from top left: Cheese in Puff Pastry; Spinach Triangles and Avocado with Shrimp.

Tyropita in a Tube Pan

Baked Shrimp
with Feta

Fried Cheese
with Tomato

1 egg plus 1 egg yolk or white, lightly beaten
1 1/3 cups dried breadcrumbs (see index for recipe)
1 1/2 Tbsp olive oil
1/2 cup minced onion
2 tsp salt or to your taste
1/4 tsp pepper
1/8 tsp Greek oregano
1 Tbsp minced fresh mint or 1 tsp. dried, crushed
1 tsp red wine vinegar
1 pound lean ground beef
1/2 pound lean ground lamb
All-purpose flour for rolling
3/4 cup oil for frying

In a large bowl, mix milk, eggs and breadcrumbs, let stay for 15 minutes. In a small skillet heat the oil and sauté the onion until soft. Add to the milk mixture and the rest of the ingredients. Mix well by hand until thoroughly blended. Cover and chill for two hours or longer. Shape into 60 meatballs about 1-inch in diameter. Roll the meatballs lightly in flour; shake off excess. Fry in hot oil until nicely browned. Lift out and drain on absorbent paper. Serve hot.

COD FISH AND POTATO SPREAD

Alimma Bakaliarou ke Patatas

1 pound potatoes (about 2 medium)
Salt and white pepper to taste
1 1/2 cups milk
3 garlic cloves or more, roughly chopped
1 pound cod fish fillet
2 Tbsp or more extra Virgin olive oil
2 Tbsp of more fresh lemon juice
1/2 cup of more mayonnaise

Scrub and wash the potatoes well. Drop them in boiling salted water and cook for 45 minutes, or until tender when pierced with a fork. Remove from heat, drain and peel them. Press them through a food mill. Set aside. While potatoes are boiling, prepare the fish. Rinse fish under cold running water, and dry with paper towels. Bring milk and garlic to a boil, add fish and simmer uncovered, for 10-15 minutes or until fish flakes easily when tested with a fork. Remove from heat. Cut fish fillets into pieces and place in a food processor, blend for 8 seconds. Then add some of the milk you cook the fish, and the garlic, potatoes and process for few seconds. Add olive oil, lemon juice, and process until well blend. Add more milk if it is too thick. Last add the mayonnaise and blend well to combine. Transfer to a bowl, cover, and chill. Serve with toasted Greek pita bread, fresh crusty bread or crackers.

COPANISTI (CHEESE SPREAD)

Kopanisti

8 ounces crumbled feta cheese
1 large garlic clove, chopped
1/4 tsp pepper
1/8 tsp pepper Cayenne
1/8 tsp paprika
1/8 tsp crushed Greek oregano
1 Tbsp wine vinegar
1/3 cup fine quality olive oil

In a food processor combine all the ingredients except the olive oil. Process the mixture until smooth. Remove the pusher from the feed tube and add the olive oil in a fine stream while the motor is running. When all the oil is added and copanisti is thick and smooth, turn off the motor. Transfer the copanisti to a covered container and chill until ready to use. Spread the copanisti on fresh crusty bread or toasted Greed pita bread. Serve as an appetizer.

EGGPLANT SPREAD (L. CHOL. L. FAT)

Melitzanosalata

1 large eggplant (about 1 1/2 pounds)
2 cloves garlic or more, crushed
1 Tbsp minced onion
1/4 cup or more good quality extra virgin olive oil
1 tsp wine vinegar
2 tsp or more fresh lemon juice
1 Tbsp fresh chopped flat leaf parsley
Salt and pepper to taste

Remove stem of the eggplant and wash well. Puncture with a fork in few places to prevent it from exploding while it bakes. Place in a baking pan and bake in a preheated 450 F (230 C) oven for 60 minutes or until soft to the touch. While hot, remove skin. Cut into pieces. In a food processor combine all the ingredients and blend well. Pour in a serving bowl and chill. Serve with fresh crusty bread, Greek pita, crackers or melba toast. Makes 2 cups.

Note: After you blended, pour in a bowl, and add 1 cup Mexican salsa. It is delicious.

EGGPLANT SPREAD
Melitzanosalata

1 large eggplant (about 1 1/2 pounds)
2 cloves garlic or more, crushed
2 Tbsp minced onion
1 Tbsp chopped parsley
Salt and pepper to taste
2 Tbsp fresh lemon juice or
2 Tbsp white wine vinegar
1/2 cup (approx.) good quality extra virgin olive oil

Remove stem from the eggplant and rinse well. Puncture with a fork to prevent it from exploding while it bakes. Place in a baking pan lined with foil and bake in a preheated 450 F (230 C) oven for 60 minutes or until soft to the touch. While hot, remove the skin and seeds, and cut into pieces. In a food processor combine all the ingredients except the oil and blend well to combine. Slowly add the oil and blend well. Pour in a serving bowl and chill. Garnish with Kalamata olives. Serve with fresh bread or toasted Greek pita bread. Makes 2-21/2 cups.

EGGPLANT- ALMOND SPREAD
Melitzanosalata

1 large eggplant (about 1 1/2 pounds)
1 clove minced garlic
1 Tbsp minced onion
2 Tbsp good quality extra virgin olive oil
1/2 cup ground almonds or walnuts
Salt and pepper to taste
2 tsp fresh lemon juice
1/2 cup or more mayonnaise

Remove stem of the eggplant and wash well. Puncture with a fork to prevent it from exploding while it bakes. Place in a baking pan and bake in a preheated 450 F (230 C) oven for 60 minutes

or until soft to the touch. While hot, remove skin or live it on if desired and cut into pieces. In a food processor combine all the ingredients except the mayonnaise and blend well. Add mayonnaise and blend for 3 seconds. Pour in a serving bowl and chill well. Serve with fresh bread, crackers or toasted pita bread. Makes 3 cups.

EGGPLANT-CHICKPEA SPREAD
Melitzanosalata me Revithia

1 large eggplant (about 1 1/2 pounds)
1 (can 15-ounces) chickpeas, drained
1/2 cup tahini (sesame-seed paste)
3 or more large garlic cloves, chopped
1 tsp ground cumin
Salt and pepper to taste
Pinch of cayenne pepper
1 Tbsp chopped flat leaf parsley

Remove stem of the eggplant and wash well. Pierce eggplant with a fork to prevent it from exploding while it bakes. Place in a baking pan and bake in a preheated 450 F (230 C) oven for 60 minutes or until soft to the tough. While hot, remove the skin, and cut into pieces. In a food processor combine all the ingredients together. Process the eggplant mixture until smooth. Pour in a serving bowl and chill well for several hours. Serve with fresh crusty bread, or toasted Greek pita bread. Makes 3-31/2 cups about.

EGGPLANT-TAHINI SPREAD
Melitzanosalata me Tahini

1 large eggplant (about 1 1/2 pounds)
1/4 cup tahini (sesame seed paste)
2 Tbsp olive oil
3 Tbsp fresh lemon juice
2 cloves garlic, minced
Salt and pepper to taste
1 Tbsp finely chopped flat leaf parsley
1/3 cup mayonnaise

Remove stem of the eggplant and wash well. Puncture with a fork to prevent it from exploding while it bakes. Place in a baking pan and bake in a preheated 450 F (230 C) oven for 60 minutes or until soft to the touch. While hot, remove skin or live it on if desired and cut into pieces. In a food processor combine all the ingredients except the mayonnaise and blend well. Add mayonnaise and blend for 3 seconds. Pour in a serving bowl and chill well for several hours. Serve with fresh bread, crackers or toasted pita bread. Makes 3-3 1/2 cups.

※❦※❦※

EGGPLANT AND CHEESE SPREAD
Melitzanosalata me Tyri Feta

1 large eggplant (about 1 1/2 pounds)
2 garlic cloves, crushed
2 Tbsp fresh lemon juice
3 Tbsp cream or milk
Salt and pepper to taste
1/2 cup or more good quality extra virgin olive oil
1/2 cup crumbled feta cheese

Remove the stem from the eggplant and rinse well. Puncture with a fork to prevent it from exploding while it bakes. Place in a baking pan lined with foil and bake in a preheated 450 F (230 C) oven for 60 minutes or until soft to the tough. While hot remove the skin and seeds and cut into pieces. In a food processor combine all the ingredients except the oil, and blend well. Slowly add the oil and blend until smooth and thick. Pour into and bowl and add the feta cheese, stir well to combine. Chill. Serve in a serving bowl with fresh bread or toasted Greek pita bread. Makes 2-21/2 cups.

※❦※❦※

FETA CHEESE PUFFS
Feta Bourekakia

8 ounces feta cheese, crumbled
1/2 cup grated Parmesan cheese
2 lightly beaten eggs
1 Tbsp. finely chopped parsley or mint
White pepper to taste
2/3 of a pound phyllo pastry (thawed)
1/2 cup or more clarified butter or margarine

In a medium sizes mixing bowl, combine cheeses, eggs and mint if desired and mix well. Take the phyllo sheets from the package, cut into three strips about 6x13-inch strip. Take one strip at a time, covering the remaining strips with a dry cloth, then with lightly dampened towel to prevent them from drying out. For each puff brush 1 sheet with hot melted butter and fold in half crosswise. Brush again with butter, and place 1 tsp. of the cheese mixture at a narrow end and, fold sides in toward the middle to enclose filling. Brush with hot melted butter and rollup into a tube shape. Repeat with the remaining phyllo sheets and cheese mixture. Place the puffs in a large buttered baking sheet and brush them with the hot butter again. Bake in a preheated 350 F (180 C) oven until golden, about 15-20 minutes. Make about 40 puffs.
Note: Cheese puffs may be frozen before or after baking. When ready to bake, bake frozen in a preheated 350 F oven until golden, about 30 minutes. Serve hot.

※❦※❦※

FRIED TYROPITAKIA IN HOMEMADE PASTRY
Tighanita Tyropitakia me Filo Spitiko

For the pastry:
3 cups all-purpose unbleached four sifted
1/4 tsp. salt
1 tsp. baking powder
1/4 cup fine quality olive oil
1 egg, lightly beaten
1/2 cup water

For the filling:
8 ounces feta cheese, crumbled
4 ounces cream cheese, at room temperature
3 Tbsp. grated Parmesan cheese
2 eggs separated
Fine quality oil for frying

In a mixing bowl sift together the flour, salt and baking powder. Cut in oil with a pastry blender, until mixture resembles coarse crumbs. Add beaten egg and water. Beat well to make soft dough. Turn out dough on lightly floured board and knead lightly until smooth. Divide dough into 2 balls. Place each one in a plastic sandwich bag and close it well, (air free). Let stay for 30-60 or longer. While the dough is resting, prepare the filling. In a bowl mix cheeses and egg yolks together. With the mixture fill the circles or dough. On a lightly floured surface, roll each ball at a time. Roll out by lightly dusting board and pastry with flour until 1/8-inch thick. With 4-inch round cookie cutter, cut out circles of dough. Place 1 tsp. of filling on one half of a circle. Brush edges with egg whites. Fold other half of circle making half-moon shape. Pinch edges together well to seal or seal by pressing with times of fork. Fry tyropitakia in hot oil until golden brown. Lift out and drain on absorbent paper. Serve hot.

GARLIC CHEESE SPREAD
Skorthalia me Tyri

1 large head of garlic
2 Tbsp good quality olive oil
8 ounces cream cheese at room temperature
1/2 cup butter or margarine at room temperature
1/2 cup ground walnuts or almonds
1 Tbsp finely chopped flat leaf parsley
1 Tbsp finely chopped mint
1 Tbsp finely chopped fresh dill
Salt and pepper to taste
2-3 Tbsp fresh lemon juice

With a sharp knife cut the root from the head of garlic. Place the garlic in the center of a piece of foil, sprinkle the cut side with the oil and salt, and then squeeze the foil around the head of garlic to seal. Bake in a preheated 400 F (205 C) oven for 45 minutes or until soft to the touch. Remove from the oven and the foil, and squeeze the head of garlic until all of the pulp is out. Combine all the ingredients in a food processor and blend well. Spoon the mixture in a serving bowl, and serve at room temperature. Serve on toasted pita bread, crackers or fresh crusty bread.

GARLIC SPREAD PIQUANT
Saltsa Skordou Pikantiki

2 heads of garlic
1 egg yolk
1 1/2 Tbsp prepared mustard
Salt and white pepper to taste
1 1/2-2 cups olive oil
3 Tbsp of more lemon juice

1 Tsp finely chopped flat leaf parsley
1 cup cream, whipped

With a sharp knife cut the garlic heads. Place the garlic in the center of a piece of foil, sprinkle the cut side with olive oil and salt, and them squeeze the foil around the garlic to seal. Bake in a preheated 400 F (205 C) oven for 45 minutes or until soft to the touch. Remove from the oven and the foil, and squeeze the garlic until all of the pulp is out. Combine the garlic, egg yolk, mustard and salt in a food processor, and blend until smooth. While the machine is running, add oil in a slow thin stream until mixture is thick and smooth. Add lemon juice one tsp at a time. Gradually add the cream and blend until mixture is thick. Add white pepper and parsley, and blend for a second. Spoon the garlic mixture in a large bowl, cover and chill. Serve on toasted Greek pita bread, crackers or fresh bread. Makes about 3 cups.

MEAT BOUREKAKIA IN HOMEMADE PASTRY
Kreatopitakia me Fillo Spitiko

For the pastry:
4 cups all-purpose flour about, sifted with
1 Tbsp baking powder and
1 tsp salt
3/4 cup good quality olive oil
2 Tbsp butter at room temperature
1 cup milk
1 lightly beaten egg
2 egg whites, beaten with 1 Tbsp water

For the filling:
1 Tbsp olive oil
1 medium onion, finely chopped
1/2 pound lean ground beef
1/2 pound lean ground lamb
1/2 cup dry white wine
Salt and pepper to taste
Pinch of Cayenne pepper
1 medium red ripe tomato, peeled, seeded
         and chopped
1/3 cup grated Parmesan or Kefalotyri cheese
1 lightly beaten egg

Prepare the pastry. In a mixing bowl cut flour in

oil and butter until mixture resembles coarse crumbs. Add milk and egg and gently toss with your fingers. Form dough into 2 balls. Place each one in a plastic sandwich bag and close it well. Let stay for 30 minutes or longer. While the pastry is resting prepare the filling. Sauté onion in oil until soft. Add meat and brown while stirring. Add wine and tomato, salt and peppers, simmer covered about 40 minutes or until sauce thickens. Remove from heat and cool. Add cheese, egg, blend well to combine. Place dough on a floured board lightly dusted with flour and flatten each ball at a time. Roll out by dusting board and pastry with flour until 1/8-inch thick. With a 4-inch round cookie cutter, cut out circles of dough. Place 1 Tbsp of filling on one half of a circle. Brush edges with egg whites. Fold other half of circle making half-moon shape. Pinch edges together well to seal or seal by pressing with tines of fork. Dip fry in hot oil until golden brown on both sides. Lay on paper towels to drain. Serve them hot.

Note: Instead of frying the bourekakia, you can bake them. Place half-moon in a buttered baking sheet. Gently brush with egg whites. Bake in a preheated 375 F (190 C) oven for 20-25 minutes. Serve them hot. Makes 30-40 bourekakia.

MEAT FILLED FLUTES
Flogheres me Kreas

2 pounds lean boneless lamb or beef, cut into
    small cubes
2 cups finely chopped onions
2 Tbsp olive oil
4 medium tomatoes, peeled, seeded and chopped
1/4 cup pine nuts
Salt and pepper to taste
Pinch Cayenne pepper
1 pound fillo pastry (thawed)
1 cup clarified melted butter, margarine or good
    quality olive oil

Sauté the meat and the onions until onions are soft and liquid evaporates. Add tomatoes, pine nuts, salt, pepper and cayenne. Cover and cook slowly until the meat is tender. Add little water

if needed. Remove from heat. Cut fillo sheets in half crosswise. Place strips on top of each other, cover with damp cloth to keep from drying while working. Take one strip at a time. Brush each strip with hot melted butter if desired and fold in half crosswise; place one Tbsp of filling at a narrow end of strip. Turn sides in toward middle to enclose filling. Brush with butter and roll up lengthwise to other end to form a roll. Place in a greased baking pan. Repeat the filling and rolling process. Generously brush each one with hot butter. Bake in a preheated 375 F (190 C) oven for approximately 15 minutes or until golden brown. Serve immediately with Tzatziki (see index for the recipe).

MEAT PUFFS
Bourekakia me kima

2 Tbsp butter or margarine
1 pound lean ground beef
1 medium onion, minced
1/4 cup dry wine
1 medium tomato, peeled, seeded and chopped
Salt and pepper to taste
1/2 cup grated Parmesan cheese
2 large eggs, lightly beaten
2 Tbsp breadcrumbs (see index)
1 pound phyllo pastry (thawed)
1 cup clarified butter, margarine (see index for
    recipe) or good quality olive oil

In a skillet, heat butter if desired, and brown meat and onion together. Add wine, when the wine evaporates add chopped tomatoes, salt and pepper. Cook slowly covered for 30 minutes. Remove from heat, and gradually add the beaten eggs, stirring constantly until they are combined, let cool. Stir in cheese, and breadcrumbs. Take the phyllo sheets from the package, cut into three strips about 6x13-inches each strip. Take one strip at a time, covering the remaining strips with a dry cloth, them with lightly dampened towel to prevent them from drying out. Every strip has 20-22 sheets. For each puff brush 1 sheet with hot melted butter and fold in half crosswise. Brush again with butter. Place 1 tsp. of the meat mixture, at a narrow end, and fold sides in toward the middle to enclose filling. Brush with melted butter and rollup into a tube shape. Repeat the filling and rolling process. Place the puffs in a large buttered baking sheet and brush them with hot melted butter, again. Bake in a preheated 350 F (180 C) oven until golden, about 15-20 minutes. Make 60-65 puffs. Serve hot.

Note: Meat puffs may be frozen before or after baking. When ready to bake, bake in a preheated 350 F oven until golden, about 30 minutes. If the butter isn't very hot, you used too much butter.

❧❀❧

MEAT TURNOVERS
Kreatopitakia

For the dough:
1/2 cup warm milk
1 pkg active dry yeast
4 large eggs
1 1/2 tsp salt
5 cups about all-purpose flour
1/2 cup melted butter or margarine
2 egg whites, beaten with1Tbsp water

For the filling:
1/2 pound lean ground beef
1/2 pound lean ground lamb
1 cup finely chopped onion
2 Tbsp olive oil
1 cup dry white wine
2 Tbsp finely chopped fresh dill
1 medium ripe tomato, finely chopped
Salt and pepper to taste
1/4 cup grated Parmesan cheese
2 Tbsp dried breadcrumbs

Prepare the dough. Dissolve yeast in warm milk. Cover; let stand 5 minutes. Place milk mixture in a large- bowl, add eggs, salt and beat well. Gradually stir in flour until dough is soft and smooth. Add more four if needed. Add warm butter little by little and knead until all the butter is used and dough is smooth. Cover; let rise in warm place free from draft until doubled in bulk. While dough is rising prepare the filling. In saucepan sauté meat and onion with oil until meat is well brown and onion is soft. Add wine, tomato, salt, pepper and 1/2 cup water, and cook until the meat has evaporated all the juices. Add

the dill, cheese and breadcrumbs, mix well to combine. Remove from heat and let cool. Punch down dough and knead. Divide dough into two parts; let rest, covered for 15 minutes. On a lightly floured surface, roll one part of the dough at the time to a circle about 1/8-inch thick. With a 4-inch round cookie cutter, cut out circles of dough. Place 1 Tbsp. of the filling on one half of a circle. Brush edges with egg whites. Fold other half of circle making half-moon shape. Pinch edges together well to seal of seal by pressing with tines of fork. Place the turnovers in a buttered baking sheet. Repeat rolling and filling until you finish. Let rise in warm place, until doubled. Gently brush with egg whites. Bake in a preheated 375 F (190 C) oven for 20-25 minutes. Serve hot. Makes about 30-40 kreatopites.

Note: Instead of baking the turnovers, you can fry them. Dip-fry them in oil until golden brown on both sides. Remove from the oil, and lay them on paper towels to drain. Serve hot.

❧❀❧

MEAT TWIRL IN PUFF PASTRY
Kreas Rolo se Sfoliata

1 pound frozen puff pastry (thawed)
1 large onion finely chopped
1 Tbsp olive oil
1 pound lean ground lamb or turkey
1 pound lean ground beef or chicken
2 cups firmly pressed down breadcrumbs, from
   day-old bread (see index for recipe)
1/3 cup red dry wine
3 Tbsp tomato sauce
1 egg
Salt and pepper to taste
3 Tbsp finely chopped fresh mint
2 Tbsp finely chopped fresh dill
2 cups grated Gouda cheese
6 thin slices boiled ham
2 Tbsp butter, margarine or good quality olive oil

Sauté the onion with 1 Tbsp olive oil until soft. Combine the first 12 ingredients together and mix well with your hand. Take the pieces of puff pastry from the box and lay them on a cutting board, and brush with butter if desired. Divide the meat mixture into two parts. Spread each part of pastry with one part of meat mixture and spread evenly leaving 1-inch around the pastry uncovered. Lay the cheese and then the ham. Brush edges with water. Start rolling-up the pastry with the filling from the wide side. Seal the edges well. Place the twirl in a greased baking pan. Repeat the same procedure with the remaining of pastry and meat mixture. Bake in a preheated 400 F (205 C) oven for 20-30 minutes or until golden. Let rest for 10 minutes. Slice the twirls with a sharp serrated knife and place on a serving platter. Serve with kritharaki (Greek orzo) or rice pilaf and salad (see index for the recipes). Serves 6-8.

MUSHROOM CHEESE TRIANGLES
Trighona me Manitaria ke Tyri

1 pound mushrooms (two or three kinds)
2 Tbsp. butter, margarine or good quality olive oil
Salt and pepper to taste
8 ounces shredded Swiss cheese
1 cup crumbled feta cheese
2 egg whites
1 Tbsp chopped flat leaf parsley
1 pound fillo pastry (thawed)
*1 cup melted clarified butter, margarine or good
       quality olive oil*

Wash mushrooms under cold running water. Dry them on absorbent towels, and slice. Sauté the mushrooms in hot butter if desired, until liquid evaporates. Remove from heat and cool. In a food processor combine all the ingredients except the fillo and the butter, and process until smooth. Take the fillo sheets from the package, cut into three strips lengthwise, about 4-inches each strip. Take one strip at a time, covering the remaining strips with a dry cloth, then with lightly dampened towel to prevent them from drying out. For each triangle take1 sheet and fold in half lengthwise, and brush lightly with hot melted butter if desired. Place 1 Tbsp. of the mushroom mixture at one end of the folded strip. Lift a corner of the strip, next to the filling, and fold it over the filling, so that it touches the opposite long side, and forms a triangle enclosing the

filling. Continue to fold up the pastry, keeping the triangular shape. Repeat filling and folding in triangles with the remaining strips and filling. Place them in greased baking sheets and brush with the hot butter again. Bake in a preheated 350 F (180 C) oven for 20-25 minutes or until golden. Serve hot. Makes 50-70 triangles.

MUSHROOM PUFFS
Bourekakia me Manitaria

For the pastry:
1 cup whole wheat flour
1/2 cup all-purpose flour
Salt and pepper to taste
1 tsp dry yeast
1 egg, beaten with
1/3 cup milk (approx.)
1/2 cup olive oil

For the filling:
3 ounces cream cheese, at room temperature
10 ounces mushrooms
1 garlic clove, minced
2/3 cup shredded Swiss cheese
3 Tbsp grated Parmesan or Kefalotyri cheese
Sesame seeds for sprinkling

In a mixing bowl combine the flours, salt, yeast, egg with the milk, 1/4 cup olive oil and cream cheese, and mix well. Knead until dough is smooth and stiff. Add more milk or flour if needed. Divide the dough into two parts. Cover; let rest at room temperature, until the filling is ready. Rinse the mushrooms under cold running water. Dry them on paper towels. Finely chop the mushrooms. Sauté the mushrooms and the garlic, in 2 Tbsp. of the remaining oil, until the liquid evaporates. Add salt, pepper, the shredded cheese, and grated cheese, and mix well to combine. On a lightly floured surface, roll out dough one part at a time to 1/8-inch thickness. Cut out circles of dough into 3-4-inches in diameter. Place 1 tsp. of filling on one half of a circle. Brush edges with a small amount of water. Gently fold other half of circle making half-moon shape. Pinch edges well together to seal or seal by pressing with tines of fork. Place the half-moon in a greased baking sheet. Brush with egg white, and sprinkle with the sesame seeds. Bake in a preheated 375 F (190 C) oven for 20-25 minutes. Serve hot.

❧❈❧

OLIVES
How to Cure Olives

Pick olives one by one, and look if they don't have any holes, or they are not blemished. Wash well with tap water. Place olives in large deep container or deep jars. Add tap water to cover, cover and let stand 24 hours. Change water every 24-hours for 7-10 days, depending how sweet or bitter you like them. After olives are ready the way you like them, drain well and prepare them for the brine. Boil water in a large pot. Let water cool completely. Wash olives well with cool water. Wash container with soap and rinse well. Drain olives and place in clean container, leave 4-inches from rim. Prepare the brine. In every 7-cups of water add 1- cup of salt, stir well. Bring to a boil and boil 5 minutes, stirring occasionally to dissolve salt. Remove from heat, let cool completely. Pour cool brine in container with the olives to cover them, leave 2-inches from rim. Let olives stay in the brine 5-10 days, depending how salty you want your olives. Pour olives and brine in a large pot. Wash container or jars and rinse well. With a slotted spoon, take olives from brine and place them in clean container, add 1 cup from the brine, 2 cups wine vinegar, 1 Tbsp. crushed Greek oregano, some slices of fresh garlic to your taste and cover with 1/2-inch above the olives with olive oil. Place 4 large layers of plastic wrap on rim of jars (if you use jars). Cover and seal well. Shake jars or container occasionally. Olives are ready for eating. Serve olives as desired.

❧❈❧

OLIVE SPREAD
Alimma Elias

1/2 cup Kalamata olives, pitted
1/2 cup Greek green olives, pitted
3 boneless anchovies
1/4 cup or more olive oil
Pepper to taste

Place the olives in a Ziploc plastic bag, close and pound with a small heavy frying pan or a mallet, until they crack. Remove the pits. Place all the ingredients in a food processor and blend for few minutes. Don't over blend. Spread on toasted slices of bread.

❧❈❧

SAUSAGE WITH ONIONS AND PEPPERS
Loukanila me Kremithia ke Piperies

3 pounds Italian hot sausage or half hot and
        half mild, sliced 1/2-inch thick
4 pounds onions, sliced thick
1/3 cup or more good quality olive oil
4 bell peppers, chopped
3 large red tomatoes, peeled, seeded and chopped
Salt and pepper to taste

In a dry frying pan sauté sausage slices until browned on both sides, but not burned. Lay them on absorbent paper. In a saucepan sauté onions with oil until soft. Add chopped peppers and sauté few minutes longer. Add chopped tomatoes, salt and pepper. Bring to a boil. Add sausage slices, cover. Reduce heat and simmer for 30 minutes or until meat is tender and liquid has evaporated. Add little water if needed. Serves 6-12.

❧❈❧

SCALLOPS GRATINEE
Ktenia Gratine

8 large scallops, fresh or frozen (thawed)
Salt and pepper to taste
2 Tbsp olive oil
5 Tbsp butter, margarine or good quality olive oil
5 Tbsp all-purpose flour
2 cups milk
2 extra large beaten eggs
1/2 cup grated Parmesan cheese
Pepper Cayenne to taste
2 Tbsp finely chopped flat leaf parsley

Season scallops with salt and pepper. Sauté scallops in hot oil, for 5 seconds on each side. Remove from heat and set aside. Prepare béchamel sauce. Melt butter if desired over medium heat, blend in flour until smooth using a whisk. Remove from heat. Gradually add milk, stirring constantly. Return to heat and cook until is thick, stirring constantly. Cook 3 minutes longer; add seasoning and blend. Remove from heat. Spoon little by little of the hot sauce into beaten eggs, stirring constantly. Add egg mixture to the sauce and cook over very low heat (do not let the sauce boil) for 2 minutes, stirring constantly. Add half the Parmesan cheese, salt, pepper and Cayenne, and stir well to combine. Grease 8 baking gratin dishes. Divide half the béchamel sauce into the prepare dishes, place one scallop on each dish and cover with the remaining sauce. Sprinkle with the remaining grated cheese. Bake in a preheated 475 F (245 C) oven for 5 minutes or until golden. Remove from oven and sprinkle with parsley. Serve immediately. Serves 8 as a first dish.

❧❀❧

SEAFOOD AU-GRATIN (IN INDIVIDUAL DISHES)
Thalasina Au-Graten se Atomika Piata

1 pound Dover sole fillets, fresh or frozen (thawed), cut into small pieces
1 pound medium raw shrimp, peeled
1 pound small sea scallops
8 ounces crab, fresh or frozen (thawed)
8 ounces cooked and shelled mussels
1/4 cup butter, margarine or good quality olive oil
2 large or more garlic cloves, crushed
Salt and pepper to taste
1 cups white wine
3/4 cup lightly pressed down grated Kefalotyri or Parmesan cheese
3/4 cup lightly pressed down coarsely grated Kaseri or Swiss cheese
4 cups medium béchamel sauce (see index for recipe)
3 extra large eggs, beaten
1/2 cup soft breadcrumbs
4 Tbsp butter for topping (divided)

In a large frying pan sauté the sole pieces, shrimp, scallops, crab and mussels in hot butter if desired, for few minutes. Season the fish with salt and pepper. Add wine and cook until the wine has evaporated. Remove the pan from the heat, and remove the fish from the liquid, to a large bowl. Prepare the béchamel sauce as directed in the recipe. Add the wine from the frying pan to the béchamel sauce. Remove from the heat and spoon little by little of the hot sauce into the beaten eggs, stirring constantly. Add egg mixture to the sauce, and continue stirring. Let cool. Mix the Parmesan and the Kaseri cheese together. Add all the cheese to the sauce except of 1 cup, and stir well to combine. Assembling the dishes. Add one half the béchamel sauce to the fish mixture, and stir well to combine. Divide the fish mixture into 12 individual au-gratin dishes, and cover with the remaining béchamel sauce. Sprinkle with the remaining cheese mixture, the breadcrumbs, and dot with the butter. Bake in a preheated 375 F (190 C) oven on the middle rack for 20 minutes or until bubbling hot and sauce has browned nicely. Serve immediately, as a first coarse. Serves 12.

❧❀❧

SHRIMP AND EGG SAGHANAKI
Gharithes me Avga Saghanaki

1 pound medium raw shrimp
1/4 cup good quality olive oil
8 large Roma tomatoes, peeled, seeded and chopped
8 beaten eggs
1/3 plus 1 tbsp grated Parmesan cheese
2 Tbsp chopped parsley
Salt and pepper to taste

Wash shrimp in lots of cold water, peel and devein them. Pat them dry on absorbent paper. In a skillet sauté shrimp in hot oil, for 2 minutes. Remove shrimp from the pan. Set aside. In the same skillet add chopped tomatoes and sauté until all juices, has evaporated. Add beaten eggs, parsley, salt and pepper. Stir well to combine. Add shrimp and cook slowly until eggs are cooked. Add cheese and stir well to combine. Remove from heat and serve. Serve with salad and fresh crusty bread. Serves 4-6.

❧❀❧

SHRIMP AND MUSHROOMS TARTLETS
Gharithes ke Manitaria Tartlettes

1 pound raw medium shrimp, peeled and deveined

1/4 cup butter or margarine
1/2 cup finely chopped onion
2 cloves garlic, minced
3/4 pound mushrooms chopped
1/2 cup dry white wine or Vermouth
1/2 cup cream or milk
Salt and pepper to taste
1 pound fillo pastry (thawed)
1 cup clarified butter, margarine or good quality
    olive oil

Lay 4 fillo sheets at a time, brushing lightly every one with hot melted butter. Cut squares of circles from prepared fillo, using cutters slightly larger than tartlets of muffin pans in which you are baking. The fillo will extend up the sides of the pans. Gently push fillo into greased pans and press gently and firmly against bottom and sides. Bake empty shells in a preheated 325 F (165 C) oven for about 8 minutes or until golden. Cool for 5 minutes. Remove from pans and fill when you are ready to serve with the shrimp mixture. Prepare the shrimp mixture. Sauté onion in hot butter until soft but not brown, add mushrooms and sauté until all liquid has evaporated. Add garlic, shrimp, salt and pepper and sauté for 4 minutes. Add wine and cook until evaporates. Add cream and cook 3 minutes longer. Remove from heat. Cool. Serve 12 big or 24 small tartlets.

❦❧

SHRIMP AND SCALLOPS TARTLETS
Gharithes ke Ktenia Tartlettes

2 cups cooked salad shrimp
2 cups cooked bay scallops
1 1/2 cups mayonnaise
1/3 cup tomato ketchup
1 1/2 Tbsp. fresh lemon juice
2 tsp. Worcestershire sauce
1 pound fillo pastry (thawed)
1 cup clarified butter, margarine or good quality
    olive oil

Mix first six ingredients together and chill. Lightly grease tartlets or muffin pans. Lay 4 fillo sheets at a time, brushing lightly every one with hot melted butter. Cut squares or circles from prepared fillo, using cutters slightly larger than tartlets or muffin pans in which you are baking, The fillo will extend up the sides of the pans.

Gently push fillo into greased pans and press gently and firmly against bottom and sides. Bake empty shells in a preheated 325 F (165 C) oven for about 8 minutes or until golden. Cool for 5 minutes. Remove from pans and fill when you are ready to serve with chilled shrimp mixture. Don't chill after you fill the shells more than 5-10 minutes, they will get soft. Serves 12 big or 24 small tartlets.

❦❧

SHRIMP STUFFED ARTICHOKES
Agkinares Ghemistes me Garithes

12 fresh cooked artichokes (see index for How to
    prepare artichokes)
36 medium cooked shrimp
2 Tbsp finely chopped flat leaf parsley
Salt and pepper to taste
6 ounces of Brie cheese, cut into 12 pieces
Some springs of parsley for decoration

Prepare artichokes as directed. Arrange shrimp on artichokes and sprinkle with salt, pepper and chopped parsley. Top each artichoke with a piece of cheese. Place in a baking sheet and broil until cheese is melted. Decorate each artichoke with parsley and serve immediately as appetizer. Serves 12.

❦❧

SHRIMP STUFFED EGGS
Avga Ghemista me Gharithes

12 hard-boiled eggs
Salt and white pepper to taste
Pinch of Cayenne pepper
1 Tbsp Dijon mustard
1 1/4 cups mayonnaise
1/2 cup chopped cooked small shrimp
1/4 cup finely chopped small dill pickles
24 whole small shrimp

Boil the eggs with salt until hard (salt helps the eggs to peel easy). Peel and cut into halves. Gently remove the yolks and press through a sieve in a bowl. Add salt, peppers, mustard, one half the mayonnaise, chopped shrimp and the pickles. Mix well to combine. Fill the egg halves with the mixture. Spread some of the remaining mayonnaise over each egg and decorate with the whole shrimp and the capers. Chill. Makes 24 halves. Serves 12-24.

SHRIMP TOMATO AND EGG SAGANAKI
Gharithes Tomates ke Auga Saganaki

1 pound medium raw shrimp
Salt and pepper to taste
4 Tbsp butter, margarine or good quality olive oil
10 large Roma tomatoes, peeled, seeded and
    chopped
2 or more cloves of garlic, crushed
1/2 bell pepper, finely chopped
1 Tbsp finely chopped flat leaf parsley
Pinch of pepper Cayenne
10 extra large eggs, beaten with
1/4 cup cream or milk
1/2 cup grated Parmesan, coarsely grated Swiss,
    or 1 1/2 cups crumbed feta cheese

Peel, devein and rinse the shrimp. Dry them on paper towels, season with salt and pepper. Sin a large not stick frying pan sauté shrimp in hot butter if desired for 2 minutes. Remove shrimp from frying pan. In the same pan add the tomatoes, chopped pepper, garlic, salt and peppers, and bring to a boil. Reduce the heat and simmer until all liquid evaporates. Add beaten eggs, cheese and parsley, stir well and add the shrimp. Cook until the eggs are cooked. Add the cheese, stir well to combine and serve hot if you used butter or hot and cold if you used oil. Serve on bed of rice as a lunch with salad and fresh crusty bread. Serves 6-10.

SHRIMP WITH OUZO
Gharithes me Ouzo

12 raw tiger shrimp (about 1 pound)
3 Tbsp good quality olive oil
1 garlic clove, crushed
Salt and pepper to taste
1/3 cup ouzo (Greek liqueur)
2 large red ripe tomatoes, peeled, seeded and
    chopped
1 Tbsp finely chopped parsley
1/3 cup cream

Rinse the shrimp in lots of cold water. Peel and devein them. Sauté in hot oil on both sides. Add garlic and sauté few minutes. Add salt, pepper,

ouzo, chopped tomatoes and parsley. Cook few minutes. Add cream and cook few minutes longer. Serve immediately as an appetizer. Serves 3-4.

SMOKED SALMON TARTLETS
Tartakia me Solomo

For the crust:
2 cups all-purpose flour (sifted)
2/3 cup chilled butter or margarine
4-5 Tbsp ice water

For the filling:
6 ounces smoked salmon, cut into small pieces
3 ounces cream cheese, at room temperature
1/4 cup butter, at room temperature
1/2 cup heavy cream
2 Tbsp fresh lemon juice
1/2 tsp Worcestershire sauce
Fresh springs of dill

Prepare the dough. Cut flour in butter with pastry blender, until mixture resembles coarse crumbs. Add 4 Tbsp. of the water, mix until pastry will hold together. Add the remaining 1 Tbsp. of water if needed. Roll out on a piece of parchment paper to a 1/8-inch thick. Cut and line 18-medium greased tart pans with pastry. Prick and bake in a preheated 450 F (230 C) oven for 10-12 minutes or until golden. Gently remove from tart pans and cool. Fill with salmon filling. While the tartlets are cooling, prepare the filling. In a food processor blend the first 6 ingredients together until smooth and creamy. Remove to a bowl, cover and chill until ready to use. Spoon the salmon mixture in a pastry bag with the star tip, and fill the cool tartlets. Decorate the tartlets with small springs of dill. Chill. Makes 18.
Note: You can use the filling to spread on canapés or on small sandwiches.

SPINACH PATE (L. CHOL. L. FAT)
Spanaki Pate

3 Tbsp olive oil
4 scallions, minced
1/2 pound fresh mushrooms, finely chopped
1 bag (16-ounces), cut leaf spinach, (thawed)

1/4 cup minced fresh dill
1 cup bread crumbs
1 egg plus 3 egg whites
1/4 cup dry milk
Salt and pepper to taste
2 cups nonfat cottage cheese.

Sauté scallions and mushrooms together with the oil until soft. In a food processor, finely chop spinach. Add the rest of the ingredients except cheese; process for 1 minute. Spoon into a bowl and fold in cottage cheese well to combine. Pour into well greased 10x10x3-inch baking dish, and pack lightly. Bake in a preheated 350 F (180 C) oven for 60 minutes. Serve hot or cold on Greek pita bread, crackers or melba toast. Serves 8-12

❦❦❦

SPINACH TRIANGLES
Trighona me Spanaki

2 pkg. (10 ounces each) frozen leaf spinach (thawed)
1 cup chopped fresh scallions or 1/4 cup minced onion
1/4 cup good quality olive oil
8 ounces feta cheese, crumbled
4 ounces farmers or ricotta cheese
3 eggs, lightly beaten
1 Tbsp minced fresh dill
1 Tbsp minced flat leaf parsley
Salt and pepper to taste
1 pound fillo pastry (thawed)
1 1/2 cups clarified butter, margarine (see index for recipe), or olive oil

Chop spinach, and squeeze as dry as possible, and place in a bowl. Sauté scallions in oil until tender but not brown. Add scallions, cheeses, eggs, parsley, dill, salt and pepper to the spinach, and mix well to combine. Take the fillo sheets from the package. Cut the fillo into three strips lengthwise about 4-inches each strip. Take one strip at a time covering the remaining strips with a dry cloth, then with lightly dampened towel to prevent them from drying out. For each triangle brush one sheet with hot melted butter if desired, fold in half lengthwise and brush again with butter. Place 1 tsp spinach mixture at one end of the folded strip. Lift a corner of the strip next to the filling and fold it over the filling, so that it

touches the opposite long side and forms a triangle enclosing the filling. Continue to fold up the pastry, keeping the triangle shape. Continue to fill and fold in triangles with the remaining strips. Place each one as- you finish in a greased baking sheet, brush again with hot melted butter. Bake in a preheated 350 F (180 C) oven for about 20-25 minutes or until golden. Serve hot. Make 70-80 triangles.

Note: Spinach triangles may be frozen before or after baking. When ready to bake, bake in a preheated 350 F oven about 30 minutes or until golden.

❦❦❦

SPINACH CHEESE SWIRLS
Spanakotyropitakia Rolo

4 scallions, finely chopped
2 Tbsp good quality olive oil
1 pound frozen leaf spinach, thawed, well drained and chopped
2 beaten eggs
1 cup pressed down coarsely grated Kasiri or Swiss cheese
1 cup crumbled Feta cheese
1/4 cup grated Parmesan cheese
1 Tbsp finely chopped fresh dill
1 Tbsp finely chopped flat leaf fresh parsley
Salt and pepper to taste
1 pkg 171/4-ounce puff pastry sheets (thawed)
1 egg, beaten with 1 Tbsp of water

While pastry thaws, prepare filling. Sauté onion in oil until soft. Add spinach, eggs, cheeses, dill, parsley, salt and pepper to onion and mix well to combine. Unfold pastry on lightly floured surface. Brush each sheet with egg. Top with filling and spread evenly. Staring at one side, roll up in a jellyroll fashion. Makes two rolls. Cut each roll into 20 (1/2-inch) slices. Place the rolls 2 inches apart on baking sheet. Brush tops with egg mixture. Bake in a preheated 400 F (205 C) oven for 15 minutes or until golden. Makes 40.

❦❦❦

STUFFED SQUID
Kalamarakia Ghemista

4 cups low sodium 100% fat free chicken broth
1/2 cup dry white wine
6 peppercorns

Juice of 1 lemon
1 garlic glove
2 bay leaves
4 extra large clean squid bags, fresh or
frozen (thawed)
12 ounces raw shrimp, peeled
5 leaves gelatin, soaked in cold water
2 Tbsp butter or margarine
4 anchovy fillets in oil, drained
3 ounces perch fillet
2 Tbsp finely chopped green olives
3 Tbsp finely chopped blanched almonds
3 Tbsp finely chopped pistachio nuts
2 Tbsp finely chopped capers
2 ounces grated Kefalotyri or Parmesan cheese
2 eggs, boiled and finely chopped
Salt and pepper to taste
Springs of fresh dill
Thin slices of lemon

In a small saucepan combine the first six ingredients. Bring to boil, add the squid, and bring again to boil. Reduce heat to medium-low and cook for 35 minutes. Add the shrimp and cook for 6 minutes. Remove from heat. Gently remove the squid and the shrimp from the broth. Drain the broth. Return broth to the heat for a minute or two and add the prepared gelatin, and stir vigorously to dissolve. When the gelatin has dissolved, remove from heat. Melt the butter if desired and sauté the perch fillet on both sides. Remove the fish fillet from the frying pan, and add the anchovy fillets, stir and mash them with a wooden spoon. Finely chop the shrimp and the perch fillet. In a bowl combine the shrimp, the fish, the mashed anchovies, olives, almonds, pistachio nuts, capers, cheese, egg, salt pepper and 1 1/2 cups about from the broth, and mix well. Chill to thicken. When is thicken enough fill the squid bags. Secure the opening with toothpicks. Chill for 60 minutes. Slice the stuffed squid with a sharp serrated knife into 1/2-inch slices. Place into a platter and smear on both sides with the prepared broth. Chill the platter with the sliced squid for 60 minutes or longer. When ready to serve decorate the platter with springs of dill and slices of lemon.

❧❦❧

TAHINI DIP (L. CHOL. L. FAT)

1 (15 ounces can) chick peas, drained
1/4-1/2 cup tahini (sesame paste)
2 Tbsp fresh lemon juice
2 garlic cloves, minced
3 Tbsp water
1/4 tsp ground cumin
2 Tbsp minced parsley
Salt and pepper to taste
Pinch cayenne pepper
Greek pita bread, toasted

Combine all the ingredients in a food processor and blend until smooth and creamy. Spoon into a serving bowl and serve with pita bread or fresh bread.

❧❦❧

TAHINI EGGPLANT SPREAD (L. CHOL. L. FAT)

Tahini Melitzanosalata

1 large eggplant (about 1 1/2 pounds)
2 or more garlic cloves, crushed
1/4 tahini (sesame paste)
2 Tbsp lemon juice or to your taste
2 Tbsp olive oil (optional)
Salt and pepper to taste

Remove stem of the eggplant and wash well. Puncture with a fork to prevent it from exploding while it bakes. Place in a baking pan and bake in a preheated 400 F (205 C) oven for 60 minutes or until soft to the touch. While hot, remove skin. Cut into pieces. In a food processor combine all the ingredients and blend well. Pour in a serving bowl and chill well. Serve with toasted Greek pita bread or fresh bread. Makes 2 1/2 cups.

❧❦❧

TARAMOSALATA

Carp Fish Caviar Spread

2 medium potatoes, boiled
9 ounces day-old shepherd bread, crust removed
1/2 jar (5-ounces) tarama (carp fish caviar)
1 Tbsp finely chopped onion (optional)
Juice of 1/2 or more lemon
1 1/2 cups good quality olive oil

Cut bread into large chunks and soak in cold water 10 minutes. Squeeze dry. In a food processor or blender, blend the tarama first for few minutes. Add the bread if desired and blend at high speed until smooth. While the machine is running, add onion, lemon juice, one tsp. at a time, add oil in a slow thin stream until mixture is thick and smooth. Chill. Serve with fresh bread or crackers.

❧❦❧

EASY TYROPITA IN A BUNDT PAN
Efkoli Tyropita sti Forma

 2/3 cup good quality olive oil
5 extra large eggs
1/2 cup each lightly pressed down coarsely grated
        Kaseri, Swiss and crumbled feta cheese
1/4 cup grated Kefalotyri, Parmesan or
        Romano cheese
1 Tbsp fresh minced mint
Pepper to your taste
Pinch of Cayenne pepper
1 1/2 cups all-purpose flour, sifted with
4 tsp baking powder
2/3 cup milk, mixed with
1 Tbsp fresh lemon juice
2 Tbsp sesame seeds (optional)

Beat oil until light. Add eggs one at a time, beating thoroughly after each addition. Add cheeses, mint and peppers, mix well to combine. Add flour alternately with the milk mixture. Pour the mixture into greased bundt pan and sprinkle with the sesame seeds if desired. Bake in a preheated 350 F (180 C) oven for 45 minutes or until golden brown. Cool slightly before slicing. Serve hot.

❧❦❧

TYROPITAKIA WITH BLUE CHEESE TRIANGLES
Cheese triangles

8 ounces blue cheese, crumbled
8 ounces cream cheese, at room temperature
4 Tbsp unsalted butter or margarine, at room
        temperature
White pepper to taste
1/2 cup coarsely chopped walnuts
1 pound about fillo pastry (thawed)
1 1/2 cups clarified melted butter or margarine
(see index for recipe)

In a bowl combine all ingredients except the fillo clarified butter together, and mix well. Follow preparation as directed in Spinach Triangles (see index for recipe).

❧❦❧

TYROPITAKIA WITH HOMEMADE PASTRY (L. CHOL.)
Tyropitakia me Fillo Spitiko Horis Holisterini

For the pastry:
1 1/2 cups fine quality olive oil (no extra virgin oil)
5 cups all-purpose flour (about)
3 tsp baking powder
1/8 tsp salt or to taste
1/2 cup lightly pressed down grated Parmesan or
        Pecorino Romano cheese or any other low
        fat hard cheese if desired
1 1/2 cups 1% milk

For the filling:
1 extra large egg white
8 ounces crumbled goat cheese or low fat feta
cheese
Pepper to taste
1 Tbsp minced mint
1 extra large egg white beaten with 1 Tbsp of water

Prepare the pastry. Sift dry ingredients together in a large bowl. Cut in oil with a pastry blender until mixture resembles coarse crumbs. Add cheese and milk and gently toss with your fingers. Add more flour if needed to make semi-soft dough. Divide the dough into 3 parts. Cover with plastic wrap, and let rest for 30 minutes. While the dough is resting prepare the filling. Beat the egg white, add cheese, pepper and mint, mix well to combine. On lightly floured surface, roll out one part of the dough, at a time to a 20-inch circle about and 1/8-inch thick. With a 33/4-inch round cookie cutter or smaller, cut out circles of dough. Place one half of a Tbsp of the filling on the middle of each of the circles. Gently fold the circles into half to make half-moon shape, use a spatula to lift the dough, if the dough sticks to surface. Gently lift the tyropitakia with the spatula one at a time and pinch edges together with your fingers well to seal. Place the tyropitakia on baking sheets lined with parchment paper. Repeat the same procedure with the remaining of dough and filling. Brush the tyropitakia with the beaten egg white. Let stand for 5 minutes to allow the egg to dry. Use the tines of a fork to prick a small vent in each tyropitaki. Bake in a preheated 375 F (190 C) oven on the middle rack for approximately 20-25 minutes or until golden brown. Serve hot. Makes about 40-60 tyropitakia.

TYROPITAKIA WITH HOMEMADE PASTRY
Tyropitakia me Filo Spitiko

For the pastry:
1 cup unsalted butter, at room temperature
1 cup good quality olive oil
1 cup milk
1 cup lightly pressed down grated Pecorino Romano or Parmesan cheese
6 cups all-purpose flour (about)
4 tsp baking powder
Pinch of salt or to taste

For the cheese filling:
1 extra large egg
12 ounces crumbled feta or goat cheese
1/8 tsp pepper
1 egg, beaten with 1 Tbsp water

Prepare the pastry. Sift dry ingredients together in a large bowl. Cut in butter and oil with a pastry blender until mixture resembles coarse crumbs. Add cheese and milk and gently toss with your fingers. Add more flour if needed to make a semi-soft dough. Divide the dough into 3 parts. Cover with plastic wrap, and let rest for 30 minutes. While the dough is resting prepare the filling. Beat egg, add cheese and pepper, mix well to combine. On lightly floured surface, roll out one part of the dough, at a time to a 20-inch circle about and 1/8-inch thick. With a 33/4-inch round cookie cutter or smaller, cut out circles of dough. Place one half of a Tbsp of the filling on the middle of each of the circles. Gently fold the circle into half to make half-moon shape, use a spatula to lift the dough, if the dough sticks to surface. Gently lift the tyropitakia with the spatula one at a time and pinch edges together with your fingers well to seal. Place the

tyropitakia on baking sheets lined with parchment paper. Repeat the same procedure with the remaining dough and filling. Brush the tyropitakia with the beaten egg. Let stand for 5 minutes to allow the egg to dry. Use the tines of a fork to prick a small vent in each tyropitaki. Bake in a preheated 375 F (190 C) oven on the middle rack for approximately 20-25 minutes, or until golden brown. Serve hot. Makes about 60-70 tyropitakia.
Note: Tyropitakia may be frozen before or after baking, as in cheese puffs (see index for the directions).

TYROPITAKIA WHEELS
Tyropitakia Rollo

8 ounces grated Pecorino-Romano or Parmesan cheese
8 ounces coarsely grated Kaseri cheese
1 pound feta cheese, crumbled
1 1/4 cups sour cream, drained
4 extra large lightly beaten eggs
White pepper to taste
1 1/2 pounds fillo pastry (thawed)
1 1/2 cups melted clarified butter or margarine (see index)

Divide Pecorino-Romano cheese if desired into four parts, set aside. Mix Kaseri and feta cheese, sour cream, eggs and pepper well to combine. Divide into four parts, set aside. Divide fillo sheets into four parts. Cover fillo sheets with a kitchen towel and then with a damp towel to prevent of drying out. Use one part at a time. Place one fillo sheet on a 20x14-inch heavy-duty foil. Gently brush fillo sheet with the hot melted butter if desired without brushing the foil. Place one more fillo sheet on top of the first, brush again with the hot butter. Sprinkle evenly with a handful of the grated Pecorino-Romano cheese. Place on another fillo sheet on top of the cheese, brush with hot butter. Sprinkle evenly with another handful of the cheese mixture. Repeat and continue until all the cheese and fillo is used. Take one part of the cheese egg mixture and spread evenly over the fillo. Gently lift layered tyropita from the wide side without the foil and roll. Wrap in with the foil, seal and freeze. Continue with the rest parts. Follow preparation as the first. When you are ready to use the rolled tyropita, thaw for 20 minutes and slice into 1/2 to 3/4-inch slices. Place slices tyropita on greased baking sheets and bake in a preheated 350 F (180 C) oven for 20-30 minutes, or until golden. Serve hot. Makes 4 rolls. Each roll makes about 20 slices.

TZATZIKI
Cucumber and yogurt spread

4 cups plain yogurt
2 Tbsp good quality olive oil
2 or more garlic cloves, crushed
2 tsp wine vinegar
1 long English cucumber, peeled, seeded, coarsely
*   grated and drained*
Salt and pepper to taste
1 Tbsp finely chopped fresh dill
1/2 Tbsp finely chopped fresh mint

Place yogurt in a strainer lined with cheesecloth or coffee filters. Place the strainer on a bowl, cover the yogurt and let drain over night in the refrigerator. Gently blend yogurt, garlic and cucumber, add oil, vinegar fresh dill, fresh mint if desired, salt and pepper to taste, blend well to combine. Chill. Serve with carrot and celery sticks, cucumber slices, crackers or pieces of bread, fried zucchini, and fried eggplants, in gyros or in shish kebob.

TZATZIKI (L. CHOL. L. FAT)
Cucumber and Yogurt Spread

4 cups non-fat or 2% plain yogurt
1 Tbsp olive oil
2 garlic cloves, crushed
2 tsp wine vinegar
1 long English cucumber, peeled, seeded, coarsely
*   grated and squeeze dry*
Salt and pepper to taste
1 Tbsp minced fresh dill
1/2 Tbsp minced fresh mint

In a bowl place a strainer lined with cheesecloth or a large coffee filter. Pour yogurt over the cheesecloth, cover and chill over night, or longer. Remove yogurt to a clean bowl, add all the ingredients, and blend well to combine. Chill. Serve with carrot sticks, celery, cucumber slices, fresh bread or toasted Greek pita bread.

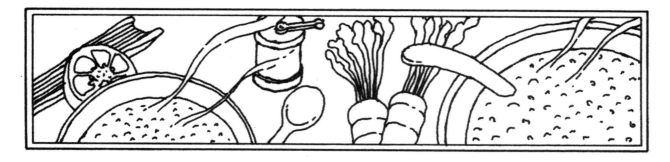

SOUPS

BEAN SOUP
Fasolada

1 pound small white beans
1 large minced onion
3 medium diced carrots
1 celery heart, diced
3 cups peeled, seeded and chopped ripe tomatoes or
1/3 cup tomato sauce
2/3 cup more or less olive oil
Salt and pepper to taste

Pick over beans carefully to remove any tiny stones, rinse under cold water and place in a large saucepan, cover with cold water. Cover saucepan and bring to a boil and boil for 10 minutes. Remove from heat, cover pan and let sit for 2 hours or overnight. Drain well and cover with hot water. Cover saucepan, bring to a boil, reduce heat and simmer for 50 minutes. Add the remaining ingredients, except the oil and salt, simmer for 45 minutes. Add oil and salt and hot water if soup is too thick. Simmer until beans are tender. Serve hot or cold. Serves 6-8.

✖✖✖

BOILED BEEF AVGOLEMONO SOUP
Vothino Vrasto Soupa Avgolemono

4 pounds beef shoulder, shank or brisket
4 small whole onions
3 carrots, cut in half
6 small whole potatoes
3 celery stalks, cut in half
1 Tbsp salt
3/4 cup long grain rice
2 eggs
Juice of 1 or more lemons
Olive oil and vinegar dressing (optional-see index)
Mustard (optional)

Trim meat of excess fat. Rinse meat in cold water. Set meat in a large pot with cold water to cover by 2 inches. Bring to the simmer, skim off any scum for several minutes, partially cover and simmer for 1 hour and 45 minutes. Add all the vegetables, salt and simmer for 60 minutes longer or until meat is tender when pierced with a fork Add more water as needed. Remove meat, cut into serving pieces and arrange on a hot serving platter. With a slotted spoon, gently remove the vegetables and arrange them around the meat pieces. Keep warm. Strain the broth, measure it; add enough hot water to make 10 cups bring to a boil, add rice and stir. Reduce heat and simmer for 20 minutes. Remove from heat. In a medium mixing bowl beat eggs until frothy, gradually beat in lemon juice. Add approximately a quarter of the hot broth, at first spoon by spoon and then a little more at a time beating constantly. Gradually add egg mixture to the soup, stirring gently to combine. Keep stirring for a few more minutes on a low heat, do not let the soup boil. Serve soup immediately, followed by the meat and the vegetables. Pass olive oil and vinegar dressing (see index) or mustard if desired. Serves 6.

✖✖✖

BOILED CHICKEN AVGOLEMONO SOUP
Kotopoulo Vrasto Soupa Avgolemono

1 whole chicken (about 5 pounds)
2 carrots, cut in half
3 stacks celery, cut into thirds
2 whole small onions
4 whole small peeled potatoes
1 Tbsp or more salt

3/4 cup long grain rice
2 eggs
Juice of 1 or more lemons

Clean and rinse chicken well. Place in a large pot and cover with cold water. Bring to a simmer, skim off any scum for several minutes, partially covered and simmer for 30 minutes. Add all the vegetables, salt and simmer for 60 minutes longer. Let chicken and vegetables stay in the broth for 30 minutes. Remove chicken and cut into serving pieces and arrange on a hot serving platter. With a slotted spoon, gently remove the vegetables and arrange them around the chicken pieces. Keep warm. Strain the broth, measure it; add enough hot water to make 10 cups, bring to a boil, add rice and stir. Reduce heat and simmer for 20 minutes. Remove from heat. In a medium mixing bowl beat eggs until frothy, gradually beat in lemon juice. Add approximately a quarter of the hot broth, at first spoon by spoon and then a little more at a time beating constantly. Gradually add egg mixture to the soup, stirring gently to combine. Keep stirring for a few more minutes on a low heat, do not let the soup boil. Serve soup immediately, followed by the chicken and the vegetables. Serves 6

CREAM OF LEEK AND POTATO SOUP
Krema Soupa me Prasa ke Patata

4 medium potatoes
3 medium leeks
1 medium onion
6 cups fresh beef or chicken stock or can fat free
    chicken broth
2 Tbsp butter or margarine
2 Tbsp flour
2 cups scalding milk
Salt and pepper to taste

Peel and roughly chop potatoes, chop the leeks and wash several times in cold running water. Roughly chop onion. Place all the vegetables in large pot, add stock if desired and bring to a boil. Reduce heat and simmer until vegetables are tender. Drain. Save the stock. Mash the vegetables through a food mill or food processor until smooth. In a medium saucepan melt butter, using a wire whisk blend in flour until smooth. Remove saucepan from the heat. Gradually add milk and stock, stirring constantly, return to heat, stirring constantly until boiling point is reached. Reduce heat and simmer for 3 minutes longer. Add seasonings and blend. Add mashed vegetables; bring to a boil and simmer for 5 minutes, stirring constantly. Serve hot, topped with croutons if desired. Serves 6.

CREAM OF LEEK-SPINACH SOUP
Krema Soupa me Prasa ke Spanaki

1 large leek
1 Tbsp butter
1 Tbsp good quality olive oil
Salt and pepper to taste
1 large potato, peeled and chopped
8 ounces fresh spinach
8 ounces fresh Swiss chard
5 cups or more fresh chicken stock of 100% fat free
    chicken broth
2 egg yolks
1 cup cream
Fresh croutons

Clean and wash leeks well. Chop and wash again thoroughly in several waters. Drain in a strainer. Set aside. Pull the stems off the Swiss chard and chop them finely and wash as the leeks. Set aside. Roughly chop the chard and wash as the leeks. Set aside. Remove roots from spinach and coarse leaves and wash as the Swiss chard. Set aside. Saute the leeks with butter and oil until soft, season with salt and pepper. Add the stock, the Swiss chard stems and the potatoes and cook slowly for 15 minutes. Add the spinach, stir and cook slowly for 15 minutes or until the vegetables and potatoes are tender. Add more stock if needed. Remove from the heat and with the hand blender puree the soup. Return to heat and bring to boil. Beat the egg yolks with the cream. Gradually add the egg mixture to the soup, stirring constantly for 2 minutes (do not let the boil). Serve immediately with croutons.

FISH AND AVGOLEMONO SOUP
Psari and Psarosoupa

2 pounds striped bass, sea bass or pike
Salt and pepper to taste
6 whole small peeled potatoes
3 carrots, cut in half
4 whole small onions
3 stalks celery, cut into thirds
2 whole medium-sized ripe tomatoes
8 cups water
1/2 (or less) cup olive oil
6 Tbsp long grain rice
2 eggs
Juice of 1 lemon
Mayonnaise

Clean and rinse fish well. Sprinkle with 1 teaspoon of salt, cover and chill. Place the vegetables, olive oil, salt and water in a large saucepan. Bring to a boil. Reduce heat and simmer for 40 minutes. Add the fish and slowly simmer uncovered, for approximately 20 minutes. Remove from heat. Let the fish stay in the broth for 20 minutes. Gently remove fish and arrange in a heated serving platter. With a slotted spoon, remove the vegetables and arrange them around the fish. Keep warm. Strain the fish stock through a strainer, using the back of a spoon, and press the tomatoes through. Make sure no fish bones or scales go into the stock. Return stock to the heat, bring to a boil, add rice and simmer for 20 minutes. In a medium mixing bowl beat eggs until frothy, gradually beat in lemon juice. Add approximately a quarter of the hot stock, at first spoon by spoon and then a little more at a time beating constantly. Gradually add egg mixture to the soup, stirring gently to combine. Keep stirring for a few more minutes on a low heat, do not let the soup boil. Serve soup immediately, followed by the fish and vegetables. Pass mayonnaise or lemon-oil dressing (see index), at the table. Serves 4-5.

Note: For a beautiful fish platter, for a buffet or dinner party, gently remove skin and bones from the cooked fish. Reform fish pieces into the shape of a fish. Cover with mayonnaise and decorate with slices of hard-boiled eggs, dill pickles and capers.

LENTIL SOUP
Fakes Soupa

1 1/2 cups lentils
8 cups hot water
1 large minced onion
3 cloves garlic, sliced
1/4 cup tomato sauce
2 small bay leaves
1/4 tsp Greek oregano
Salt and pepper to taste
1/2 cup more or less olive oil
2 Tbsp wine vinegar

Pick over lentils carefully to remove any tiny stones, rinse under cold water, and place in a medium saucepan. Cover with cold water and bring to a boil. Reduce heat, cover and simmer for 10 minutes. Drain well and add 8 cups of hot water, onion, garlic, tomato, bay leaves and oregano. Bring to a boil, reduce heat, cover and simmer for 45 minutes. Add oil, salt, pepper and vinegar; simmer for 30 minutes longer or until lentils are tender. Add more hot water if needed. Serve hot or cold. Serves 4-6.

TINY MEATBALLS AVGOLEMONO SOUP
Youvarlakia Avgolemono

1 pound lean ground beef
1 small minced onion
1 Tbsp minced parsley
Salt and pepper to taste
1/2 cup long grain rice
3 eggs
8 cups fresh beef stock or water
2 Tbsp or less butter or margarine (optional)
Juice of 1 lemon or more

Combine meat, onion, salt, pepper, half of the rice and 1 egg. Mix well by hand to combine. Shape into tiny balls. In a four-quart saucepan boil the stock. Remove from heat and drop in the meatballs. Return saucepan to heat and bring to a boil, add rice and butter if desired, stir slowly. Simmer partially covered for 30 minutes. In a mixing bowl, beat eggs until frothy. Gradually beat in lemon juice. Add approximately a quarter of the hot broth. At first, spoon by spoon, and them a little more at a time beating constantly. Gradually add egg mixture to the soup, stirring gently to combine. Keep stirring for a few more minutes on low heat, do not let the soup boil. Serve immediately. Serves 4-6.

TOMATO ORZO SOUP
Kritharaki Soupa me Tomata

8 cups fresh chicken, turkey or beef stock
1 cup ripe, peeled and chopped tomatoes or
*   1/2 cup tomato juice*
1/2 cup kritharaki (orzo Greek pasta)
Salt and pepper to taste

Bring stock and tomato to a boil. Add pasta and stir well. Reduce heat and simmer partially covered for 30 minutes. Stir occasionally. Serve hot. Serves 4.

TRAHANA SOUP
Soupa Trahanas

8 cups fresh chicken, turkey or beef stock
1/2 cup tomato juice
1/2 cup trahana (sweet or sour)
Salt and pepper to taste

Bring stock and tomato juice to a boil. Sprinkle trahana to the stock and stir well. Reduce heat and simmer partially covered. Stir occasionally. Simmer for 25 minutes. Serve hot. Serves 4.

TURKEY AVGOLEMONO SOUP
Ghalopoula Soupa Avgolemono

1 large onion, cut into fourths
4 carrots, cut into fourths
4 stalks celery, cut into fourths
1 1/2 cups long-grain rice
3 eggs
Juice of 2-3 lemons
1 turkey carcass

After you have sliced the turkey on Thanksgiving day, save bones, skin, gizzards, neck, etc. Place in large deep pot and cover with cold water. Bring to a boil. Reduce heat and simmer 4 hours. Skim off as much fat as possible. Add carrots, onion, celery and salt. Simmer 1 hour longer. As liquid cooks away add more water as needed. Strain the stock, skim off some of the fat. Chill stock overnight if you wish; it will be easier to remove the fat. Leave 3 Tbsp. of the fat if you wish; the soup will taste better. Measure it; add enough water to make 6-quarts. Bring to a boil, add rice, and stir well. Reduce heat and simmer for 20 minutes. Remove from heat. In a medium mixing bowl beat eggs until frothy, gradually beat in lemon juice. Add approximately a quarter of the hot broth, at first spoon by spoon and then a little more at a time beating constantly. Gradually add egg mixture to the soup, stirring gently to combine. Return to the heat. Reduce heat to very low. Keep stirring a few more minutes (do not let soup boil). Serve immediately.

VEGETABLE SOUP
Hortosoupa

1 cup chopped celery
3 cups peeled and cubed potatoes
1 cup chopped carrots
2 cups chopped cabbage
1 cup chopped zucchini
1 cup chopped green beans, fresh or frozen
1 cup fresh or frozen peas
3 cups ripe, peeled and chopped tomatoes
1 medium chopped onion
16 cups fresh beef, chicken or turkey stock or low
*   sodium 100% fat free chicken froth*
Salt and pepper to taste

Place all the ingredients together in a large pot and bring to boil. Reduce heat, stir well, cover, and slowly simmer for 60 minutes or until vegetables are tender, stirring frequently. If the soup is too thick, add hot stock or water and simmer for 5 minutes longer. Serve hot. Serves 6-8.

SALADS

ARTICHOKES SALAD
Agkinares Salata

12 fresh or frozen artichokes
Juice of half lemon
3 cups boiling water
1 tsp salt

If fresh prepare artichokes as directed in How to Prepare Artichokes (see index). Boil artichokes in salted water and the lemon juice for 30 minutes or until tender. Drain. Serve with oil-lemon dressing A (see index for recipe). Serves 6-12.

❧※❧

BEET APPLE WALNUT SALAD
Pantzarosalata

3 medium raw beets, scrubbed, peeled and coarsely
    grated (about 4 cups)
3 Tbsp wine vinegar
3 medium raw carrots, rinsed, peeled and coarsely
    grated (about 1 1/3 cups)
1 Tbsp. olive oil
1/2 cup sugar
1/4 tsp salt
1/4 tsp pepper
1 Tbsp. lemon juice
2 large granny smith apples, scrubbed, cored and
    cut into small cubes
1/2 cup chopped walnuts
1-1 1/2 cups mayonnaise
1 Tbsp. chopped walnuts for topping

Mix grated beets with the vinegar, let stand 60 minutes. Drain well. Then squeeze with your hands to remove excess liquid. Mix all the ingredients together. Spoon into a serving bowl or on bed of lettuce and chill. Serves 8.

❧※❧

BEET SALAD
Patsaria Salata

10-12 young beets with tops
1/2 Tbsp salt
1/2 cup or less olive oil
2 Tbsp wine vinegar

Remove leaves and stalks from beets. Retain tender leaves and stalks. Cut off leaves from stalks; cut stalks in half and wash well in cold running water. Soak beets in water for 30 minutes. Scrub beets well under cold running water to remove dirt. In a large pot place beets and stalks. Cover with cold water and add salt. Bring to a boil, reduce heat, cover and boil 45 minutes. Add leaves and boil until tender. Drain. Remove beet skin with fingers while hot under cold running water to prevent burning and staining hands. Slice beets into a bowl, add stalks and leaves. Toss with olive oil and vinegar. Serve with garlic sauce (see index) or plain, hot or cold.

❧※❧

BOILED BEEF SALAD
Moshari Vrasto Salata

2 pounds sliced boiled beef (see index)
1 medium cubed boiled potato
1 cup cooked peas
1 cup cubed cooked carrots
2 hard-boiled eggs, cut into fourths
1/3 cup more or less olive oil
1 Tbsp or more wine vinegar
Salt and pepper to taste
1 cup tartar sauce (see index)

In a serving platter, place meat in the center. Arrange vegetables and eggs around meat.

Combine oil, vinegar, salt and pepper and blend well. Pour oil mixture over meat and vegetables. Pass tartar sauce. Serve hot or cold. Serves 4-8.

CABBAGE APPLE SALAD
Laghano Milo Salata

4 cups finely shredded cabbage, rinse well and drain
1 cup grated carrots,
2 tart apples, pared, cored and cut into small cubes
Salt and white pepper to taste
1 cup chopped walnuts or pecans
1 1/2 cups less or more mayonnaise

Mix all ingredients together, cover and chill. When ready to serve, spoon into serving bowl.

CABBAGE SALAD
Lahano Salata

1 small head cabbage, finely shredded
2 medium peeled and grated raw carrots
Salt and pepper to taste
1/3 cup or less olive oil
Juice of 1 or more lemons

Place cabbage in a colander and rinse well under cold running water. Drain well. Chill. When ready to serve, toss cabbage with 4 Tbsp. olive oil, 2/3 of the lemon juice and salt and pepper. Place cabbage in serving bowl. Toss grated carrots with remaining olive oil and lemon juice and salt. Decorate cabbage by placing carrots in center of bowl. Serves 6-8.

CHICKEN OR TURKEY CABBAGE APPLE SALAD
Kotopoulo-Galopoula Lachano Milo Salata

2 cups cooked chicken or turkey, cut into small cubes and firmly pressed down
5 cups cabbage, finely shredded and firmly pressed down; rinse and drain well
2 cups grated and firmly pressed down carrot
4 large tart or mixed apples, wash, core and cut into small cubes
Salt and white pepper to taste
1 cup or more chopped walnuts or pecans
21/2 cups or more mayonnaise

Mix all ingredients together, add more mayonnaise if needed. Cover and chill. When ready to serve, spoon into serving bowl or on bed of lettuce.

MACARONI SALAD WITH FETA CHEESE
Macaroni Salata me Feta Tyri

1 pound macaroni small shells or bows
8 ounces feta cheese, crumbled
2 Tbsp finely chopped flat leaf parsley
1/8 tsp Greek oregano, crushed
Pepper to taste
1/4 cup good quality olive oil
2 Tbsp wine vinegar
24 or less Kalamata olives, pitted and cut into fourths
4 scallions, thinly sliced
1 medium red bell pepper, seeded, white membranes removed, and diced
1 medium yellow bell pepper, seeded, white membranes removed, and diced
3 Tbsp capers, rinsed
1/4 cup roasted blanched chopped almonds or pine nuts (optional)
2 medium tomatoes, cut into thin wedges

Cook the macaroni in 3 quarts boiling salted water, for 20 minutes. Drain well. Rinse with cold water, and drain again. In a large bowl combine all the ingredients together and toss well. Place the mixture in a serving bowl or serving platter and decorate with the tomato wedges. Serve chilled. Serves 6-8.

MACARONI SALAD
Macaronia Salata

1 pound bow ties macaroni
1/4 cup or more olive oil
1 yellow bell pepper
1 red bell pepper
1 green bell pepper
3 medium ripe tomatoes
2 Tbsp capers
1 Tbsp finely chopped flat leaf parsley
3 anchovy fillets, finely chopped
Juice of 1 lemon

Boil macaroni in 4 quarts boiling salted water 20 minutes or to taste. Drain well, rinse with cold water and drain again. Transfer to a large bowl, add oil and toss well. While macaroni is boiling, prepare peppers. Place peppers in a baking pan and broil in the oven or on a grill until skins are blistered. Remove from oven and place in a plastic bag, close bag and let stay 15 minutes. Prepare tomatoes. Cut tomatoes into 1/2-inch slices and lay them on a baking pan lined with parchment paper. Sprinkle tomatoes lightly with salt and bake in a 450 F (230 C) oven for 15-20 minutes. Remove from oven and chop into cubes, add to the macaroni. While the tomatoes are roasting, peel the peppers and remove the seeds. Cut peppers into small strips, and add to the macaroni. Add the rest of the ingredients and toss gently to combine. Chill the salad. Serves 4-8.

❦❦❦❦

MEAT SALAD IN A MOLD
Salata Jele me Kreas

3 Tbsp gelatin
2 cups boiling fresh beef or chicken stock
2 cups cold fresh beef or chicken stock
1 Tbsp fresh lemon juice
Salt and pepper to taste
4 cups boiled beef or chicken (see index), cut
    into cubes
1 cup coarsely chopped celery
1/3 cup or more coarsely chopped dill pickles
1/3 cup or more roasted red peppers, cut into strips
4 hard-boiled, roughly chopped eggs
1/2 cup cubed cooked carrots
1 cup cooked asparagus tips
1 Tbsp or more capers
Leaves of lettuce

Chill all the ingredients. Dissolve gelatin in boiling stock, add cold stock, lemon juice, salt and pepper, and mix well. Set aside to cool. Mix all the ingredients together in a large mixing bowl. Add gelatin and mix well to combine. Pour into 12-cup mold. Chill until firm. Gently invert the mold on a bed of lettuce on a serving platter and remove the salad from the mold. Serve cold. Serves 6-12.

❦❦❦❦

POTATO SALAD
Patatosalata

18 small red potatoes (about 4 pounds)
1 small red onion, thinly sliced
8 ounces feta cheese, crumbed (optional)
1/4 cup or more kalamata olives, petted and cut
    into fourths
2 Tbsp capers
2 Tbsp minced flat leaf parsley
3 eggs, hard-boiled, cut into fourths
2 medium tomatoes, washed and cut into wedges
Salt and pepper to taste
3/4 cup more or less olive oil
Juice of 1 or more lemons

Scrub and wash potatoes well. Drop in 4 quarts boiling salted water and cook 20-30 minutes, or until tender when pierced with a fork. Remove from heat and drain. Cut potatoes into cubes. Place potato cubes on large round platter or bed of lettuce. Sprinkle with onion, feta cheese if desired, kalamata olives, capers, parsley and tomatoes. In a small bowl or jar combine salt, pepper, olive oil and lemon juice and beat well. Spoon oil mixture over potato salad. Decorate with hard-boiled eggs. Serve warm or cold with fresh crusty bread. Serves 6-8.

❦❦❦❦

RICE SALAD WITH FETA CHEESE
Rizi Salata me Feta Tyri

2 cups long grain rice
8 ounces feta cheese, crumbed
2 Tbsp. chopped fresh mint
2 Tbsp. chopped flat leaf parsley
2 medium tomatoes, cored and diced
1 medium yellow bell pepper, seeded, white
    membranes removed, and diced
1 medium red bell pepper, seeded, white
    membranes removed, and diced
4 scallions, sliced
1 cucumber, peeled seeded and diced
3 Tbsp. capers, rinsed
24 or less Kalamata olives, pitted and cut
    into fourths
1/2 roasted chopped blanched almonds or
    pine nuts (optional)
1/4 cup olive oil
2 Tbsp. or more fresh lemon juice or wine vinegar
Salt and pepper to taste
1 medium tomato, cut into thin wedges

Cook rice in 3 quarts boiling salted water for 20 minutes or to taste. Drain well, rinse and drain again thoroughly. In a large bowl combine all ingredients and toss well. Let the salad rest 10 minutes before serving. Place rice salad in a serving bowl or platter, and decorate with tomato wedges. Serves 6-10

RUSSIAN SALAD GREEK STYLE
Rossiki Salata

3 cups cubed boiled potatoes
1 cup cooked small white dried beans
1 cup cooked peas
1 cup cubed cooked carrots
4 hard-boiled eggs, chopped
1/2 cup or more finely chopped dill pickles
2 Tbsp capers
1 1/4 cups or more mayonnaise, mixed with
1 1/2 tsp mustard
Salt and pepper to taste
2 hard-boiled eggs, cut into fourths
12 Kalamata Greek olives
Leaves of lettuce (optional)
1 boiled beet-root, rinsed well, drain and cut into
    eighths and dry well

Chill all vegetables. In a large mixing bowl, combine first 6 ingredients, add 1 Tbsp. capers, 1 cup mayonnaise mixture, salt and pepper; toss well. Spoon in a serving bowl or arrange leaves of lettuce on a serving platter and spoon salad over it. Spread remaining mayonnaise over salad. Garnish with eggs, olives beet and capers. Chill until ready to serve. Serves 10-12
Note: Add 2 cups cooked lobste, cut into cubes and increase mayonnaise to 1 3/4 cups, if desired.

SHRIMP OR LOBSTER SALAD
Garither or Astako Salata

3/4 cup mayonnaise
2 Tbsp ketchup
1/2 tsp Worcestershire sauce
3 cups roughly chopped chilled cooked shrimp or
    lobster meat

Combine first 3 ingredients and blend well. Add shrimp if desired and mix well. Chill until ready to serve. Spoon shrimp salad in a serving bowl. Sprinkle with paprika. Serves 6-10.

SHRIMP SALAD
Garithosalata

1 pound cooked medium shrimp, chilled (fresh
    or frozen [thawed])
1 romaine lettuce
1/2 cup whipping cream, whipped
3 Tbsp ketchup
1/2 cup mayonnaise
1 Tbsp fresh lemon juice
Pinch Cayenne pepper
Salt and pepper to taste
1 Tbsp brandy
1 tsp horseradish
2 Tbsp chopped flat leaf parsley
2 springs of flat leaf parsley

Separate the leaves from the lettuce, and wash well under cold running water. Pick the best tender leaves from the hart, and keep the rest for salad. Prepare the sauce. In a bowl combine all the ingredients except the lettuce and the shrimp, and mix well. Add the shrimp and fold well to combine. Arrange romaine leaves on a round platter and spoon the shrimp salad over. Decorate with the springs of parsley.

SPRING SALAD
Anixiatiki Salata

1 large romaine lettuce, washed well and
    finely shredded
4 scallions, finely sliced
1 Tbsp fresh dill, finely chopped
1/4 cup or less olive oil
1 Tbsp more or less wine vinegar or balsamic
Salt and pepper to taste

Wash all the vegetables well under cold running water. Drain well. Finely shred the romaine lettuce. Combine all the ingredients together in a serving bowl and toss well. Serve immediately. Serves 4-6.

SPRING SALMON SALAD
Salata Anixiatiki me Solomo

1 romaine lettuce
4 scallions, finely sliced
2 Tbsp finely chopped fresh dill
1 large granny smith apple, washed, cored and
*   cut into small cubes*
5 ounces finely coarsely grated Graviera (Greed
*   cheese) or Parmesan*
1 can (8-ounces) red salmon, well drained and
*   finely shredded*
1/4 cup good quality olive oil
3 Tbsp red wine vinegar or balsamic
Salt and pepper to taste

Remove coarse leaves from the lettuce and discard. Remove the leaves from the root and wash one by one in several waters. Finely shred the leaves. In a large mixing bowl combine all the ingredients except the oil, vinegar, salt and pepper and mix well. Beat the oil with the vinegar, salt and pepper until well mixed. Spoon over the salad and toss well. Chill the salad until ready to serve. Serves 4-6.

SUMMER COUNTRY STYLE SALAD
Kalokerini Horiatiki Salata

3 medium sliced tomatoes
1 thin peeled and sliced cucumber
1 medium thinly sliced red onion
1 medium bell pepper, seeded and thinly sliced
2 Tbsp capers
1/4 tsp crushed Greek oregano or 2 Tbsp chopped
*   fresh Greek oregano*
1/4 cup or more olive oil
1 Tbsp wine vinegar or balsamic
Salt and pepper to taste
8 ounces feta cheese, cut into small chunks
12-24 Kalamata Greek olives

Wash and chill all the vegetables before cutting. Place the vegetables and capers in a serving bowl. When ready to serve, place the oil, vinegar, oregano, salt and pepper in a small bowl and mix well to combine. Pour over the salad and toss gently. Add feta cheese and olives. Serve immediately. Serves 4-8.

SUMMER RICE SALAD
Kalokerini Salata me Rizi

1 1/3 cups converted rice, boiled in salted water,
*   drained well*
3 medium red ripe tomatoes, cored, seeded and cut
*   into 1/4-inch dice*
1 yellow bell pepper, seeded, white membranes
*   removed, cut into 1/4-inch dice*
1 seedless cucumber, wash well and cut into
*   1/4-inch dice*
1/2 cup finely chopped red onion
1 1/4 cups or more crumbled feta cheese
16 or more Kalamata olives, pitted and sliced
1/4 cup chopped capers
1/4 cup finely chopped fresh flat leaf parsley
3 Tbsp. finely chopped fresh mint
1/2 cup or more extra virgin olive oil
2 Tbsp or more wine vinegar or balsamic
Salt and pepper to taste
Shaves of Parmesan cheese
Springs of mint

In a large bowl, combine all the ingredients together and toss well. Spoon in a serving bowl, and decorate with Parmesan cheese and spring of mint. Let salad rest for few minutes at room temperature before serving. Serve with fresh crusty bread. Serves 6-8.

TOMATO SALAD
Ntomatosalata

3 medium ripe red tomatoes, cut into halves
*   crosswise and then into wedges*
1 thin cucumber, peeled and thinly sliced
1 bell pepper, seeds removed and thinly sliced
1 small red onion, thinly sliced
1 small bell pepper, seeds removed and
*   thinly sliced*
1/4 cup good quality olive oil
2 Tbsp or more balsamic vinegar
Salt to taste

Wash and chill the salad before slicing. Place sliced salad in a large bowl. When ready to serve, add salt, olive oil and vinegar. Toss gently to combine. Serve immediately. Serves 3 to 5.

TOMATO SURPRISE SALAD
Tomata Ekpliktiki

8 medium ripe firm round tomatoes
1 1/2 cups diced cooked breast of chicken or turkey
1/4 cup slivered toasted blanched almonds
1/4 tsp crushed tarragon
3/4 cup coarsely chopped celery
Salt and pepper to taste
2/3 cup more or less mayonnaise
Leaves of lettuce
8 springs of flat parsley

Cut out the stems of the tomatoes and discard. Wash and dry them. Cut a thin slice from the stem end of each tomato. Scoop out the pulp; remove seeds; reserve pulp. Chill all the ingredients. When ready to serve mix all the ingredients together. Fill the tomatoes. Arrange on a bed of lettuce. Decorate each tomato with a spring of flat parsley. Serve as a first course or as a lunch. Serves 4-8.

VEGETABLE SALAD
Lachanosalata

2 pounds beets (about 4 medium)
4 medium potatoes
4 medium carrots, cut into cubes and boiled
1 cup white cooked beans
1 cup cooked peas
6 pickles, finely chopped
1 bunched scallions, thinly sliced
1/4 cup finely chopped fresh dill
Salt and pepper to taste
1/3 cup or more good quality olive oil
3 Tbsp or more wine vinegar or balsamic

Scrub beets and potatoes well under cold running water to remove all dirt. In a large saucepan place the beets and cover with taped water and salt. Bring to boil, cover and boil for 30 minutes. Add the potatoes and cook for 30-45 minutes or until tender when pierced with a fork. Drain. Skin beets while are hot, under running cold water, this way it is easy to peeled them and you don't stain your hands. Cut beets into small cubes and place into a large bowl. Peel potatoes, and cut into small cubes, and add to the beets. Add the rest of the ingredients with the beets and the potatoes, and toss gently to combine. Cover the bowl and chill. Serves 4-8.

WALNUT-YOGURT AND FRUIT SALAD
Salata Frutou me Karythia ke Yiaourti

1 1/2 cups walnuts, toasted and roughly chopped
2 apples, cored and cut into cubes
1 cup seedless grapes, if large cut into half
1 cup strawberries, cut into fourths
1 banana, cut into cubes
3/4 cup or more honey
1/2 tsp cinnamon
1/8 tsp nutmeg
21/2 cups yogurt

Gently mix the fruit in a large bowl. Chill. In a separate bowl combine honey, cinnamon, nutmeg, and yogurt together. Blend well. Arrange fruit in individual bowls. Pour sauce over fruit and garnish with toasted walnuts. Serve 8-10.
Note: You can use any kind of fruit you desired.

SEAFOOD

BAKED FISH FILLETS WITH LEEKS
Filleta Psariou Me Prasa Sto Fourno

3 large potatoes
2 large leeks
1 medium onion, finely chopped
1/2 cup more or less good quality olive oil
3 garlic cloves, finely minced
6 large fillets of sole, flounder or thin
       swordfish steaks (about 2 1/2 pounds)
Sliced tomatoes 1/4-inch thick
1/2 cup slivered blanched almonds or pine nuts

Scrub the potatoes and rinse well. Drop them in boiling salted water and boil for 20 minutes. Remove from heat and let cool. Peel the potatoes and cut into 1/4-inch slices thick. While the potatoes are boiling prepare the leeks. Clean and rinse leeks well. Cut into thin slices and rinse again in a colander under cold running water. Drain them well. In a large skillet sauté leeks and onion in 1/4 cup of the olive oil until soft. Add garlic salt and pepper to taste and sauté for a minute or two. Remove from heat and let stand. Lay the potatoes in a well-greased baking dish in one layer. Spoon leek mixture over the potatoes and spread evenly. Place the fish fillets over the leek mixture and sprinkle with salt and pepper. Cover fillets with sliced tomatoes, sprinkle with salt, the remaining olive oil and almonds if desired. Bake in a preheated 350 over for 25-30 minutes depending on the sizes of the fish. Serve hot or at room temperature with salad, feta cheese, and fresh crusty bread. Serves 4-6.

❧❀❧

BAKED FISH WITH LEMON
Psari tou Fournou Lemonato

3-4 pounds whole red snapper, porgies or bluefish
1/4 cup or more olive oil
1/4 tsp. crushed Greek oregano
Juice of 1 or more lemons
Salt and pepper to taste
1/2 cup water

Ask the fisherman to clean your fish. Rinse fish well. Place in an oiled baking dish. Sprinkle with oil, lemon juice, salt, pepper and oregano. Add water to the dish and bake in a preheated 350 F (180 C) oven for approximately 45-50 minutes depending on the size of the fish. Occasionally baste with the sauce. Serve hot. Serves 4-6.

❧❀❧

BAKED FISH WITH ONIONS AND TOMATOES
Psari me Kremithia ke Tomates sto Fourno

3 pounds fresh whole trout, pike or white fish
Juice of 1/2 lemon
Salt and pepper to taste
3/4 cup good quality olive oil
1 large onion, thinly sliced
1 cup dry white wine
2 cloves garlic, crushed
2 Tbsp all-purpose flour
1/2 cup tomato sauce or 4 large ripe, peeled,
      seeded and chopped tomatoes
1/4 cup chopped flat leaf parsley
1/2 cup dried breadcrumbs, (see index)

Ask the fisherman to clean the fish for you. Rinse fish well. Sprinkle with lemon juice and season with salt. Cover, and chill while preparing the sauce. In a saucepan heat olive oil and sauté the onions until soft. Add garlic and flour and sauté few minutes longer. Add wine, tomatoes, parsley, salt and pepper. Cover and simmer for 10 minutes. Place fish in an oiled baking dish. Pour sauce over the fish and sprinkle with the breadcrumbs. Bake in a preheated 350 F (180 C) oven for 40-45 minutes, basting occasionally with the sauce. Serve hot. Serves 6.

BRAISED SHRIMP IN GARLIC SAUCE
Garithes me Skortho

1/3 cup olive oil
1/2 cup shallots, finely chopped
3-4 garlic cloves, minced
1 cup dry tomatoes in oil, chopped
1/2 cup dry Vermouth
1 cup fresh chicken stock of can fat free
    chicken broth
Salt and pepper to taste
1 1/2 pounds raw medium shrimp, peeled
1 pound bowties
3 Tbsp. melted butter, margarine or olive oil
Grated Parmesan, Kefalotyri or Romano cheese

Sauté shallots in oil until soft, add garlic and sauté few minutes longer. Add tomatoes, Vermouth, stock, salt and pepper. Cove and simmer for 20 minutes. Add shrimp and cook for 10 minutes or until tender. Remove from heat. While the sauce is simmering boil the bowties in 4 quarts of boiling salted water for 20 minutes or to your taste. Drain well and add the melted butter if desired, and toss well to combine. Place bowties in a serving platter, and generously sprinkle with grated cheese, spoon the shrimp with the sauce over the pasta and serve hot. Serve with salad and fresh crusty bread. Serves 5-6.

BREADED FLOUNDER
Gloses Pane

2 pounds flounder or sole fillets
Salt to taste
1 cup dried breadcrumbs (see index)
2 Tbsp. grated Parmesan cheese
Pepper to taste

2 eggs beaten with 1 Tbsp of water
Clarified butter or margarine for frying

Rinse fish and dry well. Cut into serving pieces and sprinkle with salt. Mix breadcrumbs with the grated cheese and pepper. Dip fish in beaten eggs, then roll in breadcrumbs to cover well. Fry in hot butter until golden brown on both sides. Serve hot with Tartar Sauté (see index), salad and French fries (see index) if desired. Serves 4-6.

CODFISH CROQUETTES
Bakaliaros Crokettes

1 pound frozen of fresh cod or haddock
    fish fillets (thawed)
21/2 cups mashed potatoes
3 egg-yolks
3 Tbsp cream or milk
1 small onion, finely chopped
1 tsp salt
1/2 tsp pepper
1 cup flour
2 egg whites, lightly beaten
1 1/2 cups fine dried breadcrumbs
Oil for frying

Chop fish finely. In a mixing bowl, mix well first seven ingredients. Chill for couple hours. Shape into small balls each about 1-inch in diameter. Roll them lightly in flour, and shake off excess flour, then in egg whites and in crumbs. Fry croquettes in hot oil until golden brown on all sides. Lift out and drain on absorbent paper. Serve hot or cold with garlic sauce (see index for recipe).

CODFISH PATTIES
Bakaliaros Tiganites

1 pound fresh or frozen (thawed) chopped cod or
    haddock fish fillets
1/3 cup milk
1 beaten egg
1 cup all-purpose flour
2 tsp baking powder
1 Tbsp olive oil
Salt and pepper to taste
1 Tbsp minced flat leaf parsley
Oil for frying

Combine milk, egg, flour, baking powder, oil, salt, pepper and parsley. Blend until smooth. Add fish and mix well. Drop from a tablespoon into hot oil and fry until brown on both sides. Serve with any salad, fresh crusty bread, and skorthalia if desired (see index for recipe). Serves 4-6.

❦❦❦

COD FISH AU-GRATIN
Bakaliaros Au-Graten

3 medium potatoes (about 2 pounds)
1 1/2 pounds cod fish fillets, fresh or
        frozen (thawed)
21/2 cups milk
1 small onion, thinly sliced
5 springs of flat leaf parsley
1 bay leaf
5 Tbsp butter, margarine or good quality olive oil
5 Tbsp all-purpose flour
Salt and pepper to taste
8 ounces medium raw shrimp, peeled, rinsed
        and dried
3 Roma tomatoes, peeled, seeded and
        finely chopped
1/4 cup butter, margarine or good quality olive oil
1/3 cup hot milk

Scrub and wash the potatoes well. Drop them in boiling salted water and boil for 30 minutes or until tender when pierced with a fork. Remove from heat and drain. They may be peeled quickly before they are cool. Mash the hot potatoes with a food processor in a bowl. Add the butter if desired, hot milk and white pepper and beat until light. Cover and let stand. While the potatoes are boiling prepare the fish. Rinse the fish fillets well and dry. Place milk in a deep frying pan and add the fillets, onion, parsley and bay leaf. Bring to a boil, reduce heat and cook slowly for 13 minutes. Remove the pan from the heat. Gently remove the fillets from the pan to a bowl, remove the skin and bones and cut into cubes. Drain and reserve the liquid. Melt butter if desired over medium heat, blend in flour until smooth using a whisk. Remove from heat and gradually add the reserved milk, stirring constantly. Return back to heat and slowly cook until mixture is thick and smooth. Remove from heat and add the fish

pieces, the shrimp, the tomatoes, salt and pepper and mix well to combine. Spoon the fish mixture in a greased casserole and spread evenly. Spoon mashed potatoes in pastry bag with a star tip and decorate over the fish mixture to cover. Bake in a preheated 350 F (180 C) oven for 30-40 minutes. Remove from oven and serve immediately with carrots and peas sautéed and salad (see index for the recipes). Serves 4-6.

❦❦❦

COD FISH GRATINEE
Bakaliaros Gratine

3 pounds potatoes
3 cups water
1 small onion, chopped
2 bay leaves
1/2 tsp. peppercorns
2 garlic cloves, chopped
2 pounds cod fish fillets, rinsed with cold water
Salt and white pepper to taste
8 Tbsp butter, margarine or good quality olive oil
9 Tbsp all-purpose flour
4 1/2 cups scalding milk
2 eggs, beaten
1/2 cup lightly pressed down grated Parmesan,
Kefalotyri or Romano cheese
5 ounces coarsely grated Swiss or Kaseri
        cheese or mixed

Scrub and wash the potatoes. Drop them in boiling salted water and boil for 45-60 minutes or until tender when pierced with a fork. When cooked, drain. They may be peeled quickly before they cool. Cut into 1/4 -inch slices and set aside. While potatoes are boiling, prepare the fish. In a saucepan add the water, onion, bay leaves, peppercorns, garlic and salt. Bring to a boil, reduce heat to medium-low and simmer for 10 minutes. Add the fish, add enough water to cover the fish and simmer for 8 minutes or until flaked. Remove from the heat and remove the fish from the broth. Flake the fish and place in a bowl. While the fish is simmering, prepare the sauce. Melt butter if desired over medium heat, blend in flour until smooth using a wire whisk. Remove from the heat and gradually add the milk, stirring constantly. Return to heat and cook until mixture is thick and smooth. Cook 3 minutes longer. Remove from heat. Spoon little by little of the hot sauce into beaten eggs if desired stirring constantly, add egg mixture to the sauce and cook over very low heat (do not let the sauce boil) for 2 minutes, stirring constantly. Add Parmesan cheese, salt and pepper, and stir well to combine. In a well-greased 14x11 1/2 x 21/2 -inch baking dish spread a layer of the sauce (1/2-inch thick about) in the bottom of the dish. Arrange the sliced potatoes in one layer, (divide the coarsely cheese into five parts) sprinkle with one part of the cheese, cover with half of the flaked fish, sprinkle with second part of the cheese and cover with half of the sauce. Repeat with potatoes, cheese, fish, cheese and finish with the sauce. Spread the sauce evenly, and sprinkle the remaining cheese over the sauce. Bake in a preheated 375 F (190 C) oven on the middle rack for 35 minutes. This dish is excellent for brunch. Serve immediately. Serves 6 for a main course or 12 as first course.

❧✠❧

CODFISH RAGOUT
Bakaliaros Ragou

2 pounds fresh or frozen (thawed) codfish or
*   haddock fillets*
1 1/2 tsp salt or to taste
1 large sliced onion
3 cloves garlic, sliced
1/2 cup more or less olive oil
4 large whole ripe, peeled, seeded and
*   chopped fresh tomatoes*
1/8 tsp pepper
1/4 cup chopped flat leaf parsley
5 medium potatoes, cut into fourths
1 cup water

Rinse fish well and cut into serving pieces. Sprinkle with salt. Chill until ready to cook. Sauté onion and garlic in oil until soft. Add tomatoes, parsley, potatoes, salt, pepper and water. Bring to a boil. Reduce heat, cover and simmer for 20 minutes. Add fish and simmer for 20 minutes longer or until fish flakes easily when tested with a fork. Serve hot or cold. Serves 4-6.

❧✠❧

FILLET OF FLOUNDER ROLLS WITH AVGOLEMONO SAUCE
Rola Glosas Avgolemono

12 flounder or sole fillets
2/3 cup fresh breadcrumbs
4 scallions, finely chopped
2/3 cup coarsely chopped shrimp
1 1/2 Tbsp. finely chopped fresh dill
2/3 cup finely chopped mushrooms
Salt and pepper to taste
2 large eggs + 1 egg yolk
Juice of one lemon about
1 cup dry white wine or Vermouth
1 tsp. lemon rind
2/3 cup cream
Fresh springs of dill for decoration and
*   lemon slices*

Rinse fillets and dry on absorbent paper towels. In a bowl add breadcrumbs, scallions, shrimp, dill, mushrooms, salt, pepper, and one egg and one egg white and mix well to combine. Place fish fillets on a cutting board. Divide the mixture onto 12 fillets. Roll fillets starting form the tall, and secure with a toothpick. Place rolled fillets in a greased baking dish and pour over the wine, one cup of water, juice and lemon rind and bake in a preheated 375 F (190 C) oven for 20-25 minutes. Remove from oven. Drain the liquid and place in a small saucepan. Boil the fish liquid in medium heat until half. Beat cream with the remaining two egg yolks, and gradually add to the fish liquid, stirring constantly. Slowly cook, stirring constantly until lightly thickens. Season the sauce and pour over the rolled fillets. Serve immediately with rice pilaf, salad and fresh crusty bread (see index for the recipes). Serves 4-6.

❧✠❧

FILLET OF SOLE WITH FETA CHEESE
Filleta Glosas me Feta

6 fillets of sole
1 finely chopped shallot
2 Tbsp butter, margarine or olive oil
Salt and pepper to taste
12 spinach leaves, washed, trimmed and dry
6 ounces feta cheese, crumbled
1 1/2 cups dry white Vermouth
1 1/2 Tbsp all-purpose flour

2 Tbsp Dijon mustard
Finely chopped parsley for decoration

Sauté half of the shallots with butter if desired, until soft, over medium-low heat. Remove from heat and let cool for few minutes. While the shallots are cooling, prepare the fillets. Season fillets with salt and pepper. Lay 2 spinach leaves on each fillet. Set aside. Combine sauté shallots with crumbled feta cheese and mix well. Divide feta mixture among fillets. Roll up each fillet from sort side to make a shape of a cylinder. Place, seam side down, in a well-greased baking dish. Pour 1/4 cup of wine over the rolls, cover and bake in a preheated 450 F (230 C) oven for 15 minutes, or until fish flakes easily with a fork. While the fish is baking prepare the sauce. Sauté the remaining shallots with the remaining butter and sauté until shallots are soft, over medium-low heat. Add the flour, and cook slowly, stirring constantly, for 1 minute. Add the remaining wine, bring to a boil; and cook slowly, add the mustard, and stir well to combine. Cook, stirring constantly until sauce thickens, season with salt and pepper to your taste. Remove from heat and serve over the fish rolls, sprinkle with chopped parsley. Serve hot. Serves 3-6.

❈❀❈

FISH AND SHELL FISH AU-GRATIN
Thalasina Ograten

2 cups water
Salt
5 peppercorns
1 bay leaf
1 pound fillets of flounder or sole, fresh or
    frozen (thawed)
1 pound raw crab, shelled, fresh or
    frozen (thawed) or scallops
1 pound medium raw shrimp, shelled, fresh or
    frozen (thawed)
6 Tbsp butter, margarine or good quality olive oil
6 Tbsp all-purpose flour
2 cups scalding milk
Salt and pepper to taste
2 Tbsp fresh lemon juice
1/2 cup pressed down grated Kefalotyri or
    Parmesan cheese

1/4 cup dried breadcrumbs (see index for recipe)
3 Tbsp butter or margarine

In a saucepan combine first four ingredients. Bring to a boil. Add fish and shelled fish if fresh, and simmer for 5 minutes. Drain, reserve 1 cup from the stock, save the rest for other use. Cut fish into 1-inch cubes. Melt butter; add flour and blend well. Add milk and fish stock, cook slowly until thickened, stirring constantly. Add salt and pepper. Cook slowly for 3 minutes longer. Add lemon juice, fish and half of the grated cheese. Mix well. Fill a greased baking dish with the mixture. Sprinkle with cheese and then with breadcrumbs and dotted with butter. Bake in a preheated 425 F. (205 C) oven for approximately 15 minutes or until bubbling hot and sauce has browned nicely. Serve immediately as an appetizer or on bed of rice for a main course. Serves 6-10.

❈❀❈

FISH BALLS AVGOLEMONO
Psari Yiouvarlakia Avgolemono

1 pound ground fish (cod, flounder, sole or
    any other fish)
1 small onion, minced
2 garlic cloves, minced
2 eggs
2 cups soft breadcrumbs or more
1 Tbsp finely chopped flat leaf parsley
Salt and pepper to taste
4 cups boiling water or fish stock
1 egg, beaten
Juice of one lemon or more

Mix the first seven ingredients together, add more breadcrumbs if needed to make a thick mixture. Shape into balls the sizes or a walnut. Remove the saucepan from the heat, and gently drop the fish balls into the boiling water. Return to the heat, bring to boil, reduce the heat and simmer for 15-20 minutes or until cooked. Remove the saucepan from the heat and spoon little by little of the hot broth into the beaten egg, stirring constantly. Gradually add egg mixture to the pot and continue stirring. Return to the heat and reduce the heat to low, cook for few minutes longer (don't let the avgolemono boil), stirring constantly. Serve hot. Serves 3-4.

FISH SHISH KEBOB
Psari Souvlaki

1/3 cup good quality olive oil
1/2 cup lemon juice
1/4 tsp onion powder
3 bay leaves
Salt and pepper to taste
3 pounds swordfish or halibut cut into 1-inch cubes
18 cherry tomatoes
12 bay leaves
1/2 cup good quality olive oil
1/2 cup lemon juice
1/2 cup minced onion
2 Tbsp minced flat leaf parsley
Salt and pepper to taste

In a glass bowl, combine the first 5 ingredients, and mix well. Add fish cubes and toss well. Cover and chill for 5 hours. Thread fish cubes, cherry tomatoes and bay leaves, alternately on 12 skewers. Grill the shish kebobs over charcoal turning and basting frequently with remaining marinade. In a serving bowl combine the rest of the ingredients. Mix well and serve with the shish kebobs. Serve hot with salad and rice pilaf (see index). Serves 6.

FRIED CODFISH WITH GARLIC SAUCE
Bakaliaros Tiganitos me Skordalia

2 pounds fresh or frozen (thawed) codfish or haddock fillets
1 2/3 cups all-purpose flour
1/2 tsp baking powder
1 1/2 tsp salt or to taste
1/8 tsp pepper
1 Tbsp olive oil
1 beaten egg (optional)
2/3 cup milk or water
Oil for frying
For the Garlic Sauce (see index)

Rinse codfish well, and dry on a paper towel, cut into serving pieces. Chill until ready to fry.

Combine flour, baking powder, salt, pepper, and egg if desired, oil and milk if desired. Blend until smooth. Dip fish into batter. Deep-fry few pieces at a time in hot oil until golden brown and crisp. Drain on absorbent paper. Serve hot with garlic sauce and beets salad (see index) or any other salad you desire. Serves 4-6.

FRIED SHRIMP WITH TOMATO SAUCE
Tiganites Garithes me Saltsa Tomatas

1 pound raw shrimp
Salt and pepper to taste
2 Tbsp dry white wine or Vermouth
2 egg white, lightly beaten
1 1/2 Tbsp cornstarch
5 Tbsp unsalted clarified butter or good quality olive oil
1 cup finely chopped white onion
3 large garlic cloves, minced garlic
2 Tbsp minced parsley
3 large red ripe tomatoes, peeled, seeded and diced (about 1 1/2 pounds)
1 8 ounces can cooked sliced mushrooms, drained (optional)
1/3 cup dry white wine or Vermouth

Rinse shrimp in lots of cold water, peel and devein. Place shrimp in a bowl, and sprinkle with salt and 2 Tbsp wine. Mix by hand until combined. Add the egg whites and work in until absorbed. Add the cornstarch and mix until smooth. Chill for at least 30 minutes. In a medium saucepan, sauté the onion in 2 Tbsp or the butter if desired over medium heat, add garlic and sauté for few more minutes. Add parsley, tomatoes and season with salt and pepper. Cook for 10 minutes. Add the mushrooms if desired and cook for 1 minute. While sauce is simmering prepare shrimp. Melt the remaining 3 Tbsp. of the butter if desired over medium heat in a frying pan. Add shrimp and cook for 1 minute. Add wine and cook until wine has evaporated. Pour shrimp into the sauce and cook for 1 minute. Remove from heat, and serve immediately. Serve with fresh crusty bread and a good wine.

Kritharaki Soup

Bean Soup

Fish Avgolemono Soup
and
Boiled Fish

Cabbage Salad

Summer Country Salad

FRIED SHRIMP
Gharithes Tighanites

1 pound raw shrimp
Salt
1 egg, lightly beaten
1/2 cup four
Oil for frying
Juice of 1 lemon

Wash shrimp in lots of cold water, peel and devein them. Dry on paper towel. Sprinkle with salt. Dip shrimp into egg a few at a time and then into flour. Shake excess flour. Fry shrimp in hot oil on both sides until golden. Sprinkle with lemon juice and serve hot. Serve with salad. Serves 2-4.

❧❀❧

FRIED SQUID
Kalamarakia Tiganita

2 pound young squid
Salt
Flour for coating
Oil for frying
Fresh lemon juice

Wash the squid in cold running water. Pull off heads. Remove backbone, guts and black skin. Wash again in a bawl of salted water, then rinse thoroughly. Pat them dry on absorbent paper. Slice into 1/2-inch rings, or if they are small leave them whole. Pat dry again. Season the squid with salt. Coat squid, with flour, shake off excess flour. Fry in hot oil until golden, no more than 3 minutes. Serve hot with fresh lemon juice and fresh crusty bread. Serves 6-8.

❧❀❧

GRILLED RED SNAPPER OR PORGY
Sinagritha ke Tsipoura sti Skara

3 pounds whole snapper or porgies
Salt and pepper to taste
1/4 cup good quality olive oil
Juice of 2 lemons
1 large red onion, thinly sliced
1/3 cup good quality olive oil
2 Tbsp chopped flat leaf parsley

Ask fisherman to clean your fish. Rinse fish well and dry on paper towels. Sprinkle with salt, cover; chill 1-2 hours. Mix olive oil with juice of half lemon. Brush fish with mixture and place on grill. Grill fish 10-12 minutes on each side depending on thickness. Occasionally brush fish with oil-lemon mixture. Place fish on serving platter. In a colander, place sliced onion and salt, rub well with your fingers. Rinse off salt under cold running water, and pat on paper towel to absorb excess water. In a mixing bowl blend olive oil and lemon juice, add salt, pepper to taste and chopped parsley, mix well. Pour over grill fish. Serve fish hot with Spring Salad or Summer Country Style Salad (see index for recipes), and French fries. Serve hot. Serves 3-4.

❧❀❧

HOW TO BOIL AND CLEAN A LOBSTER
Pos na Vrasis ke na Katharisis Astako

1 medium onion, cut in half
1 carrot, cut in half
2 stalks celery, cut in half
3 springs flat leaf parsley
1 small bay leaf
1/2 tsp peppercorns
1 Tbsp salt
3 Tbsp white vinegar
3 quarts water
2 live lobsters, (about 2 pounds each)

In a large pot, place all the ingredients, except the lobsters and boil for 30 minutes. Pick up live lobsters back of claws and plunge it into boiling water, head downward. Cover and boil for 15 minutes. Reduce heat and simmer for 10 minutes longer. Plunge it into cold water and when cool enough to handle, take the meat from the shell in the following order. Chop off the claws. Split the body lengthwise and remove and discard the stomach, a small sac just back of the head. Running from the stomach to the base of the tail is the intestinal canal. If this does not pull out with the stomach, it must be lifted out with a fork, in pieces, if necessary, and removed entirely. Crack the claws and remove the meat. If the lobster is not to be served whole, take out the meat from the body, the creamy green fat which constitutes the liver, and the coral or spawn found in female lobsters. The spongy particles between the meat and shell are not used. Serve with mayonnaise. Serves 2

❦❦❦

LOBSTER AU-GRATIN
Astakos Ograten

2 boiled lobsters (about 2 pounds each-see index)
4 medium boiled potatoes (see index)
1/4 cup tomato sauce
1/4 cup water
1/4 tsp sugar
6 Tbsp butter or margarine
8 Tbsp all-purpose flour
1 1/2 cups fresh chicken stock if possible
2/3 cup cream
Salt and pepper to taste
1/2 cup grated Kefalotyri or Parmesan cheese
1/4 cup dried breadcrumbs (see index)
1/4 cup melted butter or margarine

Remove meat from lobster and cut into dice. Peel potatoes and dice. Boil tomato sauce with the water and sugar, covered on low heat for 15 minutes. Melt butter, blend in flour, and add chicken stock and cream, cook slowly until thickened, stirring constantly. Add salt and pepper and cook for 7 minutes longer. Add tomato and blend well. Add diced lobster and potatoes, mix well to combine. Fill greased scallop shells or shallow baking dish with the mixture. Top with the grated cheese, and sprinkle with the breadcrumbs, and with the melted butter. Bake in very hot oven 425 F (220 C) oven for approximately 15 minutes. Serve immediately. Garnish with the coral if desired.

❦❦❦

MUSSELS RICE PILAF
Mythia Pilafi

1 medium onion, finely chopped
2/3 cup or less good quality olive oil
3 or more large garlic cloves, crushed
1 cup dry white wine or Vermouth
2 pounds Roma tomatoes, peeled, seeded
*   and chopped*
Salt and pepper to taste
2 Tbsp finely chopped flat leaf parsley
4 pounds mussels
1 1/2 cups converted rice

Soak the mussels 60 minutes, then scrub and rinse them in several waters. Remove the beard and discard, and place in the refrigerator until ready to use. Sauté onion in oil until soft, add the garlic and sauté for one minute. Add the wine, the tomatoes, salt, pepper and parsley, bring to boil, reduce the heat and simmer for 20 minutes, partially covered. Add the mussels, cover; and cook for 15 minutes or until they are all open. Remove from the heat, and remove the mussels in a deep plate, and keep warm. Measure the sauce and add enough water to make 3 1/2 cups. Bring to boil, add the rice, stir well and reduce the heat to medium-low, and simmer for 20 minutes or until tender, partially covered. Serve immediately the rice with the mussels, salad and fresh crusty bread. Serves 4.

❦❦❦

MUSSELS WITH SPAGHETTI
Mythia me Makaronia

1 medium onion, finely chopped
1/4 cups good quality olive oil
3 or more garlic cloves, crushed
1 cup dry white wine or Vermouth
2 pounds Roma tomatoes, peeled, seeded
*   and chopped*
Salt and pepper to taste
2 Tbsp finely chopped flat leaf parsley
4 pounds mussels
12 ounces to 1 pound spaghetti
3 Tbsp melted butter, margarine or good
*   quality olive oil*
Grated Kefalotyri or Parmesan cheese

Soak the mussels for 60 minutes, then scrub and rinse them in several waters. Remove the beard and discard, and place in the refrigerator until ready to use. Sauté onion in oil until soft, add the garlic and sauté for one minute. Add the wine, the tomatoes, salt, pepper and parsley, bring to boil, reduce the heat and simmer for 20 minutes, partially covered. Add the mussels, cover; and cook for 15 minutes or until they are all open. Remove from the heat, and remove the mussels in a deep plate, and keep warm. Cook the sauce until thickens. While the sauce and mussels are simmering prepare the spaghetti. In a 4-quart saucepan, add 3-quarts of water, bring to boil, add salt and the spaghetti, stir well. Bring to boil again, reduce the heat to medium and boil for 20 minutes or until tender, uncovered. Drain the spaghetti, place into a deep platter, spoon the hot melted butter over and sprinkle with the grated cheese. Arrange the mussels over the spaghetti and spoon the sauce over it. Serve immediately with salad and fresh crusty bread. Serves 4.

OCTOPUS IN WINE
Oktapothi Krassato

3 pounds octopus, fresh or frozen (thawed)
1/2 cup olive oil
1 cup finely chopped onion
2 cloves garlic, crushed
1 cup dry red wine
1/2 cup tomato sauce
Salt and pepper to taste

Rinse octopus well and cut into 1-inch cubes. Heat oil and sauté onion and garlic until soft. Add octopus and sauté for few more minutes; add wine and cook until wine evaporates. Add tomato sauce, salt, pepper and 1 cup water. Cover and cook slowly for 60 minutes or until tender. Serve hot, plain or with rice pilaf (see index), and salad. Serves 6.

SALMON WITH LINGUINI
Solomo me Linguini

12 ounces linguini
Salt and white pepper to taste
8 ounces salmon fillet, skin removed and
        cut into small cubes
1 medium onion, finely chopped
2 Tbsp butter, margarine or good quality olive oil
2 garlic cloves, finely minced
1/2 cup dry white wine or Vermouth
2 Tbsp finely chopped flat leaf parsley
2/3 cup cream or milk
1 Tbsp fresh lemon juice
Grated Parmesan or Kefalotyri cheese (optional)

Drop linguini in boiling salted water and boil for 20 minutes or to your taste. Drain well. Let stand. Sauté the salmon cubes and the onion with butter if desired for few minutes, or until onion is soft. Add the garlic, wine if desired, parsley to the salmon and cook slowly until wine evaporates. Add the cream and the lemon juice to the salmon mixture and stir well. Add the linguini and stir well to combine. Serve immediately, sprinkle with cheese if desired, salad (see index for the Salad recipe) and fresh crusty bread. Serves 2-3.

SEAFOOD WITH RICE PILAF
Pilafi me Thalassina

2 medium onions, finely chopped
1/2 cup good quality olive oil
1 cup squid, clean and thinly sliced
2 cups medium raw shrimp, peeled and rinse
3 pounds mussels
1 cup octopus, cut into small pieces and rinse
1 1/2 cups white wine
2 pounds ripe tomatoes, pressed through a
        food mill
Salt and pepper to taste
2 cups water
21/2 cups converted rice, rinsed and drain well
1/3 cup melted butter

Scrub the mussels with a stiff brush and pull out the hairy beards. Discard any broken mussels, or open ones that don't close when tapped. Rinse well. In a large pot sauté onion in olive oil until soft. Add all the seafood, wine and the tomatoes. Cover, and let cook for 15 minutes. Remove all the seafood from the pot to a large bowl. Discard any unopened mussels. Let all the liquid drain back to the pot. Add water to the pot and bring to a boil. Add rice salt and pepper, stir well, reduce heat and cook for 10 minutes, add the seafood to the rice and more water if needed, stir well, cover and cook for 10 minutes longer or until rice is tender. Remove from heat and pour the melted butter over. Stir well to combine. Serve hot. Serves 6

SEAFOOD WITH SPAGHETTI
Spagketi me Thalasina

12 ounces squid, buy already clean
Salt and pepper to taste

3 garlic cloves, finely minced
1/3 cup good quality olive oil
2 large ripe tomatoes, peeled, seeded and
*   cut into small cubes*
1 cup dry white wine or Vermouth
1/4 tsp or more finely chopped fresh thyme
12 ounces spaghetti
8 ounces medium raw peeled shrimp, rinse well
2 pounds mussels scrubbed and rinse well
1 pound clams scrubbed and rinse well
2 Tbsp finely chopped flat leaf parsley
1 Tbsp finely chopped fresh basil

Rinse the squid well in cold water. Pat dry. Slice in 1/2-inch thick rings, season with salt and pepper. Sauté the squid and the garlic in 4 Tbsp of the oil for 3 minutes. Add the tomatoes and sauté for few minutes longer, stirring constantly. Add the wine if desired, the thyme and cook slowly for 20 minutes. While the squid is simmering boil the spaghetti in boiling salted water for 20 minutes or to your taste. Drain and rinse with hot water, and drain again well. Transfer the spaghetti back to the pot and add the remaining olive oil and stir well to combine and keep warm. Add the shrimp, mussels and clams to the tomato mixture, stir well, cover; and cook slowly for 3-5 minutes or until the shells open. Sprinkle with parsley and basil. Serve hot over the spaghetti, with salad and fresh crusty bread. Serves 4-6.

❈❀❈

SEAFOOD WITH SPINACH AU GRATIN
Thalasina me Spanaki Au Graten

3 pounds frozen leaf spinach (thawed)
1 cup butter, margarine or good quality olive oil or
*   half of each*
1 large bunch scallions, thinly sliced
Salt and pepper to taste
1/4 cup whipping cream or milk
2 cups dry white wine or Vermouth
4 ounces grated Parmesan cheese
5 ounces coarsely grated Kaseri (Greek cheese)
31/2 pounds flounder or Dover sole fillets
2 pounds medium raw peeled shrimp or scallops
1/3 cup fresh lemon juice
1 cup all-purpose flour
5 cups scalding milk
White pepper to taste
3 extra large eggs, beaten

Drain spinach in strainer. With your hands, squeeze out excess water, and chop. Sauté scallions in 1/4 cup of olive oil if desired until soft. Add spinach to scallions, salt, pepper and stir well, sauté 10 minutes or until liquid has evaporated. Add cream if desired and cook on low heat 3 minutes. Let stand. Prepare fish. In a large frying pan add wine and 3 Tbsp butter if desired, salt and pepper, bring to boil, add fish. Cover; bring to boil again, reduce heat to low and simmer 5 minutes. Remove from heat. Remove fish, and let stock cook until reduced to 1 cup. Sprinkle shrimp if desired with lemon juice and let stand. While fish is cooling prepare béchamel sauce. In 3-quart saucepan melt remaining butter if desired over medium heat, blend in flour until smooth using wire whisk. Remove from heat and gradually add milk, and fish stock, stirring constantly. Return to heat and cook until it thickens, stirring constantly. Cook 3 minutes longer; add white pepper and blend. Remove from heat and spoon little by little of the hot sauce into the beaten eggs, stirring constantly. Add egg mixture to the sauce, and continue stirring. Let cool. Mix the Parmesan and Kaseri cheese together. Add all of cheese except of 1 cup to the sauce, and stir well to combine. Assembling the dish. Add 1 1/2 cups of the béchamel sauce to the spinach, and mix well to combine. In a greased 14x11 1/2x2 1/2-inch (about) baking dish spread the spinach mixture. Break up the fish into small pieces with your hands, arrange over the spinach, and top with 1 1/2 cups of the sauce and spread evenly. Drain and dry the shrimp from the lemon juice and arrange over the sauce, in one layer. Spoon the remaining béchamel sauce over the cheese and spread evenly. Sprinkle the remaining cheese over the béchamel. Bake the au gratin in a preheated 375 F (190 C) oven on the middle rack for 30 minutes or until bubbling hot and sauce has browned nicely. Let stand for 20 minutes. Cut and serve on rice pilaf. Serves 10 to 12.

❈❀❈

SHRIMP CROQUETTES
Gharithes Kroketes

1 pound cooked shrimp
2 Tbsp minced onion
2 Tbsp minced flat leaf parsley
2 Tbsp finely chopped celery (stem only)
2 sheets gelatin
5 Tbsp butter or margarine
5 Tbsp all-purpose flour
2 cups milk
2 egg-yolks, lightly beaten
Salt and pepper to taste
1 tsp Worcestershire sauce
2 Tbsp fresh lemon juice
Flour for rolling
3 beaten egg whites
3 cups dried fine breadcrumbs (see index)
2 Tbsp grated Parmesan cheese
Good quality olive oil for frying

Drain and pat dry shrimp, and chop. Soak gelatin in cold water. In a small-saucepan melt butter over medium-heat, blend in flour until smooth using a whisk. Gradually add milk, stirring constantly until mixture is thick and smooth. Cook 5 minutes longer. Spoon little by little of the hot sauce into egg-yolks, stirring constantly. Gradually add egg mixture to the sauce and cook over low heat for 2 minutes, stirring constantly. Squeeze gelatin dry, add to the sauce, and stir well until gelatin has melted. Add shrimp, onion, parsley, celery, salt, pepper and Worcestershire sauce, and mix well to combine. Remove from heat, let cool, and chill for 4 or more hours. Shape into cylinders, each about 2-inches in diameter. Chill again for 30 minutes. Roll them lightly in flour, shake off excess flour, them in egg whites and then in crumbs. Fry croquettes in hot oil, until golden brown on all sides. Lift out and drain on absorbent paper. Serve hot.
Serves 6-8.

SHRIMP RAGOUT WITH RICE PILAF
Garithes Ragout me Rizi Pilafi

1 pound mushrooms
4 Tbsp butter, margarine or good quality olive oil
1 medium onion, finely chopped
2 garlic cloves, crushed
1/2 bell pepper, chopped
1 1/2 pounds ripe tomatoes, peeled, seeded
    and chopped
Salt and pepper to taste
3/4 cup dry white wine or Vermouth
1 1/2 pounds medium raw shrimp, peeled
    and deveined
2 Tbsp finely chopped flat leaf parsley
2 cups converted rice
1/4 cup butter or margarine

Rinse mushrooms in gold running water, dry them on paper towels and slice. Sauté mushrooms in butter if desired, until liquid evaporates. Add onion, garlic, green pepper and sauté until soft. Add wine, tomatoes, parsley, salt, pepper and 1 cup water. Bring to a boil, reduce heat and simmer for 20 minutes, stirring occasionally. Add shrimp and simmer for 15 minutes. While the ragout is simmering prepare the rice. Place 3 quarts water in a saucepan, add salt, bring to a boil. Add rice and stir well. Reduce heat to medium and boil for 20 minutes. Drain well. Return the rice to the saucepan, add butter and stir with a fork. Place the rice in a ring mold, if desire. Invert the rice in a serving platter. Pour shrimp with sauce over rice, and serve immediately. Serve with salad and fresh crusty bread. Serves 6-8.

SHRIMP WITH LINGUINE
Garither me Linguine

2 pounds medium raw shrimp
1/2 cup more or less olive oil
2 garlic cloves, minced
3 Tbsp finely chopped flat leaf parsley
Salt and pepper
1/2 cup white wine or Vermouth
1 medium onion, finely chopped
1 (29-ounces can) whole tomatoes, chopped
1 pound linguine
Grated Parmesan or Kefalotyri Greek cheese

Peel and devein the shrimp, rinse under cold running water. Drain well. Keep them chill. In a frying pan sauté garlic with 4 Tbsp. of the olive oil for 30 seconds. Add shrimp and the parsley, salt and pepper and sauté on both sides until the shrimp is pink, about 3 minutes, add the wine and simmer for 3 minutes longer. Remove from heat. With the remaining olive oil sauté the onion until soft. Add the tomatoes, salt and pepper. Bring to a boil. Reduce heat and simmer for 50 minutes. Add shrimp to the sauce and simmer for 3 minutes. While the sauce is simmering, boil the linguine in boiling salted water for 20 minutes or to your taste. Drain well. Serve the linguine with the sauce over it, and sprinkle with grated cheese if desired. Serve hot with salad and fresh crusty bread (see index for recipe). Serves 4-6.

❦❦❦❦❦

SHRIMP WITH MUSHROOM AND RICE
Garithes me Manitaria ke Rizi

1 medium onion, finely chopped
 1/2 cup more or less good quality olive oil,
        butter or margarine
2 cups converted rice
4 1/2 cups fresh chicken stock or can low sodium
100% fat free chicken broth
Salt and pepper to taste
1/2 cup toasted slivered blenched almonds
1 pound mushrooms
3 garlic cloves or more finely minced
1/2 cup dry white wine or Vermouth
4 medium ripe tomatoes, peeled, seeded
        and chopped
1/2 cup fresh chicken stock or can low sodium
100% fat free chicken broth
1 1/2 pounds raw shrimp, peeled and deveined
8 ounces feta cheese, crumbled (optional)

Sauté onion in 3 Tbsp of the olive oil if desired until soft. Add rice and sauté few minutes. Add stock bring to boil, reduce heat to medium-low and simmer partially covered 20 minutes or until tender. Remove from heat, add almonds and stir gently with a fork. While the rice is simmering prepare mushrooms. Rinse mushrooms under cold running water. Drain and dry. Cut mushrooms into thin slices. Sauté mushrooms and garlic with remaining olive oil until all liquid evaporates. Add wine, salt, pepper, tomatoes and 1/2 cup chicken stock bring to boil and add shrimp, stir and slowly simmer 10-15 minutes. Serve hot, the rice and spoon shrimp and mushrooms over, and sprinkle with feta cheese if desired. Serve with any salad and fresh crusty bread (see index for salad recipe). Serves 6.

❦❦❦❦❦

SHRIMP WITH PIQUANT SAUCE ON RICE
Garithes me Pikantiki Saltsa

1 1/2 pounds frozen medium raw shrimp
1/4 cup olive oil
1 large shallot, finely minced
1/2 cup dry white wine or Vermouth
3 garlic cloves or more finely minced
1 cup tomato sauce
Salt and pepper to taste
1/4 tsp more or less pepper Cayenne
1/2 green bell pepper, finely minced
1 Tbsp basil, finely minced
1 Tbsp Worcestershire sauce

Keep shrimp frozen until ready to use. Place shrimp in colander and thaw rapidly in lots of cold running water. Drain and dry well. Peel and devein. In a large skillet sauté shrimp in hot oil 3 minutes. Remove shrimp from skillet to a plate and season with salt and pepper. In the same skillet add shallot and sauté until soft. Add Vermouth, garlic, tomato sauce, pepper, Cayenne and green pepper, bring to a boil, reduce heat and slowly cook 10 minutes. Add shrimp to skillet, season with salt and pepper and stir gently, and let cook slowly 6-10 minutes. Sprinkle with basil, add Worcestershire and stir gently to combine. Serve immediately on bed of rice pilaf, salad (see index for the recipes), and fresh crusty bread. Serve 4-6.

❦❦❦❦❦

SHRIMP WITH RICE
Garither Pilafi

1 pound medium raw shrimp
2 Tbsp good quality olive oil or butter
2 Tbsp finely chopped onion
1 pound ripe tomatoes, peeled, seeded and chopped
        or 1 can (16-ounces) whole tomatoes chopped
Salt and pepper to taste
1 cup converted rice
1/4 cup melted butter, margarine or olive oil

Rinse shrimp in lots of cold water, peel and devein them. Chill while preparing the sauce. Sauté onion with oil if desired until transparent. Add chopped tomatoes, salt, pepper and 1 cup water. Cover and bring to a boil, reduce heat and simmer for 10 minutes, stirring occasionally. Add shrimp and simmer for 20 minutes or until tender. While shrimp is cooking prepare rice pilaf. Place 4 cups water in a saucepan, add salt; bring to a boil. Add rice and stir well, cover, simmer for 20 minutes. Drain. Place rice back in the saucepan. Add hot melted butter if desired to rice and stir gently with a fork. Place the rice in a ring- mold, and lightly pressed down. Invert in a serving dish upside down over mold. Reverse the two. Gently remove mold. Pour shrimp with sauce over rice. Serve immediately. Serves 3.

SQUID IN WINE
Kalamarakia Krasata

2 pounds young squid
3/4 cup good quality olive oil
3 large onions, thinly sliced
3/4 cup dry wine
1 (16 ounces) can whole tomatoes, crushed
2 Tbsp chopped parsley
Salt and pepper to taste
Juice of 1 lemon or less
2 garlic cloves, crushed

Wash squid in cold running water. Pull off heads. Remove backbone, guts and black skin. Wash again in bowl of salted water; rinse thoroughly. Cut into 1/2-inch rings. Heat olive oil and sauté onions until translucent. Add squid and sauté a few minutes longer. Add wine, tomatoes, parsley, salt and pepper. Simmer covered over low heat until squid is tender, about 45-55 minutes. Sprinkle with lemon juice and serve hot or cold with fresh crusty bread. Serves 6.

STEAMED FISH
Psari Atmou

2 pounds fresh or frozen (thawed) flounder, sole or
        perch fillets
Salt and pepper to taste
1 1/2 cups milk
1 bay leaf
The rind of 1/2 lemon, cut into fourths
2 Tbsp butter
2 Tbsp good quality olive oil
2-3 bell peppers, thinly sliced
1 1/2 cups finely chopped onion
2-3 cloves garlic, crushed
2 Tbsp all-purpose flour
1/2 cup dry white wine or Vermouth
1 pound ripe tomatoes, peeled, seeded
        and chopped
3 Tbsp chopped parsley

Rinse fish well and dry. Place fish fillets in glass baking dish, sprinkle with salt and pepper and lemon juice. Chill 20-30 minutes. In large frying pan place milk, bay leaf and lemon rind and bring to boil. Add fish in one layer; cover and steam on low heat approximately 10-12 minutes or until fish is tender. With slotted spoon remove fish from the frying pan to a large plate and keep warm. Drain liquid and reserve. In large frying pan sauté in butter and oil the peppers and onion until soft. Add garlic and flour and sauté few minutes longer, stirring constantly. Add wine and cook until evaporates. Add reserved liquid, stirring constantly. Add tomatoes and cook slowly 6 minutes. Add parsley, stir well and remove from heat. Serve on bed of rice pilaf, salad, feta cheese and fresh crusty bread. Serves 4-6.

MEATS

BEEF

BAKED MEATBALLS WITH CUMIN
Soutzoukakia Sto Fourno

1 1/2 pounds ground sirloin
1/2 pound lean ground lamb or veal
2 cloves garlic, minced
1/2 tsp. or more ground cumin
Salt and pepper to taste
2 cups soft breadcrumbs (see index)
2 lightly beaten eggs
1/2 cup dry white wine or dry Vermouth
1 (29-ounces can) whole tomatoes, pressed
    through a food mill
2 Tbsp butter or good quality olive oil

Soak the breadcrumbs with the wine. Combine all the ingredients together except the tomatoes and butter, and mix well with your hand. Set aside. Cook tomato for 5 minutes. Pour half of the tomato sauce in a baking dish. Shape meat mixture into 2-inch long cylinders. Place the meatballs in the baking dish, over the tomato sauce. Pour the remaining tomato sauce over the meatballs, and dot with the butter if desired. Bake in a preheated 350 F (180 C) oven for 45-55 minutes. Serve with rice pilaf, mashed potatoes or spaghetti and salad (see index) for recipes. Serves 6.

❧❀❧

BEEF CUTLETS IN PUFF PASTRY
Kotoletes Moshariou se Sfoliata

1 pkg. puff pastry (thawed)
8 slices beef cutlets
3 Tbsp butter, margarine or olive oil
Salt and pepper to taste

1 pound mushrooms
8 large slices boiled potatoes 1/8-inch thick
8 large slices tomatoes 1/4-inch thick
8 slices Kaseri cheese 1/8-inch thick
3 Tbsp finely chopped flat leaf parsley
1 cup frozen peas, thawed and drained
Thin slices carrots, boiled
1 egg, beaten with 1 Tbsp of water

Rinse mushrooms under cold running water. Drain well and slice thinly. Sauté cutlets fast one at a time on both sides in hot butter if desired. Remove from frying pan to a dish, and season with salt and pepper. Repeat the frying procedure with the rest of the cutlets. In same pan sauté the mushrooms until all liquid evaporates, season with salt and pepper. Remove the puff pastry from the package, take one at a time and cut into fourths. Roll out each piece of pastry on a lightly floured surface to make it more than double of the size of the meet crosswise. Start with one piece of the pastry at a time, place meat on one half side of the pastry, then cover meat with mushrooms, potato, tomato, kaseri cheese, parsley, peas, and carrots. Brush pastry with egg wash and lift the other half of the pastry over the filling to cover it. Seal the edges of the pastry with the tines of a fork. Place on a greased baking sheet. Repeat this procedure until you finish with all the pastry and filling. Brush the meat puff pastries with egg wash. Bake in a preheated 400 F (205 C) over 20-30 minutes or until golden. Serve hot with salad and fresh crusty bread. Serves 8.

❧❀❧

BEEF ESCALOP WITH MARSALA SAUCE
Eskalop Moshariou me kokkino Vermouth

6 thin cutlets slices from sirloin tip, top, round or
fillet mignon of beef
Clarified butter and good quality olive oil
for frying
Salt and pepper to taste
1/2 cup Mavrothafni (Greek sweet wine) or
Marsala
1/2 cup cream

Pound cutlets with a meat mallet to 1/8-inch thick. Melt butter and oil in a large frying pan until hot but not smoking. Add cutlets two at a time and fry fast on both sides on medium-high heat. Remove from heat and place in a serving dish and keep warm, season with salt and pepper. Repeat the same procedure until you have frying all the cutlets. In the frying pan add the Marsala if desired, stir well and cook for few minutes, reduce heat to low and gradually add the cream, stirring continuously (to not let the sauce boil), season with salt and pepper and spoon over the cutlets. Serve immediately with rice or kritharaki pilaf, salad and fresh crusty bread.

❦❦❦

BEEF KAPAMA WITH RICE
Moschari Kokkinisto me Rizi

21/2 pounds lean boneless chuck, round or rump
of beef cut into serving pieces
1 Tbsp butter
2 Tbsp olive oil
1/2 cup minced onion
1 cup tomato sauce
Salt and pepper to taste
1 cinnamon stick 1/2-inch long (optional)
2 cups converted rice
1/4 cup or less butter or margarine
1/2 cup grated Kefalotyri or Parmesan
cheese (optional)

Heat butter and oil in Dutch oven and brown meat pieces few at a time. Add onion and sauté until soft. Add tomato, salt, pepper, cinnamon if desired, and 2 cups water; stir well. Bring to a boil. Reduce heat, cover and simmer until tender approximately 2 hours. As liquid cooks away add more water as needed. Remove meat from pot to a plate, and keep warm. Measure sauce, add water

to make 41/2 cups. Bring to a boil. Sauté rice with butter 5 minutes on medium heat, stirring constantly. Add rice to boiling sauce and simmer partially covered 20 minutes. Pack rice into a 6-cup ring mold. Gently invert on a platter. Arrange meat pieces around rice. Serve hot with grated cheese if desired, and salad. Serves 6.

❦❦❦

BEEF KAPAMA WITH SPAGHETTI
Moschari Kokkinisto me Spagetto

2 1/2 pounds lean boneless chuck, round or rump
of beef cut into serving pieces
2 Tbsp or less butter
2 Tbsp good quality olive oil
1/2 cup minced onion
1 cup tomato sauce
Salt and pepper to taste
1 cinnamon stick 1/2-inch long (optional)
1 pound spaghetti
1 Tbsp salt
4 quarts boiling water
1/4 cup melted butter or margarine or 2 Tbsp
of olive oil (optional)
1/2 cup or more grated Kefalotyri or Parmesan
cheese

In a Dutch oven heat butter and olive oil and brown the beef pieces few at a time. Add onion and sauté until soft. Add tomato, salt, pepper, cinnamon if desired, and 2 cups water; stir well. Bring to a boil. Reduce heat, cover and simmer until tender for approximately 2 hours. As the liquid cooks away add more water as needed. Prepare pasta. Break the spaghetti in half, drop into rapidly salted boiling water, and stir well. Cook uncovered for 20 minutes or until tender. Keep boiling and stir occasionally with a fork. Pour into a colander and rinse with warm water. Drain spaghetti well. Arrange half of the spaghetti on a large platter. Sprinkle with the half of the grated cheese, then cover with the other half of the remaining spaghetti, and top with the remaining grated cheese. Pour hot butter if desired over spaghetti, and spoon pan sauce and beef pieces over it. Serve immediately with salad. Serves 4-6.

❦❦❦

BEEF RAGOUT WITH EGGPLANT
Moschari Yiachni me Melitsanes

3 pounds lean boneless chuck, round or rump of
    beef cut into serving pieces
1/4 cup all-purpose flour
1 tsp salt
1/4 tsp pepper
1 Tbsp butter
2 Tbsp good quality olive oil
1 cup finely chopped onion
1 cup tomato sauce or 6 medium ripe tomatoes,
    peeled, seeded and chopped
2 cups water
4 pounds small narrow eggplants (3-4-inchs long)
Olive oil for frying

Mix flour with salt and pepper. Coat meat pieces with flour mixture. In Dutch oven brown meat in hot butter and oil, few pieces at a time. Add onion and sauté until soft. Add tomato sauce if desired, and water. Bring to a boil. Reduce heat, cover and simmer 1 1/2 hours or until meat is tender and sauce is thick. As liquid cooks away add more water as needed. While meat is simmering prepare eggplants. Cut stems. Rinse well and dry. Slit eggplants lengthwise, but do not cut all the way through and do not slit 1/2-inch at the each end. In a nonstick frying pan sauté eggplants with 2 Tbsp. oil on medium heat until soft on all sides. Cover pan to prevent splashing. Add more oil if needed. Add eggplants to beef ragout and spoon pot juices over them to coat well. Do not stir. Simmer 10 minutes. Serve hot, with fresh crusty bread. Serves 4-6.

❦❧❦

BEEF RAGOUT WITH PEAS
Moschari Yiachni me Araka

Follow recipe and preparation as directed in
    Beef Ragout with Eggplants (see index).
Substitute peas for the eggplant
2 pounds frozen peas or fresh
2 Tbsp butter, margarine or good quality olive oil

While meat is simmering prepare peas. Drop peas in 1 cup salted boiling water; cover and simmer for 10 minutes, add butter if desired and simmer for 5 minutes longer. Add peas to the meat and simmer for 10 minutes. Serve hot. Serves 6.

❦❧❦

BEEF SOFRITO
Moschari Sofrito

2 pounds beef cutlets
1/2 cup all-purpose flour
Salt and pepper to taste
6 Tbsp olive oil
3 Tbsp red wine vinegar
1/4 cup crushed fresh garlic
1/4 cup chopped flat leaf parsley
2 cups fresh beef stock or can fat free chicken broth

Season cutlets with salt and pepper, coat cutlets with the flour, shake off excess. Fry the cutlets in 4 Tbsp. of hot oil until brown on both sides. Remove to a large saucepan, and add the remaining olive oil. Turn the heat on and add the vinegar, cook until evaporates. Add the rest of the ingredients, bring to a boil, reduce heat and simmer until the meat is tender and the sauce thickens. Remove from heat and serve immediately on bed of rice, kritharaki (Greek orzo) or mash potatoes, salad and fresh crusty bread. Serves 6

❦❧❦

BEEF TENDERLOIN WITH MUSHROOMS
File Minion me Manitaria

2 pounds beef tenderloin, cut into very thin slices
1/2 cup Mavrothafni (Greek wine) or Marsala
1 pound mushrooms, washed, dried and
    thinly sliced
1/4 cup clarified butter
2 Tbsp good quality olive oil
1/2 cup finely chopped shallot
Salt and pepper to taste
Juice of one lemon
4 large Roma tomatoes, peeled, seeded and cut
    into small cubes
Pinch of cayenne pepper
1/2 cup cream

Sauté the mushrooms in 2 Tbsp of the butter and 1 Tbsp of the oil until all liquid has been absorbed. Add shallots and season with salt and pepper, and sauté until soft. Add lemon juice and cool for 1 minute. Add the tomatoes and cayenne pepper, and cook for few minutes. Remove from heat. Sauté the tenderloin slices with remaining butter and oil few pieces at a time. When you finish, return the meat to the frying pan, add the

Marsala, season with salt, pepper and cayenne, and cook until evaporates. Add the mushroom mixture to the meat and simmer for 2 minutes longer. Add the cream, bring to boil and remove from the heat. Serve immediately on bed of rice pilaf or kritharaki (see index for recipes). Serve with salad and fresh crusty bread. Serves 4-6.

BEEF STIFATHO
Moschari Styfatho

2 1/2 pounds lean boneless chuck of beef, cut
       into serving pieces
1/2 cup or less olive oil
1 large chopped onion
1/2 cup dry red wine
2 Tbsp wine vinegar
2/3 cup tomato sauce
2 bay leaves
3 garlic cloves, sliced
1 tsp rosemary
1 cinnamon stick 1/2-inch long
8 whole allspice
8 whole peppercorns
Salt and pepper to taste
4-5 pounds very small onions if possible

Brown meat slowly in oil few pieces at a time. Add onion and sauté until soft. Add wine and vinegar; stir well. Add the rest of the ingredients except the onions. Bring to a boil. Reduce heat, cover and simmer for 60 minutes. As the liquid cooks away, add water as needed. While meat is simmering, peel onions and cross cut root ends to prevent centers for popping out during cooking. Drop onions in a large amount of boiling water, and boil for 5 minutes; drain. Add onions to the meat and spoon pot juices over them to coat them well. Do not stir. Cover and simmer for approximately 60 minutes or until meat and onions are tender, shaking the pot occasionally. Serve hot with spaghetti or noodles and fresh crusty bread. Serves 6.

BEEF WITH OREGANO
Moschari Riganato

1/3 cup all-purpose flour
1 1/2 tsp salt

1/4 tsp pepper
3 pounds lean boneless beef, cut into serving pieces
1 cup finely chopped onion
1/4 cup olive oil
1/2 tsp crushed Greek oregano
Juice of 1 or more lemons
2 cups water
2 cups converted rice
1/4 cup melted butter (optional)

Mix flour, salt and pepper together. Coat the meat pieces, and shake off the excess. In a Dutch oven heat oil and brown meat pieces few at a time. Remove to a dish. Add onion and sauté until soft. Return meat to pot. Add lemon juice, oregano, water and cover. Cook slowly, for approximately 2 hours, or until the meat is tender and sauce is lightly thick. While meat is simmering prepare the rice. In a 3-quart, boil 8 cups water and 2 tsp. salt. Add rice, reduce heat and simmer partially covered for 20 minutes. Drain, and return to the saucepan. Add melted butter if desired and toss it with a fork. Serve meat with rice and pour sauce over. Serves 6.

BEEF WITH WINE
Oura Katsarolas me Krasi

4 pounds rump or beef
3 Tbsp olive oil
1 cup finely chopped onion
1 cup dry white wine or Vermouth
1/2 cup chopped carrots
1/2 cup chopped celery
1 Tbsp chopped flat leaf parsley
1 can (20-ounces) whole tomatoes chopped
Salt and pepper to taste

Heat oil and brown meat on all sides. Add onion and sauté until it is soft. Add wine and cook until wine evaporates, and sauté few minutes longer. Add the rest of the ingredients. Cover and cook slowly for approximately 2 hours or until meat is tender. Add water as needed. Remove meat from sauce and slice it. Press sauce through a food mill. Add meat slices to the sauce and heat through. Serve with mashed potatoes, rice pilaf or spaghetti (see index) and salad. Serves 6-8.

FILLET MIGNON ATHENIAN
Bon-File Athinaiko

2 pounds beef tenderloin (fillet mignon)
All-purpose flour for coating
6 slices stale white bread, remove all crust
1/2 cup clarified butter or margarine
Salt and pepper to taste
3 Tbsp all-purpose flour
1 cup dry Vermouth
1 cup fresh beef stock or chicken broth
1 tsp tomato paste
1/4 cup Mavrodaphne (Greek sweet wine) or
Marsala wine
1 tsp. butter

Remove skin and fat from the tenderloin with a sharp knife. Cut tenderloin into 1/2-inch thick slices, sprinkle with salt and pepper. Set aside. Sauté bread slices with clarified butter until golden. Place bread slices on a serving platter. Coat fillet slices with flour, and shake off the excess. Sauté the fillets in the same butter for few minutes on both sides. Remove from pan and place on the bread slices and keep warm. Blend the 3 Tbsp. of the flour in the pan fat. Gradually add wine, stock, tomato paste, salt and pepper, stirring constantly. Cook slowly for 5 minutes or until mixture thickens. Add the Mavrodaphne, if desired, and the butter, cook for 3 minutes longer. Pour sauce over fillets. Serve immediately. Serve with rice pilaf or Kritharaki pasta and salad (see index). Serves 6.

❦❦❦

FILLET MIGNON GRATINEE
Bon-File Gratine

3 pounds veal or beef fillet mignon (tenderloin)
Salt and pepper to taste
All-purpose flour for coating
Clarified butter and
Fine quality olive oil for frying
2 cups thick white sauce (see index)
1/2 cup grated Parmesan or Romano cheese
1/4 cup finely chopped boiled ham
1/4 cup fine dried breadcrumbs (see index)
1/4 cup melted butter or margarine

Clean fillet mignon by removing skin and fat with a sharp knife. Cut fillet into 1/2-inch thick slices.

Season slices with salt and pepper. Coat with flour and shake off excess. Sauté slices in 1 Tbsp. of the butter, and 2 Tbsp. of the oil, for 5 minutes. Turn and sauté on the other side for same length of time. Add more butter and oil if needed. Prepare white sauce as directed, add half of the grated cheese, the chopped ham, salt and pepper to your taste, and blend well to combine. Place fillets in a greased baking dish. Top each fillet equally with the white sauce. Sprinkle with remaining cheese, then breadcrumbs and lastly with melted butter if desired. Bake in a preheated 450 F (230 C) oven for 10 minutes. Serve immediately. Serve with kritharaki (orzo), boiled artichokes, and salad (see index) for recipes. Serves 6.

❦❦❦

FILLET MIGNON IN FILLO PASTRY
Bon-Fille Rollo me Fillo

1 beef tenderloin (fillet mignon) about 4 pounds
1/3 cup Madera or Marsala wine
Salt and pepper to taste
2 Tbsp butter
2 Tbsp good quality olive oil
1 pound mushrooms, sliced
1 1/2 cups white onions, thinly sliced
1 pound fillo pastry (thawed)
1/2 cup melted clarified butter or good
*   quality olive oil*

Clean the tenderloin by removing the silver skin and fat, with a sharp knife. Cut the tenderloin into 8-12 slices. Place in glass dish and season with salt and pepper. Sear the fillet slices on hot butter and oil on both sides. In the same frying pan sauté the mushrooms and the onions, add more butter and oil if needed, and cook until all the liquid has evaporated. Add the meat juices and the wine and cook until have evaporated. Remove from the heat. Divide the mushroom onion mixture into 8-12 parts. Assembled and baking. Take two fillo sheets at a time, and cover the remaining sheets with a dry cloth, then with a lightly dampened towel to prevent them from drying out. Brush one sheet with hot melted butter if desired, take the other sheet, and place on top the first one and brush it with hot melted butter. At the narrow side of the fillo, 3-inches from the end, place 1 slice of the prepared fillet mignon and top with 1 of the mushroom onion mixture. Roll up the fillo with the filling twice, fold one side in, toward the middle to enclose the filling, brush with hot butter, and roll up ounce again and fold the other side in, toward the middle to enclose the filling, and brush with hot butter, and roll up to make a roll. Repeat the same procedure with the remaining fillo and filling. Place the rolls seam side down in a greased baking pan, one at time as you finish, and brush with hot butter. With a sharp knife, make a slit on the top of each roll to release the steam. Bake in a preheated 375 F (190 C) oven on the second bottom rack for approximately 30 minutes or until golden brown. Place the rolls in a serving platter and serve immediately with boiled kritharaki or rice and salad.

FILLET MIGNON IN MADERA SAUCE
Moscharisia Filleta me Saltsa Maderas

2 pounds beef tenderloin (fillet mignon)
1/3 cup Madera wine
6 Tbsp. clarified butter or margarine
2 medium sized ripe tomatoes, peeled, seeded and finely chopped
8-ounces sliced mushrooms
Salt and pepper to taste
1/2 cup chicken broth
3/4 cup whipping cream
Chicken pate (see index) optional

Clean the tenderloin, by removing skin, and fat, with a sharp knife. Cut fillet mignon into 4 slices. Tie slices with butcher's twine to keep the round shape. Place in a dish and sprinkle with the wine, cover and chill for 2 hours. Remove fillets from wine and sauté in frying pan with 4 Tbsp. butter if desired, for 2 minutes. Turn, season with salt and pepper. Sauté on the other side for the same length of time. Remove fillets to a hot plate, and keep warm. In the same pan add wine, tomatoes and broth. Simmer for few minutes. In different frying pan, sauté mushrooms with the remaining butter, until liquid evaporates. Add the mushrooms to the wine tomato mixture, and stir well. Slowly add whipping cream, bring to a boil and cook for 3 minutes longer. Pour wine sauce over fillets. Serve with a spoonful of Chicken pate over each fillet if desired (see index for recipe). Serves 4.

FILLET MIGNON IN VERMOUTH SAUCE
Moscharisia Filleta me Saltsa Vermouth

2 pounds beef tenderloin (fillet mignon)
1/3 cup clarified butter or margarine
Salt and pepper to taste
2 Tbsp. all-purpose flour
1/2 cup dry Vermouth
1 1/2 cups fresh beef stock or chicken broth

Clean the tenderloin, by removing skin and fat with a sharp knife. Cut fillet mignon into 4 slices. Tie slices with butcher's twine to keep the round shape. Sauté in frying pan with butter for 5 minutes. Turn, season with salt and pepper. Sauté on the other side for the same length of time. Remove to a hot platter, and keep warm. In the same pan, blend in flour. Add Vermouth, stock or broth, salt and pepper. Cook slowly for 5 minutes. Pour sauce over fillets. Serve with rice pilaf, sautéed spinach and salad (see index) for recipes. Serves 4.

FRIED MEATBALLS
Keftethes Tighaniti

1 1/2 pounds lean ground sirloin
1/2 pound lean ground lamb, pork or veal
3 cups soft breadcrumbs (see index for recipe)
1/2 cup dry white wine or dry Vermouth or milk
1/2 Tbsp olive oil
1 medium onion, finely chopped
2 garlic cloves, crushed
1 Tbsp finely chopped fresh mint
1/4 tsp crushed Greek oregano
2 lightly beaten eggs
Salt and pepper to taste
All-purpose flour for coating
Oil for frying

Soak breadcrumbs in wine. Combine all the

ingredients together, except the flour and oil. Mix well with your hand. Cover and chill for 2 hours or longer. Shape mixture into balls the size of a large walnut or larger and press them down in your hands. Roll them in flour, and shake off excess flour. Heat oil and fry meatballs in medium heat, until browned on both sides and cooked through. Serve hot with boiled green vegetable or salad and fries (see index for recipes). Serves 6-8.

❦❧❦

HAMBURGERS
Biftekia

2 pounds lean ground sirloin
1 cup soft breadcrumbs (see index), soaked in
1/4 cup milk or water
1 clove garlic, minced
1/4 tsp crushed Greek oregano
Salt and pepper to taste

Combine all the ingredients together. Mix well with your hand. Press into 6 flat biftekia 1/2-inch thick. Broil for 4 minutes. Turn and broil on the other side for the same length of time, or to your taste. Serve hot with fries and salad. Serves 6.

❦❧❦

HAMBURGERS WITH BEEF AND LAMB
Biftekia me Moschari ke Arni

1 1/2 pounds lean ground sirloin
1/2 pound lean ground lamb
1 cup soft breadcrumbs (see index), soaked in
1/3 cup dry Vermouth
2 cloves garlic, minced
Salt and pepper to taste
1/4 tsp crushed Greek oregano

Combine all the ingredients together. Mix well with your hand. Press into 6 flat biftekia 1/2-inch thick. Broil for 4 minutes. Turn and broil on the other side for the same length of time, or to your taste. Serve hot with fries, rice pilaf and salad (see index) for recipes. Serves 6.

❦❧❦

LAYERED BEEF MEDALLIONS GRATINEE
Moschari Gratine

5 pounds top sirloin or eye of the round
         roast of beef
2 stalks celery, cut into fourths
3 carrots, cut into fourths
1 medium onion, peeled and cut into half
Salt to taste
10 slices white or dark sandwich bread
5 slices 1/8-inch thick boiled ham, cut into half
8 ounces coarsely grated Swiss cheese
10 slices 1/4-inch thick of medium ripe tomatoes
8 Tbsp butter or margarine
8 Tbsp all-purpose flour
2 cups fresh beef stock
3 cups milk
5 beaten eggs
Salt and pepper to taste
1/3 cup or more grated Parmesan cheese

Trim beef of excess fat. Tie the meat with butchers twine, every 2 inches crosswise. Set the meat in a large pot, cover with boiling water. Bring to a boil. Skim the broth. Reduce heat, and simmer for 1 hour. Add celery, carrots, onion and salt. Simmer for 1 hour longer, or until meat is tender. Let stand in the liquid until meat is completely cool. Remove from the liquid, remove the twine and cut into 20 equal slices. Save the stock. Prepare sauce. In a four quart saucepan, melt butter if desired over medium heat, blend in flour until smooth using a wire whisk. Remove from heat and gradually add beef stock and milk, stirring constantly. Return to heat and cook slowly stirring constantly until mixture is thick and smooth. Cook 3 minutes longer. Remove from heat. Add approximately 2 cups of the hot broth, at first spoon little by little into beaten eggs, and then little more, stirring constantly, then pour egg mixture to the sauce and cook over very low heat for 2 minutes, stirring constantly. Remove from heat. Cut bread slices the same size of the meat. In a deep well greased baking pan spread a layer of the sauce (1/4-inch thick). Lay bread slices in the prepare pan. Top bread slices starting first with meat, then with 1/3 of the shredded Swiss cheese, ham, then spread 1/3 of the sauce and sprinkle with 1/3 of the Parmesan cheese. Start again with meat first, then with 1/3 of the shredded Swiss cheese and finish with the tomato slices. Mix the béchamel sauce with the remaining Swiss cheese and 1/3 of the Parmesan cheese. Spoon remaining sauce over tomato slices and spread evenly to cover. Sprinkle with the remaining Parmesan cheese. Bake in a preheated 400 F (205 C) oven for approximately 30 minutes or until bubbling hot and sauce has browned nicely. Let stand for 20 minutes. Serves 10.

Note: With the remaining stock you can make kritharaki pilaf and serve it with layered beef medallions.

❧✣❧

LEMON ROAST BEEF SUPREME
Moschari Psito Katsarolas me Lemoni

4 pounds top sirloin, rump or eye of the round
3 Tbsp. or less olive oil
Salt and pepper to taste
1 tsp or more granulated garlic
Juice of 1 lemon, or more
1/2 cup dry Vermouth
3 Tbsp cornstarch
1/2 cup dry red wine or Vermouth

Tie roast with butcher's twine every 2-inches crosswise. In a Dutch oven brown meat on all sides in hot oil. Add lemon juice and season with salt, pepper and garlic. Add wine if desired and 1/2 cup water to pot. Reduce heat to medium-low, cover and simmer 30 minutes. Turn meat with a tong, sprinkle with salt, pepper and garlic. Cover and simmer 30 minutes. Turn meat frequently, cook approximately 3 hours. As liquid cooks away add more water as needed, 1/2 cup at a time. Remove from heat. Let rest 15 minutes. Remove twine and carve into slices. While roast is resting prepare gravy. Strain pot juices. Pour off fat. Add enough water or fresh stock to make 2 1/2 cups. In small saucepan bring juices to a boil; mix cornstarch with 1/2 cup water to a paste. Slowly add to stock stirring constantly. Cook slowly 2 minutes. Serve roast with gravy, mashed potatoes or rice pilaf, sautéed spinach, and salad, or to your desire (see index). Serves 6-8.

❧✣❧

MEATBALLS AVGOLEMONO
Youvarlakia Avgolemono

1 pound lean ground beef
1/2 pound lean ground lamb or veal
1/2 cup long grain rice
1/2 cup minced onion
3 beaten egg whites
Salt and pepper to taste
1 Tbsp fresh finely chopped dill or flat leaf parsley or both
2 Tbsp or less butter or margarine (optional)
4 cups fresh beef stock or water
1/3 cup dry white wine or Vermouth
2 Tbsp cornstarch
3 beaten egg yolks
Juice of 1 or more lemons

Combine first 8 ingredients and mix well with your hand. Shape into meatballs the size of a small walnut. In a Dutch oven bring stock or water, wine and butter if desired to a boil. Remove from heat and gently drop meatballs one by one. Return pot to the heat, bring to a boil, reduce heat and simmer covered 1 hour. Mix corn starch with 1/4 cup water to a thin paste. Slowly add to meatballs stirring constantly. Simmer 5 minutes longer. Beat egg yolks with lemon juice. Gradually spoon some of the hot meatball liquid, stirring constantly. Pour over meatballs, and stir gently to combine. Remove from heat and serve immediately. Serves 6-8.

❧✣❧

MEATBALLS WITH SPINACH
Keftethes me Spanaki

1 pound cooked beef, finely diced
1 pound spinach
3 Tbsp butter, margarine or light olive oil
4 Tbsp flour
1 cup milk
1 egg
1/4 cup grated Parmesan or Kefalotyri cheese
Salt and pepper to taste
Flour for coating
Butter and olive oil for frying

Remove roots and coarse leaves for spinach and wash in several waters. Place spinach in a small saucepan with little salt and cook slowly without water for few minutes. Drain well and finely chop. Prepare the béchamel. Melt butter if desired over medium heat, blend in flour until smooth using a whisk. Remove from heat and gradually add milk, stirring constantly. Return to heat and cook until mixture is thick and smooth, stirring constantly. Season the sauce with salt and pepper. Remove from the heat. In a large mixing bowl combine all the ingredients except the flour, butter and oil and mix well with your hand. Cover and chill for 60 minutes or longer. Shape mixture into balls the sizes of a large walnut. Roll them in flour and shake off excess flour. Heat butter and oil and fry the meatballs until lightly brown on both sides. Place the meatballs on absorbent papers. Serve hot with salad (see index for recipe) and fresh crusty bread. Serves 4-6.

≈≈≈≈

MEAT PATTIES IN MARSALA SAUCE
Biftekia me Saltsa Marsala

2 pounds lean ground sirloin
1 1/2 cups soft breadcrumbs (see index), soaked in
1/3 cup Marsala sweet wine
2 large garlic cloves, minced
Salt and pepper to taste
1/4 tsp. or more crushed Greek oregano
1/2 cup clarified butter or margarine
12-16-ounces any kind of mushrooms
3 medium ripe tomatoes, peeled, seeded and
        finely chopped
1/2 cup fresh beef or chicken stock or can of
        fat free chicken broth
1 cup Marsala sweet wine
3/4-1 cup whipping cream

Wash mushrooms under cold running water. Dry them on absorbent towels, and slice. Set aside. Combine six first ingredients together. Mix well with your hand. Press into 6-8 flat round biftekia 1/2-inch thick. Sauté with 5 Tbsp. hot clarified butter if desired on medium heat for 4 minutes. Turn other side and sauté for 4 minutes longer. Remove from frying pan. Keep warm. In the same pan add wine, the chopped tomatoes and the broth. Simmer for few minutes. Sauté mushrooms in different pan with the remaining butter until liquid evaporates. Add mushrooms to the wine sauce, and stir. Slowly add whipping cream and bring to a simmer, and cook for 3

minutes. Add the biftekia to the sauce and simmer for a minute. Serve the biftekia with the wine sauce over it and serve immediately. Serve with pasta, mashed potatoes or rice pilaf (see index for recipes). Serves 6-8.

≈≈≈≈

MEAT STUFFED CREPES
Crepes Ghemistes me Kima

1 cup all-purpose unbleached flour
1 cup milk
4 extra large eggs
1 cup melted butter, margarine or good
        quality olive oil
Salt and pepper to taste
1 medium onion, minced
1 1/2 pounds lean ground beef
2 garlic cloves, crushed
1/2 cup dry white wine or Vermouth
1 large ripped tomato, peeled, seeded and
        finely chopped
2 Tbsp finely chopped flat leaf parsley
1 large egg, beaten
2 Tbsp dried breadcrumbs
5 medium ripped tomatoes, peeled, seeded and
        finely chopped
1 large garlic clove, crushed
1/2 cup or more grated Kefalotyri or Parmesan
        cheese

Place flour in a mixing bowl and beat in milk, eggs, 3 Tbsp of the melted butter if desired, salt, and pepper with a wire whisk. Beat until smooth. Let rest for 15 minutes or longer. Lightly grease a small frying pan 7-inch and pour in about two Tbsp of batter. Move the pan so that the batter spreads to the outer of the pan. Cook for 1 minute. Loosen with a spatula and flip over. Brown the crepe on the other side. Repeat the same procedure until you finish with all the batter. Stack the crepes on a dish. Makes about 16-18 crepes. Prepare the meat sauce. Sauté onion in oil if desired until soft, add the ground meat, and the garlic and stir breaking up clumps until brown. Add the wine and cook until evaporates. Add salt, pepper and parsley to the meat and stir well to combine. Bring to boil, reduce heat to medium-low and cook for 45 minutes, stirring occasionally. Add water if needed. Remove from the heat and add the beaten egg and the breadcrumbs, stir well. Let cool. While the meat is cooling prepare the sauce. In a 2-quart saucepan add 2 Tbsp oil, the tomatoes and the garlic, stir and bring to boil, reduce heat to medium-low and cook for 5 minutes. Stuff the crepes with the meat mixture and place them in a greased baking dish seam side down. Spoon the sauce over the crepes evenly and sprinkle with the grated kefalotyri cheese. Bake in a preheated 350 F (180 C) oven for 15 minutes. Serve immediately with salad and fresh crusty bread. Serves 4-6.

SMALL MEATBALLS WITH PILAF
Mikra Keftethakia me Pilafi

1/2 pound lean ground beef
1/2 pound lean ground lamb
1/2 pound lean ground pork or veal
2 cups soft breadcrumbs (see index)
1/4 cup water
2 beaten eggs
1 tsp Worcestershire sauce
Salt and pepper to taste
1 Tbsp finely chopped fresh mint or dill or both
1 medium finely chopped onion
1/4 cup butter, margarine or good quality olive oil
1 Tbsp all-purpose flour
1/2 cup dry white wine or dry Vermouth
2 cups fresh beef stock or can low sodium
        100% chicken broth

Combine the first ten ingredients together, and mix well with your hand. Shape into meatballs, the size of a small walnut. Sauté with the butter if desired on medium heat on all sides. Remove meatballs to a plate. Strain pan fat to a saucepan, and blend in flour. Add wine, stock, salt and pepper and stir well. Bring to a simmer. Gently add meatballs, cover and cook slowly for 15 minutes. Serve with rice pilaf and salad (see index for recipes). Serves 4-6.

STUFFED FLANK STEAK ROLL UP
Brizola Moscharou Ghemisti Rollo

1/2 cup finely chopped onion
6 Tbsp butter, margarine or 1/4 cup
        good quality olive oil
1/2 cup chopped chicken livers
1/2 cup chopped mushrooms
1/2 cup chopped ham
2 chopped hard-boiled eggs
1 beaten egg
1/2 cup cooked peas
1 cup soft breadcrumbs (see index)
Salt and pepper to taste
2 1/2 pounds whole round or flank steak
1/2 cup dry white wine or Vermouth (optional)
1 cup tomato sauce

Sauté onion in 4 Tbsp. of the butter if desired until transparent. Add the chicken livers and the mushrooms, sauté few minutes longer. Remove from heat. Add all the ingredients except wine and tomato. Stir well to combine. Let stand. On a cutting board, place steak flat. Begin to halve steak's thickness but do not cut through to other side; keep meat in one piece that can be opened. This makes it easier to stuff and rollup. Flatten with mallet until meat is 1/2-inch thick. Spread stuffing over meat, up to 1-inch from edges. Then very carefully rollup meat lengthwise, tucking in stuffing like a jelly-roll. To keep the roll closed, tie meat sides and ends with twine. In a Dutch oven brown meat roll in the remaining butter if desired on all sides. Add wine, tomato sauce and 1 cup water, salt and pepper to taste. Cover and cook slowly for approximately 2 hours or until meat is tender and sauce is thick. Add water as needed. Remove twine and slice the meat. Arrange meat slices on a serving platter, spoon pot juices over, and serve with mashed potatoes, spaghetti or rice pilaf and salad. Serves 5-6.

STUFFED GROUND MEAT ROLLUP
Rollo me Kyma Ghemisto

3/4 cup finely chopped onion
1/4 cup butter, margarine or olive oil
2 cups soft breadcrumbs (see index)
2 lightly beaten eggs
1/2 cup dry white wine (optional) or water
1 pound lean ground beef
1 pound lean ground lamb
Salt and pepper to taste
1 Tbsp finely chopped fresh mint

1/8 tsp crushed Greek oregano
1 cup shredded Kaseri or Swiss cheese (optional)
6 hard boiled eggs, shelled
1 1/2 cups tomato sauce
1/2 cup all-purpose flour

Sauté onion with 2 Tbsp. of the butter if desired until transparent. In a large bowl mix breadcrumbs, the beaten eggs and wine and let stay for 5 minutes. Add meat, salt, pepper, mint, oregano and mix well to combine. Divide the meat mixture in half. With your hands flatten out half of the mixture evenly on a 9x7-inch waxed or parchment paper sheet, which has been generously sprinkled with flour. Sprinkle evenly half of the shredded Kaseri cheese if desired on the meat, and arrange 3 of the whole hard-boiled eggs down the center of the flattened meat mixture lengthwise 1/2-inch from edges. Then very gently lift the waxed paper and meat together lengthwise and rollup around the eggs once. Seal the edges. Repeat with the second half the same way. Boil tomato, 1 1/2 cups water, salt and pepper in a small saucepan for 5 minutes. Pour half of the tomato sauce in a deep baking dish. Remove waxed paper. Place meat rolls in the baking dish and pour sauce over, and dot with the remaining butter. Bake in a preheated 350 F (180 C) oven for 45-55 minutes. Arrange meat rolls on a serving platter. Slice meat and pour sauce over. Serve hot with French fries of mashed potatoes and salad. Serves 6.

Note: Substitute beef for the lamb if desired.

❧❦❧

STUFFED MEAT ROLL
Rollo me Kreas

1 large shallot finely chopped (about 1/2 cup)
3 Tbsp butter
3 Tbsp good quality olive oil
1/2 cup cleaned, rinsed and chopped chicken livers
1 1/2 cup chopped mushrooms
1/2 cup chopped boiled ham
2 extra large eggs, hard-boiled and chopped
2/3 cup frozen peas (thawed)
1 cup soft breadcrumbs
Salt and pepper to taste
2 medium carrots, lightly cooked and cut into
    fourths lengthwise

3 pounds whole round, flank steak or top sirloin
1 cup dry red wine
2 cups tomato sauce
Twine

Sauté shallot in 2 Tbsp butter and 2 Tbsp oil until soft. Add chicken livers and mushrooms and sauté for few minutes longer. Remove from the heat. Add all the ingredients except the carrots, meat, the wine and the tomato sauce. Gently stir to combine. Let stand. Place the steak flat on a cutting board. Begin to halve the steak thickness but to not cut through to other side; keep meat in one piece that can be opened. This makes it easier to stuff and rollup. Flatten with a meat mallet until meat is 1/2-inch thick, or thinner. Cut pieces of twine 3-inch longer than the meat crosswise and place on a cutting board 1-inch apart and two pieces of twine lengthwise. Season the meat with salt and pepper on both sides. Gently place the meat on the twine. Spread stuffing over the prepare meat, up to 1 inch from edges. Arrange the carrots over the filling lengthwise. Then very carefully rollup the meat lengthwise and tucking in stuffing as you go, like jelly roll. Tie the meat sides and ends with the twine. In a large saucepan to fit the meat roll, add the remaining butter and oil and brown the meat on all sides. Add the wine, tomato sauce and 1cup water, salt and pepper to taste. Bring to boil, reduce the heat to simmer, cover and cool slowly for 90 minutes or until meat is tender and sauce is thick, (turning the roll every 15 minutes). Add water if needed. Remove the meat from the pan and place on a cutting board. Remove the twine and cut into slices. Gently transfer to a serving platter and spoon pan juices over the meat. Serve with rice pilaf, mashed potatoes or spaghetti, salad and fresh crusty bread. Serves 6-8.

❧❦❧

TAS KEBOB
Kreas Kokinisto

3 pounds beef, veal or lamb, fat removed and cut
    into the sizes of walnuts
3 Tbsp good quality olive oil
Salt and pepper to taste

Pinch of pepper Cayenne
1 large onion, finely chopped
2/3 cup dry white wine or Vermouth
1 (29-ounces can) whole tomatoes, crushed

Brown the meat in hot oil, on all sides. Season the meat with salt and pepper, and Cayenne. Add the onion and sauté until soft. Add the wine and stir well, and cook for few minutes. Add the tomatoes and 1 cup water, bring to boil, cover, reduce heat to simmer and cook 60-90 minutes or until the meat is tender and the sauce is thick. Serve hot on rice pilaf, mush potatoes or pasta, salad (see the index for recipes) and fresh crusty bread. Serves 6.

LAMB

ATZEM PILAF
Atzem Pilafi

4 pounds lean and boneless leg of lamb
2 Tbsp good quality olive oil
1 medium onion, finely chopped
2 pounds ripe tomatoes
Salt and pepper to taste
1-inch cinnamon stick
2 cups water
1/4 cup butter
2 cups converted rice (rinse well)

Rinse lamb and dry with paper towels. Cut into 1/2-inch cubes. Brown lamb with olive oil, stirring frequently. Add onion and sauté until soft. Wash and core tomatoes and cut in half crosswise. Squeeze one tomato half at a time with your hand to remove seeds. Place cut side of tomato on wide side of grater and grate tomato until all the tomato pulp is grated and only the skin is left. Discard the skin and repeat with the remaining tomatoes. Add the pulp to the meat, salt, pepper, cinnamon and the water. Cover, bring to a boil, reduce heat and simmer for approximately 30-40 minutes or until tender. Add 3 cups water to the pot and bring to a boil. Let stand. In a frying pan melt the butter, add rice and sauté few minutes or until every piece of rice is coated with butter and has a golden color. Add the rice to the meat and stir well. Reduce heat and simmer for 20 minutes. Remove

from heat and remove the cinnamon stick. The dish will look moist and creamy. Serve hot with salad. Serves 6.

BAKED CHEESE STUFFED LEG OF LAMB
Arni Gemisto me Feta Cheese sto Fourno

1 leg of lamb (8 pounds about)
Salt and pepper to taste
1/2 cup chopped fresh flat leaf parsley
1 pound (about) hard feta cheese, cut into
        1/2-inch thick slices
Garlic slivers (optional)
6 pound potatoes, peeled and cut into fourths
lengthwise
2 tsp granulated garlic
1 tsp Greek oregano, crushed
Juice of 2 or more lemons
1/4 cup good quality olive oil
5 whole fresh or can artichoke hearts, drained
Twine

Ask your butcher to bone, butterfly, and pound the leg of lamb. Prepare the artichokes, leaving only the harts, cut each into half if you use fresh. Remove the lamb from the refrigerator and let stand for 60 minutes. While the lamb is standing, prepare the potatoes. Place the potatoes into a large deep baking pan, and sprinkle with half of the granulated garlic, half of the oregano, salt pepper, and toss well with your hands. Arrange the fresh artichokes between the potatoes. Sprinkle with lemon juice and 2 Tbsp of olive oil, and 2 cups of water. Bake in a preheated 450 F (230 C) oven on the second lower rack, for 60 minutes. Wipe the lamb with paper towels and sprinkle with pepper only the cheese is salty. Sprinkle with the parsley and arrange the feta cheese. Roll and tie the lamb with twine strings 1-inch apart or elastic net, ask the butcher for one. Place slivers of garlic if desired into deep narrow gashes cut in meat. Place lamb on top of the potatoes (fat side down), sprinkle with half of the lemon juice, oil, garlic, oregano, salt and pepper. Roast uncovered for 30 minutes. Turn the lamb upside down (fat side up), sprinkle with the remaining lemon juice, olive oil, granulated garlic, oregano, salt and pepper. If you use can artichoke hearts, add them now, and arrange between the potatoes. Reduce temperature to 375 F (190 C), and bake for 30-45 minutes longer or until meat is in to your taste. Add water if needed. Remove the meat from the pan. Remove strings from the meat. Slice the meat and serve with potatoes and artichokes. Serves 8-10.

❦❧❦❧❦

BAKED LAMB COUNTRY STYLE IN FILLO PASTRY
Arni Exohiko me Fillo

2 1/2 pounds lean boneless leg of lamb, cut into
    6 thick slices
1 cup melted clarified butter or good quality
    olive oil
Salt and pepper to taste
2 medium potatoes, peeled and cut into
    1/8-inch thick slices, lengthwise
6 ounces Kaseri, Swiss or any other kind cheese
    you desire, cut into 6 slices
3 medium carrots, cut 1/8-inch thick lengthwise
2 medium ripe tomatoes, cut in 1/4-inch thick slices
2 Tbsp. finely chopped fresh flat leaf parsley
12 Tbsp. frozen peas (thawed)
24 or more sheets filo pastry (thawed)

Brown meat pieces in 1 Tbsp. of butter if desired, on all sides, add more butter if needed. Take three fillo sheets at a time, and cover the remaining sheets with a dry cloth, then with a lightly dampened towel to prevent them from drying out. Brush one sheet with hot melted butter if desired, take the other two sheets, and place on top the first and brush them with hot melted butter. At the narrow side of the fillo, 3-inches from the end, place one potato slice, slightly brush with the hot melted butter, and sprinkle with salt and pepper as you go. Top with a piece of the meat, then a slice of the cheese, two slices of the carrots, then again with a slice of potato, a slice of tomato, sprinkle with parsley, and top with the peas. Fold the 3-inches overhanging of fillo over the filling. Rollup the fillo with the filling twice, fold one side in, toward the middle to enclose the filling, brush with hot melted butter, and rollup ounce again and fold the other side in, toward the middle to enclose the filling and brush with hot melted butter, and rollup to make a bundle. Repeat the same procedure with the remaining fillo and filling. Place the bundles seam side down in a greased baking pan, one at a time as you finish, and brush with hot melted butter. With a sharp knife, make a slit on the top of each bundle to release the steam. Bake in a preheated 350 F (180 C) oven for approximately 60 minutes or until golden brown. Serve hot. Serves 6.

❦❧❦❧❦

BAKED LAMB SHANK WITH KRITHARAKI YOUVETSI

6 lamb shanks
Salt and pepper to taste
1 Tbsp butter (optional)
2 Tbsp good quality olive oil
21/2 cups can whole tomatoes, finely chopped
liquid included
4 cups boiling water
1 pound kritharaki (Greek pasta orzo)
Grated Parmesan cheese (optional).

Remove excess fat from the shanks. Wash them well and place into a deep baking pan. Season the meat with salt, pepper, butter if desired and olive oil. Place the pan on the second lower oven rack. Bake in a preheated 400 F (204 C) for 45 minutes. Turn the meat up side down add the tomatoes and 2 cups of the water. Return to oven. Reduce temperature to 350 F (180 C) and bake for 45 minutes. While the meat is baking, prepare the pasta. In a four-quart pot add 3 quarts of water, bring to a boil, add salt and the pasta, stir well and boil for 10 minutes uncovered. Drain the pasta and add to the meat and the remaining 2 cups of boiling water. Stir the pasta well to prevent of lumping and sticking. Bake for 20 minutes or until the pasta is tender, stir occasionally, add water as needed. The dish will look moist and creamy. Serve meat and pasta hot and sprinkle with Parmesan cheese if desired, and spring salad. Serves 6.

❦❧❦❧❦

BAKED LAMB WITH KRITHARAKI
Arni Youvetsi Me Kritharaki

41/2 pounds lean lamb (shoulder or leg), cut into
    serving pieces

2 Tbsp or more good quality olive oil
1 Tbsp butter or margarine (optional)
6 large ripe tomatoes, peeled, seeded and finely
*   chopped or 2 1/2 cups finely chopped can*
*   whole tomatoes*
3 cups boiling water
Salt and pepper to taste
1 cinnamon stick 1/2-inch long (optional)
1 pound kritharaki (Greek pasta) orzo
Grated Parmesan or Kefalotyri cheese

Brown meat pieces in oil, on all sides. Remove from heat. In a large baking casserole place browed meat pieces, tomato sauce, butter, cinnamon stick if desired and 3 cups of boiling water. Bake meat in a preheated 350 F (180 C) oven for 90 minutes, or until meat is tender. While the lamb is baking, in a large pot bring to a boil 4 quarts of water. Add 1 Tbsp. salt and the kritharaki, and stir well. Boil kritharaki for 10 minutes. Drain; add to the youvetsi, stir and continue baking until liquid is absorbed, for 20 minutes, or until pasta is tender, stirring occasionally. Add more water if needed. The dish will look moist and creamy. Serve hot with grated cheese and salad. Serves 4-6.

❧❧❧

BAKED SPINACH STUFFED LEG OF LAMB
Arni Ghemisto me Spanaki sto Fourno

1 leg of lamb (6-8 pounds about)
2 Tbsp good quality olive oil
2 pounds fresh spinach, leaves only, wash
*   and drain well*
8 garlic cloves, sliced
Salt and pepper to taste
5 pounds potatoes, peeled and cut into
*   fourths lengthwise*
1 1/2 tsp granulated garlic
1 tsp. Greek oregano, crushed
Juice of 2 or more lemon juice
2-3 Tbsp olive oil (optional)

Ask your butcher to bone and pound the leg of lamb. Remove lamb from the refrigerator and let stand, until you prepare the spinach. Sauté the garlic slices in hot oil just for 1 minute, in a medium heat. Add spinach, return heat to high and sauté spinach until is wilted and liquid evaporates. Stuff the lamb with the spinach mixture. Roll and tie the lamb with twine strings

or elastic net, ask the butcher for one. Place potatoes into the pan, and sprinkle with half of the granulated garlic, half of the oregano, salt pepper, and toss well. Place lamb on top of the potatoes (fat side down), sprinkle with half of the lemon juice, garlic, oregano, salt and pepper; add 2 cups water to the pan and 2-3 Tbsp. of olive oil, if desired. Roast uncovered in a preheated 450 F (230 C) oven on the second lower rack, for 45 minutes. Turn the lamb upside down (fat side up), sprinkle with the remaining lemon juice, oregano, salt and pepper. Reduce temperature to 350 F (180 C), and bake for 60-90 minutes longer or until meat and potatoes are tender. Add water if needed. Remove meat from the pan. Return the pan with the potatoes back in the oven, turn the broiler, and broil for 3-5 minutes. Being careful not to burn them. Remove strings from the meat. Slice the meat and serve with potatoes and salad. Serves 8-10.

❧❧❧

BAKED STUFFED BREAST OF LAMB
Stithos Arnou Yiemisto

1 1/2 pounds lean ground beef
1 medium onion, finely chopped
3 Tbsp good quality olive oil
1/2 cup dry Vermouth
3/4 cup converted rice
1/3 cup pine nuts or slivered blanched almonds
Salt and pepper to taste
6 pounds breast of lamb
Juice of 1 or more lemon

Ask your butcher to make a pocket on the breast of lamb and remove as much fat as possible. Set aside. Sauté ground meat and onion with 1 Tsp. of the oil, until onion is soft and the meat juices has evaporated. Add wine and simmer until wine has evaporated. Add rice stir, and sauté all together for 2 minutes. Add 3/4 cup hot water, pine nuts if desired, salt and pepper. Cover and cook slowly for 5 minutes. Season the breast of lamb, inside the pocket with salt and pepper. Pack stuffing into pocket and sew edges together to seal the stuffing. Place the breast in a roasting pan. Brush top with the remaining oil and sprinkle with lemon juice, salt and pepper. Bake in a preheated 400 F (205 C) oven for 30 minutes. Add 1 cup water to the pan and cover. Reduce heat to 350 F (180 C) oven and bake for approximately 2 hours, or until the meat is tender. Serves 6-8.

BAKED STUFFED EASTER LEG OF LAMB
Paschalino Ghemisto Arni Fournou

1 whole leg of lamb, 6-8 pounds
1 1/2 pounds lean ground sirloin
3/4 cup finely chopped onion
2 Tbsp good quality olive oil
3/4 cup dry white wine or Vermouth
3/4 cup converted rice
1/3 cup pine nuts or slivered blanched almonds
1 1/2 tsp granulated garlic
1/2 tsp. Greek oregano
Salt and pepper to taste
Juice of 2 or more lemons
5 pounds potatoes, peeled and cut in
        fourths lengthwise
2-3 Tbsp olive oil (optional)

Ask your butcher to bone and pound lamb. Sauté ground meat and onion with oil until meat juices have evaporated. Sauté 5 more minutes stirring constantly. Add wine and cook until wine has evaporated. Add rice, sauté 3 minutes longer. Add 1 cup hot water, pine nuts, salt and pepper. Cover and simmer 5 minutes. Stuff lamb with meat mixture. Roll lamb and tie with twine or elastic net (ask your butcher for one). Place potatoes in baking pan, sprinkle with half the granulated garlic, half the oregano, salt and pepper, toss well, and add 2 cups water. Place the leg of lamb on top of the potatoes, (fat side down) and sprinkle with half of the lemon juice, the half of the garlic, half of the oregano, salt, pepper and the olive oil if desired. Bake in a preheated 450 F (230 C) oven for 45 minutes. Turn the leg of lamb upside down (fat side up), sprinkle with the remaining garlic, oregano, salt and pepper. Reduce the temperature to 350 F. and bake for 45 minutes longer or until meat is tender. Remove the meat from the pan. Place potatoes back in the oven, turn the broiler and broil for 3-5 minutes longer.

Being careful not to burn them. Remove strings from meat and carve into slices. Serve hot stuffed lamb with the potatoes, and salad. Serves 6-10.

EASTER BAKED STUFFED SUCKLING LAMB
Paschalino Arni Ghemisto Tou Fournou

1 whole lamb, approximately 20 pounds
4 pounds lean ground beef
1 1/2 cups finely chopped onion
1/4 cup butter or olive oil
1 cup dry white wine or Vermouth
2 cups converted rice
3/4 cup or more pine nuts or slivered
        blanched almonds
Salt and pepper to taste
Juice of 2 or more lemons
1/2 cup melted butter or olive oil
6 pounds red or white potatoes, peeled and cut
        into fourths
1 tsp granulated garlic
1/2 tsp Greek oregano

Remove liver, heart, kidney and spleen from lamb cavity. Reserve for other use. Cut and separate body from legs. Rinse lamb inside and out with cold running water. Sprinkle cavity with salt. Sauté ground meat and onion with butter if desired, until meat juices evaporate. Sauté 5 more minutes stirring constantly. Add wine and cook until wine has evaporated. Add rice and sauté together 3 minutes. Add 2 cups hot water, pine nuts, salt and pepper; cover and simmer 5 minutes. Stuff lamb cavity with meat mixture. Close cavity by sewing with heavy thread. In large roasting pan place potatoes, sprinkle with salt, pepper, 1/2 tsp. granulated garlic and 1/4 tsp. Greek oregano, and toss well. Add 3 cups water. On a rack lay both pieces of the lamb. Sit rack on edges of roasting pan. Lay both pieces of lamb on rack. Rub outer surfaces with lemon juice. Brush with melted butter if desired and sprinkle with salt, pepper, the remaining granulated garlic and oregano. Roast in preheated 350 F. (180 C.) oven 2 hours. Gently turn lamb upside down, and bake approximately 2 hours longer or until tender. Remove lamb from rack to a cutting board. Let stand 30 minutes. Return potatoes to lowest rack in oven, turn button to broil, and broil 8-10 minutes to get them crispy, careful not to burn them. Carve meat and serve hot with potatoes, artichokes and peas, and salad (see index for recipes). Serves 10-12.

❦❦❦

EASTER BAKED SUCKLING LAMB
Pashalino Arni Psito Sto Fourno

1 whole lamb, approximately 20-25 pounds, cut into half crosswise (separate the cavity from the legs)
1/4 cup olive oil
Juice of 3-4 lemons
Salt and pepper to taste
Greek oregano
Granulated garlic
10 pounds potatoes any kind, peeled and cut in fourths

Rinse lamb inside and out with cold water. Sprinkle cavity with salt and pepper and close by sewing with heavy thread. Place potatoes in baking pan, sprinkle with salt, pepper, Greek oregano and granulated garlic and toss well. Place lamb over potatoes, sprinkle with half the lemon juice, and olive oil, salt, pepper granulated garlic and oregano. Add 1 1/2 cups of water to the pan. Place the baking pan on the bottom rack of the oven and bake in a preheated 450 F (230 C) oven for 45 minutes. Turn the lamb once and sprinkle with remaining lemon juice and olive oil, salt, pepper and oregano. Reduce heat to 400 F (190 C) and bake for 60 minutes longer or until meat is tender. Add more water to the pan if needed. Gently remove meat from the pan and cover to keep warm. Return the pan with the potatoes in the oven on the bottom rack and turn on the broiler if the potatoes are not cooked. Broil potatoes 15 minutes, being careful not to burn them. Carve meat and serve hot with potatoes.

❦❦❦

FRIED LAMB LIVER WITH SAUCE PIQUANT
Sykoti Tighanito me Saltsa Pikantiki

4 medium onions, thinly sliced
3 garlic cloves, minced
3 Tbsp or less butter, margarine or olive oil
3 Tbsp olive oil
Salt and pepper to taste
1 Tbsp Worcestershire sauce
1 Tbsp prepared mustard
1 Tbsp wine vinegar
2 pounds baby lamb liver

In a small saucepan sauté onions and garlic with the butter if desired until soft. Add salt and pepper, cover and simmer until tender. Add the Worcestershire sauce, mustard and vinegar, stir well and cook slowly for few minutes. Remove from heat. Rinse liver thoroughly and dry on paper towels. Cut liver into 1x2-inch slices. Fry quickly in hot olive oil, on both sides. Place liver on a serving platter, season with salt and pepper. Spoon the sauce piquant over fried liver, and serve immediately. Serves 5 as a main course or 8-10 as a first course.

❦❦❦

GRILLED LAMB CHOPS
Arnisia Paithakia sti Skara

12 lamb chops or (4 pounds leg, cut into 1/2-inch slices)
1 tsp Greek oregano
1/2 tsp salt
1/4 tsp pepper
Juice of 1 lemon
1/4 cup olive oil

Mix lemon juice and oil together. Combine oregano, salt and pepper together. Season chops with oregano mixture. Baste them with lemon and oil mixture on both sides and grill. Grill chops on both sides, basting frequently. Serve hot with French pries, rice pilaf or kritharaki pasta and salad (see index for recipes). Serves 4-6.

❦❦❦

GYROS
Gyros

8 pita bread (see index for recipe) or bought
Good quality olive oil
2 pounds lean lamb, cut into 1 1/2 x 1/2-inch thin strips
1/2 tsp crushed Greek oregano
Salt and pepper to taste
2 medium red ripe tomatoes, cut into thinly wedges
1 medium red onion, thinly lengthwise slices

2 cups shredded lettuce
1 1/2-2 cups cucumber and yogurt dip (see index)

Brown strips of lamb with the oil. Add oregano, salt, pepper and 1/2 cup water. Cook the meat slowly for 15 minutes or until it is cooked and dry. Lightly brush pita bread with olive oil and grill for a minute or less on both sides, don't brown the pita, just enough to soften. Place pita bread on a piece of waxed paper. Divide meat into 8 portions. Fill pita with meat pieces, tomato, onions, lettuce and cucumber and yogurt dip. Roll up pita bread to enclose the filling, then wrap with the waxed paper. Serve hot with French fries. Serves 4-8.

Note: Substitute lean pork loin or beef for the lamb.

LAMB AND MUSHROOMS WITH KRITHARAKI

Arni ke Manitaria me Kritharaki

2 pounds boneless lamb, cut into small cubes
1 medium onion, finely chopped
1/3 cup butter, margarine or olive oil
1 Tbsp flour
Salt and pepper to taste
1/2 cup dry Vermouth or white wine
5 medium red ripe tomatoes, peeled, seeded
  and chopped
1/2 pound mushrooms
1 pound kritharaki (Greek orzo pasta)
2 Tbsp or more butter, margarine or good
  quality olive oil
Grated Parmesan or Kefalotyri

Sauté the onion in butter if desired until soft, add lamb pieces and sauté until brown on all sides. Add flour, stirring constantly for few minutes. Add salt, pepper and the wine and cook until wine evaporates. Add tomatoes, and 1 cup of water, cover and simmer on low-heat for 1 hour. While the meat is simmering, prepare the mushrooms. Wash the mushrooms under cold running water. Dry and slice them, and add to the meat. Cook until the meat is tender and sauce is thick. While the food is simmering boil the kritharaki, in 4 quarts of boiling salted water, stirring frequently for 20 minutes or to your taste on low-heat. Drain well. Add the butter if desired and toss well to

combine. Serve the kritharaki with the meat and sauce, and sprinkle with the grated cheese. Serve hot with salad and fresh crusty bread. Serve 5-6.

LAMB CHOPS CUTLETS

Kotoletes Arniou Pane

3 pounds boneless lamb chops, 1/2-inch thick
2 eggs, beaten with 1 Tbsp. of water
1 1/2 cups dried breadcrumbs (see index)
1/4 cup grated Parmesan cheese
Salt and pepper to taste
Clarified butter, margarine or olive oil (see index)

Place one chop at a time between two pieces of plastic wrap or waxed paper and lightly pound to a thickness of 1/4-inch. Combine breadcrumbs, cheese, salt and pepper together. Dip chops one at a time in egg and them into breadcrumbs mixture until completely covered. Press it between your hands to stick well. Fry in hot butter if desired, on both sides, on medium heat. Serve hot with Au-Gratin Potatoes, rice pilaf or kritharaki pasta (see index for recipes). Serves 4-6.

LAMB CHOPS IN PUFF PASTRY

Arnisia Paithakia se Sfoliata

1 pkg puff pastry (thawed)
8 ounces chicken lives
3 ounces butter or margarine
1/4 tsp crushed thyme
1 1/2 Tbsp brandy
Salt and pepper to taste
8 large lamb chops, fat removed
2 Tbsp good quality olive oil
1 egg, beaten with 1 Tbsp water

Carefully clean and rinse livers, drain well and chop. In a skillet melt 2 Tbsp. butter, add chopped lives and sauté slowly for 2-3 minutes or until they are no longer pink, stirring occasionally. Season the lives with salt pepper, and thyme. Let cool for 10 minutes. Place the livers into a food processor container, add 3 Tbsp butter and the brandy, blend until smooth and creamy. Brown the lamb chops on both sides in hot oil and season with salt and pepper. Place on absorbent paper to drain. Remove the puff pastry from the box. Roll out each piece of pastry until almost doubled in size and cut into fourths. Divide the liver mixture into 8 parts and place on each pastry and spread evenly. Place one lamb chop over each piece of pastry. Roll pastry around the chop to enclose it, living the bone out. Brush the edges of the pastry with water and press to seal. Place the prepare lamb chops in a greased baking pan of dish and brush them with the egg wash. Let stand for 5 minutes. Bake in a preheated 400 F (205 C) oven for 20-30 minutes or until golden. Serve hot with macaroni gratinee, spiced roasted potatoes, or rice pilaf and salad (see index for recipes). Serves 8.

LAMB FRICASSEE
Arni Frikasse

2 pounds lean boneless lamb, cut into chunks
1 bunch of scallions, chopped
2 Tbsp of butter or margarine
2 Tbsp of olive oil
2 Tbsp or more finely chopped fresh dill
Salt and pepper to taste
2 cups hot water
3 heads endives or romaine lettuce
2 eggs
Juice of 1 or more lemon
3 tsp cornstarch

In a Dutch oven brown lamb on all sides. Add onion and sauté until soft. Add dill, salt, pepper and 2 cup water. Cover and cook slowly for 1 hour. While meat is simmering wash the vegetables and cut into small pieces about 2-inches long. Add prepared vegetables to the meat and continue to cook until meat and vegetables are tender. Remove from heat. Carefully drain liquid from pan into a measuring cup, add water to make 1 1/4 cups. Transfer liquid to a small saucepan, and bring to a boil. Mix cornstarch with 1/4 cup water to a smooth paste. Gradually add to liquid, stirring until boiling and thickened. Reduce heat and cook for 2 minutes. In a bowl beat eggs until frothy, add lemon juice, beating

constantly. Slowly add approximately 1 cup of the hot sauce at first spoon by spoon, and then a little more at a time beating constantly. Gradually add egg mixture to the sauce. Pour avgolemono sauce into the lamb and stir gently with a fork to combine. Shake the pot few times. Serve immediately. Serves 4.

LAMB KAPAMA WITH RICE
Arni Kokkinisto me Rizi
Substitute lamb for the beef

Follow recipe and preparation as directed in beef kapama with rice (see index for recipe)

LAMB KAPAMA WITH SPAGHETTI
Arni Kokkinisto me Spagetto
Substitute lamb for the beef

Follow recipe and preparation as directed in Beef kapama with spaghetti. (see index for recipe).

LAMB RAGOUT WITH EGGPLANT
Arni yiachni me Melitsanes

4 pounds lean leg of lamb, cut into 3/4-inch slices
1/4 cup all-purpose flour
1 tsp salt
1/4 tsp pepper
1 Tbsp butter
2 Tbsp good quality olive oil
1 cup finely chopped onion
1 cup tomato sauce or 6 large ripped tomatoes,
        peeled, seeded and chopped
2 cups water
4 pounds small narrow eggplants (5-6-inches long)
Olive oil for frying

Mix flour with salt and pepper. Coat meat pieces with the flour mixture. In a large non- stick frying pan brown meat pieces in hot butter and oil, few at a time. Remove to a large saucepan. Repeat with the rest of the meat pieces. Add onion to the frying pan and sauté until soft. Add to the meat. Add tomato sauce if desired, and water (add less water if you used fresh tomatoes). Bring to boil. Reduce heat, cover; and simmer for approximately 90 minutes or until tender and sauce is thick. As the liquid cooks away add more water as needed. While the meat is simmering prepare the eggplants. Cut the stems from the eggplants. Rinse well and dry. Slit eggplants lengthwise, but do not cut all the way through, and do not slit 1/2-inch at each end. In a nonstick frying pan sauté eggplants with 2 Tbsp of the olive oil on medium heat until soft on all sides. Cover pan to prevent splashing. Add more oil if needed. Add eggplants to the lamb ragout and spoon pot juices over them to coat them well. Do not stir. Simmer for 10 minutes. Serve hot, with fresh crusty bread. Serves 5-6.

❦❦❦

LAMB RAGOUT WITH PEAS
Arni Yiachni me Araka

Substitute lamb for the beef

Follow recipe and preparation as directed in Beef ragout with peas (see index for recipe).

❦❦❦

LAMB ROLL UPS IN FILLO PASTRY
Arni Exohiko Rolo me fillo

2 1/2 pounds lean boneless leg of lamb, cut into small cubes
3 Tbsp butter, margarine or olive oil
Salt and pepper to taste
1/2 cup dry white wine or Vermouth
1 bunch scallions, thinly sliced
3 medium carrots, thinly sliced
1 cup peas, fresh or frozen (Thawed)
1/3 cup lightly pressed down chopped dill
1 cup lightly pressed down grated Parmesan or Kefalotyri cheese
1 pound fillo pastry (thawed)
1 cup melted clarified butter, margarine or olive oil

Brown lamb cubes in oil if desired on all sides and season with salt and pepper. Add wine and let simmer for 30 minutes. Add scallions, carrots, peas and cook for 10 minutes or until all liquid evaporates. Remove from heat. Let cool, add dill, cheese and stir well to combine. Take three fillo sheets at a time, and cover the remaining sheets with a dry cloth, then with a lightly dampened towel to prevent them from drying out. Brush one sheet with hot melted butter if desired, take the other two sheets, and place on top the first one and brush them with hot melted butter. At the narrow side of the fillo, 3-inches from the end, place 1/6 of the meat filling. Fold the 3-inches overhanging of fillo over the filling. Roll up the fillo with the filling twice, fold one side in, toward the middle to enclose the filling, brush with hot butter, and rollup ounce again and fold the other side in, toward the middle to enclose the filling, and brush with hot melted butter, and roll up to make a roll. Repeat the same procedure with the remaining fillo and filling. Place the rolls seam side down in a greased baking pan, one at a time as you finish, and brush with hot melted butter. With a sharp knife, make a slit on the top of each roll to release the steam. Bake in preheated 350 F (180 C) oven for approximately 50-60 minutes or until golden brown. Place the rolls in a serving platter and decorate with springs of dill. Serve hot with salad. Serves 6.

❦❦❦

LAMB SOUVLAKIA
Lamb Shishkebab

1 leg of lamb (5-6 pounds), remove excess fat, boned and cut into 1-inch cubes
2 tsp crushed Greek oregano
2 tsp salt
1/2 tsp or less pepper
1/2 cup olive oil
Juice of 1 lemon
12 skewers
12 Greek pita bread
12 large pieces of waxed paper
2 medium tomatoes, cut into thinly wedges
1 medium onion, cut into thinly sliced lengthwise
2 cups or more shredded lettuce
2 cups or more tzatziki (Cucumber and Yogurt dip - see index for recipe)

Mix oil and lemon juice together. Combine oregano, salt and pepper together. Coat lamb cubes with the oregano mixture. Thread lamb cubes on 12 skewers. Grill over hot charcoal, turning and basting frequently with lemon and oil mixture. Place each of the pita bread on a piece of waxed paper. Remove meat from the skewer and place on the pita bread, and then top with tomato wedges, onion, lettuce and tzatziki. Roll up pita bread to enclose the filling, then wrap with the waxed paper. Serve hot with French fries. Serves 6-12.

❦❦❦❦

LAMB WITH ARTICHOKES AVGOLEMONO
Arni me Agginares Avgolemono

3 pounds lean lamb shoulder, cut into
      6 serving pieces
1 bunch scallions, chopped
1/4 cup fine quality olive oil
2/3 cup dry white wine or dry Vermouth
Salt and pepper to taste
9 artichokes, fresh or 3 boxes artichoke
      hearts frozen (thawed)
Juice of 1 lemon or more
3 Tbsp butter or margarine
3 Tbsp all-purpose flour
3 egg yolks

In a Dutch oven sauté lamb in oil on both sides, add scallions and sauté until onions are soft. Add wine, salt, pepper and 2 cups boiling water. Cover, and simmer for 90 minutes, or until meat is tender. While meat is simmering, prepare artichokes as directed in How to Prepare Artichokes (see index). Drain and save 3 cups of the liquid. In a 4-quart casserole, place boiled artichokes and top with lamb. Cover and bake in a preheated 350 F (180 C) oven for 30 minutes. While casserole is baking, prepare avgolemono sauce. Melt butter if desired and blend in flour until smooth. Gradually add reserved artichoke liquid, stirring constantly until boiling point is reached. Reduce heat and cook slowly for 5 minutes longer. Beat egg yolks lightly, add lemon juice beating constantly. Add 1 cup of hot sauce at first spoon by spoon and then a little more at a time, beating constantly. Gradually add egg mixture to sauce and stir gently to combine. Add salt and pepper if needed. Pour over casserole. Serve immediately. Serves 6.

❦❦❦❦

LAMB WITH PEAS AVGOLEMONO
Arni me Araka Avgolemono

21/2 pounds lean boneless lamb, cut into
      serving pieces
1 bunch scallions, chopped
2 Tbsp butter
2 Tbsp olive oil
2 Tbsp finely chopped fresh dill
Salt and pepper to taste
1 bag (20-ounces) frozen peas
1 cup water
2 eggs
Juice of 1 or more lemons

In a Dutch oven brown lamb pieces in hot butter, on all sides, add scallions and sauté until soft. Add 1 cup of water, dill, salt and pepper; cover and simmer for 1 1/2 hours. Add peas and simmer for 15 minutes or until meat and peas are tender. Add more water if needed. Remove from heat. In a bowl beat eggs until frothy. Add lemon juice beating constantly. Slowly add approximately 1 cup of the hot pot juices, at first spoon by spoon, and then a little more at a time beating constantly. Gradually add egg mixture to the sauce. Pour avgolemono sauce into the pot, stirring gently with a fork to combine. Return to a low heat and keep stirring for few minutes longer, don't boil it because the eggs will curl. Serve immediately. Serves 4.

❦❦❦❦

LAMB YOUVETSI WITH KRITHARAKI
Arni me Kritharaki Youvetsi

21/2 pounds boneless lamb, cut into 15-18 pieces
2 Tbsp olive oil
1 large onion, chopped
2 garlic cloves, minced
2/3 cup white Vermouth
Salt and pepper to taste
Pinch of Cayenne pepper
1 cup tomato sauce
8 ounces mushrooms
1 pound kritharaki (Greed pasta orzo)
2-3 Tbsp melted butter, margarine or good
      quality olive oil
Grated Parmesan or Kefalotyri

Sauté meat pieces in oil until brown. Add onion and sauté until soft, add garlic and Vermouth and cook until wine evaporates. Add salt, pepper, cayenne, tomato sauce and 1 cup of water. Bring to a boil, reduce heat to low, cover and simmer for 60-90 minutes. Stir the meat very carefully as not to break it apart. While meat is simmering, prepare the mushrooms. Rinse mushrooms under cold running water. Dray them on paper towels, cut into thin slices and add to the meat. Simmer for 30 minutes longer or until meat is tender. Add water as needed a little at a time. While meat is simmering prepare the kritharaki. Boil kritharaki in 4 quarts of boiling salted water for 20 minutes or to your taste. Drain well and add the melted butter if desired, toss well to combine. Serve the kritharaki with the meat and sauce and sprinkle with grated cheese. Accompany with salad and fresh crusty bread. Serves 5-6.

❧❦❧

LEG OF LAMB COUNTRY STYLE
Arni Exohiko

1 leg of lamb (6-8 pounds)
Juice of 1 lemon
2 garlic cloves, slivered
1/2 tsp crushed Greed oregano
Salt and pepper to taste
3 large sheets of parchment paper and
2 brown grocery paper bags or
2 sheets heavy-duty aluminum foil

Mix salt, pepper and oregano together. Make 8 deep slits in meat and insert some salt mixture and garlic slivers. (Remove before serving if desired). Rub meat with lemon juice and sprinkle with salt mixture. Wrap first tightly with parchment paper, closing ends as you would a parcel to keep juices in. Wrap again tightly with brown bags. If you don't use foil. Tie with twine like you tie a roast. Place in a baking pan and brush surface of paper with oil to keep from burning. Bake in preheated 350 F (180 C) oven 2 1/2 hours. Remove papers and carve the meat. Serve hot with Lemon spiced roasted potatoes, Carrots sautéed and Spring salad (see index for recipes), and fresh crusty bread. Serves 6-8.

❧❦❧

ROASTED LEG OF LAMB WITH POTATOES
Arni Psito me Patates

1 leg of lamb approximately 8 pounds
5 pounds red or white potatoes, peeled and cut
*   into fourths*
Salt and pepper to taste
1 1/2 tsp or less granulated garlic
2 or more garlic cloves, slivered (optional)
1/2 tsp crushed Greek oregano
1 tsp finely chopped fresh rosemary
Juice of 2 or more lemons
3 Tbsp good quality olive oil

Place potatoes in large roasting pan. Sprinkle with salt, pepper, granulated garlic and oregano, rosemary and toss well. Remove excess fat from meat. Insert slivers of garlic into deep narrow gashes cut in meat (remove before serving if desired). Place meat on top of potatoes (fat side down), sprinkle with half the lemon juice, half the oil, salt, pepper, oregano, and granulated garlic; add 2 cups water to pan. Roast uncovered in preheated 400 F (205 C) oven 30 minutes. Turn meat upside down (fat side up), sprinkle with remaining lemon juice, oil, salt, pepper, oregano and granulated garlic. Reduce temperature to 350 F. (180 C) and bake 2 1/2 hours longer or until meat and potatoes are tender. Add water if needed. Remove pan from oven and remove meat. Let stand 20 minutes before carving. Return potatoes and place on bottom rack of oven. Turn broiler and broil 6-10 minutes, watching carefully not to burn. Carve meat and serve hot with potatoes and salad. Serves 6-8.

❧❦❧

SUCKLING LAMB ON A SPIT
Arnaki tis Souvlas

1 whole lamb, approximately 20 pounds
Salt and pepper to taste
1 whole lemon, cut in half
Juice of 1 lemon, mixed with
1 cup olive oil

Pull liver, heart and spleen from the lamb cavity and leave the kidneys. Wipe the lamb inside and out with a damp cloth. Sprinkle cavity with salt and pepper; close with strong twine. Place lamb on the spit. Push spit through center from between the back legs, along the spine and through the neck. Tie the spine with the spit every 3 inches with wire. Pull front legs forwards and tie securely onto the spit with wire. Press back legs along the spit and cross them above it, again securing with wire. Rub outer surfaces with lemon and sprinkle with salt and pepper. Set a fire in a pit. When the charcoal is glowing; put spitted lamb in position and start cooking. Turn lamb slowly over the fire. Begin with spit well away from fire if possible, basting occasionally with lemon-oil mixture. When the lamb is evenly browned, move close to the fire and move most of the charcoal to the areas of the legs and shoulders. The total cooking time depends on the size of the lamb, and the weather, if the weather is cold it takes longer. Takes approximately 6 hours. The lamb is ready when the meat begins to crack on the legs, shoulder blade, and when the fork goes through the meat easily. Gently remove from the spit and carve. Serve hot with spiced roasted potatoes, artichokes with peas, tyropita, salad, Easter bread, red eggs and good wine (see index for recipes).

PORK

PORK WITH CELERY AVGOLEMONO
Hirino me Selino Avgolemono

*2 1/2 pounds lean boneless pork, cut into
    serving pieces*
2 medium onions, finely chopped
2 Tbsp butter or margarine (optional)
1/4 cup olive oil
Salt and pepper to taste
2 cups water
3 pounds Italian celery
2 Tbsp cornstarch
3 egg yolks
Juice of 1 or more lemons

Brown meat pieces on all sides. Add onions and sauté until soft. Add salt, pepper and water. Cover and cook slowly 80 minutes or until meat is tender. Stirring occasionally. While meat is simmering, prepare celery by removing roots of each plant. Retain tender leaves. Cut in fourths. Wash celery thoroughly in plenty of water. Drain. In large saucepan add water. Bring to a boil. Add celery and boil 2 minutes. Drain and add to meat. Stir gently, add 2 cups water, cover and simmer 15 minutes or until celery is tender. Add salt if needed. Remove pot juices, and add enough water to make 2 cups. Transfer liquid to a small saucepan. Bring to a boil. Mix the cornstarch with 1/4 cup of water to make a paste. Slowly add to the liquid stirring constantly. Cook slowly for 3 minutes. Beat egg yolks with the lemon juice. Gradually add some of the boiling sauce, stirring vigorously. Add egg mixture to the sauce and cook over very low heat for 2 minutes, stirring constantly. Do not let the sauce boil. Pour avgolemono sauce into the pot and stir gently with a fork to combine. Serve immediately. Serves 4-6.

ROAST PORK LOIN
Hirino Psito

4 pounds pork loin
Juice of half lemon or more
1 Tbsp good quality olive oil
Salt and pepper to taste
1 1/4 cups low sodium 100% fat free chicken broth
1 1/2 cups dry white wine or Vermouth
1/2 cup minced shallots
1 garlic clove or more, minced
3 Tbsp butter, margarine or olive oil
1/2 pound mushrooms
1/4 cup finely chopped flat leaf parsley
1 tsp Worcestershire sauce

Place a rack in a roasting pan, and place the roast on the rack. Rub the roast on all sides with the oil and sprinkle with the lemon juice, salt and pepper. Add 1 cup of the chicken broth to the pan, and bake in a preheated 350 F (180 C) oven for 1 1/2 hours. Turn the roast and add 1 cup of the wine if desired over the roast and bake for 30 minutes longer or until roast is tender. Add more broth to the pan if needed. Remove from the oven. Transfer the roast on a cutting board, let stand. Prepare the sauce. Remove most of the fat from the roasting pan and discard. In frying pan sauté shallots in butter until soft, add garlic and sauté few minutes longer. Wash the mushrooms under cold running water. Dry them well and slice thinly. Add to the onions and sauté until liquid evaporates. Add parsley, wine, Worcestershire sauce, the remaining chicken broth and the drippings. Slowly simmer until sauce lightly thickens. Carve the roast and arrange on a serving platter. Spoon sauce over the roast and serve hot on bed of rice pilaf. Serve with salad and fresh crusty bread, (see index for recipes). Serves 6-8.

VEAL

VEAL CUTLETS
Kotoletes Pane

3 pounds rump or veal
Salt and pepper to taste
1 1/2 cups fine dried breadcrumbs (see index)
1/4 cup grated Kefalotyri, Parmesan or
      Romano cheese
2 beaten eggs with 1 Tbsp. of water
Clarified butter (see the index for recipe)
Good quality olive oil for sautéing

Cut veal into 1/3-inch slices. Pound the slices between 2 sheets of plastic wrap, with a mallet, to expand them about double and to thin them down by half. Salt and pepper the veal slices lightly. Mix breadcrumbs with cheese. Dip cutlets into beaten eggs, then into breadcrumb and shake off excess. Sauté cutlets in 1 Tbsp of the butter, and 2 Tbsp of the oil, for about 2 minutes on each side. Add more butter and oil if needed. Serve immediately with French fries, pasta or rice pilaf and salad, (see the index for the recipes). Serves 6.

VEAL CUTLETS AU GRATIN
Mosharaki Kotoletes Au-Graten

4 pounds veal for cutlets
Salt and pepper to taste
1 cup or more flour for dredging
6 Tbsp butter, good quality olive oil or mixed
      for sautéing
3 medium onions, finely chopped

1/2 cup butter, margarine or good quality olive oil
1 pound fresh mushrooms, finely chopped
3 1/2 cups soft breadcrumbs (from a day old
      French or Italian bread)
1/4 cup finely chopped fresh flat leaf parsley
1/2 cup coarsely chopped blanched toasted
      almonds
2 beaten eggs
8 ounces coarsely grated Kaseri or Swiss cheese
      or mixed
6 Tbsp butter, margarine or good quality olive oil
6 Tbsp flour
3 1/2 cups fresh veal stock or low sodium
      100% fat free chicken broth
2 cups milk
3 beaten eggs
1/2 cup grated Parmesan cheese

Sauté onion with the butter if desired until onion is transparent. Add the mushrooms and sauté until browned and liquid has been absorbed. Remove from heat, set aside. Add breadcrumbs, parsley and tarragon to the onion mushroom mixture, and mix well, and sauté 2 minutes longer. Remove from heat, add almonds, one half of the grated Kaseri cheese if desired, beaten eggs, salt, pepper and mix well to combine. Set aside. With the leftover pieces and the bone prepare the stock. Place veal cutlets one at a time between two pieces of plastic wrap and pound with a meat mallet each one until 1/4-1/8-inch thick. Lightly season with salt and pepper them, dredge in flour and shake off excess. Sauté few pieces at a time for about 45 seconds or until golden brown on each side in butter and oil or oil if desired, (add more oil as needed) over medium heat. Set aside. Prepare the sauce. In a saucepan, melt butter if desired oven medium heat, blend in flour until smooth using a wire whisk. Remove from heat and gradually add turkey stock and milk, stirring constantly until mixture is thick and smooth. Cook 3 minutes longer. Remove from heat. Spoon little by little of the hot sauce into beaten eggs stirring constantly, add egg mixture to the sauce and cook over very low heat (do not let the sauce boil) for 2 minutes, stirring constantly. Add Parmesan cheese, salt and pepper, and stir well to combine. In a well-greased 15x11x2 1/2-inch baking dish place prepare veal cutlets until you have finish with all. Starting from the beginning, spread between each slice of the cutlets with the onion mushroom filling. Spoon the sauce over veal cutlets and spread evenly to cover. Sprinkle with the remaining grated Kaseri cheese. Bake in a preheated 400 F (200) oven for approximately 30 minutes or until golden brown. Serve immediately on bed of kritharaki and rice pilaf and salad. Serves 8-16.

VEAL CUTLETS WITH CHEESE
Kotoletes Pane me Tyri

3 pounds rump of veal
Salt and pepper to taste
1 1/2 cups fine dried breadcrumbs (see index)
1/4 cup grated Kefalotyri, Parmesan or
     Romano cheese
Clarified butter (see index)
Fine quality olive oil
Equal slices Kaseri or Swiss cheese

Cut veal into 1/3-inch slices and pound with mallet between 2 sheets of plastic wrap to expand them about double and thin them down by half. Salt and pepper veal lightly. Mix breadcrumbs with cheese. Dip cutlets into beaten eggs, then into breadcrumbs; shake off excess. Sauté cutlets in 1 Tbsp. of the butter and 2 Tbsp. of the oil for about 2 minutes. Turn on other side and place a slice of cheese on each cutlet, cover and sauté 2 minutes more. Add more butter and oil if needed. Serve immediately with French fries, pasta or rice pilaf and salad (see index for recipes). Serves 6.

GAME

DEER STIFATHO
Elafi Stifatho

Substitute 3 pounds of any piece of deer, cut into serving pieces, for the Hare or Rabbit.

Follow recipe and preparation as directed in Hare or Rabbit Stifatho (see index for recipe).

GRILLED DEER STEAKS
Brizoles Elafiou sti Skara

6 deer steaks
1 recipe for marinade as directed in Hare or
     Rabbit Stifatho (see index for recipe)
Salt and pepper to taste
1/4 cup olive or salad oil
Fresh lemon juice (optional)

Follow recipe and preparation for marinade. Place marinade and steaks in large heavy- duty Ziploc; zip and leave to marinate for 36-48 hours in refrigerator. Shake plastic bag occasionally. Lift steaks out of marinade and dry with paper towels. Generously brush steaks with oil and season with salt and pepper. Place in a preheated grill rack and grill for 5-7 minutes on each side or to your taste. Serve immediately with lemon juice if desired. Serves 6.

HARE OR RABBIT KAPAMA WITH PASTA
Kouneli Kapama me Zimariko

1 hare or rabbit fresh or frozen (thawed), cut into
     serving pieces
1 recipe for marinade as directed in Hare or
     Rabbit Stifatho (see index for recipe)
3 Tbsp butter
3 Tbsp olive oil
1 can (20-ounces) whole tomatoes, pressed through
     a food mill
Salt and pepper to taste
1 cinnamon stick 1/4-inch long
1 pound spaghetti or any other kind of pasta
4 quarts boiling water and
1 Tbsp salt
1/4 cup melted butter
1/2 cup or more grated Parmesan cheese

Follow recipe and preparation for marinade. Place marinade and meat pieces in a heavy- duty Ziplo; zip it and marinate for 36-48 hours in the refrigerator. Shake the plastic bag occasionally. Lift meat pieces out of marinade and dry with paper towels. Drain the marinade and reserve 1/ 2 cup of the liquid. Heat butter and oil and sauté meat pieces. Add the reserved liquid, tomato, salt, pepper and cinnamon stick; cover, bring to a boil and cook slowly for approximately 1 1/2 hours, Add water if necessary. Break spaghetti in half and drop into rapidly boiling salted water and boil uncovered for 20 minutes or until tender. Keep boiling and stir occasionally with a fork. Pour into a colander and drain well. Arrange half of the pasta on a large platter. Sprinkle with half of the cheese, cover with the remaining pasta and sprinkle again with the remaining cheese. Spoon the hot butter over pasta. Spoon sauce and rabbit kapama over pasta. Serve immediately with salad and fresh crusty bread. Serves 4-6.

HARE OR RABBIT STIFATHO
Kouneli, Lagos Stifatho

Marinate:
3 stalks celery, finely chopped
2 carrots, finely chopped
1 medium onion, finely chopped
2 cloves garlic, crushed
2 Tbsp flat leaf parsley, finely chopped
3 whole cloves
2 bay leaves, crushed
12 black peppercorns
1/4 cup olive oil
21/2 cups dry red wine or Vermouth
1/4 cup wine vinegar
*1 hare or rabbit, fresh or frozen (thawed), cut
	into serving pieces*
Other Ingredients:
1/2 cup or more olive oil
1/2 cup tomato sauce
1 bay leaf
1 tsp rosemary
12 black peppercorns
Salt and pepper to taste
1 cinnamon stick 1/2-inch long
5 whole allspice
2 pounds small white onions

Combine marinade ingredients in a large mixing bowl and stir well. Pour in a large heavy-duty plastic Ziploc, add meat pieces, zip it and leave to marinate for 36-48 hours in the refrigerator. Lift meat out of marinade and dry with paper towels. Drain the marinade and reserve the liquid. Heat olive oil and brown the meat pieces. Add the reserved liquid, tomato, bay leaf, rosemary, peppercorns, salt, pepper, cinnamon, allspice and 1 cup water; cover. Bring to a boil and cook slowly for approximately 60 minutes. While meat is simmering, prepare the onions as directed in Beef Stifatho (see index for recipe). Add onions and simmer for 60 minutes longer or until meat and onions are tender. Serve hot with noodles, salad and fresh crusty bread (see index for recipes). Serves 4-6.

ROASTED LEG OF DEER
Bouti Elafiou Fournou

1 leg of deer
*1 recipe for marinade as directed in Hare or
	Rabbit Stifatho (see index for recipe)*
1 1/2 cups dry red wine or Vermouth
1/2 cup melted butter or margarine
Salt and pepper to taste

Follow recipe and preparation for marinade. Make 12 deep slits in the meat. Place meat in prepared marinade, cover and leave for 36-48 hours in refrigerator. Turn meat occasionally. Lift meat out of marinade. Place leg on rack of roaster. Sprinkle with wine, brush with butter and season with salt and pepper on all sides. Add 1 cup water to the pan. Roast uncovered in a preheated 350 F (180 C) oven, allowing 15 minutes per pound or to your taste. Turn leg after 1 hour. Baste meat frequently add water to the pan as often as necessary. Make gravy from the pan juices if desired. Serve hot. Serves 6-8 depending on size of leg.

Stuffed Grape Leaves

Eggplant Mousaka

Beef Kapama
with
Rice

Fried Meatballs

POULTRY

BAKED LEMON CHICKEN
Kotopoulo Psito Lemonato

1 chicken (about 5 pounds)
Juice of 1 large lemon
Salt and pepper to taste
1/4 tsp or more granulated garlic
1/4 tsp crushed Greek oregano

Remove backbone from the chicken, save it for stock. Wash chicken thoroughly and place in a roasting pan, skin side down. Sprinkle chicken with half of each lemon juice, salt, pepper, garlic and oregano. Pour 1 cup water in the pan. Bake in a preheated 450 F. oven for 30 minutes. Gently turn chicken up side down and sprinkle with the remaining lemon juice, salt, pepper, garlic and oregano. Return to oven and bake 30-50 minutes longer or until golden. Add water if needed.

※ ❀ ※

BRAISED CHICKEN IN WINE
Kotopoulo Krasato

6 chicken breasts, boneless, skinless and
        fat removed
3 Tbsp olive oil
3 Tbsp butter or margarine
2 Tbsp all-purpose flour
1 cup dry white wine or Vermouth
1 Tbsp. brandy
3 large cloves garlic, crushed
1 bay leaf
1 Tbsp fresh parsley, finely chopped
Salt and pepper to taste
12 small white onions
1 pound fresh mushrooms, rinsed and sliced

Peel onions, cross cut root ends to prevent centers for popping out during cooking. Drop them in boiling water, bring to boil and boil for 5 minutes. Drain, let stand. While the onions are boiling, prepare the mushrooms. Sauté the mushrooms with 2 Tbsp of each butter and oil until all the liquid evaporates. Add the boiled onions and sauté few minutes longer, season with salt and pepper. Let stand. Season the chicken breasts with salt and pepper. Lightly brown the chicken breasts in the remaining oil and butter on both sides. Remove chicken pieces from the pan to a 6-quart saucepan. Add flour to the frying pan, stir well with a wire whisk and cook for 2 minutes on medium heat. Add wine, brandy, garlic, bay leaf, parsley, salt, pepper and 1 cup chicken stock or broth. Bring to boil and cook slowly for 5 minutes. Add the mixture to the chicken. Add the prepare mushrooms and onions to the chicken. Cover and cook slowly for 15-20 minutes or until chicken is tender. Serve with rice pilaf and salad (see index for recipes). Serve hot. Serves 6.

※ ❀ ※

BREAST OF CHICKEN CUTLETS WITH CHEESE
Stithos Kotas Pane me Tyri

3 whole chicken breasts, boned and skinned
Salt and pepper to taste
2 eggs, beaten with 1 Tbsp of water
1 1/2 cups fine dried breadcrumbs
2 Tbsp or more grated Parmesan cheese
Clarified butter, margarine or good quality
        olive oil for frying
Equal slices Kaseri or Swiss cheese

71

Place the breasts of chicken one at a time between two pieces of plastic wrap or waxed paper, and lightly pound to a thickness of 1/4-inch. Lightly season with salt and pepper. Combine breadcrumbs and cheese together. Dip prepare chicken breasts one at a time into egg and them into bread crumbs until completely covered and pressed them with your hands. Brown chicken in hot butter, oil or mixed until golden. Turn cutlets on the other side and place a slice of cheese on each cutlet, cover and brown until cheese is melted. Add more butter as needed. Remove cutlets in a serving platter and keep warm. Serve immediately. Serves 6.

❦❦❦

CHICKEN BREAST WITH WINE (L. CHOL. L. FAT)
Stithos Kotas Krasato

3 whole chicken breasts, skinned, fat removed and
    cut into halves
1 Tbsp olive oil
3 Tbsp all-purpose flour
1 1/2 cups dry white wine or Vermouth
1 Tbsp cognac or brandy
Salt and pepper to taste
2 large garlic cloves, minced
1 bay leaf
2 medium carrots, cut into small pieces
1 Tbsp fresh flat leaf minced parsley
1 1/2 cups fresh chicken stock or can fat free
    chicken broth
18 small white onions
2 Tbsp olive oil
1 pound small fresh mushrooms, wash well and
    cut onto halves

Rinse chicken breasts well and place in a 6-quart saucepan. Blend flour in hot oil, and cook 2 minutes, stirring constantly. Add wine, brandy, salt, pepper, garlic, bay leaf, carrots, parsley, and the chicken stock if desired. Bring to a boil, and cook slowly for 5 minutes. Add to the chicken. Peel onions, crosscut root ends to prevent centers for popping out during cooking. Drop onions in boiling water and boil them for 5 minutes. Drain. Add onions to the chicken. Sauté fresh mushrooms with the 2 Tbsp. of olive oil. Add to

the chicken. Cover, and cook slowly for 45-55 minutes or until chicken and vegetables are tender. Serve hot with rice pilaf, salad, and fresh crusty bread (see index for recipes). Serves 6.

❦❦❦

CHICKEN AND CHEESE STUFFED PEPPERS
Kotopoulo ke Piperies Gemistes me Tyri

3 pounds chicken
1/3 cup or less olive oil
2 pounds Roma tomatoes, peeled, seeded and
    finely chopped
6 garlic cloves, finely minced
Salt and pepper to taste
4 green chili sweet peppers
4 ounces feta cheese, crumbed
4 ounces cottage or ricotta cheese
1/2 cup or less olive oil

Remove the fat from the chicken and rinse well. Remove the skin from the chicken if desired and cut into serving pieces. Brown the chicken pieces in 3 Tbsp of the oil on all sides in a deep frying pan. Add tomatoes, garlic, salt and pepper to the chicken. Bring to boil, reduce heat and simmer until tender, covered. Add water if needed. Rinse and dry peppers. Cut tops off peppers and discard; remove inner seeds. Lightly sauté the peppers in the remaining oil on all sides, being gently when you turn not to tear them. Remove from the frying pan to a plate. Mix the feta and cottage cheese if desired with little pepper and stuff the peppers. Place stuffed peppers around the chicken pieces in the frying pan and simmer for 6-7 minutes longer. Serve hot plain or with rice pilaf or kritharaki (see index for recipe), and fresh crusty bread. Serves 4.

❦❦❦

CHICKEN AND PEPPERS WITH RICE PILAF
Kotopoulo ke Piperies me Rizi Pilafi

1 chicken (about 3 pounds), cut into serving pieces
3 Tbsp butter, margarine or olive oil
2 large onion, thinly sliced lengthwise
5 garlic cloves, thinly sliced
4 large red bell peppers, cut into half and
    then into fourths

4 large red bell peppers, cut into half and
    then into fourths
2 jalapeno peppers or any other hot peppers,
    seeded and thinly sliced
1 can (20-ounces) whole tomatoes, crushed
1/2 tsp crushed tarragon
Salt and pepper to taste
1/2 cup dry white wine
41/2 cups fresh chicken stock or fat free
    chicken broth
2 cups converted rice

In a frying pan heat oil if desired and brown the chicken pieces on both sides. Transfer to a Dutch oven. Set aside. Add onions to the pan and sauté until soft, add garlic, and peppers and sauté few minutes longer. Spoon the onion mixture over the chicken. Add tomatoes, salt, pepper, wine and one cup water. Bring to boil, reduce heat and simmer for 45-60 minutes or until chicken is tender. While chicken is simmering prepare the rice pilaf. Bring stock or broth to boil, add rice, stir, reduce heat and simmer partially covered for 20 minutes. Serve chicken and pepper over rice pilaf. Serve with salad and fresh crusty bread. Serves 4-5.

CHICKEN OR TURKEY CROQUETTES
Kotopoulo or Galopoula Krokettes

2 cups cooked chicken or turkey, minced
1 cup thick béchamel sauce (see index for recipe)
2 egg yolks, beaten
Salt and pepper to taste
1 Tbsp grated Parmesan or Romano cheese
1/8 tsp onion powder
1 1/2 cups dry fine breadcrumbs (see index)
1 egg plus 2 egg whites, beaten with 1 Tbsp water
Clarified butter or margarine (see index) or
    olive oil for frying

Combine chicken, white sauce, egg yolks, salt, pepper, cheese and onion and mix well. Shape croquettes into 3-inch long cylinders and roll them in fine crumbs. Dip croquettes in egg, then in crumbs and fry in hot butter on both sides, until golden brown. Drain on absorbent paper. Serve hot. Serves 4.

CHICKEN OR TURKEY FILLETS IN WINE SAUCE
Filleta Kotas or Galopoulas me Saltsa Krasiou

21/2 pounds chicken or turkey fillets
2 Tbsp olive oil
2 Tbsp butter
1 large shallot, finely minced
Salt and pepper to taste
3 Tbsp all-purpose flour
2/3 cup dry white Vermouth or wine
2/3 cup fresh orange juice
2/3 cup fresh chicken or turkey stock or
    100% fat free chicken broth
Segments of one orange
1 pound kritharaki (Greek pasta orzo)
1/4 cup or more melted butter, margarine or
    olive oil

Pound the slices of chicken if desired between 2 sheets of plastic wrap, with a mallet to expand them about double and to thin them down by half. These are your chicken or turkey fillets; cover and chill them until you are ready to sauté them. Prepare the kritharaki by dropping in 4 quarts of boiling salted water, stir well, reduce heat to medium-low and boil partially covered for 30 minutes or to your taste. Drain and rinse with warm water. Drain again well. Return to the pot and add the butter if desired and stir well to combine. While the kritharaki is boiling prepare the chicken or turkey fillets. Salt and pepper the meat slices lightly and sauté for about one and half minutes on each side in 1 Tbsp of the oil and 1 Tbsp of the butter (add more if needed). Remove the slices of chicken or turkey from the frying pan to a warm plate as you finish them, and keep warm. Add the shallot to the pan and sauté until soft. Add the flour and sauté for a minute stirring constantly. Gradually add wine, orange juice and stock or broth to the onion, stirring constantly until sauce thickens. Add the orange segments and the fillets to the sauce, let them simmer for few minutes. Serve fillets of chicken hot with the sauce on bed of kritharaki and salad. Serves 4-6.

CHICKEN OR TURKEY RICE GRATINEE
Kotta or Galopoula me Rizi Gratine

*31/4 cups fresh chicken or turkey stock or
        100% fat free chicken broth*
1 1/2 cups converted rice
*2 cups cooked breast of chicken or turkey,
        cut into small cubes*
21/4 cups finely chopped celery
1 1/2 tsp. curry powder or 3/4 tsp. crushed tarragon
2/3 cup toasted slivered blanched almonds
1 cup dried cranberries (optional)
1/4 cup minced onion
1/4 cup fresh lemon juice
*13/4 cups or more mayonnaise or half real and
        half low fat mayonnaise*
Salt and pepper to taste
*3/4 cup more or less grated Kefalotyri or
        Parmesan cheese*

Bring stock to a boil. Pick over rice carefully to remove any tiny stones. Rinse rice in a strainer under cold running water. Add rice to the boiling stock, and stir well. Reduce heat and simmer partially covered for 20 minutes. Remove from heat. Combine all the ingredients (except half of the cheese) together, toss well with two forks. Add more mayonnaise if needed. Spoon into a well greased casserole dish. Sprinkle with the remaining grated cheese and bake in a preheated 450 F (230 C) oven for 15 minutes. Serve hot. Serves 6-8.

CHICKEN OR TURKEY WITH MUSHROOM-PEA GRATINEE
Kotta or Galopoula me Manitaria ke Araka Gratine

1 1/2 pounds button mushrooms
2 Tbsp butter or margarine
1 1/2 cups grated onion
1 cup dry white Vermouth or wine
*3 cups cooked breast of chicken or turkey, cut
        into small cubes and firmly pressed down*
2 cups frozen peas (thawed and drain well)
*1/3 cup or more toasted slivered blanched
        almonds (optional)*
1/2 tsp crushed tarragon
Salt and white pepper to taste
Pinch of Cayenne pepper
*1 cup of each lightly pressed down coarsely grated
Kaseri and Swiss cheese*
*5 Tbsp butter, margarine or good quality light
        olive oil*

5 Tbsp of all-purpose flour
*31/2 cups hot fresh chicken or turkey stock or
100% fat free chicken broth*
2 cups scalding milk
3 extra large eggs, beaten
*1/3 cup lightly pressed down grated
        Parmesan cheese*

Wash the mushrooms under cold running water, dry them well, and cut into slices. In a frying pan sauté the mushrooms in butter if desired until liquid almost evaporates. Add onions and sauté until soft, add Vermouth if desired and cook until wine evaporates. Set aside. In a saucepan, melt butter over medium heat, and blend in flour until smooth using a wire whisk. Remove from heat and gradually add chicken or turkey stock if desired and milk, stirring constantly until mixture is thick and smooth. Cook 3 minutes longer. Remove from heat. Spoon little by little of the hot sauce into eggs stirring constantly. Add egg mixture to the sauce and cook over very low heat (do not let the sauce boil) for 2 minutes, stirring constantly. Remove from heat. Add the Parmesan cheese, stir well and taste it, add salt if needed and white pepper. In a large bowl combine all the ingredients, except 1/2 cup of the coarsely grated cheese, and 1 1/2 cups of the sauce and mix well. Spoon the mixture into a well-greased casserole dish. Spoon the remaining sauce over and spread evenly. Sprinkle with the remaining shredded cheese. Bake the casserole in a preheated 375 F (190 C) oven for 15-20 minutes, or until lightly golden. Remove from oven and serve hot over kritharaki. Serves 6-10.

CHICKEN RICE PILAF IN MUSHROOM MARSALA SAUCE
Kotopoulo me Manitaria me Saltsa Marsalas

4 half chicken breasts, boneless and skinless
Salt and pepper to taste
*4 Tbsp of good quality olive oil, butter or
        margarine*
*1 cup fresh chicken stock or can 100%
        fat free chicken broth*
1/2 cup chopped onion
12 ounces mushrooms

2 garlic cloves, crushed
1/2 cup sweet Marsala
1/4 cup whipping cream
1 1/2 cups converted rice
2 Tbsp butter, margarine or good quality olive oil

Sauté chicken breasts in 2 Tbsp of olive oil if desired, on both sides, until golden. Season the chicken with salt and pepper to taste and add the stock or broth. Cover the chicken and simmer for 15 minutes about, or until tender. Remove from heat. While chicken is simmering prepare the sauce. Wash mushrooms under cold running water, drain well, dry them on paper towels, and slice them. Sauté onion in butter if desired until soft. Add sliced mushrooms, garlic and sauté until liquid evaporates. Season mushrooms with salt and pepper. Add Marsala and cook for few minutes longer. Add cream, cook for a minute and serve. While mushrooms are simmering prepare the rice pilaf. Drop rice in 3 quarts of boiling water, stir, reduce heat, to medium, and cook for 20 minutes. Drain well. Return rice to pot, add butter if desired, and toss well with fork. Serve hot chicken on bed of rice, and top with mushroom Marsala sauce, cabbage carrot salad and fresh crusty bread (see index for recipe).

CHICKEN ROLL-UPS
Rola Kotopoulou

2 Tbsp butter or good quality olive oil
1/2 cup minced shallots
13/4 cups fresh breadcrumbs
1 Tbsp minced flat leaf parsley
1 Tbsp minced of dill
4 large dried apricots, finely chopped
2 Tbsp toasted pine nuts or toasted
*   blanched almonds*
Salt and pepper to taste
1 egg, beaten
1 cup pressed down coarsely grated
*   Gruyere cheese*
2 whole boneless chicken breasts, skinned and split
8 thin slices Prosciutto
Melted butter or good quality olive oil for brushing

Sauté shallot in butter if desired until soft. Add breadcrumbs and sauté a few minutes longer. Add the rest of the ingredients except Prosciutto, and mix well to combine. Remove from heat, cover, and set aside. Prepare chicken breasts. Place each chicken breast between 2 sheets of plastic wrap; pound with a meat mallet, until 1/4-inch thickness. Remove top sheet of plastic; place 2 slices Prosciutto over each breast. Place plastic sheet back over Prosciutto, and turn upside down. Remove top sheet of plastic; spread with the bread mixture. Roll-up; tie with kitchen string. Place rolls in a greased baking dish, and brush with butter if desired. Bake in a preheated 375 F (190 C) oven approximately 30 minutes. Let cool 10 minutes. Remove strings and cut chicken breasts into 1-inch slices. Place on a serving platter, and pour pan juices over. Serve chicken roulades with rice pilaf and salad (see index for recipes), and fresh crusty bread. Serves 4.

CHICKEN STIFATHO
Kotopoulo Stifatho

Substitute 4-5 pounds chicken for the beef.

Follow recipe and preparation as directed in Beef Stifatho (see index for recipe).

CHICKEN WITH EGG CREAM SAUCE
Kotopoulo me Krema Avgou

1 whole fryer chicken (about 4 pounds)
1 Tbsp. salt
2 carrots, cut into half
3 stalks celery, cut into fourths
2 whole small onions, peeled
2 cups converted rice
41/2 cups from the chicken stock
1/2 cup toasted blanched slivered almonds
5 Tbsp butter or margarine
5 Tbsp all-purpose flour
3 cups from the chicken stock
1 1/2 cups milk
3 extra large egg, beaten
1/2 cup or more grated Parmesan cheese
2 cups frozen or fresh peas, cooked
Salt and White pepper to taste

Clean and rinse chicken well. Place in large pot and cover with cold water. Add salt and bring to a boil. Skim off broth. Reduce heat and cook slowly partially covered for 1 hour. Add vegetables and cook 30 minutes longer. Remove chicken from broth. Remove bones and skin from chicken, and cut into small pieces. Set aside. In saucepan place 41/2 cups stock. Bring to a boil, add rice, stir and cook slowly partially covered 20 minutes. Remove from heat. Add toasted almonds and toss well with a fork. Pack rice into 6-cup ring mold. Unmold in large round platter. Arrange chicken pieces around rice. While rice is cooking prepare sauce. In medium saucepan, melt butter over medium heat, and blend in flour until smooth using wire whisk. Gradually add chicken stock and milk, stirring constantly until mixture is lightly thick and smooth. Cook 3 minutes longer, stirring constantly. Remove from heat. Spoon little by little of the hot sauce into egg yolks, stirring constantly. Add egg mixture to sauce and cook over very low heat 4-5 minutes, stirring constantly. Remove from heat. Add cheese and stir well; add salt and pepper. Spoon half the sauce over chicken and rice pilaf. Pour other half of sauce in sauce dish. Fill center of rice mold with cooked peas. Serve hot with salad (see index for the salad recipe). Serves 6-8.

Note: This dish is excellent for buffet.

❦❦❦

CHICKEN WITH GARLIC
Kotopoulo me Skortho

1 fryer or broiler chicken (about 3 pounds), cut
    into serving pieces
1/4 cup olive oil
3 cloves garlic or more, sliced
1/2 cup dry white wine or Vermouth
Juice of 1/2 or more lemon
Salt and pepper to taste
1 tsp crushed Greek oregano
1 cup water

In a Dutch oven brown chicken pieces in oil. Add garlic and sauté few minutes longer. Add wine, lemon, salt, pepper, oregano and water, and stir well to combine. Cover and simmer for approximately 1 hour or until chicken is tender. Serve with noodles, rice pilaf or fries and salad (see index for recipes). Serves 4.

❦❦❦

CHICKEN WITH OKRA
Kotopoulo me Bamies

1 fryer or broiler chicken (about 3 pounds), cut
    into serving pieces
1/4 cup olive oil
1 can (16-ounces) whole tomatoes, crushed or
    pressed through a food mill
Salt and pepper to taste
2 pounds fresh or frozen baby okra

Clean and prepare okra. The pods of okra are so sticky that special care is needed to avoid breading them during the cleaning. Wash them well and remove the stems. In a Dutch oven heat oil and brown chicken pieces. Add tomatoes, salt, pepper and 1 cup water. Cover and cook slowly for 45 minutes. Neatly add okra to the chicken. Cover and cook slowly 30 minutes (depending on the size of the okra) or until tender. Do not overcook. Occasionally shake pot but do not stir. Arrange chicken and okra in a serving platter and serve hot. Serves 4.

❦❦❦

QUAILS WITH RICE PILAF
Ortykia Pilafi

6 fresh of frozen quails (thawed)
1/4 cup good quality olive oil
1 medium onion, finely chopped
1 (16-ounces) can whole tomatoes, crushed
1 cinnamon stick 1/2-inch long
Salt and pepper to taste
1/4 cup butter, margarine or good quality olive oil
2 cups converted rice

Rinse quails and dry. In large frying pan heat oil and brown the quails on both sides. Transfer to a 6-quart saucepan. Set aside. Add onion in the frying pan and sauté until soft and tender. Add tomatoes, cinnamon, salt and pepper to the onion, bring to a boil, reduce heat, cover; and simmer for 10 minutes. Poor onion tomato mixture and 1cup water to the quails, cover and simmer for15-20 minutes or until quails are tender. Add more water if needed. Remove the quails from the pan to a large serving platter, cover and keep warm. Measure the sauce and add water to make 5 cups. Bring to a boil, rinse rice in a strainer under cold running water (to get rid of the starch). Sauté rice in butter if desired for 5 minutes. Add rice to the boiling sauce, stir well and cool slowly partially covered 20 minutes or until tender. Place rice into a serving bowl. Serve quails and rice hot with grated cheese if desired, salad and fresh crusty bread.

❧❧✧❧❧

ROASTED SPICED CHICKEN AND POTATOES
Psito Kotopoulo me Patates Mirothates

3 pounds red or white potatoes, peeled and cut
    into fourths
Salt and pepper to taste
1 tsp granulated garlic
1/2 tsp crushed Greed oregano
1 broiler chicken (about 3 pounds) cut into half
1/4 cup or less olive oil
Juice of 1 or more lemons

Arrange potatoes in roasting pan. Sprinkle with salt, pepper, 2/3 of the garlic and half the oregano. Toss well. Rinse chicken under cold running water. Dry and place chicken halves over potatoes with skin side down. Sprinkle chicken with lemon juice, oil, salt, pepper, the remaining garlic and oregano. Add 2 cups water to pan. Bake in a preheated 350 F. (180 C.) oven approximately 1 hour. Turn chicken upside down and bake 30 minutes longer or until chicken is tender. Add water if needed. Remove chicken from pan to a cutting board. Return potatoes to oven on lower rack and turn broiler on. Broil 5-10 minutes. Been careful not to burn them. Cut chicken into serving pieces, and place into a serving platter, arrange potatoes around. Serve hot with salad. Serves 4.

❧❧✧❧❧

ROASTED STUFFED TURKEY
Galopoula Ghemisti

1 turkey (about 16 pounds)
3 Tbsp good quality olive oil
1 medium finely chopped onion
2 pounds lean ground beef
1/2 cup dry white wine or Vermouth
1 cup converted rice
1/2 cup pine nuts or toasted slivered
    blanched almonds
1 pound roasted chestnuts
Salt and pepper to taste

Juice of 1 lemon
4 Tbsp cornstarch

The night before, roast chestnuts. With a knife, cut two crisscross slashes on each chestnut shell. Arrange in baking pan, in one layer and broil 10 minutes or until shells are open. Remove shells and peel inner skins, cut into fourths. Cover turkey with cold water and add 4 Tbsp salt, and soak 1 hour. Rinse well and set aside. While turkey is soaking prepare stuffing. Brown meat in oil, stirring constantly breaking up clumps, add onion and sauté until soft, and meat juices evaporate. Add wine and cook until wine evaporates. Add rice and sauté 2 minutes. Add 1 cup water; cover and simmer 5 minutes. Remove from heat, add pine nuts, chestnuts, salt and pepper, and mix well to combine. Stuff turkey cavity with meat mixture and close up opening. Place turkey in enamel roasting pan. Sprinkle with lemon juice, salt and pepper. Add 2 cups water to pan. Roast turkey in preheated 325 F. (165 C.) oven 1 1/2 hours. Cover with foil and roast approximately 1-1 1/2 hours longer or until turkey is golden and tender. If roasting pan is stainless steel, roast turkey in preheated 450 F. (230 C) oven for the same cooking time as above. Remove turkey from roasting pan. Set aside. Strain pan juices in small saucepan. Pour off fat. Measure and add water to make 3 1/2 cups. Bring to a boil; mix cornstarch with 1/2 cup water to a paste. Slowly add to stock stirring constantly. Cook slowly 2 minutes. Remove from heat and pour in a gravy dish. Spoon stuffing in a serving bowl. Carve turkey and arrange in a serving platter. Serve turkey with stuffing, mash potatoes and salad. Serves 8-10.
Note: With the neck and giblets make delicious avgolemono soup, for first dish if desired.

❧❧✧❧❧

STUFFED BREAST OF CHICKEN
Stithos Kottopoulo Ghemisto

6 half chicken breasts, skinless and boneless
1/4 cup finely chopped shallots
1/4 cup butter or margarine at room temperature
1 1/2 cups coarsely chopped mushrooms

2 Tbsp finely chopped flat leaf parsley
2 Tbsp fresh lemon juice
1/2 tsp dry tarragon, crushed
Salt and pepper to taste
1 egg, beaten
1/3 cup coarsely chopped pine nuts
3/4 cup pressed down coarsely grated Kaseri or
Swiss cheese or mixed
1 1/2 cups all-purpose of flour
2 eggs, beaten with 1 Tbsp of water
2 cups dried breadcrumbs mix with
3 Tbsp grated Parmesan cheese
Egg cream sauce (see index for recipe)

Place chicken breasts one at a time between two pieces of plastic wrap or parchment paper and lightly pound to thickness of 1/4-inch. Sauté shallots in butter until soft add mushrooms and sauté until liquid evaporates. Remove from heat. Combine all ingredients except flour, eggs, breadcrumbs and grated Parmesan cheese, and mix well. Divide mixture into 6 parts. Take one part of mixture at a time and place on one of the prepared chicken breasts, and roll up to enclose the filling. Repeat with remaining chicken breasts and filling. Roll one at a time in flour the stuffed chicken breasts, shake off the excess flour. Dip them in egg and then into breadcrumbs mixture until completely coated. Place in well-greased baking pan, one next to each other. Bake stuffed chicken breasts in a preheated 375 F (190 C) oven 20 minutes or until chicken is cooked. Serve with rice pilaf and spoon egg cream sauce over it. Serve with salad and fresh crusty bread, (see index). Serves 6.

❦❦❦

TURKEY BREAST CUTLETS ROLL UPS
Kotoletes Ghalopoulas Rolla

12 thin sliced turkey breast cutlets
Salt and pepper to taste
6 thin slices Kaseri or Swiss cheese, cut each
into half
3 Tbsp finely chopped flat leaf parsley
2 eggs, well beaten with 2 Tbsp. water
2 cups fine dried breadcrumbs (see index
for recipe)
1/4 cup grated Parmesan cheese
1/4 cup clarified butter
2 Tbsp olive oil

1 cup dry white wine or Vermouth
3 shallots, finely chopped
1 cup fresh turkey stock or can fat free
chicken broth
1 large ripe tomato, peeled, seeded and cut
into small cubes
3/4 cup whipping cream

Pound turkey cutlets between 2 pieces of parchment paper, until they are paper thin. Sprinkle turkey slices with salt and pepper. Place half pieces of cheese at one end of slice. Sprinkle with the parsley. Fold in sides and roll up jellyroll fashion, enclosing cheese. Dip rolls in egg and then into breadcrumbs. Let dry on parchment paper for 10 minutes. (Can be made a day ahead to this point). After drying, cover rolls and refrigerate. Bring to room temperature before cooking. In a skillet, heat the butter and the oil and sauté rolls slowly until golden brown on all sides. Remove from pan and keep warm. Add shallots and wine and bring to a boil, cook until reduce lightly. Add stock if desired, salt and pepper, reduce heat, and cook for 10 minutes. Add the tomatoes, bring to a boil and simmer 2 minutes. Stir in cream and bring back to a boil, simmer for 1 minute. Pour sauce over rolls. Serve immediately on bed of rice pilaf, country style salad and fresh crusty bread. Serves 6-8.

❦❦❦

TURKEY BREAST CUTLETS
Stithos Ghalopoulas Kotoletes

1/2 breast of turkey, skinned and cut into
1/2-inch slices
2 cups all-purpose flour
2 eggs, beaten with 1 Tbsp water
2 1/2 cups dried fine breadcrumbs (see index)
1/3 cup grated Parmesan or Romano cheese
Salt and pepper to taste
Clarified butter or margarine (see index) or
olive oil for frying

Place turkey cutlets between two pieces of plastic wrap or waxed paper, one at a time, and lightly pound to a thickness of 1/4-inch. Combine breadcrumbs, cheese, salt and pepper together and mix well. Dredge cutlets one at a time in flour, then dip in egg and then into breadcrumbs mixture, until completely covered. Fry in hot butter if desired on medium heat until golden brown on both sides. Repeat with the remaining cutlets, adding more butter as needed. Serve immediately with French fries, salad, feta cheese and fresh crusty bread. Serves 4-6.

❦❦❦

TURKEY MEATBALLS WITH CUMIN (L. CHOL. L. FAT)

Soutzoukakia

2 pounds lean ground turkey
2 garlic cloves, crushed
1/2 tsp or more ground cumin
Salt and pepper to taste
2 cups soft breadcrumbs (see index for recipe)
4 lightly beaten egg whites
1/2 cup dry Vermouth, white wine or skin milk
1 (29-ounces can) whole tomatoes, pressed
    through a food mill
2 Tbsp good quality olive oil

Soak breadcrumbs in wine if desired. Combine all ingredients, except tomatoes and olive oil, and mix well with your hand. Cook tomato 5 minutes on medium heat. Pour half the tomato in a baking dish. Shape meat mixture into 2-inch long cylinders. Place in the baking dish over tomato sauce in one layer. Pour remaining tomato sauce over meatballs, and sprinkle with oil. Bake dish in preheated 350 F (180 C) oven on middle rack 45-55 minutes or until cooked through. Serve with rice pilaf, or spaghetti and salad (see index for recipes). Serves 6-8.

❦❦❦

TURKEY MOSAIC IN FILLO PASTRY

Ghalopoula Mosaiko Pollo se Fillo

3 pounds ground turkey (breast and thigh mixed)
2 eggs
1 cup boiled and drained converted rice
Salt and pepper to taste plus a pinch of
    Cayenne pepper
3/4 tsp dried crushed tarragon
2/3 cup Vermouth
1 cup plus 2 half and half
2 Tbsp. chopped fresh flat leaf parsley
8 ounces chopped mushrooms
2 Tbsp butter, margarine or good quality olive oil
1 bunch scallions, finely sliced
4 ounces Swiss or Kaseri cheese, cut into
    1/4-inch dice
4 ounces good quality boiled ham, cut into
    1/4-inch dice
3/4 cup slivered blanched almonds, toasted until
    golden brown
1/4 cup toasted pine nuts
1 1/2 pounds fillo pastry (thawed)
1 cup melted clarified butter, margarine or good
    quality olive oil for brushing the fillo

In a mixer, mix well the first 8 ingredients. Set aside. Sauté mushrooms in hot butter if desired until all liquid evaporates. In a large bowl fold the turkey mixture and the rest of the ingredients except the fillo and the butter, well to combine. Divide turkey mixture into 6 parts. Lay two sheets of fillo on a large cutting board, brush with hot melted butter, and cover again with two more sheets of fillo and brush with the hot butter. Repeat the same procedure one more time. Take one part of the turkey mixture and place at the wide end of fillo to within 3-inches, and 2-inches of edges of the narrow side, and spread evenly. Fold the top 3-inches to cover the filling, roll up twice. Then fold the sides in toward the middle to enclose filling. Brush with the hot butter and roll up over crosswise to the other end to form a tube. Place in greased baking pan. Repeat the filling and rolling process. Generously brush with the hot butter. Pierce 2 steam holes 1/2-inch in diameter in top of fillo with the point of a knife, going down through the fillo to the filling. Bake in a preheated 375 F (190 C) oven for 30-45 minutes or until golden brown. Remove from oven, slice into 3-4 slices slantwise and serve hot with Egg Cream Sauce, String Beans with Tomato and Potatoes, and Salad (see index for recipes). Serves 12-18.

❦❦❦

TURKEY OR CHICKEN SOUFFLÈ

Stithos Ghalopoulas or Kotas Soufflé

2 cups cooked breast of turkey or chicken, cut
    into small cubes
7 Tbsp butter
8 Tbsp all-purpose flour

2 cups scalding milk
7 eggs, separated
Salt and white pepper to taste
1 Tbsp finely chopped fresh tarragon
1 cup lightly pressed down coarsely grated
Kefalograviera, Gruyere or Swiss cheese

Prepare the béchamel sauce. Melt butter over medium heat blend in flour until smooth using a wire whisk. Cook for 2 minutes, stirring continuously. Remove from heat and gradually add milk, stirring constantly, return to heat and cook until mixture is thick and smooth. Cook for 3 minutes longer, stirring constantly; add seasoning and blend. Remove from the heat. Beat egg yolks and gradually add to the sauce mixture stirring constantly. Add the turkey, cheese and tarragon and stir well to combine. Cool completely. Beat egg whites with a pinch of salt until hold stiff peak but not dry. Gently fold in the turkey mixture. Spoon the mixture in a greased 10-cup soufflé dish. Bake in a preheated 375 F (190 C) oven on the middle rack, for approximately 30 minutes or until golden. Remove from the oven and serve immediately with salad. Serves 8-10.

TURKEY WITH EGG-CREAM SAUCE GRATINEE

Ghalopoula me Krema Avgou Gratine

4 cups cooked turkey, cut into 1/2 -inch cubes
41/2 cups boiling turkey stock or
        100% fat free chicken broth
2 cups converted rice
1 pound chestnuts, roasted, peeled and chopped
3/4 tsp crushed dried tarragon
Salt and pepper to taste

3 cups cooked and drained fresh or frozen peas
7 Tbsp butter or margarine
7 Tbsp all-purpose flour
33/4 cups scalding turkey stock or
        100% fat free chicken broth
21/4 cups scalding milk
4 extra large eggs, beaten
3/4 cup lightly pressed down grated Parmesan,
        Kefalotyri or Romano cheese
1 cup lightly pressed down coarsely grated
        Swiss cheese

Drop rice in boiling stock, stir; simmer partially covered 20 minutes. In large bowl, combine rice, turkey, chestnuts, tarragon and peas; toss well. Add seasoning if needed. In 4-quart saucepan melt butter if desired over medium heat, blend in flour with whisk until smooth. Cook 2 minutes more stirring constantly. Remove from heat and gradually add stock and milk, stirring continuously. Return to heat and cook until mixture is thick and smooth. Cook 3 minutes more. Remove from heat. Spoon hot sauce little by little into beaten eggs, until you have added 1/3 of sauce, stirring constantly. Add egg mixture to sauce and cook over very low heat 2-3 minutes (do not let sauce boil), stirring constantly. Remove from heat, add grated Parmesan if desired, and stir well. Season with salt and pepper if needed. Add 2/3 of sauce to turkey-rice mixture and toss well. Spoon mixture on greased 14x11 1/2 x21/2 -inch baking casserole. Spoon remaining sauce over and spread evenly, sprinkle with grated Swiss cheese. Bake casserole in preheated 375 F (190 C) oven on middle rack 15-20 minutes or until bubbling and golden color. Serve hot with salad. Serves 8-12.

HOMEMADE PASTRY & PITA

BUTTERNUT-PUMPKIN SQUASH CHEESE PITA

Kolokythopita me Tyri

*2 cups of each cooked and mashed butternut
        and pumpkin squash*
2 medium onions, finely chopped
5 extra large eggs
*1 cup of each grated and lightly pressed down
Kaseri and Swiss cheese*
*1/3 cup grated and lightly pressed down
        Parmesan or Kefalotyri cheese*
2 Tbsp finely chopped fresh mint
1/4 cup finely chopped fresh dill
Salt and pepper to taste
*1 pound fillo pastry (thawed) or homemade
        pastry (see index for recipe)*
*1 cup clarified melted butter, margarine or
        good quality olive oil*

Wash the squashes and cut into half and remove the seeds and soft mesh surrounding them. Place the squashes into a baking pan lined with foil, and bake in a preheated 350 F (180 C) oven on the middle rack for 1 1/2-2 hours or until soft to the tough. Remove from oven and let cool. When cool enough scoop out the flesh and process in a food processor or with a food mill. Sauté the onion in 1/4 cup of the butter if desired until soft. Remove from heat and let stand. In a large mixing bowl add the mashed squash and fold in eggs one at a time. Add the rest of the ingredients except the fillo pastry and the butter if desired and stir well to combine. Grease a 11x17x3-inch baking pan. Line pan with half of the fillo sheets, brushing every other sheet with hot melted butter if desired. The sheets will extend up the sides of the pan. Spoon in the squash mixture and spread evenly. Take one fillo sheet and folded into half crosswise and cover the squash mixture, brush with the hot butter. Repeat the procedure with a second fillo sheet and place over the first sheet and brush again with hot butter. Fold overhanging fillo sheets over the filling to enclose it and brush with hot butter. Top with the rest of the fillo sheets brushing every other one with hot butter, and tuck in overhanging sheets inside the pan. Generously brush top with hot butter. Score top layers of fillo all the way to the filling with a sharp serrated knife into three lines lengthwise. Bake in a preheated 350 F (180 C) oven on the middle rack for 50-60 minutes or until golden brown. When you are ready to serve, cut through scored lines and them into 3x3-inch squares or rectangles. Serve hot if you used butter or at room temperature if you used oil. Serves 12 or more.

❧❦❧

BUTTERNUT OR PUMPKIN SQUASH PITA

Kolokythopita

*4 cups cooked and mashed butternut or
        pumpkin squash or half and half*
1/2 tsp salt
5 extra large eggs
1/3 cup milk
1/4 tsp. cinnamon
Pinch of nutmeg (optional)
1/4 cup melted clarified butter or margarine
3 Tbsp or more sugar
*1 pound fillo pastry (thawed) or homemade
        pastry (see index for recipe)*
*1 cup melted clarified butter or margarine
        (see index)*

Wash squash, cut into half and remove seeds and soft mesh surrounding them. Place squash into a baking pan lined with foil, and bake in a preheated 350 F (180 C) oven in the middle rack for 2 hours or until soft to the touch. Remove from oven. When cool enough cut pieces with a knife and process in a food processor or with a food mill. Place squash in large mixing bowl and fold in eggs one at a time. Add milk, sugar, butter, cinnamon and nutmeg if desired and mix gently with a spatula to combine. Grease a 16x11x3-inch baking pan. Line pan with half of the fillo sheets, brushing every other sheet with hot butter if desired. The sheets will extend up the sides of the pan. Spoon in the squash mixture and spread evenly. Take one fillo sheet, fold it in two, and cover the pumpkin mixture and brush with the butter. Take a second fillo sheet, fold it in two, place over the first sheet and brush with hot butter. Fold overhanging fillo sheets over the filling to enclose it and brush with hot butter. Top with the rest of the fillo sheets brushing every other one with hot butter, and tuck in overhanging sheets inside the pan. Brush top with hot butter. Score top layers of fillo all the way to the filling with a sharp serrated knife into three lines lengthwise. Bake in a preheated 350 F (180 C) oven for 50-60 minutes or until golden brown. When you are ready to serve, cut through scored lines into 3x3-inch squares or rectangles. Serve hot or at room temperature. Serves 12 or more.

❦❧❦

CHICKEN OR TURKEY AND HAM PITA

Kotopoulo or Galopoula ke Zampon Pita

2 medium onions, finely chopped
1 Tbsp butter, margarine or olive oil
8 ounces grated Kaseri cheese
4 ounces boiled ham, cut into small cubes
8 ounces cooked breast of chicken or turkey,
*   cut into small cubes*
Salt and pepper to taste
7 Tbsp butter, margarine or olive oil
8 Tbsp all-purpose flour
2 cups milk
5 extra large eggs, beaten

1/4 cup grated Parmesan or Kefalotyri cheese
1 pound fillo pastry (thawed) or homemade pastry
(see index for recipe)
1 cup melted clarified butter, margarine or olive oil

Sauté the onion with the butter if desired until soft. Remove from heat. In a large mixing bowl combine 5 first ingredients together and mix well. Prepare the béchamel sauce. Melt butter if desired over medium heat, blend in flour until smooth using a whisk. Remove from heat and gradually add the milk, stirring constantly until mixture is thick and smooth. Cook 2 minutes longer; add seasoning and blend. Remove from heat and spoon little by little of the hot sauce into beaten eggs, stirring constantly. Gradually add egg mixture to the sauce, reduce the heat and cook over very low heat for 2-3 minutes, stirring constantly (do not let the sauce boil). Remove from heat and add the Parmesan cheese if desired and stir well. Gradually add sauce to the mixture in the bowl and mix well to combine. Grease a 14x11x3-inch baking pan. Line pan with 10 fillo sheets or half of the fillo sheets from the box, brushing every other sheet with hot melted butter if desired. The sheets will extend up the sides of the pan. Spoon in the mixture and spread evenly. Take one fillo sheet and folded in two and cover the filling and brush with the hot butter. Take second fillo sheet and folded in two and place over the first sheet and brush with hot butter. Fold overhanging fillo sheets over the filling to enclose it and brush with hot butter. Top with the rest of the fillo sheets brushing every other one with hot butter, and tuck in overhanging sheets inside the pan. Brush top with hot butter. Score top layers of fillo all the way to the filling with a sharp serrated knife into three lines lengthwise. Bake in a preheated 350 F (180 C) oven for 50-60 minutes or until golden brown. When you are ready to serve, cut through scored lines into 3x3-inch squares or rectangles. Serve hot. Serves 12 or more.

❦❧❦

CHICKEN OR TURKEY AND SPINACH PITA

Kotopoulo or Galopoula ke Spanaki Pita

1 1/2 pounds lean ground chicken or turkey
1/4 cup olive oil
Salt and pepper to taste
2 bunches scallions, cleaned, washed and
    finely chopped
5 extra large eggs
1 pound feta cheese, crumbled
1/4 cup grated Parmesan or Kefalotyri cheese
1 1/2 pounds frozen cut leaf spinach (thawed and
    squeezed dry)
1/4 cup finely chopped dill
1/4 cup finely chopped flat leaf parsley
1 pound fillo pastry or homemade pastry
    (see index for recipe)
1 cup clarified melted butter, margarine or
    good quality olive oil

Sauté chicken if desired with the oil, stir breaking up clumps until brown and meat juices have evaporated. Add scallions, salt and pepper, sauté until tender but not brown. Remove from heat. In a large mixing bowl beat eggs, add feta, grated cheese, spinach, dill and parsley and stir well. Add ground chicken mixture and mix well to combine. Grease a 13x11x3-inch or larger baking pan. Line pan with 10 sheets of the fillo, brushing every other sheet with hot butter if desired. The sheets will extend up the sides of the pan. Spoon in the chicken-spinach mixture and spread evenly. Cover the filling with 2 fillo sheets and brush with hot butter. Fold overhanging fillo over the filling to enclose it. Top with the rest of the fillo brushing every other one with hot butter and tuck in overhanging sheets inside the pan. Brush top with hot butter. Score top eight layers of fillo with a sharp serrated knife into three lines lengthwise. Bake in a preheated 350 F (180 C) oven for 50-60 minutes or until golden brown. Cut through scored lines and then into squares or rectangles when you are ready to serve. Serve hot. Serves 12-16 as a first course or 6-8 as a main course.

❦

CHICKEN OR TURKEY PITA

Kotopita or Galopita

7 Tbsp butter, margarine or good quality olive oil
8 Tbsp flour
2 cups milk
Salt and pepper to taste
1/4 cup grated Parmesan or Kefalotyri cheese
4 ounces shredded Kaseri or Swiss cheese
3 cups cooked chicken or turkey breast, cut
    into small cubes
8 extra large beaten eggs
Pepper to taste
1/2 cup chopped blanched almonds
1 pound fillo pastry (thawed)
3/4 cup melted clarified butter, margarine or
    good quality olive oil

Prepare béchamel. Melt butter if desired over medium heat, blend in flour until smooth using a whisk. Remove from heat. Gradually add milk, stirring constantly. Return to heat and cook until is thick and smooth stirring constantly. Cook 3 minutes longer; add seasoning and blend. Remove from heat. In a large bowl beat the eggs. Spoon little by little of the hot sauce into eggs, stirring constantly. Add chicken or turkey, pepper, salt if needed, cheese and almonds to the egg mixture and mix well to combine. Grease an 11x17x3-inch baking pan. Line pan with one half of the fillo sheets brushing every other one with hot melted butter. The sheets will extend up the sides of the pan. Spoon in the chicken or turkey mixture and spread evenly. Take one fillo sheet and folded into half crosswise and cover the filling and brush with hot melted butter. Repeat the same procedure with a second fillo sheet and place over the first sheet and brush again with the butter. Fold overhanging fillo sheets over the filling to enclose it. Top with the rest of fillo sheets, brushing every other one with hot melted butter and tuck in overhanging sheets inside the pan. Generously brush top with butter. Score top layers of fillo sheets all the way to the filling with a sharp serrated knife into three lines lengthwise. Bake in a preheated, 350 F (180 C) oven on the middle rack for 50-60 minutes or until golden brown. When you are ready to serve, cut through scored lines and then cut into 3x3-inch squares or rectangles. Serve hot or at room temperature if you used oil. Serves 12 or more.

❧❦❧

CHICKEN PITA IN PUFF PASTRY
Kotopita me Sfoliata

1 pkg. Puff pastry (thawed)
1 chicken about 4 pounds
1 medium onion, cut into half
1 carrot, cut into fourths
2 stalks celery, cut into fourths
1 bunch scallions, finely chopped
3 Tbsp butter or fine quality olive oil
Salt and pepper to taste
Pinch of Cayenne pepper
4 extra large eggs, beaten
1 cup lightly pressed down coarsely grated
  kasseri or Swiss cheese
1 Tbsp of more fresh finely chopped tarragon or
  1/2 tsp dried
1/4 cup toasted blanched almonds, chopped or
  pine nuts
1 egg, beaten with 1 Tbsp of water
1 Tbsp melted butter and mix with 1 Tbsp of
  milk for brushing

Clean and rinse chicken well. Cut into four pieces. Drop the chicken pieces, and the onion in 6 cups boiling salted water. Bring to a boil, reduce heat to medium, cover and boil for 30 minutes. Add carrots and celery to the chicken and cook for 30 minutes longer or until tender. Remove from heat. Remove chicken from the stock. Remove skin and bones, and cut into small dice, and place into a large bowl. Set aside. Sauté scallions in oil until soft. Remove from heat, and add to the chicken. Add salt and pepper, cayenne pepper, the beaten eggs, the cheese, the tarragon, and the nuts, mix well to combine. Set aside. Prepare puff pastry as directed in the pkg. Grease a 13x11x1 1/2 -inch baking pan. Line pan with one sheet of the puff pastry, the sheet will extend up the sides of the pan. Spoon in the chicken mixture and spread evenly. Brush ends with egg wash. Cover the chicken mixture with the second sheet of puff pastry, and press the bottom and the top ends of the pastry together to seal well (like you do with pie). Brush pita with butter and

milk mixture. Score the top of the pita with a sharp knife into 3x3-inch squares. Bake in a preheated 350 F (180 C) oven for 60 minutes or until golden brown. Cut and serve hot. Serves 6 as a main course or 12 as a first course.
Note: With the stock you make a delicious chicken soup (see index for recipe), as a first dish., salad and chicken pita.

❧❦❧

CLARIFIED BUTTER OR MARGARINE
Diylismeno Voutyro ke Margarine

Melt butter or margarine in a saucepan over medium-low heat until it melts and foams. Watch it carefully, avoid of browning or burning. Remove from heat and let stand until cool. Chill over night. Using a spoon, scrape off the foam and discard. With the spoon remove a piece of the butter to make a hole on the side of the pan. Tilt the pan to remove the milk, which is in the bottom of the pan. Slowly spoon clarified butter into a jar, being careful not to take any of the milk. Store clarified butter in the refrigerator or freezer until you are ready to use.

❧❦❧

HOMEMADE PASTRY FOR TYROPITAKIA
Filo Spitiko yia Tyropitakia

Pastry A:
2/3 cup butter or margarine, chilled
1 1/2 cups evaporated milk
41/2 cups all-purpose flour (about)
3 tsp. baking powder and
1 1/2 tsp or less salt

In a large mixing bowl sift together flour, salt and baking powder. Cut in butter if desired with a pastry blender until mixture resembles coarse crumbs. Add milk and gently toss with your fingers. Add more flour as needed to make soft dough. Form dough into a ball. Let rest for 30 minutes. Use according to recipe directions.

Pastry B:
1 cup unsalted butter, at room temperature
1 cup fine quality olive oil
1 cup milk
1 cup lightly pressed down grated Kefalotyri,

Parmesan or Pecorino Romano cheese
6 cups all-purpose unbleached flour (about)
4 tsp baking powder
Pinch of salt or to taste

In a large mixing bowl sift together flour, baking powder and salt. Cut in butter and oil with a pastry blender until resembles coarse crumbs. Add milk and gently toss with your fingers. Add more flour as needed to make soft dough. Divide dough into three parts, cover with plastic wrap. Let rest for 30 minutes. Use according to recipe directions.

Pastry C:

1 cup butter, at room temperature
1 cup fine quality olive oil
1 cup plain yogurt
6 cups all-purpose unbleached flour (about)
4 tsp baking powder
1 1/2 tsp salt

In a large mixing bowl sift together flour, baking powder and salt. Cut in butter and oil with a pastry blender until resembles coarse crumbs. Add yogurt and gently toss with your fingers. Add more flour as needed to make soft dough. Divide dough into three parts. Cover with plastic wrap. Let rest for 30 minutes. Use according to recipe directions.

☙❧

HOMEMADE PASTRY FOR PITA

Fillo Spitiko

3 cups all-purpose unbleached flour
1/2 tsp salt
1 cup warm water
1 Tbsp good quality olive oil
3/4 cup melted clarified butter or margarine

In a mixing bowl combine flour, water, salt and oil. Beat well to make soft dough. Add more water if needed. Turn out dough on lightly floured board and knead until smooth and elastic about 5 minutes. Divide dough into 2 balls. Place each one in a plastic sandwich bag and close it well. Let the dough stay for 30-60 minutes. Place dough on a floured board dusted with flour, and flatten each ball with dowel. Roll out the dough by dusting board and pastry lightly with flour

until the size of the pan. Brush off any flour from the dough. Generously brush the pastry with hot melted butter if desired, lift one end and fold in the middle of the fillo lengthwise. Repeat this process for the other side. Brush only one side (one-half) with butter and fold to cover the other half. Brush again with butter and fold into three layers. Place fillo pastry on large plate dusted with flour and cover with plastic wrap and chill. Repeat this process with the other ball of dough. When you place the second fillo pastry in the refrigerator the first one is ready to roll out again. Place pastry on the board and flatten with the dowel Gently roll out by dusting board and pastry with flour until the size has become 2-inches larger than the pan. Grease a 13x17x2-inch baking pan. Gently roll fillo on the dowel and place in the pan the fillo will extend up the sides of the pan. Set a side. Repeat this process with the other pastry, which was in the refrigerator. Place filling in the pan on top the first fillo, and spread evenly. Cover with the second filo. Brush ends with melted butter, roll both fillo sheets together and press to close well, (like you do with the pie). Generously brush the top of the pita and the edges with hot butter. Bake in a preheated 400'F (205 C) oven for 30 minutes or until puffs up, then reduce heat to 350'F (180 C) and bake for 15-20 minutes longer or until golden brown. Remove from oven and pierce in few places with a toothpick for the steam to come out. Wait for 15 minutes. Cut into pieces and serve hot.

☙❧

KREATOPITA WITH HOMEMADE PASTRY

Kreatopita me Fillo Spitiko

8 ounces of each lean ground beef, lamb and pork
3 Tbsp olive oil
1 medium onion, finely chopped
2 garlic cloves, minced
1/2 cup dry white wine or Vermouth
3 large Roma tomatoes, peeled, seeded and
        finely chopped
1 tsp finely chopped fresh thyme
Salt and pepper to taste
2 fresh leaves of sage, finely minced
2 eggs, beaten

2 Tbsp finely chopped flat leaf parsley
1/3 cup grated Parmesan or Kefalotyri cheese
2 Tbsp dried breadcrumbs (see index for recipe)
1 recipe homemade pastry for pita
    (see index for recipe)

Sauté the ground meat and onion with the olive oil, stirring constantly breaking up clumps as it browns. Add garlic and sauté a minute or two. Add wine and cook for 3 minutes. Add tomatoes, thyme, salt, pepper, sage and 1/2 cup water and simmer for 30 minutes, stirring occasionally, add more water if the meat mixture is to dry. Remove from heat and let cool. Add the eggs, parsley, cheese and breadcrumbs and mix well to combine. While the meat filling is simmering, prepare the homemade pastry as directed. Follow preparation and baking as directed. Serve hot as a first course or as a main course, and with salad (see index for recipe, for the salad to your taste).

❧❧❧

LAMB PITA
Arnaki Pita

3 pounds lean boneless lamb, cut into very
    small cubes the size of a dime
1/4 cup finely chopped onion
2 Tbsp good quality olive oil
4 beaten eggs
Salt and pepper to taste
4 ounces shredded Kaseri, Swiss cheese or mixed
1 pound filo pastry (thawed)
3/4 cup melted clarified butter, margarine (see
    index for recipe) or good quality olive oil

Sauté lamb cubes and onion with oil until onion is soft and liquid has evaporated. Add 1/2 cup water, salt and pepper. Cover and cook slowly for 20 minutes. Remove from heat. Set aside to cool for 15 minutes. Add cheese and beaten eggs. Stir well to combine. Grease a 14x11 1/2x3-inch baking pan. Line pan with one half of the fillo sheets, brushing every other one with hot melted butter if desired. The fillo sheets with extend up the sides of the pan. Spoon in the lamb mixture and spread evenly. Take one fillo sheet and folded into half crosswise and cover the middle of the filling, brush with hot butter. Repeat the same

procedure with a second fillo sheet and place over the first sheet and brush again with the butter. Fold overhanging fillo sheets over the filling to enclose it. Top with the rest of fillo sheets, brushing every other one with hot butter and tuck in overhanging sheets inside the pan. Generously brush top with hot butter. Score top layers of fillo sheets all the way to the filling with a sharp serrated knife into three lines lengthwise. Bake in a preheated 350 F (180 C) oven on the middle rack for 50-60 minutes or until golden brown. When ready to serve, cut into the score lines and then cut into 3x3-inch squares or rectangles. Serve hot or at room temperature if you used oil. Serves 12 or more.

❧❧❧

LEEK AND RICE PITA
Prasopita

1 1/2 pounds leeks
1/4 cup butter, margarine or olive oil
1/4 cup sort grain rice
1 cup milk
Salt and pepper to taste
5 extra large eggs
8 ounces crumbed feta cheese
8 ounces shredded Swiss or Kaseri cheese
1 pound fillo pastry (thawed)
1 cup clarified melted butter, margarine or good
    quality olive oil

Clean and wash leeks well. Chop finely and rinse again in a colander under cold running water. Drain well. Sauté leeks in butter if desired on medium heat until soft. Add rice, milk, salt and pepper, cook slowly for 10 minutes. Remove from heat and cool. In a large mixing bowl beat the eggs, add the cheeses and the leek mixture and stir well to combine. Grease a 14x11x3-inch baking pan of dish. Line pan with half of the fillo sheets, brushing every other sheet with hot melted butter if desired. The sheets will extend up the sides of the pan. Spoon in the leek mixture and spread evenly. Take one fillo sheet and folded in two and cover the leek mixture, brush with hot butter. Repeat with second sheet and place over the first. Fold overhanging fillo over the filling to enclose it. Top with the rest of the fillo sheets brushing every other one with hot butter, and tuck in overhanging sheets inside the pan. Brush top with butter. Score top layers of fillo all the way to the filling with a sharp serrated knife into three lines lengthwise. Bake in a preheated 350 F (180 C) oven for 50-60 minutes or until golden brown. When you are ready to serve, cut through scored lines into 3x3-inch squares or rectangles. Serve hot. Serves 12 or more.

※◦✕◦※

LEEK CHEESE PITA
Prasotyropita

3 medium leeks (about 3 cups)
3 Tbsp butter, margarine or good quality olive oil
1 1/2 pounds Ricotta or Farmer's cheese
8 ounces crumbled feta cheese
1/4 cup grated Kefalotyri or Parmesan cheese
6 extra large beaten eggs
Salt and pepper to taste
31/2 Tbsp butter, margarine or good quality
     olive oil
4 Tbsp flour
1 cup milk
1 pound fillo pastry (thawed)
3/4 cup melted clarified butter, margarine (see
     index for recipe) or good quality olive oil

Clean and wash leeks well. Chop finely and rinse again in a strainer under cold running water, to get rid of the sand. Drain well. Sauté leeks in butter if desired on medium heat until soft. Remove from heat. Set aside. Prepare béchamel sauce. Melt butter if desired over medium heat, blend in flour until smooth using a whisk. Remove from heat and gradually add milk, stirring constantly. Return to heat, and cook until is thick and smooth, stirring constantly. Cook for three minutes longer; add seasoning and blend. Remove from the heat. In a large bowl beat the eggs and spoon little by little of the hot sauce, stirring constantly. Add Ricotta, Feta, and Kefalotyri cheese, pepper and leeks, mix well to combine. Add salt if needed. Grease an 11x17x3-inch baking pan. Line pan with one half of the fillo sheets, brushing every other one with hot melted butter if desired. The fillo sheets will extend up the sides of the pan. Spoon in the leek cheese mixture and spread evenly. Take one fillo sheet and folded into half crosswise and cover the filling and brush with the hot butter. Repeat the same procedure with a second filo sheet, and place over the first sheet and brush again with the butter. Fold overhanging fillo sheets over the filling to enclose it. Top with the rest of the fillo sheets, brushing every other one with hot butter and tuck in overhanging fillo sheets inside the pan. Brush top with hot butter. Score top layers of fillo sheets all the way to the filling with a sharp serrated knife into three lines lengthwise. Bake in a preheated 350 F (180 C) oven on the middle rack for 50-60 minutes or until golden brown. When you are ready to serve, cut through the scored lines. Then cut into 3x3-inch squares or rectangles. Serve hot or at room temperature if you used olive oil. Serves 12-15 as a first course or 6-8 as a main course.

※◦✕◦※

MIXED VEGETABLES PITA
Hortopita

1 1/2 pounds fresh spinach
1 1/2 pound fresh Swiss card
1 pound leeks
1 bunch scallions
Salt and pepper to taste
2 Tbsp finely chopped fresh dill
2 Tbsp finely chopped fresh flat leaf parsley
2 Tbsp finely chopped fresh mint
3 Tbsp long grain rice
12 ounces feta cheese, crumbed
8 ounces cottage or ricotta cheese
1/3 cup grated and lightly pressed down
     Parmesan or Kefalotyri cheese
1 pound fillo Pastry (thawed), or homemade pastry
     for pita (see index for recipe)
1 1/4 cup good quality light olive oil (about)

Remove roots and coarse leaves from spinach. Wash in several waters, drain and finely chop. Remove coarse leaves and stems from Swiss chard. Wash in several waters, drain and finely chop. Cut roots and coarse leaves from leeks and wash well. Chop finely and rinse again in a colander under cold running water. Drain well.

Cut roots from the scallions rinse well and slice finely. In a large mixing bowl place the spinach, the Swiss chard and sprinkle with salt. Crush the vegetables with your hands well. Place in a colander to drain for 60 minutes or longer. Transfer the vegetables back to the mixing bowl, add the rest of the ingredients except the pastry and 1 cup of the olive oil. Mix well to combine. Grease a 16x11x3-inch baking pan. Line pan with half of the fillo sheets, brushing every other sheet with olive oil. The sheets will extend up the sides of the pan. Spoon in the vegetable mixture and spread evenly. Take one fillo sheet and folded in two crosswise and cover the vegetable mixture and brush with olive oil. Take a second fillo sheet and folded in two and place over the first sheet and brush with oil. Fold overhanging fillo sheets over the filling to enclose it and brush with oil. Top the rest of the fillo sheets brushing every other sheet with oil, and tuck in overhanging sheets inside the pan. Brush top with oil. Score top layers of fillo all the way to the filling with a sharp serrated knife into three lines lengthwise. Bake in a preheated 350 F (180 C) oven for 50-60 minutes or until golden brown. When you are ready to serve, cut through scored lines into 3x3-inch squares or rectangles. Serve hot, at room temperature or cold. Serves 12 or more.

❧❀☙

MUSHROOM-HAM AND CHEESE PITA
Manitaria-Zampon and Tyri Pita

2 pounds mushrooms
2 Tbsp light olive oil
2 medium onions, finely chopped
8 ounces grated Swiss cheese
6 ounces boiled ham, cut into small cubes
1 bell pepper, finely chopped
2 Tbsp finely chopped fresh mint
Pinch of Greek oregano, crushed
5 extra large eggs, beaten
Salt and pepper to taste
1 pound fillo pastry (thawed) or homemade pastry
  (see index for recipe)
1 cup good quality light olive oil

Wash the mushrooms under cold running water,

and dry well. Roughly chop the mushrooms and sauté in the oil until liquid almost evaporates, season with salt and pepper. Add the onions and sauté until soft and dry. Remove from heat. In a large mixing bowl combine all the ingredients except the fillo pastry and the oil and mix well. Grease a 14x11x3-inch or larger baking pan. Line pan with half of the fillo sheets, brushing every other sheet with olive oil. The sheets will extend up the sides of the pan. Spoon in the mushroom mixture and spread evenly. Take one fillo sheet and folded in two and cover the mushroom mixture, brush with the oil. Take second fillo sheet and folded in two and place over the first sheet and brush with oil. Fold overhanging fillo sheets over the filling to enclose it and brush with oil. Top with the rest of the sheets bushing every other one with the oil, and tuck in overhanging sheets inside the pan. Brush top with oil. Score top layers of fillo all the way to the filling with a sharp serrated knife into three lines lengthwise. Bake in a preheated 350 F (180 C) oven for 50-60 minutes or until golden brown. When you are ready to serve, cut through scored lines into 3x3-inch squares or rectangles. Serve hot. Serves 12 or more.

❧❀☙

MUSHROOM AND LEEK IN FILLO PASTRY
Manitaria ke Prasa se Fillo

8 ounces small mushrooms
1 1/2 pounds leeks (two large)
3 Tbsp butter, margarine or good quality olive oil
Salt and pepper to taste
2 Tbsp. all-purpose flour
1 cup milk
4 ounces shredded Kaseri cheese
4 ounces shredded Swiss cheese
1/4 cup grated Parmesan or Kefalotyri cheese
4 extra large lightly beaten eggs
1/2 cup chopped almonds or walnuts (optional)
1 pound fillo pastry (thawed)
1 cup melted clarified butter, margarine (see index
  for clarified butter), good quality olive oil
  or half of each

Wash mushrooms rapidly, dry, remove steams and thinly slice. Set aside. Clean and wash leeks well. Chop finely and rinse again in a strainer under cold running water. Drain well. Sauté mushrooms in butter if desired over high heat, 5-6 minutes or until they begin to brown. Stir in leeks and sauté over medium heat 3-4 minutes or until soft but not brown. Season with salt and pepper and stir well to combine. Stir in flour and sauté a few minutes. Slowly add milk, stirring constantly until mixture slightly thickens. Remove from heat. Slowly add eggs, cheeses and almonds if desired, stir well. Let cool. Divide fillo sheets and filling into five parts. Use one part of fillo at a time. Cover other parts with kitchen towel and cover that with a damp towel to prevent drying out. Lay two sheets of fillo on a 20x14-inch heavy-duty foil. Gently brush sheets with hot melted butter if desired without brushing the foil. Lay two more sheets fillo, brush again with hot melted butter. Take one part of the filling and place at the wide side end and spread evenly. Gently lift layered pita from the wide side without the foil and roll. Repeat this process with remaining fillo and filling. Place each roll in a greased baking pan, seam side down. Make slits to release steam. Brush with hot melted butter. Bake in a preheated 350 F oven until golden brown about 40-45 minutes. Slice diagonally into 2-inch slices or longer. Serve hot if used butter or room temperature if used olive oil. Makes five rolls.

❦❦❦

PUMPKIN CHEESE PITA WITH HOMEMADE PASTRY
Kolokytha ke Tyri me Fillo Spitiko

6 cups coarsely grated pumpkin, firmly packed
1/4 cup butter or margarine
3/4 cup minced shallot
Salt and pepper to taste
2 Tbsp finely chopped flat leaf parsley
2 Tbsp finely chopped dill
6 ounces of each coarsely grated Swiss and Gouda cheese
1 cup pressed down grated Kefalograviera (Greek cheese), Parmesan or Romano cheese
6 extra large eggs, beaten
1 recipe of homemade pastry (see index for recipe)

Wash the pumpkin and cut into large pieces, peel, remove the seeds and soft mash surrounding them. Then coarsely grate the pumpkin. Melt the butter if desired in a large nonstick frying pan, add the grated squash and sauté on low heat until soft and all the liquid has absorbed. Add the shallot, season with little salt and pepper and sauté until the shallot is transparent. Remove from the heat, and let cool for 10 minutes. Add parsley, dill and cheeses, and gradually add the beaten eggs, stirring well to combine. The pumpkin filling is ready to use. Prepare the homemade pastry as directed in the recipe.

❦❦❦

RUSTIC SPINACH PITA
Spanakopita Horiatiki

For the fillo:
4 cups all-purpose unbleached flour sifted (approx.)
1 1/2 tsp baking powder
1 1/4 tsp salt
3/4 cup good quality olive oil
1 cup lukewarm water

For the filling:
1 large leek (about 1 pound)
1 large onion, finely chopped
1 bunch scallions, finely sliced
1 cup or more good quality olive oil
4 bunches spinach or 2 pounds frozen (thawed)
Salt and pepper to taste
1/2 cup finely chopped and lightly pressed
*   down fresh dill*
1/2 cup finely chopped and lightly pressed
*   down flat leaf parsley*

Prepare the fillo. In a mixing bowl sift three cups of the flour, baking powder and salt. Add the olive oil and rub between your palms. Add the water and knead well, add more flour as needed to make soft dough. Divide into five parts, the first two parts put it together, and form it into a ball, form the other three into balls. Cove with plastic wrap and let the dough rest for 1-2 hours. While the dough is resting, remove roots and coarse leaves from spinach. Wash in several waters, drain well and chop, let stand. Clean and wash the leek well. Chop finely and rinse again in a strainer under cold running water. Drain well and place in large saucepan with the onion and scallions, sauté in 3/4 cup olive oil on medium-low heat until soft, season with salt and pepper. Add the spinach and sauté until wilted and liquid evaporates. Remove from heat and add the dill and parsley, stir well to combine. Place one ball at a time, on a board lightly dusted with flour. Roll out with a rolling pin by dusting board and pastry with flour until the size has become 3 1/2-inches larger than the pan. Grease a 12x16x3-inch baking pan. Gently roll fillo on the rolling pin and place in the pan, and brush with the remaining olive oil. The fillo will extend up the sides of the pan. Repeat the rolling with one more ball of dough, the size of the pan. Spoon filling in the pan and spread evenly. Repeat the rolling with the third and four balls of dough, and roll out the size of the pan. Place one at a time over the filling, and brush the top of each one and the extending fillo with olive oil. Roll and press the ends to close well. Brush again the ends with oil. Score top layers of fillo with a sharp serrated knife into 3-4 lines lengthwise. Bake the pita in a preheated 350 F (180 C) oven for 50-60 minutes or until golden brown. When you are ready to serve, cut through scored lines into 3x3-inch squares or rectangles. Serve hot of cold. Serves 12 or more.

❧❧❧

SCALLIONS CHEESE PITA
Kremythotyropita

3-4 bunches scallions (about 3 cups)
3 Tbsp butter, margarine or good quality olive oil
31/2 Tbsp butter, margarine or olive oil
4 Tbsp all-purpose flour
1 cup milk
1 1/2 pounds Farmer's or ricotta cheese
8 ounces feta cheese, crumbled
*1/4 cup grated Kefalotyri, Pecorino Romano
       or Parmesan cheese*
6 extra large eggs, beaten
Salt and pepper to taste
1 pound fillo pastry (thawed)
*3/4 cup melted clarified butter, margarine or
       good quality olive oil*

Clean and wash scallions well and slice finely. Sauté scallions in butter if desired on medium

heat until soft. Remove from heat. Set aside to cool. Prepare béchamel sauce. Melt butter if desired over medium heat, blend in flour until smooth using a wire whisk. Remove from the heat and gradually add milk, stirring constantly. Return to heat and cook until is thick and smooth stirring constantly. Cook for three minutes longer; add seasoning and blend. Remove from the heat. In a large bowl beat the eggs and spoon little by little of the hot sauce, stirring constantly to combine. Add Farmer's cheese if desired, feta and Parmesan cheese if desired, scallions and season with salt and pepper, mix well to combine. Grease an 11x17x3-inch baking pan. Line the pan with one half of the fillo sheets, brushing every other sheet with the hot butter if desired. The fillo sheets will extend up the sides of the pan. Spoon in the scallion-cheese mixture and spread evenly. Take one fillo sheet and folded into half crosswise and cover the filling and brush with the hot butter. Repeat the same procedure with a second fillo sheet, and place over the first sheet and brush again with the butter. Fold overhanging fillo sheets over the filling to enclose it. Top with the rest of the fillo sheets brushing every other one with hot butter and tuck in overhanging sheets inside the pan. Generously brush top with hot butter. Score top layers of fillo all the way to the filling with a sharp serrated knife into three lines lengthwise. Bake in a preheated 350 F (180 C) oven on the middle rack for 50-60 minutes or until golden brown. When you are ready to serve, cut through scored lines and them into 3x3-inch squares or rectangles. Serve hot or at room temperature if you used olive oil. Serve 12-15 as a first course or 6-8 for main course.

❧❧❧

SPANAKOPITA A
Spanakopita

*4 pounds fresh spinach or 2 pounds frozen cut leaf
       spinach (thawed), well drain and chopped.*
2 bunches chopped scallions
1/4 cup chopped fresh flat leaf parsley
1/4 cup chopped fresh dill
5 extra large beaten eggs

Salt and pepper to taste
1 pound crumbled Feta cheese, or 8 ounces Feta
cheese and 1 pound Ricotta or Farmer's cheese
1/4 cup grated Parmesan or Kefalotyri
Greek cheese
1 pound fillo pastry (thawed) or Homemade Pastry
(see index for recipe)
1 cup melted clarified butter, margarine (see index
for recipe), or good quality olive oil

If spinach is fresh, remove roots and coarse leaves. Wash the spinach well, several times in cold water, to get rid of the sand. Drop the spinach in 1 cup boiling water, cover and bring to a boil. Stirring and turning the spinach until is wilted. Remove from heat and drain in a strainer. With your hands, squeeze out excess water, and chop. Place in a large bowl to cool. Gently sauté scallions in 1/4 cup of the oil until tender but not brown. Add sautéed scallions, cheeses, eggs, parsley, dill, salt and pepper to the spinach and mix well to combine. Grease an 11x17x3-inch about baking pan. Line pan with one half of the fillo sheets, brushing every other sheet with hot melted butter if desired. The sheets will extend up the sides of the pan. Spoon in the spinach mixture and spread evenly. Take one fillo sheet and folded into half crosswise and cover in the middle of filling and brush with hot butter. Fold overhanging fillo over the filling to enclose it. Top with the rest of fillo sheets, brushing every other one with hot butter and tuck in overhanging sheets inside the pan. Generously brush top with hot butter. Score top layers of fillo sheets all the way to the filling with a sharp serrated knife into three lines lengthwise. Bake in a preheated 350 F (180 C) oven on the middle rack for 50-60 minutes or until golden brown. When you are ready to serve, cut through the scored lines and then into squares or rectangles. Serve hot if you used butter or at room temperature if you used oil. Serve hot or cold if you used olive oil. Serves 12 as a first course or 6 as a main course. If you desired to make the pita with homemade pastry, follow recipe and preparation as directed in homemade pastry (see index for recipe).

SPANAKOPITA WITH PUFF PASTRY

Spanakopita me Sfoliata

1 pkg. Puff pastry (thawed)
1 pound frozen cut leaf spinach (thawed)
1 pound leeks
3/4 cup more or less fine quality olive oil
1 bunch scallions, finely chopped
2 Tbsp chopped fresh dill
2 Tbsp chopped fresh flat leaf parsley
1/2 cup chopped fresh fennel
8 ounces feta cheese, crumbled
1/3 cup lightly pressed down grated Parmesan
or Kefalotyri Greek cheese
3 eggs, beaten
Salt and pepper to taste
1 egg, beaten with 1 Tbsp water
1 Tbsp melted butter mixed with 1 Tbsp milk for
brushing

Drain spinach in a strainer. Drain. Squeeze the spinach with your hands to remove the excess liquid and chop, and place in a large bowl. If you are using fresh spinach prepare as directed in spanakopita A (see index for the directions). Clean and wash leeks well. Chop finely and rinse again in a strainer under cold running water, to get rid of the sand. Drain well. Sauté the leeks and the scallions in oil on medium heat until soft. Remove from heat. Add dill, parsley, fennel, feta cheese, kefalotyri cheese if desired, the beaten eggs, salt and pepper to the spinach and mix well to combine. Set aside. Prepare puff pastry as directed in the pkg. Grease a 13x11x1 1/2-inch baking pan. Line pan with one sheet of the puff pastry, the sheet will extend up the sides of the pan. Spoon in the spinach leek mixture and spread evenly. Brush ends with egg wash. Cover the spinach leek mixture with the second sheet of puff pastry, and press the bottom and the top ends of the pastry together to seal well (like you do with a pie). Brush pita with butter and milk mixture. Score the top of the pita with a sharp knife into 3x3-inch squares. Bake in a preheated 350 F (180 C) oven for 60 minutes or until golden brown. Cut and serve hot. Serves 6 as a main course or 12 as a first course.

SPINACH TART WITH PUFF PASTRY
Tarta Spanaki me Sfoliata

2 pounds fresh spinach (about 2 bunches)
1/2 cup minced shallot
2 Tbsp butter, margarine or good quality olive oil
1 cup thick béchamel sauce (see index for recipe)
4 extra large eggs
*5 ounces of each coarsely grated Kaseri and
     Gouda cheese*
*3/4 cup pressed down grated Kefalotyri or
     Parmesan cheese*
2 Tbsp finely chopped fresh dill
Salt and pepper to taste
1 pkg. frozen puff pastry (thawed)

Remove roots and coarse leaves from spinach and cut into small pieces. Wash spinach and drain well. Place spinach in 1 cup boiling water and bring to boil, stirring constantly. Remove from heat and drain well in a strainer. Cool spinach enough to handle and with your hands; squeeze out excess water. Sauté shallots with the butter if desired, until soft. Add spinach and sauté a few minutes. Prepare béchamel sauce as directed. In a large mixing bowl beat eggs and gradually add béchamel sauce, beating constantly with a wire whisk. Add the cheeses, spinach mixture, dill, salt and pepper and stir well to combine. Line bottom and sides of a 9x13x1-inch baking dish with puff pastry. Spoon spinach-cheese mixture in the prepared dish and spread evenly. Bake in a preheated 375 F (190 C) oven on the middle rack for 45 minutes or until a cake tester inserted in center comes out clean. Remove from heat and let cool for 10 minutes. Cut and serve while hot.

※※※

SUMMER YELLOW SQUASH PITA
Kolokythopita

*4 pounds summer yellow squash, trimmed,
     washed and grated*
1 medium sized onion, finely chopped
6 extra large eggs
8 ounces feta cheese, crumbled
8 ounces Cottage or Ricotta cheese
*1/2 cup lightly pressed down grated Kefalotyri or
     Parmesan cheese*
1/4 cup finely chopped flat leaf parsley
1/3 cup finely chopped dill

Salt and pepper to taste
1 pound fillo pastry (thawed)
*1 1/4 cups melted clarified butter, margarine or
     good quality olive oil*

Sprinkle squash lightly with salt and place in a colander to drain, for about 60 minutes or longer. When ready to use the squash, squeeze the moisture out by pressing down with your hand. Sauté onion with olive oil if desired until soft. Remove from heat. In a large mixing bowl, beat eggs, add the cheeses, parsley, dill and pepper and mix well. Add the drained squash and stir well to combine. Grease a 14x11x3-inch or little larger baking pan. Line with 10 fillo sheets, brushing every other sheet with hot melted butter if desired. The sheets will extend up the sides of the pan. Spoon in the squash mixture and spread evenly. Cover squash mixture with 2 fillo sheets and brush with hot melted butter. Fold overhanging fillo over the filling to enclose it. Top with the rest of the fillo sheets brushing every other one with butter, and tuck in overhanging sheets inside the pan. Brush top with hot melted butter. Score top layers of fillo with a sharp knife into 3-4 layers lengthwise. Bake in a preheated 350 F. (180 C) oven for 50-60 minutes or until golden brown. When you are ready to serve, cut through scored lines, and then into 3x3-inch squares or rectangles. Serve hot if you used butter or hot or cold if you used oil. Serves 12 or more.

※※※

TYROPITA A
Cheese Pita

*4 1/2 Tbsp butter, margarine or good quality
     olive oil*
5 1/4 Tbsp all-purpose flour
1 1/2 cups scalding milk
6 extra large eggs, lightly beaten
1 pound crumbled feta cheese
*1/4 cup lightly pressed down grated Parmesan
     or Kefalotyri cheese*
8 ounces Farmer's or Ricotta cheese
White pepper to taste
*3/4 cup melted clarified butter, margarine (see
     index for recipe) or good quality olive oil*
1 pound fillo pastry (thawed)

Prepare béchamel sauce (white sauce). Melt butter if desired over medium heat, blend in flour until smooth using a whisk. Remove from heat. Gradually add milk, beating vigorously with a whisk. Return sauce over medium heat stirring constantly until mixture is thick and smooth. Cook 3 minutes longer. Remove from heat. In a large bowl beat eggs and spoon hot sauce little by little, beating constantly. Add cheeses and pepper; mix well to combine. Grease a 14x11x3-inch baking pan. Line pan with half of the fillo sheets, brushing every other sheet with hot butter if desired. Sheets will extend up the sides of the pan. Spoon in cheese mixture and spread evenly. Take one fillo sheet and fold it in half crosswise and cover the filling in the middle, brush with hot butter. Repeat the same procedure with a second fillo sheet, place over the first sheet and brush again with butter. Fold overhanging fillo sheets over the filling to enclose it. Top with the rest of the fillo sheets brushing every other one with hot butter, and tuck in overhanging sheets inside the pan. Generously brush top with butter. Score top layers of fillo sheets all the way to the filling with sharp serrated knife into three lines lengthwise. Bake in a preheated 350 F. oven on the middle rack for 50-60 minutes or until golden brown. When you are ready to serve, cut through scored lines, then into 3x3-inch squares or rectangles. Serve hot or at room temperature if you used olive oil. Serves 12 or more.

❦❀❦

TYROPITA B

1 pound crumbled feta cheese
8 extra large lightly beaten eggs
1 cup milk
1/2 cup good quality olive oil
1/2 cup melted clarified butter, margarine (see index for recipe) or good quality olive oil
Pepper to taste
1 pound fillo pastry (thawed)

Mix cheese, eggs, milk, oil and pepper. Grease a 14x11 1/2 -inch baking pan. Line pan with 4 fillo sheets, brushing every other sheet with hot melted

butter if desired. Sprinkle evenly with a ladleful of cheese mixture. Place two more fillo sheets on top of the cheese mixture (do not brush with butter). Sprinkle again evenly with another ladleful of cheese mixture. Repeat and continue until all the cheese is used. Then layer remaining fillo sheets, brushing every other sheet with hot butter. Score top layers of fillo sheets all the way to the filling with a sharp serrated knife into three lines lengthwise. Bake in a preheated 350 F (180 C) oven on the middle rack for 50-60 minutes or until crisp and golden brown. When you are ready to serve, cut through scored lines into 3x3-inch squares. Serve hot or at room temperature if you used olive oil. Serves 12 or more.

❦❀❦

TYROPITA SOUFFLÉ
Kaseropita

3 ounces grated Parmesan or Kefalotyri cheese
7 ounces coarsely grated Kaseri cheese
6 ounces coarsely graded Swiss cheese
1/2 tsp white pepper
6 extra large lightly beaten eggs
31/2 cups milk
3/4 cup melted clarified butter or margarine
*   (see index)*
1 pound fillo pastry (thawed)

Mix cheeses with the pepper. Grease a 14x11 1/2x3-inch baking pan. Line pan with 6 fillo sheets brushing every other sheet with hot melted butter. Sprinkle evenly with a handful of the cheese mixture. Place 2 more fillo sheets on top of the cheese mixture; brush with hot melted butter. Sprinkle again evenly with a handful of the cheese mixture. Repeat and continue until all cheese is used. Then layer the remaining fillo sheets, brushing every other sheet with hot melted butter. Generously brush top with hot butter. Cut tyropita soufflé with a sharp serrated knife into 3x3-inch squares or rectangles. Beat eggs with milk. Pour over tyropita. Chill for 2-3 hours or more. Bake in a preheated 300 F (150 C) oven for 90 minutes or until crisp and golden brown. Serve immediately. Serves 12 or more.

❦❀❦

TYROPITA WITH CLUB SODA
Tyropita me Club Soda

1 pound fillo pastry (thawed)
1/2 cup or more good quality light olive oil
21/2 cups crumbled feta cheese
2/3 cup each pressed down coarsely grated Kaseri
    and Gouda cheese
Pepper to taste
4 extra large eggs
1 1/4 cups club soda

Combine cheeses and pepper together and mix well. Line two fillo sheets on large piece of foil, brush with olive oil and sprinkle with cheese mixture. Push prepared fillo with your fingers without the foil, starting form narrow side of the fillo going all the way to the other end. Gently lift it and place in a 9x13x1-inch baking pan, on the narrow side of the pan. Repeat the same procedure until you have finish with the fillo and the filling. Beat the eggs until frothy add the soda and beat again. Spoon the egg mixture evenly over the tyropita. Bake in a preheated 350 F (180 C) oven on the middle rack for 45-55 minutes or until golden brown. Serve hot.

TYROPITA WITH SEMOLINA IN HOMEMADE PASTRY
Tyropita me Simigthali se Filo Spitiko

1 recipe homemade pastry for pita
    (see index for recipe)
4 cups milk
1/2 cup fine semolina
4 Tbsp more or less butter or margarine
5 extra large eggs
1 pound feta cheese, crumbed
1 cup of each grated and lightly pressed down
    Kaseri and Swiss cheese

Salt and white pepper to taste
2 Tbsp finely minced fresh mint (optional)

Scald the milk and gradually add semolina, stirring constantly. Reduce heat to low and cook until the mixture thickens and is smooth and creamy. Remove from heat, add the butter and stir well to combine. Cover the cream and let cool at room temperature until you prepare the pastry. While the cream is cooling prepare the homemade pastry. Follow recipe and preparation as directed in the recipe (see index for homemade pastry for pita). When you are ready the use the filling, beat the eggs in a large mixing bowl, add the cheeses, salt, pepper and mint if desired, and mix well. Add cream and stir well to combine. Bake as directed. Serve hot.

ZUCCHINI CHEESE PITA
Kolokythotyropita

1/2 cup finely chopped onion
4 medium-sized zucchini, trimmed, washed and
    cut into cubes
Salt and pepper to taste
3 extra large beaten eggs
1/3 cup heavy cream or evaporated milk
1 1/2 cups grated Kefalotyri or Parmesan cheese
1 cup cooked long grain rice
1 pound fillo pastry (thawed)
1 cup melted clarified butter, margarine (see index
    for recipe) good quality olive oil or mixed

Sauté onion with oil and butter if desired until onion is soft. Add zucchini and sauté until tender. Combine onion-zucchini mixture, salt, pepper, eggs, cream, grated cheese, and rice and mix thoroughly. Prepare and bake as directed in Spinach Pita A (see index for directions).

PASTA & RICE

BAKED MACARONI WITH MEAT SAUCE
Makaronia me Kyma Fournou

1 recipe meat sauce A, B, or C (see index for recipe)
1 pound elbow macaroni, boiled
2/3 cup grated Parmesan cheese
2 Tbsp melted butter or good quality olive oil

Follow recipe and preparation as directed in Meat Sauce. Boil macaroni as directed in Boiling Macaroni (see index), reduce cooking time from 20 minutes to 12. Drain well. Add butter if desired and stir well. Place half the macaroni in a greased casserole, cover with half the meat sauce and sprinkle with half the cheese. Continue with remaining macaroni, meat sauce and top with te remaining cheese. Cover and bake in preheated 350 F (180 C) oven 30 minutes, Serve immediately with salad and fresh crusty bread. Serves 4-6.

※◆※◆※

BOILED KRITHARAKI OR RICE
Kritharaki Vrasto

1 pound kritharaki (Greek pasta orzo) or
        converted rice
1 Tbsp salt or to taste
4 quarts boiling water
1/4 cup or more butter
1/4 cup pine nuts
1/2 cup or more grated Parmesan or Kefalotyri

Drop kritharaki into rapidly boiling and salted water, stir well. Reduce heat, partially cover and boil 20-25 minutes or until tender to your taste. Keep boiling and stir occasionally with a spoon. Pour into a strainer and rinse well with warm water. Drain well. Arrange half the kritharaki on a platter; sprinkle with half the cheese, cover with remaining kritharaki and top with remaining cheese. In a small frying pan place butter and pine nuts, cook until nuts have a golden color. Spoon hot butter with pine nuts over kritharaki. Serve hot, plain or with meat. Serves 4-6.
Note: If you use meat sauce, tomato sauce or any other sauce, reduce butter or don't use at all.

※◆※◆※

BOWTIES WITH MUSHROOMS
Fioghakia me Manitaria

1 pound mixed mushrooms
3 large garlic cloves, minced
3 Tbsp or more butter, margarine or olive oil
Salt and pepper to taste
1/2 cup chopped dry tomatoes
1/2 cup whipping cream
1 pound bowties, boiled
Grated Parmesan cheese

Wash mushrooms under cold running water. Dry on absorbent towels, and slice. Sauté mushrooms in hot butter if desired until liquid evaporates. Add minced garlic and sauté few minutes, season with salt and pepper, and dry tomatoes and simmer 1 minute, then slowly add cream and simmer 3 minutes. In large bowl place boiled bowties, pour mushroom sauce over and toss well. Sprinkle with Parmesan. Serves 4-6.

※◆※◆※

BOWTIES WITH SPINACH AND FETA
Fiogaki me Spanaki

2 bunches of spinach
1 large leek
2 large garlic cloves, minced

1/4 cup or less butter, margarine or olive oil
2 Tbsp capers
1 large red ripe tomato, peeled, seeded
    and chopped
2 Tbsp chopped fresh dill
2 Tbsp chopped flat leaf parsley
Salt and pepper to taste
1/2 pound feta cheese, crumbled
1 pound bowties
2 Tbsp melted butter, margarine or olive oil
Grated Parmesan, Kefalotyri or Romano cheese

Remove the leaves from spinach and wash in several waters, to remove the sand. Drain well and dry, between two kitchen towels. Chop finely. Set aside. Clean and wash leek well. Chop finely and rinse again in a strainer under cold running water. Drain well. Sauté leek in butter if desired on medium heat until soft, add garlic and spinach and sauté few minutes longer. Add capers, tomato, dill, parsley, salt and pepper. Bring to a boil. Reduce heat and simmer for 30 minutes, or until sauce thickens. Add feta cheese, stir well and simmer on low heat for 3 minutes. Remove from heat. While sauce is simmering prepare the bowties. Boil the macaroni in boiling salted water, for 20 minutes or to your taste. Drain well. Add melted butter if desired and toss well to combine. Serve bowties with sauce, and sprinkle with grated cheese. Serve hot. Serves 4-6.

COUSCOUS WITH ALMONDS AND RAISINS
Kouskous me Amigdala ke Stafithes

1 cup couscous
1 cup water
2 Tbsp fresh lemon juice
Salt and pepper to taste
2 shallots, thinly sliced
1/3 cup or less butter, margarine or good
    quality olive oil
1 red bell pepper, thinly sliced
1/2 green bell pepper, thinly sliced
1/3 cup toasted slivered blanched almonds
1/3 cup golden raisins
1 medium tomato, peeled, seeded and chopped
1/3 cup pitted and chopped Kalamata olives
2 Tbsp small capers
1/4 cup finely chopped flat leaf parsley

In small saucepan combine water, salt, lemon juice and 3 Tbsp olive oil if desired. Bring water to boil, remove from heat, add couscous, stir well. Cover. Let stand 5 minutes. While couscous is soaking, combine all ingredients in large mixing bowl. Fluff couscous with fork, add to bowl with other ingredients and mix well. Serves 4-6.

CRACKED WHEAT PILAF
Pligouri Pilafi

3 Tbsp butter, margarine or 2 Tbsp of good
    quality olive oil
1 cup coarse cracked wheat
4 cups fresh chicken stock or can of
    100% fat free chicken broth
1/4 cup tomato sauce
Pepper to taste
1/3 cup more or less grated Parmesan cheese
    (optional)

In a 3-quart saucepan sauté cracked wheat in hot butter if desired, stirring constantly for 5 minutes. The wheat must be nicely coated with butter. Add the stock, tomato sauce and pepper, stir, bring to boil, reduce heat and slowly simmer, partially covered for 20 minutes or until the wheat is tender, stir frequently. The dish will look moist and creamy. Serve hot with grated cheese. Serves 4 as a side dish or 2 as a main dish.

KRITHARAKI PASTA PILAF
Kritharaki Pilafi

1/4 cup butter or margarine
2 cups kritharaki (Greek orzo pasta)
4 1/2 cups boiling fresh beef stock, fresh chicken stock or can 100% fat free chicken broth
1/3 cup tomato sauce
Salt and pepper to taste
Grated Parmesan cheese

Sauté kritharaki in butter if desired, 5 minutes or until golden, stirring constantly. Add boiling stock or broth with tomato sauce, salt and pepper. Stir and cook in medium-low heat covered for 15 minutes or to your taste. Stir occasionally. Serve with grated cheese. Serves 6-8.

KRITHARAKI VEGETARIAN
Kritharaki yia Fytofagous

1 large onion, thinly sliced
1/2 cup or less olive oil
2-3 garlic cloves, thinly sliced
12 ounces mushrooms, thinly sliced
4 narrow eggplants (4-5-inches long), cut in cubes
2 narrow zucchini (4-5-inches long), cut into cubes
2 bell peppers any kind, cut into cubes
3 pounds red ripe tomatoes, peeled, seeded
    and chopped
1/3 cup lightly pressed down chopped flat
    leaf parsley
Salt and pepper to taste
Pinch of Cayenne pepper
1 pound kritharaki (Greek pasta orzo)
3 Tbsp more or less melted butter, margarine
    or olive oil
Grated Parmesan or Kefalotyri

Sauté onion in oil until soft, add the garlic and sauté until the liquid evaporates. Add the rest of the ingredients, except the kritharaki, the butter and the grated cheese. Simmer on medium-low heat for 45 minutes or until the vegetables are tender. While the vegetables are simmering prepare the kritharaki. Boil the kritharaki in 4 quarts of boiling salted water for 20 minutes or to your taste. Drain well, add the butter if desired and toss well to combine. Serve the kritharaki top with the vegetables and sprinkle with the grated cheese. Accompany with feta cheese and fresh crusty bread.Serves 4-6.

❦❦❦

LINGUINE WITH MORTADELLA
Makaronia me Mortathela

1/4 cup or less butter, margarine or olive oil
1 cup finely chopped onion
2 slices bacon, cut into small cubes
8 ounces mortadella, cut into small cubes
Salt and pepper to taste
2/3 cup dry red wine
1 can (29-ounces) whole tomatoes, crushed
1 pound thick linguine
Grated Parmesan or Kefalotyri cheese

In a 3-quart saucepan melt butter if desired and sauté onion, until soft. Add the bacon, mortadella, salt and pepper, and sauté until soft. Add the wine and cook until evaporates. Add tomatoes, reduce heat, cover, and low-simmer for 30 minutes or

until sauce is thick. While the sauce is simmering boil the linguine in four-quart boiling salted water for 20 minutes or to your taste. Drain the pasta well. Serve the linguine with the sauce and sprinkle with the grated cheese. Serve hot with salad and fresh crusty bread. Serves 4-5.

❦❦❦

MACARONI WITH PEPPERS
Makaronia me Piperies

1 large onion, thinly sliced
1/3 cup more or less olive oil
2 garlic cloves, thinly sliced
3 Tbsp all-purpose flour
12 ounces mushrooms, thinly sliced
3 pounds red ripe tomatoes, peeled, seeded and chopped
1 of each, green, yellow and red peppers, cut in cubes
1/4 cup lightly pressed down chopped flat leaf parsley
Salt and pepper to taste
Pinch of Cayenne pepper
1 pound any kind of macaroni
1/4 cup or less melted butter, margarine or good quality olive oil
Grated Parmesan or Kefalotyri

Sauté onion in oil until soft. Add garlic and sauté until liquid evaporates. Add flour and sauté few minutes longer, then add 1 cup water stir well, and remaining ingredients, except the macaroni, the butter and the grated cheese. Bring to a boil and simmer on medium-low heat for 30 minutes. While the sauce is simmering prepare the macaroni. Boil macaroni in 4 quarts of boiling salted water for 20 minutes or to your taste. Drain well, add the butter if desired and toss well. Serve the macaroni with the sauce and sprinkle with grated cheese. Accompany with feta cheese and fresh crusty bread. Serves 4-6.

❦❦❦

MACARONI PASTITSIO MEATLESS
Pastitsio Horis Kreas

1 large onion, finely chopped
1/4 cup butter or good quality olive oil
Salt and pepper to taste
3 large cloves garlic, crushed
3 pounds 2-3 kind of mushrooms
1 cup dry white wine or Vermouth
1 pound Roma tomatoes, peeled, seeded and

finely chopped
Pinch of cayenne pepper
1 1/2 pounds small elbow or any other pasta
2 Tbsp melted butter or olive oil
3/4 cup plus 3 Tbsp all-purpose flour
15 Tbsp butter or 1/2 cup good quality olive oil
6 cups scalding milk
6 extra large eggs, beaten
White pepper to taste
1 cup grated Parmesan cheese
21/2 cups coarsely grated Swiss cheese or
*   1 pound crumbled feta cheese*

Rinse mushrooms thoroughly. Drain, dry and thinly slice. Set aside. In large non-stick frying pan sauté onion in 2 Tbsp butter if desired until soft. Lightly season with salt and pepper, add garlic and sauté a few minutes longer. Remove onion mixture to a bowl. In same frying pan sauté mushrooms with remaining butter if desired until all liquid has absorbed. Lightly season with salt and pepper. Add wine and cook until evaporates. Add tomatoes, onions and cayenne pepper, and cook 15 minutes uncovered. In 6-quart pot boil pasta in boiling salted water 10 minutes. Drain, rinse and drain again, return to pot. Add melted butter if desired and toss well. Set aside. Prepare béchamel sauce. In 4-quart saucepan melt butter if desired over medium heat, blend in flour until smooth using a wire whisk. Remove from heat and gradually add milk, stirring continuously, and cook until mixture is thick and smooth. Cook 3 minutes longer. Remove from heat. Spoon hot sauce little by little into beaten eggs stirring constantly. Add egg mixture to sauce and cook over very low heat (do not let sauce boil) 2 minutes, stirring constantly. Remove béchamel from heat, lightly season with salt and white pepper and add 3/4 cup Parmesan cheese; stir well to combine. Cover and set aside. In greased 14x11 1/2 x21/2-inch baking dish, spread evenly 1/3 of pasta, sprinkle with 1/2 cup Swiss cheese if desired and 1 cup béchamel sauce and spread evenly. Spoon half of mushroom mixture and spread evenly. Sprinkle with 1/2 cup of Swiss cheese. Repeat layers, pasta, cheese, béchamel, mushroom mixture, cheese, and pasta. Spoon remaining béchamel over pasta and spread

evenly, and sprinkle with remaining Parmesan cheese. Bake in a preheated 350 F (180 C) oven for 45 minutes or until golden brown. Let stand for 30 minutes before cutting. Serve hot. Serves 8 as a main course or 12 to 15 as a first course.

❧❀❧

MACARONI PASTITSIO VEGETARIAN
Pastitsio yia Fytofagous

1 pound carrots
2 pounds mushrooms
2 pounds fresh spinach
1/4 cup butter or good quality olive oil or
*   half of each*
1/4 cup fresh dill, finely chopped
1/4 cup chopped fresh flat leaf parsley
Salt and pepper to taste
1 large onion, finely chopped
3 large garlic cloves, crushed
1 1/2 pounds small elbow macaroni or
*   any other pasta*
2 Tbsp melted butter or olive oil
1 cup all-purpose flour
15 Tbsp butter or 1/2 cup good quality olive oil
*   or half and half*
7 cups scalding milk
6-8 eggs, beaten
1 cup grated Parmesan cheese
21/2 cups coarsely grated Swiss cheese or
*   1 pound crumbled feta cheese*

Trim, wash, peel and shred carrots. Set aside. Trim, wash and dry mushrooms, chop finely. Set aside. Remove roots and coarse leaves from spinach and wash thoroughly. Dry and finely chop spinach. Set aside. In large non-stick frying pan sauté carrots in 1 Tbsp. butter if desired, until tender. Lightly season with salt and pepper. Remove from pan to large bowl, set aside. In same pan sauté mushrooms in 2 Tbsp butter until all liquid has evaporated. Add onions and garlic, lightly season with salt and pepper, and sauté until onion is soft. Remove to same bowl. Sauté spinach with 1 Tbsp butter on high heat until all liquid has evaporated. Remove to bowl. In 6-quart pot boil pasta in boiling salted water 10 minutes. Drain, rinse and drain again, return to pot. Add melted butter if desired and toss well. Set aside. Prepare béchamel. In 4-quart saucepan, melt butter if desired over medium heat, blend in flour until smooth using a wire whisk. Remove from heat and gradually add milk; cook until mixture is thick and smooth. Cook 3 minutes longer. Remove from heat. Spoon hot sauce little by little into beaten eggs stirring constantly, add egg mixture to sauce and cook over very low heat (do not let sauce boil) 2 minutes, stirring constantly. Remove béchamel from heat, lightly season with salt and pepper, add 3/4 cup Parmesan, and stir well to combine. Cove and set aside. In vegetable mixture add dill, parsley, salt and pepper and mix well. In greased 14x11 1/2 x21/2-inch baking dish spread evenly 1/3 of the pasta, sprinkle with 1/2 cup Swiss cheese if desired and 1 cup béchamel, spread evenly. Spoon half the vegetable mixture, spread evenly. Sprinkle with 1/2 cup Swiss cheese. Repeat layers, pasta, vegetables mixture and pasta. Spoon remaining béchamel sauce over pasta and spread evenly, and sprinkle with remaining Parmesan. Bake in preheated 350 F (180 C) oven 45 minutes or until golden brown. Let stand 30 minutes before cutting. Serve hot. Serves 6 to 8 as main course or 12 to 15 as first course.

❦

MACARONI PASTITSIO
Makaronia Pastitsio

*21/2 pounds lean ground beef or 1 1/2 pounds
        beef and 1 pound ground lamb*
1/2 cup finely chopped onion
2 Tbsp good quality olive oil
1/2 cup dry white wine or Vermouth (optional)
Salt and pepper to taste
*1 can (16-ounces) whole tomatoes, pressed through
        a food mill, or (1 cup tomato sauce)*
1 cinnamon stick 1/2-inch long
1 beaten egg (optional)
2 Tbsp dried breadcrumbs (see index for recipe)
1 1/2-2 pounds macaroni 1/8-inch thick or penne
6 quarts boiling water
2 Tbsp salt
*1/2 cup or less melted butter, margarine or
        good quality olive oil*
1 1/2-2 cups grated Parmesan or Kefalotyri cheese
7 cups medium white sauce (see index for recipe)
6 extra large beaten eggs

Heat oil, sauté onion until soft, add ground meat,

stir, breaking up clumps until brown. Add wine and sauté few minutes longer. Add tomato, cinnamon, salt, pepper and 1/2 cup water. Cover; cook slowly for 45 minutes. Remove from heat. Let stay 10 minutes. Then add breadcrumbs and egg. Stir well to combine. Boil macaroni in boiling salted water for 10 minutes. Drain. Rinse and drain again well, return to pot. Add melted butter if desired and 3/4 cup of the grated cheese. Toss well. Place half of the macaroni in a deep 11x17x3-inch greased baking pan. Top with meat mixture. Cover with remaining macaroni. Prepare white sauce as directed. Spoon little by little of the hot sauce into eggs, stirring constantly. Slowly add egg mixture to the sauce and cook over very low heat for 2-3 minutes, stirring constantly. Do not let the sauce boil. Add half of the remaining cheese and stir well to combine. Pour sauce over macaroni, and spread evenly. Sprinkle with the remaining cheese. Bake in a preheated 350 F (180 C) oven for 45 minutes or until golden brown. Let it stand for 30 minutes before cutting. Serve hot as a main course with salad or as first course. Serves 8-12.

❦

MACARONI GRATINEE
Makaronia Gratine

1 pound elbow macaroni
3 Tbsp. melted butter, margarine or olive oil
1/3 cup grated Parmesan cheese
White pepper to taste
1 1/3 cups lightly pressed shredded Kaseri cheese
1 cup lightly pressed shredded Swiss cheese
4 extra large eggs, lightly beaten
21/2 cups milk

Boil macaroni in 4 quarts boiling and lightly salted water 12 minutes. Drain well, add melted butter, cheeses and pepper and toss well. Place mixture in well-greased 9x13x 21/2-inch baking dish or casserole. Beat eggs with milk and pour over macaroni mixture. Let stand 30 minutes at room temperature. Bake in preheated 350 F (180 C) oven 30-40 minutes or until golden brown. Serve immediately. Serves 6-8.

❦

MACARONI RAGOUT
Makaronia Ragou

1 1/2 pounds lean ground top sirloin
1/2 cup butter, margarine or good quality olive oil
1 cup finely chopped onion
2 garlic cloves, finely minced
1 stalk of celery, cut into small dice
1 medium carrot, cut into small dice
1 bell pepper, cut into small dice
Salt and pepper to taste
6 medium red ripe tomatoes, peeled, seeded, chopped
1/2 cup flat leaf parsley, chopped
12 ounces mushrooms
1-1 1/2 pounds kritharaki (Greek pasta orzo)
1 cup more or less grated Parmesan or Kefalotyri
2/3-1 cup cream

Sauté onion with 2 Tbsp. olive oil if desired, until soft. Add ground meat and garlic; stir, breaking up clumps as you brown. Add celery, carrot, bell pepper, salt and pepper; stir well and sauté a few more minutes. Add tomatoes, bring to boil, reduce heat to medium-low and simmer 45 minutes or until meat is tender. While meat sauce is simmering prepare mushrooms. Wash mushrooms under cold running water. Dry on paper towels and cut into thin slices. Sauté mushrooms in 2 Tbsp. butter or oil until liquid has been absorbed. Add prepared mushrooms to meat sauce and cream; simmer a few minutes more. While ragout is simmering, prepare kritharaki. Boil kritharaki in 6 quarts boiling salted water, stir well, and boil 20 minutes or until tender, stirring occasionally. Remove from heat and drain well. Melt 4 Tbsp. butter if desired and pour over kritharaki; toss well. Spoon kritharaki on serving platter, sprinkle with grated cheese and spoon ragout over it. Serve immediately with grated cheese. Serves 6-8.

❦❦❦

MACARONI WITH HAM AND CHEESE GRATINEE
Makaronia me Zambon ke Tyri Gratine

1 pound Vermicelli
Salt
1/4 cup melted butter or margarine
5 eggs, beaten
1 cup milk
White pepper to taste
8-ounces boiled ham, cut into 1/4 -inch cubes
2/3 cup grated Kefalotyri or Parmesan
1 1/2 cups lightly pressed coarsely grated Kaseri
    or Swiss cheese

In a large pot boil 4 quarts of water. Add 1 Tbsp. salt and the Vermicelli and stir well. Boil for 4 minutes. Drain well. Place pasta in a large bowl. Mix eggs with the milk and add to the pasta, stir well. Add remaining ingredients and toss well to combine. Spoon mixture into well-greased casserole and spread evenly. Bake in a preheated 350 F (180 C) oven for 30 minutes or until golden brown. Cut into squares and serve immediately. Serves 6-8 for first course or as side dish.

❦❦❦

MACARONI WITH MEAT SAUCE GRATINEE
Makaronia me Kima Grarine

1 pound lean ground top sirloin
1/4 cup butter, margarine or good quality olive oil
1 cup finely chopped onion
2/3 cup white Vermouth
3 medium red ripped tomatoes, peeled seeded, diced
Salt and pepper to taste
1 cinnamon stick 1/2-inch long
1 cup water
1 pound elbow macaroni
1 cup lightly pressed coarsely grated Kaseri
    or Swiss cheese
1 cup lightly pressed grated Parmesan
    or Kefalotyri
4 extra large eggs, beaten
2 cups milk

Sauté onion in 2 Tbsp. oil if desired until soft, add ground meat, stir breaking up clumps as you brown. Add wine, tomatoes, salt, pepper, cinnamon and water. Cover and cook slowly 45 minutes or until liquid evaporates and meat is cooked, stirring occasionally. Remove from heat and remove cinnamon stick. While meat sauce simmers prepare macaroni. Boil macaroni in 4 quarts boiling salted water 15 minutes. Drain well and add remaining 2 Tbsp. butter if desired; toss well. In well-greased casserole, lay 1/2 the macaroni and spread evenly. Sprinkle with 1/4 cup Parmesan cheese if desired. Spoon meat sauce over and spread evenly. Cover with remaining macaroni and sprinkle with 1/4 cup Parmesan cheese. Beat eggs with milk, add coarsely grated Kaseri cheese and remaining Parmesan cheese, and mix well. Pour over casserole. Let stand 30 minutes at room temperature. Bake in preheated 350 F (180 C) oven 30 minutes or until golden brown. Let stand 15 minutes. Cut and serve. Serves 6-8.

❦⚜❦

MACARONI WITH MUSHROOMS
Makaronia me Manitaria

1 pound mushrooms
1 large onions, finely chopped
1/4 cup or less butter, margarine or good
      quality olive oil
1 large carrot, finely diced
1 bell pepper, finely chopped
1/2 cup red Vermouth
6 medium red ripe tomatoes, peeled, seeded
      and chopped
1/4 cup finely chopped flat leaf parsley
Salt and pepper to taste
1 pound spaghetti
2 Tbsp melted butter, margarine or good
      quality olive oil
Grated Parmesan or Kefalotyri

Trim mushrooms and wash under cold running water. Dry and slice thinly. Set aside. Sauté onion in butter if desired until soft. Add sliced mushrooms and sauté until liquid evaporates. Add carrots and bell pepper and sauté few minutes longer. Add Vermouth, tomatoes, parsley, salt and pepper. Bring to a boil. Reduce heat and simmer on a medium-low heat for 30 minutes, stirring occasionally. Remove from heat. While sauce is simmering prepare macaroni. Boil macaroni in 4 quarts of boiling salted water for 20 minutes or to your taste. Drain well. Add melted butter if desired and toss well to combine. Serve spaghetti with the sauce and sprinkle with grated cheese over it. Serve hot. Serves 4-6.

❦⚜❦

MACARONI WITH MUSSELS
Makaronia me Muthia

1 pounds thin spaghetti
1 1/2 pounds mussels

1/3 cup or more olive oil
1 pound ripe tomatoes, peeled seeded and chopped
2 garlic cloves, crushed
1 Tbsp finely chopped flat leaf parsley
Salt and pepper to taste
2 Tbsp capers
Grated Parmesan or Kefalotyri cheese

Boil spaghetti in salted water 15 minutes or until tender. Drain well. While spaghetti boils, prepare mussels. Scrub mussels with knife and rinse thoroughly. Steam mussels open with 1 1/2 cups of water in covered saucepan. Remove from heat. Remove mussels from pan, and discard any that didn't open. Remove flesh from the shell. Set aside. Strain stock through piece of cheesecloth and set aside. Prepare sauce. In saucepan, add oil, tomatoes, stock, salt and pepper. Bring to boil and add garlic and parsley. Cover and simmer 15 minutes, add mussels, capers and simmer until mussels are tender and sauce thickens. Spoon sauce over spaghetti, and sprinkle with grated cheese. Serve hot with salad and fresh crusty bread. Serves 4-6.

❦⚜❦

MACARONI WITH SHRIMP
Makaronia me Garith

1-1 1/2 pounds medium size raw shrimp
1/3 cup butter, margarine or good quality olive oil
1 medium leek
1 cup finely chopped onion
1/2 cup white Vermouth
2 garlic cloves, finely minced
4 medium size red ripe tomatoes, peeled,
      seeded and chopped
Salt and pepper to taste
1 pound bow ties
2/3 cup grated Parmesan or Kefalotyri cheese
      (optional)

Clean and wash leek well. Chop finely and rinse again in strainer under cold running water. Drain well. Sauté leek and onion in 2 Tbsp. butter if desired until soft. Add Vermouth, garlic, tomatoes, salt and pepper. Cover and simmer 30 minutes. Rinse shrimp under cold running water, drain well and add to sauce, simmer 10 minutes or until shrimp is tender. While sauce is simmering, prepare macaroni. Boil bow ties in 4 quarts boiling salted water 15-20 minutes or to taste. Drain well. Melt remaining butter if desired and pour over bow ties, toss well. Spoon macaroni on serving platter, sprinkle with 1/4 of the grated cheese if desired and spoon shrimp with sauce over it. Serve immediately with remaining grated cheese. Serves 4-6.

MACARONI WITH POLPETTES
Makaronia me Polpettes

1/2 pound lean ground beef
1/2 pound lean ground pork or lamb
1 beaten egg
2 Tbsp finely chopped flat leaf parsley
1 Tbsp finely chopped mint
1/2 cup dried breadcrumbs (see index for recipe)
1/2 cup dry white wine or Vermouth
1/2 cup minced onion
1 garlic cloves or more, crushed
1/4 cup grated Parmesan or Kefalotyri cheese
Salt and pepper to taste
Olive oil
1 can (29-ounces) whole tomatoes, chopped
5 leaves fresh basil, finely chopped
1 pound thin spaghetti
3 Tbsp melted butter, margarine or good
         quality olive oil
Grated Parmesan or Kefalotyri cheese

Combine first 11 ingredients, mix well with hand. Shape into balls the size of a walnut. Brown a few at a time in a little olive oil on both sides. Set aside. Prepare sauce. In saucepan combine tomatoes, basil, salt and pepper. Bring to boil, cover, reduce heat, simmer 45 minutes. Add polpettes to sauce, simmer 15 minutes longer. While sauce simmers, boil spaghetti in 4 quarts salted water 20 minutes or to taste. Drain well, place on serving platter. Pour melted butter over spaghetti and sprinkle with grated cheese. Spoon polpettes and sauce over spaghetti. Serve hot with salad and fresh crusty bread. Serves 4-5.

MACARONI WITH TOMATO
Makaronia me Tomata

6 cups fresh chicken broth or (can 100% fat free)
1/2 cup tomato sauce
Pepper to taste

1/4 cup butter or 3 Tbsp good quality olive oil
2 cups kritharaki (Greek orzo) or elbow macaroni
1/2 cup or more grated Parmesan cheese

In 4-quart saucepan sauté kritharaki with butter if desired 5 minutes, stirring constantly. Pasta must be nicely coated with butter, and become golden brown. Add broth, tomato sauce and pepper to kritharaki and stir well. Bring to boil. Reduce heat to low and simmer partially covered 20 minutes or until pasta is tender, stir frequently. The dish will look moist and creamy. Serve hot with grated cheese and salad. Serves 4.

MACARONI WITH VEGETABLES
Makaronia me Lachanika

1 pound small zucchini or any other squash
1 pound small long-thin eggplant
1 large bell pepper
1 Tbsp finely chopped flat leaf parsley
1 Tbsp finely chopped fresh dill
2 garlic cloves, finely chopped
2 large red ripe tomatoes, peeled, seeded, chopped
1 small onion, finely chopped
1/3 cup good quality olive oil
1 pound macaroni any kind
1/4 cup melted butter, margarine or olive oil
         (optional)
Grated Parmesan of Kefalotyri cheese

Wash and trim vegetables and cut into cubes. Set aside. In four-quart saucepan sauté onion in oil, until soft. Add all vegetables, tomatoes, and 1 cup water, salt and pepper to taste. Cover; bring to a boil, reduce heat and simmer 15 minutes, or until vegetables are tender. While vegetables are simmering, prepare macaroni. Boil macaroni in salted water for 20 minutes or until tender to your taste. Drain well. Place macaroni in a serving platter, spoon over the melted butter if desired, and sprinkle with grated cheese. Spoon sauce over the macaroni. Serve hot with feta cheese and fresh crusty bread. Serves 4-6.

MACARONI VEGETARIAN IN FILLO PASTRY
Makaronia yia Fytofagous se Fillo

1 1/4 pounds elbow macaroni

Lamb Youvetsi

Lamb Souvlaki

Roasted Chicken with Potatoes

Meat Stuffed Vegetables

1/4 cup finely chopped flat leaf parsley
1 1/2 pounds mushrooms, chopped (any kind)
4 large garlic cloves, crushed
6 ounces coarsely grated Swiss cheese
6 ounces coarsely grated Gouda or Kaseri cheese
1/4 cup grated Parmesan cheese
Freshly grated pepper to taste
1 cup whipping cream
1 pound fillo pastry (thawed)
2/3 cup melted clarified butter, margarine or
    good quality olive oil

Drop macaroni in boiling and lightly salted water, bring to boil, reduce heat and boil 15 minutes. Drain well. Set aside. In nonstick frying pan sauté mushrooms in 3 Tbsp butter until all liquid is absorbed. Add garlic and sauté few minutes longer. Add whipping cream and pepper, stir well and bring to boil. Remove from heat, add to macaroni. Add cheeses and stir well. In greased 14x11 1/2x21/2-inch baking casserole, lay half of the fillo sheets, brushing every other one with hot melted butter. The sheets will extend up sides of pan. Spoon macaroni mixture and spread evenly. Take one fillo sheet and fold it in half; place on middle of pan, brush with hot butter. Repeat with a second fillo sheet as the first, and brush again with hot butter. Fold overhanging fillo sheets, brushing every other one with hot butter. Top with remaining fillo sheets, brushing every other one with hot butter, and tuck in overhanging sheets inside the pan. Generously brush top with hot butter. Score top fillo layers all the way to filling into 2-3 lines with sharp serrated knife. Bake in preheated 350 F (180 C) oven on middle rack 30-45 minutes or until golden brown. Remove from oven, let cool 30 minutes. Cut through scored lines, then into squares and serve. Serve hot with salad.

❦❦❦

RICE AND KRITHARAKI PILAF
Rizi and Kritharaki Pilafi

1/4 cup butter or margarine
1 cup converted rice
1 cup kritharaki (Greek orzo)
5 cups boiling fresh chicken stock or can of
    low sodium 100% fat free chicken broth
Salt and pepper to taste

1/2 cup grated Parmesan cheese

In 3-quart saucepan sauté rice and kritharaki in hot butter if desired 5 minutes, stirring constantly. Add boiling stock, salt and pepper to mixture, stir well. Reduce heat and simmer on low covered 20 minutes. Stir frequently. Dish will look moist and creamy. Serve with grated cheese. Serves 6.

❦❦❦

RICE OR KRITHARAKI WITH MUSHROOM PILAF
Rice or Kritharaki me Manitaria Pilafi

1 pound kritharaki (Greek orzo)
1/4 cup good quality olive oil
12 ounces mushrooms, any kind
1 small bunch sliced scallions or 1/3 cup
    minced shallots
1/2 cup or more slivered blanched toasted
    almonds or pine nuts (optional)
2 large or more garlic cloves, minced
1/2 cup dry white Vermouth (optional)
8 ounces or less snow peas fresh or
    frozen (thawed), cut into julienne
Salt and pepper to taste
1/4 cup butter
Grated Kefalotyri or Parmesan cheese

In 4-quart saucepan add 12 cups water, bring to boil, add kritharaki, and stir well. Reduce heat to medium and simmer 20 minutes, stirring frequently. Drain well. While kritharaki is simmering, prepare mushrooms. Wash mushrooms well under cold running water and dry on paper towels. Thinly slice mushrooms and set aside. Sauté sliced mushrooms in olive oil until all liquid evaporates. Add scallions and garlic if desired and sauté until soft. Add almonds if desired and sauté few minutes longer stirring constantly. Add Vermouth if desired and cook until evaporates. Add snow peas and cook a few minutes longer. Add kritharaki to mushroom mixture and stir gently to combine. Add butter and grated cheese and toss well. Remove from heat and serve immediately. The dish will look moist and creamy. Serves 4 as a main course or 6-8 as a side dish.

❦❦❦

RICE OR KRITHARAKI WITH PINE NUTS PILAF
Rízi or Kritharaki me Koukounari Pilafi

1/2 cup butter, margarine or more good
    quality olive oil
1 bunch scallions, finely sliced
1 large or more garlic clove, minced
1/4 cup or more pine nuts or slivered blanched
    almonds (optional)
2 cups converted rice or kritharaki (Greek orzo)
1/2 cup white wine or Vermouth
4 1/2 cups boiling water for rice and 5 1/2 cups
    for kritharaki
Salt and pepper to taste
1/4 cup lightly pressed chopped fresh dill
2 Tbsp finely chopped fresh mint

Sauté shallots in oil until soft, stirring constantly. Add garlic, pine nuts and rice if desired stirring constantly and sauté a few minutes or until rice coated completely with oil. Add wine, stir and cook until evaporates. Season with salt and pepper, add water, dill and mint, stir well, cover; slowly cook 20 minutes or until tender. Remove from heat and serve.

※◦ズ◦※

RICE PILAF (PLAIN)
Ryzi Pilafi Aplo

3 quarts boiling water
1 Tbsp. salt
2 cups converted rice
1/2 cup or less melted butter or margarine

Add salt and rice to boiling water, stir and boil partially covered on medium heat for 20 minutes. Place in a strainer and pour hot water over to remove the loose starch and separate the grains. Drain well and transfer to the saucepan. Add hot butter and toss with two forks. Serve hot with any dish you desired. Serves 6.

※◦ズ◦※

RICE PILAF
Ryzi Pilafi

1/4 cup butter or margarine
2 cups converted rice
4 1/2 cups boiling fresh chicken stock or can of
    100% fat free chicken broth)
Salt and pepper to taste

In 3-quart saucepan sauté rice in hot butter if desired 5 minutes, stirring constantly. Rice must be nicely coated with butter. Add boiling stock, salt and pepper; stir and simmer in medium-low heat covered 20 minutes. Serve hot. Serves 6.

※◦ズ◦※

RICE PILAF WITH ALMONDS
Rizi Pilafi me Amygdala

4 1/2 cups boiling fresh or low sodium
    100% chicken broth
Salt and pepper to taste
2 cups converted rice
1/4 cup butter or margarine
1/2 cup slivered blanched almonds

Pick over rice and rinse in a strainer under cold running water. Drain well. Add rice to boiling stock, stir and cook in medium heat partially covered 20 minutes. While rice is cooking prepare almonds. Melt butter in small frying pan, add almonds and sauté on low-medium heat until golden but not brown. Add hot butter almond mixture to rice and toss well with two forks. Serves 6.

※◦ズ◦※

RICE PILAF WITH MORTADELLA
Rizi Pilafi me Mortathela

1/4 cup butter or margarine
1 large shallot, finely chopped
6 ounces mortadella, cut into cubes
3/4 cup finely chopped celery
2 cups converted rice
1/4 cup tomato sauce
4 1/2 cups boiling fresh chicken stock or
    fat free chicken broth
1/2 cup grated Parmesan of Kefalotyri cheese

In 4-quart saucepan melt butter if desired and sauté shallot until soft. Add mortadella and celery and sauté few minutes longer. Add rice and sauté until rice is coated with butter, stirring constantly. Add tomato sauce and stock, stir well and cover, reduce heat to low-simmer 20 minutes or to taste. Remove from heat and add grated cheese. Serve immediately. Serves 4-6.

※◦ズ◦※

RICE WITH EGG CREAM SAUCE
Rizi me Krema Avgou

*4 cups boiling fresh chicken stock or can of
        low sodium 100% fat free chicken broth*
2 cups converted rice
3 Tbsp butter or margarine
3 Tbsp all-purpose flour
*2 cups fresh chicken stock or can of
        100% fat free chicken broth*
1 cup milk
2 beaten eggs
1/2 cup or more grated Parmesan cheese
Salt and pepper to taste
1/2 cup toasted slivered blanched almonds
2 cups frozen or fresh peas, cooked

Add rice to boiling stock, stir and cook slowly covered 20 minutes. Remove from heat. Add almonds and toss well with two forks. Pack rice into 6-cup ring mold. Invert in large round serving platter. Fill center of rice mold with cooked peas. While rice is simmering, prepare sauce. Melt butter if desired in 2-quart saucepan over medium heat, blend in flour until smooth using wire whisk. Gradually add chicken stock and milk, stirring constantly until thick and smooth. Cook 3 minutes more. Remove from heat. Spoon hot sauce little by little into well-beaten eggs stirring constantly. Add egg mixture to sauce. Return to heat and cook over very low heat 4-5 minutes, stirring constantly. Remove from heat. Add cheese, salt if needed and pepper; stir well. Pour sauce over rice pilaf. Serve hot with any kind of meat or poultry. Serves 6.

RICE WITH GRAPE LEAVES AND PINE NUTS
Rizi Pilafi me Ambelofila ke Koukounaria

1/2 cup or more good quality olive oil
1 large bunch scallions or 2 small, finely sliced
2 large garlic cloves, minced
2 cups converted rice
*1/4 cup or more pine nuts or slivered blanched
        almonds (optional)*
4 1/2 cups boiling water
Salt and pepper to taste
*12-14 medium sized tender fresh grape leaves or
        canned, finely chopped*
1/4 cup pressed down chopped fresh dill
3 Tbsp finely chopped fresh mint
Juice of one or more lemons

If grape leaves are fresh, cut off steams and rinse thoroughly under cold running water. Plunge grape leaves one by one into boiling water, a few at a time and boil 4 minutes. Drain well and finely chop. If grape leaves are canned, pick tender ones, rinse as with fresh ones and cook only 2 minutes. Rinse and drain. Sauté scallions in oil until soft, stirring constantly. Add garlic, pine nuts and rice, stir and sauté a few minutes or until rice is coated completely with oil. Season with salt and pepper, add chopped grape leaves, water, lemon juice, dill and mint, stir well, cover and cook 20 minutes or until rice is tender. Remove from heat and serve hot or at room temperature.

RICE WITH PEAS
Ryzi me Araka

*1/3 cup or less butter, margarine or good
        quality olive oil*
2 cups converted rice
Salt and pepper to taste
*41/2 cups boiling chicken stock or can of
        low sodium 100% fat free chicken broth*
1 1/2 cups fresh or frozen peas (cooked)

In 3-quart saucepan sauté rice in hot butter 5 minutes, stirring constantly. Rice must be nicely coated with butter. Add stock, salt and pepper to rice, and stir well. Simmer in medium-low heat covered 20 minutes. Add peas to rice, toss gently with two forks. Pack rice-peas mixture in 8-cup ring mold. Invert in round serving platter and serve. Serves 6.

SAUCES

BÈCHAMEL SAUCE
Saltsa Béchamel

THIN BÉCHAMEL SAUCE
For gravies, sauces, scalloped and soups:
2 Tbsp butter, margarine or good quality olive oil
2 Tbsp all-purpose flour
2 cups scalding milk
Salt and white pepper to taste

MEDIUM BÉCHAMEL SAUCE
For au-gratin, mousaka and pastitsio:
5 Tbsp butter, margarine or good quality olive oil
5 Tbsp all-purpose flour
2 cups scalding milk
Salt and white pepper to taste

THICK BÉCHAMEL SAUCE
For croquettes, pites and soufflés:
7 Tbsp butter, margarine or good quality olive oil
8 Tbsp all-purpose flour
2 cups scalding milk
Salt and white pepper to taste

Melt butter if desired over medium heat, blend in flour until smooth using a wire whisk. Cook 2 minutes longer, stirring constantly. Remove from heat and gradually add milk, stirring constantly, return to heat and cook until mixture is thick and smooth. Cook 3 minutes longer, add seasoning and blend. Remove from heat. Makes 2 cups.

BÈCHAMEL SAUCE WITH EGGS
Saltsa Béchamel me Avga

3 or less beaten eggs
1 recipe Béchamel Sauce (see index for recipe)

Follow preparation as directed in White Sauce. Spoon hot sauce little by little into beaten eggs, stirring constantly. Gradually add egg mixture to sauce and cook over very low heat for 2-3 minutes, stirring constantly. Do not let sauce boil. Remove from heat. Use as recipe directs.

COCKTAIL SAUCE
Saltsa Cocktail

1 cup mayonnaise
1/4 cup ketchup
1/4 cup cream, whipped
1 tsp. Worcestershire sauce
1/2 tsp. prepared mustard

Mix all ingredients well and chill until needed. Serve with crawfish, crab, lobster or shrimp.

CURRY SAUCE
Saltsa Curry

2 Tbsp. butter or margarine
1 Tbsp. finely chopped onion
2 Tbsp. all-purpose flour
1 cup fresh chicken stock or can fat free chicken broth
1 cup milk
1 tsp curry powder
Salt and pepper to taste

Melt butter and sauté onion until soft. Blend in flour until smooth using wire whisk. Gradually add stock and milk, stirring constantly until mixture is slightly thick and smooth. Add curry, salt and pepper. Simmer on low heat 10 minutes stirring constantly. Serve on cold meat or fish, hard-boiled eggs, lobster, shrimp and rice pilaf.

DRESSING FOR FISH AND MEAT
Latholemono yia Psari ke Kreas

*1 large red or sweet onion, cut lengthwise in
    very thin slices*
1 cup fine quality virgin olive oil
Juice of 1 lemon or more
Salt and pepper to taste
2 Tbsp. chopped flat leaf parsley

Combine oil, lemon, salt and pepper in a bowl. Beat with fork until well blended. Add onion slices and parsley to oil mixture and mix well. Serve on broiled fish or boiled meat.

❦❦❦

DRESSING FOR SALAD AND MEAT
Lathoxytho

1 cup fine quality virgin olive oil
1/4 cup wine vinegar or balsamic
1 tsp. Greek oregano
Salt and pepper to taste

Combine all ingredients in a blender and blend well. Use the dressing for salads or boiled meat.

❦❦❦

DRESSING FOR SALAD FISH AND MEAT
Latholemono

1 cup fine quality virgin olive oil
Juice of 1 lemon or more
Salt and pepper to taste

Combine all ingredients in a bowl. Beat with fork until well blended. Serve with salads, boiled vegetables, broiled fish of boiled meat.

❦❦❦

EGG CREAM SAUCE
Krema Avgou

5 Tbsp butter or margarine
5 Tbsp all-purpose flour
3 cups turkey stock or can fat free chicken broth
1 1/2 cups milk
4 egg yolks, beaten
1/2 cup grated Parmesan cheese
Salt and pepper to taste

In a saucepan, melt butter if desired over medium heat, blend in flour until smooth with wire whisk.

Remove from heat. Gradually add stock and milk, stirring constantly. Return to heat continuously stirring until mixture is slightly thick and smooth. Cook 3 minutes more. Remove from heat. Spoon 2 cups hot sauce little by little into egg yolks stirring constantly. Add egg mixture to sauce and cook over very low heat 4-5 minutes, stirring constantly (do not let sauce boil). Remove from heat. Add cheese, salt and pepper to taste, stir well to combine. Serve hot with Turkey Mosaic in Fillo Pastry, and Rice Pilaf.

❦❦❦

FISHERMEN'S SAUCE
Saltsa to Psara

3 Tbsp good quality olive oil
1 or more garlic clove, minced
4 large ripe tomatoes, peeled, seeded and chopped
Salt and pepper to taste
1/4 Tsp Greek oregano
1 pound boneless and skinless any fish, cut into cubes
1 pound macaroni to your taste
1/4 cup or less melted butter, margarine or good quality olive oil
Grated Parmesan or Kefalotyri cheese

In a small saucepan sauté garlic in oil for few seconds. Add chopped tomatoes, salt, pepper and oregano. Cover; bring to a boil, reduce heat to low and simmer for 15 minutes. Add fish and water if sauce is too thick. Bring to a boil, reduce heat and simmer for 15 minutes or until fish flakes easily with fork. Remove from heat. While the sauce is simmering, prepare the macaroni. Boil macaroni in 4 quarts of boiling salted water for 20 minutes or to your taste. Drain well. Place macaroni in a serving platter and spoon hot butter if desired over. Sprinkle with the grated cheese, and spoon sauce and fish over the macaroni. Serve hot with salad and crusty fresh bread. Serves 4-6.

❦❦❦

GARLIC SAUCE WITH ALMONDS
Skorthalia me Amygthala

6 garlic cloves, chopped

1/2 pound stale Italian bread, crust removed
    and sliced
1/2 tsp salt
1 cup finely ground blanched almonds
1 1/2 cups fine quality olive oil
3 Tbsp wine vinegar

Follow preparation as directed in Garlic Sauce with Bread (see index). Serve as directed.

❦❦❦

GARLIC SAUCE WITH BREAD
Skorthalia me Psomi

6 garlic cloves, chopped
1 pound stale Italian bread, crust removed,
    and sliced
1/2 tsp salt
1 1/2 cups fine quality olive oil
3 Tbsp wine vinegar

Soak bread in water 5 minutes. Squeeze dry. Place garlic, salt and bread in a food processor or blender for about 1 minute. Remove pusher from the feed tube and add oil and vinegar in a fine stream while motor is running. When all the oil and vinegar is added and garlic sauce is thick and smooth, turn off motor. Transfer sauce to a covered glass container and chill until needed. When you are ready to serve, the sauce in a serving bowl. Serve with fried codfish, fried eggplant or grilled, fried zucchini or grilled, and boiled beets (see index for recipes).

❦❦❦

MEAT SAUCE A
Saltsa me Kyma

2 Tbsp good quality olive oil
1 medium onion, finely chopped
1 1/2 pounds lean ground beef
1/2 cup dry white wine or Vermouth
1 can (29-ounces) whole tomatoes or fresh,
    pressed through a food mill
Salt and pepper to taste
1 cinnamon stick 1/2-inch long
1 cup water

Sauté onion in oil until is soft, add ground meat, stirring and breaking up clumps until brown. Add remaining ingredients and stir well. Cover and

cook slowly 45 minutes or until liquid is absorbed and meat is cooked, stirring occasionally. Remove from heat and remove cinnamon. Serve hot on pasta or rice. Serves 4-6.

❦❦❦

MEAT SAUCE B
Saltsa me Kyma

2 Tbsp good quality olive oil
1 medium onion, finely chopped
2 or more garlic cloves, minced
1 1/2 pounds lean ground lamb
1/2 cup dry white wine or Vermouth
1 can (29-ounces) whole tomatoes or fresh,
    pressed through a food mill
Salt and pepper to taste
1 Tbsp finely chopped flat leaf parsley
1 cup water

Sauté onion in oil until soft, add garlic and lamb. Stir breaking up clumps until brown. Add remaining ingredients, stir well. Cover and cook slowly 60 minutes or until all liquid is absorbed and meat is cooked, stirring occasionally. Serve hot on pasta or rice. Serves 4-6.

❦❦❦

MEAT SAUCE WITH MUSHROOMS
Saltsa me Kima ke Manitaria

1 medium onion, finely chopped
3 Tbsp of less good quality olive oil
1/2 cup grated carrots
1/2 cup minced celery
1 pound lean ground beef or lamb
1/2 cup white wine or Vermouth
5 medium red ripe tomatoes, peeled, seeded
    and chopped
Salt and pepper to taste
1 cinnamon stick 1/2-inch long
1 cup water
1/2 pound mushrooms
1 pound small elbow macaroni
3 Tbsp melted butter, margarine or olive oil
Grated Parmesan or Kefalotyri cheese

Sauté onion in oil until soft, add carrots and celery and sauté few minutes longer. Add ground meat, stirring and breaking up clumps as it browns. Add wine, tomatoes, salt, pepper, cinnamon and water.

Bring to a boil, reduce heat and simmer 50 minutes. While sauce is simmering prepare mushrooms. Wash mushrooms under cold running water. Dry, slice them, and add to sauce. Cook 15 minutes more or until liquid is absorbed and meat is cooked, stirring occasionally. Remove from heat and remove cinnamon. While sauce is simmering, boil macaroni in 4 quarts salted water for 20 minutes or to taste. Drain well and add melted butter if desired; toss well to combine. Serve macaroni with the sauce and sprinkle with grated cheese. Serve hot with salad and fresh crusty bread. Serves 4-6.

PIQUANT SAUCE FOR GRILLED VEGETABLES
Saltsa Pikantiki yia Psita Lachanika

3/4 cup tahini (sesame paste)
Juice of 1 or more lemon or to your taste
1/2 tsp or more cumin or to your taste
Salt and pepper to taste
1/2 cup or more water

Combine all ingredients in small bowl, mix well. Add more water if needed to make a thin sauce.

RAGOUT SAUCE
Saltsa Ragout

2 Tbsp. butter
2 Tbsp good quality olive oil
1 large chopped onion
1 Tbsp all-purpose flour
Salt and pepper to taste
1 can (29-ounces) whole tomatoes or fresh,
    pressed through the food mill
1 bay leaf
1 green pepper, finely chopped
1 cup chopped mushrooms
1 Tbsp chopped flat leaf parsley
1 cup fresh stock or can low sodium
    100% fat free chicken broth

Sauté onion in hot butter and oil until onion is soft. Add flour and stir until brown. Add remaining ingredients and stir well to combine. Bring to a boil. Reduce heat to medium-low. Cover and simmer 45-60 minutes or until sauce thickens, stirring frequently. Serve hot on pasta or rice. Serves 4-6.

TAHINI SAUCE PIQUANT
Saltsa Tahini Pikantiki

1 cup tahini (sesame paste)
Water
Juice of one lemon
1/2 tsp or more ground cumin
Salt and pepper to taste

Add as much water to the tahini as needed until it becomes a thin paste, stirring constantly with a whisk. Add lemon juice, cumin, salt and pepper, stirring constantly. Cover the sauce and chill for 2 hours or more. Serve with fried or grilled zucchini, eggplant and green tomatoes.

TARTAR SAUCE
Saltsa Tartar

1 cup mayonnaise
1 1/2 Tbsp finely chopped dill pickles
1 1/2 Tbsp finely chopped capers
1 tsp prepare mustard
1 Tbsp finely chopped onion
Pepper to taste

Combine all the ingredients and mix well. Chill until needed. Serve with fish, meat or tongue.

TOMATO SAUCE
Saltsa Tomatas

3 Tbsp olive oil
1 medium onion, finely chopped
2 or more garlic cloves, minced
1 (29-ounces can) whole tomatoes or fresh,
    pressed through a food mill
Salt and pepper to taste
1/2 cup water

Sauté onion in hot oil until soft. Add garlic and sauté 1 minute longer. Add the rest of the ingredients and stir well. Cover and simmer slowly for 45 minutes or until sauce thickens, stirring frequently. Serve hot on pasta or rice. Serves 4-6.

VEGETABLES

HOW TO PREPARE ARTICHOKES
Pos na Katharisis tis Anginares

Clean artichokes by removing 5 layers of leaves and trim carefully around base with sharp knife. Slice 2-inches off tips of artichokes and steams. Leave them whole. Scoop out spiny choke below leaves and above heart. Rub each one well with cut-side of lemon and then immerse in bowl of cold water (to prevent darkening). Keep them in water until you are ready to cook. Boil artichokes in boiling salted water and the juice of half lemon 30 minutes or until they are tender. Drain.

ARTICHOKES AU-GRATIN
Agkinares Au-Graten

6 large fresh, can or frozen artichokes, thawed,
*   boiled (see index for preparation)*
3 Tbsp butter, margarine or 2 Tbsp good
*   quality olive oil*
1/3 cup dried breadcrumbs (see index for recipe)
1 cup grated Parmesan cheese
2 cups medium white sauce (see index for recipe)
2-3 well-beaten eggs

Prepare artichokes as directed in Boiling Artichokes. Drain well. Lay on paper towels to absorb excess moisture. Generously grease baking dish and sprinkle with breadcrumbs. Cut artichokes in half again lengthwise and place in one layer in prepared dish. Sprinkle with 1/3 o the cheese and dot with butter. Prepare sauce. Follow recipe and preparation as directed in medium white sauce. Spoon hot sauce little by little into eggs, stirring constantly. Gradually add egg mixture to sauce and cook over very low heat

2 minutes, stirring constantly. Remove from heat. Add half remaining cheese, salt and pepper, stir well. Pour over artichokes and spread evenly. Sprinkle remaining cheese over sauce. Bake in preheated 350 F (180 C) oven 40 minutes or until golden brown. Serve immediately. Serves 6.

ARTICHOKES A LA POLITA
Agkinares A La Polita

12 fresh of frozen artichokes
1 bunch scallions, chopped
1 cup or less good quality olive oil
6 whole small white onions, peeled
12 whole small new potatoes
6 small carrots, peeled, cut into 1-inch long pieces
1 celery heart, cut into 1-inch long pieces
1/4 cup chopped fresh dill
Salt and pepper to taste
3 cups water
Juice of 1 or more lemon

Prepare artichokes as directed in How to Prepare Artichokes (see index). In small frying pan sauté scallions with oil until soft, remove from heat. Arrange vegetables in 6-quart saucepan and add sautéed scallions, salt, pepper, water and lemon juice. Cover and cook slowly approximately 1 hour or until vegetables are tender. Add water as needed. Serve hot or cold with feta cheese and fresh crusty bread. Serves 6.

MEAT STUFFED ARTICHOKES
Agkinares Ghemistes

12 large fresh artichokes or frozen bottoms
*   of artichokes (thawed)*

1/2 pound lean ground beef
1/2 pound lean ground lamb
1 medium onion, finely chopped
2 Tbsp good quality olive oil
1/2 cup dry white wine or Vermouth
1 ripe tomato, peeled, seeded and chopped
Salt and pepper to taste
1 Tbsp chopped fresh dill
1 cup medium béchamel sauce (see index for recipe)
2 egg-yolks, or less beaten
1/2 cup or less grated Parmesan cheese

Prepare artichokes as directed in boiled artichokes (see index for How to Prepare artichokes). Leave them whole. Drain well. Lay artichokes on paper towels, upside down to absorb excess moisture. Sauté onion in oil until soft, add ground meat, stirring constantly breaking up clumps until brown. Add wine and cook until it evaporates. Add salt, pepper, tomato and 2/3 cup water. Cover and cook slowly 60 minutes or until all liquid evaporates. Place artichokes in greased baking dish right side up. Fill artichokes with meat mixture. While meat is simmering, prepare béchamel as directed. Spoon little by little of hot sauce into beaten egg-yolks, stirring constantly. Add egg mixture to sauce and cook over very low heat 2 minutes, stirring constantly. Remove from heat, and add half the grated cheese. Place 1 Tbsp sauce on each artichoke to cover meat. Sprinkle with remaining grated cheese. Bake in preheated 350 F (180 C) oven 30 minutes or until golden brown. Serve immediately as a first course. Serves 6-12.

❦❦❦

ARTICHOKES MOUSAKA
Mousaka me Agginares

12 large fresh artichokes
Juice of 1/2 lemon
1 medium onion, finely chopped
1 Tbsp good quality olive oil
1/2 pound lean ground beef
1/2 pound lean ground lamb
1/2 cup dry white wine or Vermouth
1 ripe tomato, peeled, seeded and chopped
Salt and pepper to taste
1 Tbsp chopped fresh dill
4 cups medium béchamel (see index for recipe)
4 well-beaten eggs

1 cup more or less grated Parmesan cheese
1/2 cup dried breadcrumbs (see index for recipe)

Prepare artichokes as directed in How to Prepare Artichokes (see index). Boil artichokes in 2 cups boiling salted water and juice of 1/2 lemon 15 minutes. Drain well. Sauté onion in oil until soft. Add ground meat, stirring constantly breaking up clumps until brown. Add wine and cook until it evaporates. Add salt, pepper, tomato and 2/3 cup water. Cook slowly covered approximately 60 minutes. Prepare béchamel as directed. Spoon hot sauce little by little into well-beaten eggs, stirring constantly. Add egg mixture to sauce and cook over very low heat 2 minutes, stirring constantly (do not let sauce boil). Remove from heat. Add half the cheese and mix well. Set aside. Generously grease baking dish and sprinkle with breadcrumbs. Place artichokes in one layer. Cover with meat sauce. Spoon béchamel over meat and spread evenly. Sprinkle with remaining cheese. Bake in preheated 350 F (180 C) oven 45 minutes or until golden brown. Serves 12 as a first course or 6 as a main course.

❦❦❦

ARTICHOKES WITH PEAS
Akginares me Araka

6 fresh artichokes or 2 pkg. frozen
3 pounds fresh peas, shelled or 20-ounces frozen
1 bunch of scallions, chopped
1/2 cup more or less good quality olive oil
1/4 cup chopped fresh dill
Juice of 1 or more lemons
Salt and pepper to taste
1 1/2 cups of water

Prepare artichokes as directed in How to Prepare Artichokes (see index). Heat oil and sauté scallions until soft. Arrange artichokes in a 4-quart saucepan; add fresh peas, dill, lemon juice, salt pepper and 1 1/2 cups of water. Cover and cook slowly 1 hour or until artichokes and peas are tender. Serve hot or cold with feta cheese and fresh crusty bread. Serves 6 as a main course.
Note: If artichokes and peas are frozen, add 1 cup water. If artichokes are fresh and peas are frozen, add peas thawed, 5 minutes before the end of cooking.

❦❦❦

BAKED BEANS
Fasolia Gigantes Fournou

1 pound dried lima beans or other large white beans
2/3 cup or more good quality olive oil
2 medium onions, finely chopped
4 garlic cloves, minced
4 medium size ripe tomatoes, pressed through
    a food mill
2 Tbsp finely chopped flat leaf parsley
Salt and pepper to taste
1/4 tsp Cayenne pepper (optional)
1/2 tsp dry mustard
1 cup boiling water

Pick over beans; place in colander and rinse well under cold running water. Place beans in medium saucepan and cover with water. Bring to a boil and boil for 10 minutes covered. Turn off heat, let stand 2 hours or longer. Drain well. Sauté onions in oil until soft. Add remaining ingredients and beans. Bring to a boil. Reduce heat and cook slowly for 30 minutes. Stir occasionally. Turn into a casserole, cover and bake in a preheated 325 F (165 C) oven for approximately 1 hour or until beans are tender. As liquid cooks away add more as needed. Serves 6.

❦❦❦

BAKED EGGPLANTS WITH CHEESE
Melitzanes me Tyri sto Fourno

4 pounds large eggplants
1 cup or more all-purpose flour
2 eggs, beaten with 2 Tbsp water
Good quality olive oil for frying
1 large onion, finely chopped
2 Tbsp olive oil
2 clove garlic or more, minced
3 medium ripped tomatoes, peeled, seeded
    and chopped
1 Tbsp. minced flat leaf parsley
Salt and pepper to taste
2/3-1 pound kasseri, Swiss cheese or mixed,
    cut into 1/8-inch thin slices
2/3 cup lightly pressed down grated
    Parmesan cheese
2 Tbsp. melted butter or margarine
1/3 cup fine dried breadcrumbs (see index)

Remove stems, wash eggplants well. Peel and cut in 1/3-inch slices crosswise. Add salt to flour; dredge eggplant slices, shake off excess. Dip slices one at a time in egg and fry in hot oil on both sides until golden brown. Drain on paper towels. Sauté onion in oil until soft, add garlic and sauté a few minutes more. Add tomatoes, parsley, salt and pepper, cover and simmer 30 minutes. Remove from heat. Place half the eggplant slices in baking dish in one layer, close together. Cover with half the cheese slices, then, cover with half the tomato mixture. Sprinkle with half the grated cheese. Repeat with remaining eggplant slices, remaining cheese slices and tomato mixture. Sprinkle with remaining grated cheese. Top with buttered breadcrumbs. Bake in preheated 375 F (190 C) oven 30 minutes. Serve immediately. Serves 6-10.

Note: For low fat, you can bake instead of frying the eggplant slices. Brush eggplant slices with olive oil and sprinkle with little salt, on both sides. Dredge eggplant slices with the flour and shake off excess. Dip one at a time in egg and then into breadcrumbs mixture until completely covered and pressed between your hands. Place eggplant slices in a baking sheet, lined with parchment paper. Bake in a preheated 450 F (230 C) oven on the second lower rack for 20-30 minutes or until golden brown. Remove from oven and place in a platter. Repeat with the rest of the eggplant slices, using the same parchment paper. Follow the rest of the preparation as directed above.

❦❦❦

BAKED EGGPLANT WITH FETA CHEESE
Melitzanes me Tyri Feta sto Fournou

This is a low fat dish:
4 pounds large eggplants
Salt and pepper to taste
Good quality olive oil for brushing
1 (29-ounces can) whole tomatoes, finely chopped
2 large cloves garlic, crushed
1 large yellow, red or green bell pepper,
    finely chopped
2 Tbsp or less olive oil
12 ounces feta cheese, crumbled

Remove stems, wash eggplants well. Peel if desire and cut into 3/4-inch slices crosswise. Brush eggplant slices with olive oil and arrange in baking sheet lined with parchment paper, turn oiled side down. Brush top again with oil and bake in a preheated 500 F (260 C) oven on second lower rack 20 minutes. Remove from oven and transfer to platter. Repeat with remaining eggplant slices, using same parchment. While eggplants are baking, prepare sauce. In small saucepan combine chopped tomatoes and liquid, garlic, yellow pepper if desired, salt, pepper and oil. Bring to a boil, reduce heat and simmer 30 minutes. Place baked eggplant slices in 9x13x3-inch baking dish in layers. Cover with tomato sauce. Sprinkle with feta cheese, and press cheese down with a spoon into the sauce. Bake in preheated 375 F (190 C) oven 30 minutes. Serve hot with fresh crusty bread. Serves 6 as a main course or 8-12 as a first course.

꒐꒰꒱꒐

BAKED VEGETABLE CASSEROLE
Lachanika Fournou

4 medium potatoes
4 pounds round eggplants, about 3 large
3 pounds zucchini
Good quality olive oil
Salt and pepper to taste
2 large onions, thinly sliced
4 large cloves of garlic, thinly sliced
1 cup chopped flat leaf parsley
6 large red ripped tomatoes, cut into 1/4-inch slices
1 cup soft breadcrumbs (see index for recipe)
1 cup grated Parmesan cheese

Remove stems, wash eggplants well. Cut in half-inch slices, crosswise. Set aside. Trim zucchini and rinse well. Cut into 1/2-inch slices, lengthwise. Brush eggplant slices with olive oil, and arrange in baking sheet oiled side down, lined with parchment paper. Brush again with oil and sprinkle with salt, bake in a preheated 500 F (245 C) oven for 15-20 minutes or until golden brown. Remove from oven, and place in a dish. In same baking pan arrange and bake zucchini slices as eggplant. Sauté onion in 3 Tbsp. olive oil until soft, add garlic and sauté a few minutes more, season with salt and pepper, add parsley. While preparing vegetables, wash and brush potatoes. Boil in salted water 20 minutes. Remove from water, peel and cut into 1/4-inch slices. In a greased 14x11 1/2 x2 1/2-inch baking casserole, place potatoes into a layer close together. Place prepared eggplants into a layer close together,

sprinkle with 3 Tbsp. grated Parmesan cheese, and pepper. Cover eggplant with zucchini into a layer close to each other and sprinkle with 3 Tbsp. grated cheese and pepper. Then top with onion mixture, and spread evenly, sprinkle with 3 Tbsp. grated cheese. Place tomatoes slices on top of onion mixture, slightly overlapping pattern. In small bowl combine soft breadcrumbs, remaining cheese, salt, pepper and 1/3 cup of olive oil, mix well. Spread evenly over casserole. Bake in preheated 375 F (190 C) oven 45 minutes. Serve hot or cold. Serves 6 as main course with feta cheese and fresh crusty bread, or 12 as side dish with meat, poultry or fish.

꒐꒰꒱꒐

BRAISED BEANS
Fasolia Yiachi

1 pound any kind large white beans
2/3 cup olive oil
1 medium onion, finely chopped
4 medium size ripe tomatoes, pressed through
     a food mill or 1/2 cup tomato sauce
1 Tbsp finely chopped flat leaf parsley
Salt and pepper to taste
1/4 tsp Cayenne pepper (optional)
1 cinnamon stick 1/2-inch long
1 1/2 cups boiling water

Pick over beans, place in colander and rinse well under cold running water. Place beans in medium saucepan and cover with water. Bring to a boil and boil 10 minutes. Turn off the heat, let stand 2 hours or longer. Drain well. While beans are standing, prepare sauce. Sauté onion in oil until is soft. Add remaining ingredients and beans. Stir well to combine. Bring to a boil. Reduce heat, cover and cook slowly 45 minutes or until beans are tender and sauce thickens. Stir occasionally. Add hot water as needed. Remove cinnamon before serving. Serve hot or cold. Serves 4-6.

꒐꒰꒱꒐

BRAISED CAULIFLOWER
Kounoupithi Yiachi

1 large cauliflower
1 1/2 tsp salt
1/2 cup or less olive oil

1/2 cup finely chopped onion
3 medium ripe tomatoes, pressed through a food mill
Salt and pepper to taste
1 cinnamon stick 1-inch long (optional)

Remove green leaves, cut off and discard thick stems and any bruised or dirty spots from cauliflower. Cut into flowerets and place in deep bowl of salted water, let stay 40 minutes or longer. Drain and rinse well. Drain again. Sauté onion in oil until soft, add tomato, salt, pepper, cinnamon if desired and 1/2 cup water. Bring to a boil. Add flowerets, stir gently, cover and cook slowly for 30-45 minutes or until tender and sauce thickens. Shake pan occasionally, do not stir. Serve hot or cold. Serves 4-6.

❧❀❧

BRAISED OKRA
Bamies Yiachni

1/2 cup of less olive oil
1 medium onion, finely chopped
3 large ripe tomatoes, peeled, seeded and chopped
    or 1 can (16-ounces) whole tomatoes, chopped
2 Tbsp. finely chopped flat leaf parsley
Salt and pepper to taste
2 pounds fresh okra or 3 pkg. Frozen (thawed)

Sauté onion in oil until soft. Add tomatoes and liquid, parsley, salt and pepper. Cover, bring to a boil, reduce heat and simmer 15 minutes. Neatly add okra to sauce. Cover and simmer approx. 30-45 minutes, depending on size of okra, or until tender. Do not over cook. Occasionally shake saucepan, but do not stir. Serve hot or cold, with feta cheese and fresh crusty bread. Serves 4.

❧❀❧

BRIAMI

1 pound narrow zucchini cut into 1/2-inch thin slices
1 pound narrow eggplants (4-5-inches long), cut into 1/2-inch thin slices
1 pound potatoes, peeled, cut into fourths and cut into 1/2-inch thin slices
2 pounds ripe tomatoes, chopped
2 onions, cut into half, and then cut into thin slices, lengthwise
3 large cloves garlic, thinly sliced
1/4 cup finely chopped flat leaf parsley
Salt and pepper to taste

3/4 cup or less fine quality olive oil
1 cup water

In medium baking pan, place all ingredients, toss well and spread evenly. Place pan in oven on second bottom rack, bake in a preheated 375 F (190 C) oven for approximately 60-75 minutes or until vegetables are tender. Add water if needed. Serve hot or cold. Serves 4-6.

❧❀❧

CABBAGE RAGOUT
Lachano Yiachi

1 medium head cabbage or Savoy cabbage
1/2 cup or less olive oil
1 cup onion, finely chopped
4 medium size ripe tomatoes, pressed through a food mill or 1/2 cup tomato sauce
1 cinnamon stick 1/2-inch long
Salt and pepper to taste

Remove and discard outside cabbage leaves, remove core. Cut in small pieces. Rinse well under cold running water. Drain well. Sauté onion in oil until soft, add remaining ingredients and cabbage, stir well. Cover and cook slowly 45-55 minutes or until cabbage is tender. Remove cinnamon stick before serving. Serve hot or cold with grilled pork chops, hamburgers or plain with feta cheese and fresh crusty bread. Serves 6.

❧❀❧

CARROT CABBAGE AND SPINACH CASSEROLE
Karota, Lachano and Spanaki sto Fourno

1 small head of cabbage, shredded (1 1/2 pounds shredded)
3 pounds carrots, peeled and thinly sliced
2 bunches fresh spinach, leaves only
2 scallions, finely sliced
1/3 cup or less butter, margarine or good quality olive oil
6 eggs
12 ounces coarsely grated Cheddar cheese
Salt and pepper to taste
6 Tbsp whipping cream or milk

Remove roots and coarse leaves from spinach, wash thoroughly. Drain well and dry between two kitchen towels, and roughly chop. Set aside. In large nonstick frying pan sauté cabbage with 2

Tbsp butter if desired, stir well, cover pan and sweat over moderate heat 4 minutes. Uncover; raise heat; cook and stir constantly until liquid evaporates and cabbage is tender. Remove to a dish and set aside. In the same pan sauté carrots with 2 Tbsp butter, as with the cabbage. Remove to a dish and set aside. Using the same pan, sauté scallions with remaining butter until soft. Add spinach and sauté on high until spinach is wilted and liquid evaporates. You need 3 large bowls. In first bowl beat well 2 eggs, add 1/3 of the cheese and 2 Tbsp. cream, salt and pepper, mix well. Add prepared carrots and toss well. In second bowl, do the same with cabbage. In third bowl, do the same with spinach mixture and remaining eggs, cheese and cream, and toss well to combine. Grease well a 121/4x101/4x21/4-inch baking dish. Layer 1/2 the cabbage mixture and spread evenly. Top with 1/2 the carrot mixture and spread evenly. Then cover carrots with all the spinach mixture and spread evenly. Cover spinach mixture with carrot mixture, and last with cabbage mixture. Cut a piece of parchment to size of pan and brush with melted butter or oil, place greased side down to cover the mixture, and press down. Bake in preheated 375 F (190 C) oven 20-30 minutes. Remove from oven. Cool 10 minutes. Remove paper from top of pan. Slice and serve. Serves 8-12. This recipe is for a big crowd.

❧⚜❧

CARROT AND HAM SOUFFLÈ
Soufflé Karota ke Zambon

3 cups coarsely grated carrots
3 Tbsp butter, margarine or good quality olive oil
1 pound boiled ham, cut into small cubes
5 Tbsp butter, margarine or olive oil
5 Tbsp all-purpose flour
2 cups scalding milk
6 extra large eggs, well beaten
White pepper to taste
8 ounces each coarsely grated Kaseri and
*   Swiss cheese*
1/2 cup dried breadcrumbs (see index for recipe)

Place carrots in a large saucepan, cover and let slowly simmer until all liquid evaporates, stirring occasionally. Add 2 Tbsp of the butter and the ham, and simmer until ham almost melts, stirring constantly. Remove from heat. Prepare béchamel. Melt butter if desired over medium heat, blend in flour until smooth using a whisk. Remove from heat. Gradually add milk, stirring constantly, until mixture is thick and smooth. Cook 3 minutes longer; add pepper and blend. Remove from heat. Spoon little by little of the hot sauce into beaten eggs, stirring constantly. Gradually add egg mixture to sauce and cook over very low heat 2-3 minutes (do not let sauce boil). Remove from heat. Add cheeses, and carrot-ham mixture and stir well to combine. In well-greased casserole, sprinkle 1/4 cup breadcrumbs. Pour in mixture and spread evenly. Sprinkle with remaining breadcrumbs and dot with remaining 1 Tbsp butter. Bake in preheated 350 F (180 C) oven on middle rack 30 minutes or until golden brown. Serve immediately.

❧⚜❧

EGGPLANT MOUSAKA
Melitzanes Mousaka

6 pounds round eggplants, about 4 large
Good quality olive oil for brushing and cooking
Salt and pepper to taste
1 1/2 pounds lean ground beef
1/2 pound lean ground lamb
1 cup minced onion
1/2 cup dry wine
1 can (16-oounces) whole tomatoes, chopped or
*   pressed through a food mill*
1 cinnamon stick 1/2-inch long
1 Tbsp minced parsley
6 extra large eggs
2 Tbsp dry breadcrumbs
1 cup grated Parmesan, or Romano cheese
12 Tbsp butter, margarine or 9 of Tbsp good
*   quality olive oil*
13 Tbsp all-purpose flour
5 cups milk
White pepper to taste

Remove eggplant stems and rinse well. Peel if desire and cut in 1/2-inch slices crosswise. Brush slices lightly with olive oil and arrange in baking sheet, oiled side down, lined with parchment. Brush again with oil, and bake in preheated 450F oven 20 minutes. Remove from oven. While eggplants bake prepare meat sauce. Sauté onion and meat in 1 Tbsp. oil until soft. Add wine and sauté few minutes longer. Add tomato, 1/2 cup water, salt, pepper and cinnamon stick. Cover; cook slowly 45 minutes. Remove from heat, and remove cinnamon stick. Add breadcrumbs, 2 Tbsp. grated cheese, parsley and 2 beaten eggs. Stir well. Let stand. Prepare white sauce. Melt butter if desired over medium heat, blend in flour until smooth using whisk. Remove from heat and gradually add milk, stirring constantly, return to heat and cook until mixture is thick and smooth. Cook 3 minutes longer; add seasoning and blend. Remove from heat. Spoon little by little of hot sauce into 4 beaten eggs, stirring constantly. Add egg mixture to sauce and cook over very low heat 2-3 minutes, stirring constantly. Add 1/2 cup of grated cheese and stir well. In 14x12x3-inch greased baking pan, Place half the prepared eggplant slices in a layer very close to each other. Cover with meat mixture; add remaining eggplant slices. Pour white sauce to cover eggplants and spread evenly. Sprinkle with remaining grated cheese. Bake in preheated 350 F (180 C) oven 45 minutes or until golden. Let stand 20 minutes to cool before cutting. Cut into squares to serve. Serves 6-12.

❦❦❦

EGGPLANT MOUSAKA-VEGETARIAN
Melitzanes Mousaka yia Fytofagous

6 pounds round eggplants, about 4 large
Olive oil
Salt and pepper to taste
3 large potatoes
2 large onions, cut into thinly slices lengthwise
2 20-ounces each cans whole tomatoes with
*   tomato sauce, finely chopped*
3 garlic cloves or more, minced
1 large bell pepper, finely chopped
1/2 cup finely chopped and lightly pressed down
flat leaf parsley
1/4 cup dried breadcrumbs (see index for recipe)
1 1/2 pounds or less crumbled feta cheese, or
coarsely grated Kasseri, Provolone or Swiss cheese
1/2 cup olive oil
13 Tbsp all-purpose flour
5 cups scalding milk

6 eggs, well beaten
3/4 cup grated Parmesan or Romano cheese

Remove eggplant stems and rinse well. Cut into 1/2-inch slices crosswise. Lightly brush eggplant slices with olive oil and arrange in a baking sheet, lined with parchment, oiled side down. Brush again with the oil, and lightly sprinkle with salt, and bake in preheated 450 F (230 C) oven 20 minutes or until brown. Remove from oven, and remove from sheet to a plate. Repeat with rest of eggplants until you have baked all. While eggplants are baking, scrub potatoes and boil in boiling salted water 20 minutes. Remove from heat, drain and peel. Slice potatoes into 1/4-inch thick. Set aside. Sauté onions in 3 Tbsp. olive oil, until soft, add tomatoes, garlic, chopped bell pepper, season with salt and pepper. Bring to boil and simmer until sauce is very thick. Add parsley and breadcrumbs to sauce and stir well to combine. Let stand. Prepare béchamel. In 4-quart saucepan heat oil, over medium heat, blend in flour until smooth using a whisk. Remove from heat and gradually add milk, stirring constantly, return to heat and cook until mixture is thick and smooth, stirring constantly. Cook 3 minutes longer; add seasoning and blend. Remove from heat. Spoon little by little of hot sauce into beaten eggs, stirring constantly. Slowly add egg mixture to sauce and cook over very low heat 2-3 minutes, stirring constantly (do not let sauce boil). Add 1/2 cup of the grated cheese and stir well to combine. Remove from heat. In 14x12x3-inch baking pan or dish, arrange potato slices close to each other, and brush with olive oil. Then half the prepared eggplant slices, in a layer very close to each other. Spoon tomato sauce over eggplants and spread evenly. Sprinkle with feta cheese. Then top with remaining eggplant slices. Pour béchamel over and spread evenly. Sprinkle with remaining grated cheese. Bake in preheated 350 F (180 C) oven 45 minutes or until golden brown. Let stand 20-30 minutes to cool before cutting. Cut into squares to serve. Serves 8-12.

❦❦❦

EGGPLANT-MACARONI MOUSAKA
Melitzanes ke Makaronia Mousaka

3 pounds round eggplants, about 2 large
Good olive oil for brushing and cooking
Salt and pepper to taste
1 1/2 pounds lean ground beef
1/2 pound lean ground lamb
1 cup minced onion
1/2 cup dry wine or Vermouth
*1 can (16-ounces) whole tomatoes, chopped or
     pressed through a food mill*
1 cinnamon stick 1/2-inch long
1 Tbsp minced flat leaf parsley
2 Tbsp dry breadcrumbs
6 extra large eggs
1 pound noodles
2 Tbsp melted butter, margarine or olive oil
*1 cup grated Parmesan, Kefalotyri or
     Romano cheese*
*12 Tbsp or less butter, margarine or good
     quality olive oil*
13 Tbsp all-purpose flour
5 cups milk
White pepper to taste

Remove eggplant stems and rinse well. Peel if desire and cut in 1/2-inch slices, crosswise. Brush eggplant slices lightly with olive oil and arrange in baking sheet, oiled side down, lined with parchment. Brush again with the oil, and bake in a preheated 450 F (220 C) oven 20 minutes. Remove from oven. While eggplants are baking prepare meat sauce. Sauté onion and meat in 1 Tbsp. olive oil until soft. Add wine and sauté few minutes longer. Add tomato, 1/2 cup water, salt, pepper to taste and cinnamon stick. Cover; cook slowly 45 minutes. Remove from heat, add parsley, breadcrumbs, 2 Tbsp. grated cheese and 2 beaten eggs, stir well. Let stand. While meat sauce is cooking, prepare noodles. Boil noodles in 4 quarts boiling salted water 8 minutes. Drain well. Add butter and 1/4 cup grated cheese, toss well. Let stand. In 14x12x3-inch baking pan, place prepared eggplant slices in a layer very close to each other. Cover with meat mixture; then add noodles and spread evenly. Prepare béchamel. Melt butter if desired over medium heat, blend in flour until smooth using whisk. Remove from heat and gradually add milk, return to heat stirring constantly until mixture is thick

and smooth. Cook 3 minutes longer; add salt and white pepper and blend. Remove from heat. Spoon little by little of hot sauce into 4 beaten eggs, stirring constantly. Add egg mixture to sauce and cook over very low heat 2-3 minutes, stirring constantly. Add 1/2 cup grated cheese and stir well. Remove from heat and pour béchamel to cover noodles and spread evenly. Sprinkle with remaining grated cheese. Bake in preheated 350 F (180 C) oven 45 minutes or until golden. Let stand 20 minutes to cool before cutting. Cut into squares to serve. Serves 6-12.

❦❦❦

EGGPLANT LITTLE SHOES
Melitzanes Papoutsakia

12 narrow eggplants 4-5-inches long
Olive oil for sautéing
1 Tbsp. olive oil
1 1/2 pounds lean ground beef
1/2 pound lean ground lamb
1 cup minced onion
1/2 cup dry white wine or Vermouth
*1 16-ounces can whole tomatoes, pressed through
     a food mill*
1 Tbsp. minced flat leaf parsley
Salt and pepper to taste
1 beaten egg
2 Tbsp dried breadcrumbs (see index for recipe)
1 1/2 cups medium white sauce (see index for recipe)
1 egg plus 1 egg yolk, beaten
1/2 cup grated Parmesan cheese

Remove eggplant stems, rinse well and dry. Sauté in nonstick frying pan with olive oil, on medium heat, covered, until soft on all sides. Remove from heat, transfer to baking pan. Make a deep slit from one end to the other lengthwise, without cutting bottom of eggplants. With 2 spoons push eggplant from the slit out to shape a shoe and make a hollow for the filling. Sprinkle with little salt. Sauté onion in oil until soft, add ground meat, stir, breaking up clumps until brown. Add wine and sauté few minutes longer. Add tomato, 1 cup water, salt and pepper. Cook 30-45 minutes until liquid evaporates. Remove from heat. Add breadcrumbs, 2 Tbsp. grated cheese, parsley and beaten egg. Stir well. Stuff eggplants. Prepare white sauce as directed. Spoon little by little of hot sauce into beaten eggs stirring constantly. Add egg mixture and cook over low heat 2 minutes, stirring constantly, (do not let sauce boil). Remove from heat, and add half the remaining grated cheese. Place 1 Tbsp. sauce on each little shoe to cover meat. Sprinkle with remaining grated cheese. Bake in preheated 350 F (180 C) oven 30 minutes or until golden brown. Serves 6 as a main course or 12 as a first course.

❧⌘❧

EGGPLANT WITH SAUSAGE
Melitzanes me Loukanika

1 large onion, peeled and cut into half crosswise
    and thinly sliced crosswise again
2 pounds small eggplants
2 pounds bell peppers (any kind)
2 pounds red ripe tomatoes, peeled, seeded and
    chopped or 1 can 20-ounces whole peeled
    tomatoes, chopped
Salt and pepper to taste
1/2 cup olive oil
2 pounds sausage, hot or mild and cut into 1/2-inch
    slices or homemade (see index for recipe)

Sauté onion slices in 2 Tbsp oil. Remove from pan and let stand. Remove eggplant stems and rinse well. Peel if desire and cut in 1/2-inch slices, crosswise. Brush eggplant slices lightly with olive oil and arrange in a baking sheet lined with parchment, oiled side down.. Brush again with oil and sprinkle lightly with salt, and bake in preheated 450 F (230 C) oven 15-20 minutes or until golden brown. Remove from oven. Let stand. Remove stems and seeds from peppers and cut into 8 pieces. Sauté peppers in remaining oil, and season with salt and pepper. Remove from heat. In 6-quart saucepan arrange into layers the eggplant slices, peppers, onion, and tomatoes with the liquid. Sprinkle with pepper. Repeat until you finish with all the vegetables. Cook slowly 20 minutes. While vegetables simmer, fry or broil sausage slices on both sides. Add sausage slices to vegetables, lightly press down with spoon and simmer 10 minutes longer. Serve hot with rice pilaf (see index) feta cheese and fresh crusty bread. Serves 6.

❧⌘❧

EGGPLANTS IMAM BAILDI A (L. FAT)
Melitzanes Imam Baildi

10 narrow eggplants, 5-6-inches long
Olive oil for sautéing
3 large onions, thinly sliced
1/2 cup more or less olive oil
4 large or more garlic cloves, thinly sliced
4 large ripe tomatoes, peeled, seeded and chopped
    or 1 can 20-ounces whole tomatoes chopped
1/2 cup chopped flat leaf parsley
Salt and pepper to taste

Remove eggplant stems, rinse well and dry. Sauté eggplants in nonstick frying pan with little olive oil, on medium heat, covered, until soft on all sides. Remove from heat, and transfer to a baking pan or dish. Make a deep slit from one end to the other lengthwise without cutting the bottom of the eggplants. With 2 spoons push eggplant from the slit out to shape a shoe and make a hollow for the filling. Sprinkle with little salt. Set aside. Sauté onion with oil until soft. Add garlic, tomatoes, parsley, salt and pepper, cover and cook for 20 minutes. Fill the mixture into the slits in each eggplant. Spoon the rest on top. Cover and bake in a preheated 350 F (180 C) oven for 30-45 minutes. Serve hot or cold with feta cheese and fresh crusty bread. Serves 5.

❧⌘❧

EGGPLANTS IMAM BAILDI B (L. FAT)
Melitzanes Imam Baildi

4 pounds large eggplants
Olive oil for brushing
Salt
3 large onions, thinly sliced
2 Tbsp. or more olive oil
5 large ripe tomatoes, peeled, seeded and chopped
    or 1 can (29-ounces) whole tomatoes, chopped
4 or more garlic cloves, thinly sliced
1/2 cup chopped flat leaf parsley
Salt and pepper to taste

Remove eggplant stems and rinse well. Peel if desired and cut into 3/4-inch slices, crosswise. Brush slices with olive oil and arrange in baking sheet lined with parchment, oiled side down. Brush top again with oil, sprinkle with salt and bake in preheated 500 F (260 C) oven on second lower rack 20 minutes. Remove from oven and transfer to a platter. Repeat with rest of eggplant slices, using same parchment. While eggplants are baking, prepare sauce. Sauté onion with oil until soft. Add garlic, tomatoes, parsley, salt and pepper, cover and cook slowly 20 minutes. Place half the baked eggplant slices in 9x13x3-inch baking dish in layers close to each other. Cover with half the onion-tomato mixture and spread evenly. Repeat with eggplants and onion-tomato mixture. Bake in preheated 375 F (190 C) oven 30 minutes. Serve hot or cold with feta cheese and fresh crusty bread. Serves 6 as a main course or 8-12 as a first course.

EGGPLANTS PANE
Melitzanes Pane

3 large eggplants about 3 pounds
1 cup all-purpose flour
2 eggs, beaten with 2 Tbsp water
2 cups dried breadcrumbs (see index for recipe)
1/3 cup grated Parmesan cheese
Salt and pepper to taste
Good quality olive oil, clarified butter or margarine (see index for recipe) for frying

Remove eggplant stems, rinse well, peel if desired. Cut in 1/3-inch slices crosswise. Sprinkle with salt, set aside. Combine breadcrumbs, cheese and pepper and mix well. Dredge eggplant slices with the flour and shake off excess. Dip one at a time in egg and then into breadcrumbs mixture until completely covered and pressed between your hands. Fry in hot oil if desired, on both sides on medium heat until golden brown. Drain on paper towels. Place in a serving platter and serve hot with Skorthalia sauce or Tzatziki dip if desired (see index). Serves 4-8.
Note: For low fat dish, you can bake instead of frying the eggplant slices if desire. Generously brush eggplant slices with olive oil and sprinkle with little salt, on both sides. Dredge eggplant slices with the flour and shake off excess. Dip one at a time in egg and them into breadcrumbs mixture until completely covered and pressed between your hands. Place eggplant slices in a baking sheet, lined with parchment paper. Bake in a preheated 450 F (230 C) oven on the second lower rack for 20-30 minutes or

until golden brown. Remove from oven and place in a serving platter. Repeat with the rest eggplant slices, using the same parchment paper. Serve as above.

EGGPLANT AND MEAT PATTIES
Melitzanokeftethes me Kima

1 large eggplant (about 1 pound), rinse and
    cut into cubes
1 medium onion, finely chopped
3 Tbsp good quality olive oil
Salt and pepper to taste
1 pound lean ground beef or lamb
1 egg
1/3 cup dried breadcrumbs (see index for recipe)
2 Tbsp finely chopped flat leaf fresh parsley
2 Tbsp finely chopped fresh mint
2 Tbsp grated Kefalotyri or Parmesan cheese
Flour for coating
Olive oil for frying

In a frying pan sauté the eggplant cubes and onion in three Tbsp of olive oil, and let slowly cook for 10 minutes or until soft. Remove from heat. In a large mixing bowl combine all the ingredients except the flour and the olive oil and mix well with your hand. Chill for 60 minutes or longer. Shape mixture into balls the size of a large walnut or larger. Roll them in flour and shake off excess flour. Heat oil and fry the melitzanokeftethes until brown on both sides and cooked through. Place on absorbent papers. Serve hot, with fries, salad (see index for the recipes), feta cheese and fresh crusty bread. Serves 4-6.

EGGPLANT PATTIES
Melitzanokeftethes

21/2 pounds narrow eggplants, 5-6-inch long
1 medium potato, boiled, peeled and mashed
3 beaten eggs
3 cloves of garlic, crushed
1/2 cup finely chopped onion
1 Tbsp finely chopped fresh flat leaf parsley
1 Tbsp finely chopped fresh dill
1/3 cup grated Kefalotyri or Parmesan cheese
1 cup or more fine ground dried breadcrumbs
    (see index for recipe)
2 Tbsp olive oil
Salt and pepper to taste
Oil for frying

All-purpose flour for coating

Remove stems of the eggplants and wash well. Puncture with a fork to prevent it from exploding while they bake. Place eggplants in a baking pan lined with foil and bake in a preheated 400 F (205 C) oven for 30 minutes or until soft to the touch. While hot, remove the skin. Cut into pieces. In a food processor combine all the ingredients and pulse few times (to not make it smooth). Transfer the mixture to a bowl. Add more breadcrumbs if needed. With floured hands, shape into little balls. Roll them in flour, shake off excess and flatten them. Pour enough oil into a frying pan to cover the bottom. Heat oil and fry patties until brown on both sides. Drain on absorbent paper towels. Serve hot or cold with tzatziki (yogurt and cucumber sauce) or skorthalia (garlic sauce), if desired and fresh crusty bread, (see index for the recipes).

HOMEMADE FRENCH FRIES
Patates Tiganites

4 large potatoes
6 cups oil for frying
Salt

Peel potatoes, wash and dry. Cut in 1/4-inch slices then in 1/4-inch strips. Heat oil in a deep pot on high heat. Gently add half the potatoes and stir well. Reduce heat to medium-high and fry potatoes until golden, stirring occasionally. Remove from oil with slotted spoon and place on paper towels to drain. Sprinkle with salt. Repeat same procedure with other half of potatoes. Place in serving dish and serve hot. Serves 4-6. Note: Drain the oil and save in the refrigerator for the next use.

LEEKS AND MUSHROOMS GRATINEE
Prasa ke Manitaria Gratine

3 pounds leeks
1 1/2 pounds any kind of mushrooms
4 Tbsp butter, margarine or good quality olive oil
71/2 Tbsp butter, margarine or olive oil
71/2 Tbsp all-purpose flour

4 cups milk
4 beaten eggs
8 ounces shredded Swiss, Kaseri cheese or both
1/2 cup toasted chopped walnuts (optional)
1/4 cup grated Parmesan cheese
Salt and white pepper to taste

Clean and wash leeks well. Thinly slice leeks. Wash mushrooms under cold running water, and dry on paper towels. Thinly slice mushrooms. Sauté leeks in 2 Tbsp. of hot butter if desired, until soft, and season with salt and pepper. Remove to a dish. In same pan sauté mushrooms with remaining butter, until liquid evaporates, and season with salt and pepper. Prepare sauce. In saucepan, melt butter if desired over medium heat, blend in flour until smooth using wire whisk. Remove from heat and gradually add milk, stirring constantly until mixture is thick and smooth. Cook 3 minutes longer. Remove from heat. Spoon little by little of hot sauce into beaten eggs stirring constantly, add egg mixture to sauce and cook over very low heat (do not let sauce boil) 2 minutes, stirring constantly. Add Parmesan, salt and pepper to sauce and stir well to combine. In greased casserole spoon 1 1/2 cups of sauce, and spread evenly. On top spread leeks, and sprinkle with 1 cup shredded cheese. Then spread mushrooms, and sprinkle with 1 cup shredded cheese and the chopped walnuts. Spoon hot sauce over walnuts and spread evenly. Sprinkle with remaining shredded cheese. Bake in preheated 400 F (200 C) oven 30 minutes or until golden. Serve immediately, with meat or poultry. Serves 6-8.

LEEKS GRATINEE
Prasa Gratine

2 pounds leeks
1/4 cup butter or margarine
8 ounces shredded Swiss cheese
1/3 cup or more dried breadcrumbs

Clean and wash leeks well. Cut in 1/2-inch slices and rinse again in a strainer under cold running water. Drain. Boil leeks in boiling and lightly salted water, until are not quite tender. Remove from heat and drain well. Melt half the butter if desired. In well-greased casserole spread half the leeks, sprinkle with half the shredded cheese, then half the melted butter. Repeat with leeks, cheese and butter. Sprinkle with breadcrumbs, add more if needed, and dot with the remaining butter. Bake in preheated 450 F (230 C) oven 15 minutes. Serve immediately as a first course or side dish.

LEEKS AU-GRATIN
Prasa Ograten

4 pounds leeks
1 Tbsp olive oil
4 ounces bacon, cut into small cubes
2 Tbsp finely chopped flat leaf parsley
1 cup of each grated Kaseri and Swiss cheese
5 Tbsp butter, margarine or olive oil
5 Tbsp all-purpose flour
2 cups milk
4 eggs, beaten
1/4 cup grated Parmesan cheese
Salt and white pepper to taste

Clean and wash leeks well. Cut in thin slices, rinse again in colander under cold running water. Drain. Drop leeks in a boiling salted water, and boil 10-15 minutes or until tender. Remove from heat and drain well. While leeks are boiling, sauté bacon with olive oil until brown but not burned. Add leeks and sauté a few minutes longer, stirring constantly. Add white pepper and stir. Remove from heat. Prepare béchamel . Melt butter if desired over medium heat, blend in flour until smooth using whisk. Remove from heat and gradually add the milk, stirring constantly. Return to heat and cook until mixture is thick and smooth, stirring constantly. Cook 3 minutes longer; add white pepper and blend. Spoon little by little of hot sauce into eggs, stirring constantly. Gradually add egg mixture to sauce and cook over very low heat (do not let sauce boil) 2 minutes, stirring constantly. Remove from heat. In large mixing bowl combine all ingredients except Parmesan cheese and mix well. Spoon mixture in well greased 9x13x2-inch casserole and spread evenly. Sprinkle with Parmesan. Bake in preheated 350 F (180 C) oven 35-40 minutes.

Remove from oven and serve immediately as a side dish or main dish.

LEEKS WITH CRACKED WHEAT
Prasa Yiachni me Blougouri

Substitute cracked wheat for rice. Follow recipe as directed in Leeks with Rice (see index). Add cracked wheat, simmer stirring frequently until liquid is absorbed, about 30 minutes. Serve hot if use butter, or hot or cold if use oil, with feta cheese and fresh crusty bread. Serves 4.

LEEKS WITH RICE
Prasa Yiachni me Rizi

5 medium leeks
1/2 cup or less butter, margarine or good
*   quality olive oil*
1 can (8-ounces) whole tomatoes, chopped
Salt and pepper to taste
1/2 cup converted rice
2 cups water

Clean and wash leeks well. Chop into 1-inch long and rinse again in strainer under cold running water to get rid of sand. Drain well. Sauté leeks with butter if desired, until soft. Add chopped tomatoes, salt, pepper and 2 cups water. Bring to a boil, reduce heat and simmer 15 minutes. Add rice to leeks, stir, cover and simmer until liquid has been absorbed, about 20 minutes. Serve hot if use butter, or hot or cold if use oil, with feta cheese and fresh crusty bread. Serves 4.

MASHED POTATOES GREEK STYLE
Patates Poure

6 medium potatoes
1/3 cup or more butter or margarine
1 1/2 cups scalding milk
Salt and pepper to taste

Scrub and wash potatoes. Drop them in boiling salty water and cook until tender, when pierced with a fork. When done, drain, and peel quickly before they get cool. Mash the hot potatoes with a food mill. Melt butter if desired in a saucepan, add mashed potatoes, and sauté few minutes. Slowly add scalding milk, stirring constantly until potatoes absorb all milk and become light and fluffy. Add milk if needed. Season mash potatoes with salt and pepper. Serves 6-8.

❦❦❦

MEAT STUFFED CABBAGE LEAVES
Lahonodolmathes me Kyma

1 large or 2 medium Savoy cabbage
2 Tbsp butter, margarine or olive oil
1 medium onion, finely chopped
1 1/2 pound lean ground beef
1/2 pound lean ground lamb
1/2 cup converted rice
1 large ripe tomato, peeled, seeded and finely
    chopped or 1/4 cup tomato sauce
2 Tbsp finely chopped flat leaf parsley
2 Tbsp finely chopped dill
Salt and pepper to taste
3 cups fresh beef stock or water
Stock or fat free chicken broth for the sauce
21/2 Tbsp cornstarch
2 eggs, well beaten
Juice of 1 lemon or more

Remove outside leaves of cabbage and cut around the stem and discard. With a sharp knife, remove core as deeply as you can and discard. Gently separate cabbage leaves one by one as you go. Plunge the cabbage leaves one by one into boiling water and press them down with a large straining spoon and boil for 4-5 minutes for the tough leaves or until are tender, and less for the tender leaves. Remove from boiling water to a large bowl and let them cool. Cut leaves in half if they are large and remove thick stems and reserve. Line bottom of a large Dutch oven with reserved thick stems to prevent stuffed cabbage from burning. Sauté onion in hot butter if desired until soft. Combine ground meat, onion, rice, tomato, parsley, dill, salt and pepper. Mix thoroughly with your hand. Place 1 Tbsp of the meat mixture on each of the half leaves. Fold base of leaf over filling, then fold in, sides and wrap into a roll. Place rolls in layers close to each other, seam side down. Repeat this process until you have finish all the cabbage leaves and the meat

mixture. Cover rolls with any tore leaves. Place an inverted heavy plate on top of the rolls. Add 3 cups stock or water, cover and cook slowly for approximately 60 minutes or until cabbage is tender. Arrange stuffed rolls on a serving platter. Keep warm. Drain pan juices, and add stock or chicken broth to make 2 1/2 cups. Transfer stock to a small saucepan. Bring to a boil. Mix cornstarch with 1/4 cup water to a paste. Slowly add to the stock stirring constantly. Cook slowly for 2 minutes. Spoon little by little of the hot sauce into eggs, stirring constantly. Slowly add egg mixture and the lemon juice to the sauce and cook over very low heat for 2-3 minutes, stirring constantly, (do not let the sauce boil). Season the sauce with salt and pepper. Remove from heat. Spoon the sauce over stuffed cabbage rolls, or pour sauce in a gravy dish. Serve immediately cabbage rolls with the sauce. Serves 6-8 as a main course or 12 as a first course.

❦❦❦

MEAT STUFFED GRAPE LEAVES
Dolmathakia with Meat Avgolemono

1 jar (16 ounces) grape leaves
1 pound lean ground beef
1/2 pound lean ground lamb
3/4 cup converted or long grain rice
1 medium finely chopped onion
Salt and pepper to taste
2 Tbsp. finely chopped fresh dill or 1/2 tsp. dried
1 Tbsp. finely chopped fresh mint or 1/4 tsp.
    dried crushed
1/4 cup butter or margarine
3 cups fresh beef stock or water
2 Tbsp. corn-starch
3 egg-yolks
Juice of 1 or more lemon

Remove grape leaves from the jar and rinse thoroughly. Plunge grape leaves one by one into boiling water, few at a time and boil for 2 minutes. Rinse them and drain. Cut off stems from leaves and reserve. Pick out few hard leaves. Line a Dutch oven with reserved stems and hard leaves. Combine meat, rice, onion, salt, pepper, dill and mint. Mix well with your hand until thoroughly blended. Place 1-tsp. filling on underside of each grape leaf. Fold base of leaf over filling, then fold in sides and wrap into a roll. Place rolls in layers close together, seam-side-down. Add butter and juice of half lemon. Place an inverted heavy plate on top of stuffed grape leaves. Add stock or water. Cover, cook slowly for approximately 45-55 minutes or until grape leaves are tender. Let stand for 15 minutes. Gently remove from pot and arrange into a serving platter. Drain stock from pot, add water or stock to make 2 cups. Transfer stock to a small saucepan, bring to a boil. Mix the corn-starch with 1/4 cup cool water to a paste. Slowly add to the stock, stirring constantly. Cook slowly for 5 minutes. Beat egg-yolks with the remaining lemon juice, gradually add some of the boiling sauce, stirring vigorously. Add egg mixture to the sauce and cook over very low heat for 2-3 minutes, stirring constantly. Don't boil the sauce. Spoon avgolemono sauce over stuffed grape leaves. or serve avgolemono sauce in a gravy dish. Serve immediately. Serves 6-10.

❧❀❧

MEAT STUFFED MUSHROOMS
Manitaria Gemista me Kima

24 large fresh button mushrooms (about 2" diameter)
Salt and pepper to taste
2 Tbsp olive oil
1 medium onion, finely chopped
8 ounces lean ground beef
8 ounces lean ground lamb
1/2 cup dry white wine or Vermouth (optional)
1 medium ripe tomato, peeled, seeded and
*   finely chopped*
1 Tbsp finely chopped flat leaf parsley
For the béchamel sauce:
33/4 Tbsp butter or good quality olive oil
33/4 Tbsp all-purpose flour
1 1/2 cups milk
2 eggs, beaten
Salt and white pepper to taste
1/2 cup grated Parmesan cheese
1/4 cup butter (optional)

Wash and drain mushrooms. Remove stems and reserve for other use. Sprinkle mushroom caps with salt and pepper. Place mushrooms in a baking pan lined with parchment. Bake in preheated 350 F (180 C) oven on middle rack 15 minutes. Prepare stuffing. Sauté onion in oil until soft. Add ground meat, stirring breading up clumps until brown. Add wine and cook until evaporates. Add salt, pepper, tomatoes and 2/3 cup water. Cover and cook slowly 45 minutes or until all liquid evaporates. Add parsley and stir well. While meat simmers prepare béchamel. Melt butter if desired over medium heat, blend in flour until smooth using wire whisk and cook 3 minutes. Remove from heat and gradually add milk, stirring constantly. Return to heat and cook stirring continuously until mixture is thick and smooth. Cook 2 minutes longer. Add seasoning and blend. Remove from heat. Spoon little by little of hot sauce into eggs, stirring constantly. Add egg mixture to sauce and cook over very low heat (do not let sauce boil), 2 minutes, stirring constantly. Remove from heat and add half the cheese. Place mushrooms in baking pan lined with parchment. Stuff each mushroom with meat mixture, then place 1 Tbsp béchamel on top of each mushroom to cover meat. Sprinkle each one with remaining cheese and place one small piece of butter on each mushroom if desired. Bake in preheated 350 F (180 C) oven 30 minutes or until golden brown. Serve immediately as a first course or as a lunch or dinner with a salad and fresh crusty bread. Serves 6-12.

❧❀❧

MEAT STUFFED PEPPERS
Piperies Ghemistes me Kyma

12 medium bell peppers
1 medium onion, minced
1 pound lean ground beef
1/2 pound lean ground lamb or pork
3 Tbsp olive oil
2 cloves garlic, minced
1/3 cup dry white wine or Vermouth
1 can (29-ounces) whole tomatoes, or 6 large ripe
*   tomatoes, pressed through a food mill*
2/3 cup converted rice
1 Tbsp minced flat leaf parsley
Salt and pepper to taste

Wash and dry peppers. Cut off tops of peppers and reserve; remove inner fibers and seeds, poke into few places with a fork. Set aside. Sauté onion in 2 Tbsp olive oil until soft, add ground meat, stirring breaking up clumps until brown. Add garlic and sauté few minutes longer. Add wine, 1 cup tomato puree, and bring to a boil. Add rice, and cook 5 minutes. Add parsley, salt and pepper. Fill prepared peppers with meat mixture and cover with reserved covers. Place peppers in deep baking casserole, add remaining tomato and olive oil. Cover. Place casserole on second lower rack in oven and bake peppers in preheated 350 F (180 C) 60 minutes or until tender. Serve hot, with feta cheese and fresh crusty bread. Serves 6.

❧❀❧

MEAT STUFFED TOMATOES
Ghemistes Domates me Kreas

12-14 medium round firm ripe tomatoes
1 pound lean ground beef
1/2 pound lean ground pork or lamb
1/3 cup olive oil
1/2 cup finely chopped onion
3/4 cup rice
1/2 cup dry white wine or Vermouth (optional)
Salt and pepper to taste
Some sugar (optional)
6 medium potatoes, peeled and cut into fourths
1/4 tsp granulated garlic
1/2 cup fine dried bread crumbs.

Wash and dry tomatoes. Cut off tops of tomatoes and reserve. Scoop out pulp and sprinkle cavities with a little sugar if desired. Turn tomatoes upside down to drain and set aside. Press pulp through food mill and reserve. Heat 2 Tbsp. oil and sauté onion and meat, breaking up clumps as it browns. Add wine if desired, rice, salt and pepper, sauté a few minutes longer. Add 1/2 cup remaining tomato pulp, cover and cook slowly 5 minutes. Fill tomatoes with meat mixture, cover with reserved tops and place in deep baking dish. Season potatoes with salt, pepper and garlic and toss well. Arrange potatoes between tomatoes. Spoon remaining oil over tomatoes and sprinkle with breadcrumbs. Add 1 1/2 cups remaining tomato pulp and 1 tsp. sugar if desired. Place pan on lower rack and bake in a preheated 375 F (190 C) oven for 90 minutes or until tomatoes are

cooked. Serve hot. Serves 6-7.

❧❀❧

MEAT STUFFED VEGETABLES
Lachanika Ghemista me Kyma

3 small eggplants (4-inches long and
   1 1/2-2-inches thick)
6 medium firm red round tomatoes
3 medium bell peppers, any color
3 zucchini the sizes of the eggplants
Sugar (optional)
1/2 cup olive oil
1 cup finely chopped onion
1 pound lean ground beef
1/2 pound lean ground lamb
1/2 pound lean ground pork, veal or beef
3/4 cup converted rice or long grain
2 Tbsp fine-minced fresh mint
Salt and pepper to taste
1/2 cup dry white wine or Vermouth (optional)
1/2 cup fine dried breadcrumbs (see index for recipe)
6 medium potatoes, peeled and cut into fourths
1/4 tsp or more granulated garlic

Wash and dry vegetables. Slice off tops of eggplants. Scoop out inside to within 1/2-inch of skin and poke into few places with a fork. Sprinkle cavities with salt and set aside. Slice off tops from tomatoes and reserve; scoop out pulp and sprinkle cavities with a little sugar if desired. Turn upside down and set aside. Press pulp through a food mill and reserve. Cut off tops of peppers and reserve; remove inner fibers and seeds and poke into few places with a fork. Cut off ends of zucchini and with an apple corer, or a baby spoon, scoop out pulp and sprinkle cavities with salt and set aside. Heat 3 Tbsp oil and sauté onion and meat together, breaking up clumps as it browns. Add rice, salt and pepper, sauté few minutes longer. Add wine if desired and 1 cup from reserved tomato pulp. Cover and slowly cook 5 minutes. Fill vegetables with meat mixture, cover with reserved covers and place in deep baking pan. Season potatoes with salt, pepper and garlic and toss well; arrange potatoes between vegetables. Spoon remaining oil over vegetables. Sprinkle tomatoes with breadcrumbs. Pour remaining tomato pulp and 1 cup water into pan. Place pan on lower rack in oven and bake in preheated 375 F (190 C) 90 minutes or until vegetables are tender. Serve hot. Serves 6-8.

✖❈✖

MEAT STUFFED ZUCCHINI AVGOLEMONO
Kolokythakia Ghemista Avgolemono

8 medium zucchini (5-inches long)
1 pound lean ground lamb or beef, or half and half
1/4 cup minced onion
2 Tbsp good quality olive oil
1 medium ripe tomato, peeled, seeded, chopped
2 Tbsp minced flat leaf parsley
2 Tbsp minced fresh dill
1/3 cup converted rice
1/4 cup dry white wine or Vermouth
Salt and pepper to taste
2 cups fresh beef stock, or low sodium
        100% fat free chicken broth
3 Tbsp cornstarch
1/2 cup cream, milk or water
2 extra large eggs, beaten
Juice of 1 lemon

Trim ends from zucchini, wash well and dry. With apple corer, scoop pulp out from zucchini. Sauté onion in butter if desired until soft. In large bowl combine ground meat, onion, chopped tomato, parsley, dill, rice, wine, salt, pepper and mix well with hand. Stuff zucchini shells with meat mixture. Arrange stuffed zucchini in Dutch oven, upright. Add stock or broth, cover and cook slowly for 60 minutes. Remove from heat. Let stand uncovered 15 minutes. Gently arrange stuffed zucchini on platter, keep warm. Drain pot juices, add stock or broth to make 2 cups, and pour in small saucepan. Bring to boil. Mix cornstarch with 1/2 cup cream if desired to a paste. Slowly add to stock, stirring constantly with whisk. Cook slowly 5 minutes. Add lemon juice to the beaten eggs. Spoon little by little of the hot sauce into eggs whisking constantly. Add egg mixture to the sauce and cook over very low heat for 2-3 minutes whisking constantly (don't let the sauce to boil). Spoon the sauce over stuffed zucchini. Serve immediately. Serves 4 as a main course or 8 as a first course.

✖❈✖

MUSHROOM TART
Tarta me Manitaria

1 pkg. Puff pastry (thawed)
2 pounds mushrooms
1 Tbsp butter or margarine
1 bunch scallions, thinly sliced
1 small garlic clove, minced
Salt and pepper to taste
1 pound coarsely grated Kaseri or Swiss cheese
4 extra large eggs
1/2 cup milk
1 cup cream
4 tsp cornstarch

Wash mushrooms under cold running water. Dry well. Sauté mushrooms in butter if desired until all liquid evaporates. Add scallions and garlic and sauté until soft. Season mixture with salt and pepper. Grease 9x13x2-inch baking dish. Prepare pastry as directed on box. Lay pastry on baking dish and sides. Spoon mushroom mixture on pastry and spread evenly. Beat eggs with milk, cream and cornstarch, add cheese, and pepper and mix well. Spoon egg cheese mixture over mushrooms and spread evenly. Bake in preheated 400 F (205 C) oven 30-40 minutes or until golden brown. Serve immediately.

✖❈✖

MUSHROOM-SQUASH SOUFFLÈ
Manitaria ke Kolokythi Soufflé

18 slices of white or dark bread
1/4 cup butter, margarine or olive oil
1/3 cup finely chopped onion
1 1/2 pounds mushrooms
2 1/2 pounds zucchini
Salt and pepper to taste
Pinch of Cayenne
5 ounces each coarsely grated Kaseri, and Swiss
1/4 cup grated Parmesan cheese
7 eggs, beaten with
5 cups milk

Wash mushrooms under cold running water. Dry on paper towels, and slice thinly. Wash zucchini, cut both ends, and shred. Place shredded zucchini in kitchen towel, and squeeze dry. Sauté onion in butter until soft. Add mushrooms and zucchini and cook on medium high heat, until liquid evaporates. Remove from heat and cool. In mushroom mixture combine rest of ingredients except eggs and milk, and mix well. In greased baking dish, place six slices of bread in one layer. Spread half the mushroom mixture. Place second layer of bread, and spread remaining mushroom mixture, and cover with remaining 6 slices of bread. Pour over egg mixture on top of bread, and poke with fork. Cove with plastic wrap, and chill 3 hours or until the bread absorbed milk mixture. Bake in preheated 375 F (190 C) oven 45 minutes or until golden. Serve immediately. Serves 6 as a main course or 12 as a first course.

❦❦❦

OVEN DRIED TOMATOES
Kseres Tomates Fournou

Red ripe firm Roma tomatoes
Coarse salt
Good quality olive oil
Chopped garlic, to your taste

Remove stem from tomatoes, cut in half lengthwise. Remove as many seeds as you can. Lay tomatoes skin-side-down on rack in baking pan lined with parchment. Sprinkle with coarse salt and let stand 60 minutes or longer. Bake in preheated 200 F (95 C) oven on middle rack 5-6 hours. Remove from oven and let cool. Place tomatoes and garlic in layers into sterilized jars and cover with good quality virgin olive oil and seal. Keep in refrigerator. Return to room temperature before serving.

❦❦❦

PEAS WITH MUSHROOMS
Araka me Manitaria

1 bunch scallions, chopped
1/2 cup or less olive oil
1/2 pound fresh mushrooms, thinly sliced
1 bag (20-ounces) frozen peas or fresh
2 Tbsp fresh dill, finely chopped
Salt and pepper to taste
Juice of 1/2 lemon

Sauté scallions in oil until soft. Add mushrooms and sauté until all juices evaporate. Add peas, dill, salt, pepper and 1/2 cup water, stir. Cover and cook slowly 15 minutes. Add lemon juice, cover and cook slowly 5 minutes longer or until tender. Serve hot or cold, with feta cheese and fresh crusty bread. Serves 4-6.

❦❦❦

PEAS WITH SCALLIONS
Arakas me Kremithakia

1 bunch scallions, chopped
1/2 cup or less olive oil
2 bags (1 pound each) frozen peas
Salt and pepper to taste
3 Tbsp fresh chopped dill
1/2 cup water

Sauté scallions in oil until soft. Add peas, salt, pepper and water. Stir, cover, bring to a boil, reduce heat to simmer and cook 10 minutes or until tender. Serve hot or cold with feta cheese and fresh crusty bread. Serves 6-8.

❦❦❦

PEAS WITH TOMATO
Araka me Ntomates

1 bunch scallions, chopped
1/2 cup or less olive oil
1 (8-ounces) can whole tomatoes, chopped or 3 large ripe tomatoes, peeled, seeded and chopped
1 Tbsp or more fresh dill, finely chopped
Salt and pepper to taste
1/2 cup water
1 bag (20-ounces) frozen peas or fresh

Sauté scallions in oil until soft. Add chopped tomatoes, dill, salt, pepper and water. Stir, cover and cook slowly 15 minutes. Add peas and stir. Cover and cook slowly 10-15 minutes longer or until tender. Serve hot or cold, with feta cheese and fresh crusty bread. Serves 4-6.

❦❦❦

POTATO CROQUETTES
Patates Krokettes

3/4 cup grated Kefalotyri (Greek cheese) or Parmesan cheese
5 cups mashed potatoes
2 Tbsp butter, margarine or good quality olive oil
1 Tbsp minced parsley
Dash of white pepper
3 egg yolks
Flour for dredging
3 egg whites, beaten
1 1/2 cups fine dried breadcrumbs (see index)
Oil for frying

In mixing bowl, combine cheese, potatoes, butter if desired, parsley, pepper and egg yolks, and mix well. Shape into small balls, the sizes of a walnut and roll in flour, egg and then crumbs. Chill 60 minutes or longer. Fry croquettes in hot oil 375 F (190 C) until golden brown on all both sides. Lift out and drain on absorbent paper. Serve hot.

～⋇∾⋇∾⋇～

POTATO PATTIES
Patatokeftethes

3 pounds potatoes
1 cup fresh grated Parmesan cheese
1 Tbsp minced flat leaf parsley
Salt and pepper to taste
4 extra large eggs
Flour for dredging
Oil for frying

Scrub potatoes and rinse. Boil in salted water 30 minutes or until tender. Drain well. Peel potatoes and press through food mill. In mixing bowl combine all ingredients except flour and oil and mix thoroughly. Cover and chill 60 minutes or longer. Shape into round patties, rather thick. Roll in flour, shake off excess and flatten. Fry in hot oil 375 F (190 C) until golden brown on both sides. Serve hot as a side dish. Serves 6-12.

～⋇∾⋇∾⋇～

POTATO MOUSAKA
Patates Mousaka

10 medium potatoes, about 4 pounds
1 cup minced onion
2 Tbsp olive oil
1 pound lean ground beef
1 pound lean ground lamb, or beef
1/2 cup dry white wine or Vermouth
1 (16-ounces) can whole tomatoes, finely chopped
or pressed through a food mill or
2 pounds Roma tomatoes, peeled, seeded and
      finely chopped
Salt and pepper to taste
1 cinnamon stick 1/2-inch long
1 Tbsp minced flat leaf parsley
2 Tbsp or more olive oil or melted butter for brushing
5 cups medium white sauce (see index for recipe)
4 extra large eggs, well beaten
1 cup grated Parmesan cheese
White pepper to taste

Wash and scrub potatoes well, then place in 8-quart pot, cover with water, and add 1 Tbsp salt. Bring to boil, reduce heat to medium and boil 15 minutes. Drain, peel and slice potatoes into 1/4-inch thick lengthwise. While potatoes are boiling prepare meat sauce. Sauté onion in oil until soft. Add meat, breaking up clumps as it browns. Add wine and sauté few minutes longer. Add tomato, 1/2 cup water, salt, pepper, cinnamon and parsley. Stir, cover and cook slowly 45 minutes. Remove from heat. Let stand. *Assembling the dish:* Arrange sliced potatoes in 14x12x3-inch greased baking pan or dish half the potatoes in a layer, and cover all empty spaces with pieces of potatoes. Brush with olive oil if desired and sprinkle with 1/4 cup grated cheese. Cover with meat sauce. Then cover with remaining sliced potatoes, and brush with remaining olive oil. Prepare white sauce as directed. Spoon little by little of hot sauce into beaten eggs, stirring constantly. Slowly add egg mixture to sauce and cook over very low heat 2 minutes, stirring constantly. (Don't let sauce boil). Remove from heat. Add 1/2 cup grated cheese, salt and white pepper and stir well. Spoon sauce over potatoes to cover and spread evenly. Sprinkle remaining grated cheese over sauce. Bake in preheated 350 F (180 C) oven 45 minutes or until golden brown. Let stand 20 minutes to cool before cutting into squares to serve. Serve hot. Serves about 12.

～⋇∾⋇∾⋇～

POTATO SOUFFLÈ
Patates Soufflé

5 cups hot mashed potatoes
3 Tbsp butter
3/4 cup warm milk
1 1/2 cups grated Kaseri or Swiss cheese
4 egg yolks, beaten until very light
4 egg whites, stiffly beaten
Salt and white pepper to taste

In large mixing bowl, combine all ingredients except egg whites, and mix on medium speed 3 minutes. Fold in egg whites. Pile soufflé in well-greased soufflé dish. Set dish in a pan containing hot water and bake in preheated 375 F (190 C) oven on middle rack 30 minutes. Serve immediately to prevent falling. Serve as a side dish with roasted meat or chicken. Serves 6-8.

❧❀❧

POTATO-MUSHROOM AU-GRATIN
Patates ke Manitaria Au-Graten

1 pound mushrooms
1 pound small potatoes
1/2 cup shallots, finely chopped
1 Tbsp good quality olive oil
1 Tbsp butter or margarine
Salt and pepper to taste
1 Tbsp finely chopped flat leaf parsley
5 Tbsp butter, margarine or good quality olive oil
    or mixed
5 Tbsp all-purpose flour
2 2/3 cups scalding milk
3 beaten eggs
5 ounces coarsely grated Swiss cheese
1/4 cup grated Parmesan cheese

Trim mushrooms and wash under cold running water. Dry and cut into fourths. Scrub and rinse potatoes, drop in lightly salted boiling water, and boil 20 minutes. Remove from water, peel and cut into 1/2-inch cubes. Sauté onion in oil and butter if desired, until soft. Add mushrooms to onions and sauté until all liquid evaporates, add potatoes and sauté few minutes longer, add parsley and season with salt and pepper. Remove from heat. Set aside. Prepare béchamel. In small saucepan, melt butter if desired over medium heat, blend in flour until smooth using wire whisk. Remove from heat and gradually add milk, stirring constantly. Return to heat and simmer until mixture is thick and smooth. Cook 3 minutes longer. Remove from heat. Spoon little by little of hot sauce into beaten eggs, stirring constantly, add egg mixture to sauce and cook over very low heat (do not let sauce boil) 2 minutes, stirring constantly. Season with salt and pepper and add shredded cheese and mix well. In well-greased baking dish, spoon mushroom potato mixture and spread evenly. Pour béchamel over and spread evenly, and sprinkle with Parmesan. Bake in preheated 350 F (180 C) oven 30 minutes or until golden brown. Serve immediately. Serves 4-6.

❧❀❧

POTATOES LEEKS AND CABBAGE GRATINEE
Patates Prasa ke Lachano Gratinee

2 pounds small potatoes
3 medium leeks
1 pound green cabbage, cored and thinly shredded
3 Tbsp butter or margarine
Salt, black and cayenne pepper to taste
1/2 pound coarsely grated Swiss cheese
1 cup whipping cream
3/4 cup fresh chicken stock or can low sodium
    and 100% fat free broth

Parboil potatoes in boiling salted water 5 minutes. Drain well; peel and thinly slice; let stand. Trim and wash leeks well, thinly slice and rinse again in strainer under cold running water. Drain well. In skillet sauté leeks in butter if desired, on medium heat 2 minutes. Add cabbage; toss to blend; cover, and let sweat 4 minutes. Uncover; raise heat, and cook, stirring until liquid evaporates. Generously grease 11-inch round and 2-inch deep baking casserole or dish. Layer 1/3 of potatoes in prepared casserole. Top with 1/2 the leek and cabbage mixture and 1/2 the cheese (reserve 1/2 cup cheese for top). Sprinkle with salt and peppers. Repeat layering. Arrange remaining potatoes on top. In same skillet, bring cream and broth to boil; pour over potatoes. Sprinkle reserved cheese over, and spread evenly. Bake casserole in preheated 325 F (165 C) oven 1 hour or until potatoes are tender when pierced with a fork. Serve hot. Serves 6-8.

❧❀❧

POTATO-CHEESE GRATINEE
Patates ke Tyri Gratine

3 pounds potatoes, peeled and shredded
1/2 cup whipping cream
1/2 cup strained yogurt
2 eggs
2 Tbsp prepared mustard
4-ounces coarsely grated Cheddar cheese
3 Tbsp butter, cut into small cubes
Salt and pepper to taste
Pinch of Cayenne pepper

With your hands squeeze shredded potatoes, and place them in a bowl. In a large bowl beat eggs, add cream, yogurt, mustard, cheeses, salt and peppers, and mix well. Add potatoes and mix well to combine. Spoon in well greased casserole dish and spread evenly, and dot with the butter. Bake in a preheated 350 F (180 C) oven for 60 minutes, or until golden brown. Serve hot.

❧❀❧

RICE STUFFED ARTICHOKES
Anginares Ghemistes me Rizi

10 artichokes, prepared (see index for Meat
*   Stuffed Artichokes)*
Juice of 1 lemon
1 cup converted rice
3/4 cup good quality olive oil
3 scallions, thinly sliced
1/4 cup tomato sauce
2 Tbsp. finely chopped flat leaf parsley
2 Tbsp. finely chopped dill
1 Tbsp. finely chopped mint
Salt and pepper to taste

In bowl combine all ingredients except artichokes and half the oil, mix well. Fill artichokes with filling and place in large saucepan in one layer. Add 3 cups water, the remaining oil salt, pepper and the juice of the lemon. Cover, bring to a boil, reduce heat and simmer until artichokes and rice are tender. Add more water if needed. Serve hot or cold. Serves 5 as a main course or 10 as a first course.

❧❀❧

RICE STUFFED CABBAGE LEAVES
Lahanodolmathes me Rizi

1 large or 2 medium Savoy cabbage
3/4 or more cup butter, margarine or 1/2 cup
*   or more good quality olive oil*
2 cups finely chopped onion
2 cups converted rice or long grain
1/2 cup pine nuts or slivered blanched almonds
2 Tbsp. finely chopped flat leaf parsley
Salt and pepper to taste
1 cup water or can of low sodium
*   100% fat free chicken broth*
2 medium ripe tomatoes pressed through food mill
4 cups water or 100% fat free chicken broth
1 cup milk or 1/2 cup milk and 1/2 cup cream

2 Tbsp. + 1 tsp. cornstarch
2 eggs, well beaten
Juice of 1 lemon or more
1/2 cup toasted slivered blanched almonds (optional)

Clean and prepare cabbage as directed in meat stuffed cabbage leaves (see index for recipe). Sauté onion in hot butter if desired until soft, add rice and sauté for few minutes longer. Add pine nuts if desired, tomato, water or broth, parsley, salt and pepper. Stir, cover and cook slowly for 5 minutes. Remove from heat. Place 1 Tbsp. of the rice mixture on each of the half leaves. Fold base of leaf over filling, then fold in sides and wrap into a roll. Place rolls in layers, close to each other, seam side down. Place an inverted heavy plate on top of rolls. Add water or broth, cover, and cook slowly for approximately 60 minutes or until cabbage is tender. Gently arrange stuffed cabbage rolls on a serving platter. Keep warm. Drain pan juices, add water or broth to make 2 cups. Transfer stock to a small saucepan. Add milk if desired and bring to a boil. Mix corn starch with 1/2 cup water or broth to a paste. Slowly add to the stock stirring constantly. Cook slowly for 2 minutes. Spoon little by little of the hot sauce into eggs, stirring constantly. Slowly add egg mixture and the lemon juice to the sauce and cook over very low heat for 2-3 minutes, stirring constantly. Remove from heat. Spoon sauce over stuffed rolls and sprinkle toasted almonds over if desired. Serve immediately. Serves 6 as a main course or 12 as a first course.
Note: You can omit the eggs if desires. Serves plain, spoon pan juices and sprinkle toasted almonds over if desired.

❧❀❧

RICE STUFFED GRAPE LEAVES
Dolmathakia me Rizi

1 jar (16 ounces) grape leaves
4 cups grated onions (4 large onions about)
1 cup olive oil
2 cups sort or long grain rice
1 1/3 cups boiling water
1/2 cup finely chopped fresh dill or 1 tsp. dried
1/3 cup finely chopped fresh mint or 3/4 tsp. dried,
crushed

Salt and pepper to taste
1/2 cup or more chopped blanched almonds or
1/3 of cup pine nuts
21/4 cups boiling water
Juice of 1 or more lemons

Remove grape leaves from jar and rinse thoroughly. Plunge grape leaves one by one into boiling water, few at a time and boil 2 minutes. Rinse and drain. Cut off stems from leaves and reserve. Pick out few hard leaves and set aside. Line bottom of Dutch oven with reserved stems and hard leaves. Sauté onion with 1/2 cup olive oil until soft. Add rice and sauté for few minutes. Add boiling water, dill, mint, salt and pepper. Cover and cook slowly 5 minutes. Remove from heat. Cool. Add almonds if desired, mix thoroughly. Place 1 tsp. filling on underside of each grape leaf. Fold bale of leaf over filling, then fold in sides and wrap into a roll. Place rolls in layers close together, seam-side-down. Add remaining oil and lemon juice. Place an inverted heavy plate on top of stuffed grape leaves. Add boiling water. Cover, cook slowly 45 minutes or until grape leaves are tender and pot juices have evaporated. Let stand 1/2 hour to cool. Gently remove from pot and arrange onto a serving platter. Decorate with thin lemon slices. Serve warm or cold with plain yogurt if desired.

❦❧❦

RICE STUFFED TOMATOES AND PEPPERS
Ghemistes Domates ke Piperies

6 medium round firm ripe tomatoes
6 medium bell peppers
Some sugar (optional)
1 cup minced onion
3 cloves minced garlic
1 cup olive oil
1 cup long or sort grain rice
1 small grated zucchini
1 small grated eggplant
2 Tbsp, minced parsley
1 Tbsp. minced fresh mint
Salt and pepper to taste
6 medium potatoes, peeled and cut into fourths
1/4 tsp or more granulated garlic
1/4 cup fine dried breadcrumbs

Wash and dry the tomatoes and peppers. Cut off

tops of tomatoes and reserve. Scoop out pulp and sprinkle cavity with a little sugar if desired. Turn tomatoes upside down and set aside. Cut off tops of peppers and reserve. Remove inner fibers and seeds, poke into few places with a fork. Set aside. Chop large tomato pulp pieces, the rest press through a food mill and reserve. Sauté onion with 1/2 cup oil until soft. Add garlic and sauté few minutes longer. Add grated zucchini and eggplant, the chopped tomato, salt and pepper, stir and cook slowly 5 minutes. Add 1 cup boiling water, rice and stir, cover and cook slowly 5 minutes. Remove pot from heat. Add parsley and mint. Fill tomatoes with rice mixture, cover them with reserved covers and place in a deep baking pan. Add 1 cup of reserved tomato pureed to the rest of rice mixture and stir, fill peppers with rice mixture and cover with reserved covers. Place with stuffed tomatoes. Season potatoes with salt, pepper and garlic and toss well. Arrange potatoes between tomatoes and peppers. Spoon remaining oil over tomatoes and sprinkle with breadcrumbs. Pour reserved tomato pureed. Place pan on lower rack in oven and bake in preheated 375 F (190 C) 90 minutes or until tomatoes and peppers are tender. Serve hot or cold. Serves 6.

❦❧❦

RICE STUFFED VEGETABLES
Lachanika Ghemista me Rizi

3 small eggplants (4-inches long and
1 1/2-2-inches thick)
6 medium firm red round tomatoes
Sugar (optional)
3 medium bell pepper, (any color)
3 zucchini the same size as the eggplants
1 1/4 cups minced onion
4 garlic cloves, minced
1 1/4 cups more or less olive oil
3 large red ripe tomatoes, peeled, seeded, chopped
1 1/2 cups, long grain rice
1/2 cup minced flat leaf parsley
1/4 cup minced mint
1 Tbsp or more minced dill
6 medium potatoes, peeled and cut into fourths
1/4 tsp or more granulated garlic
1/4 cup fine dried breadcrumbs (see index for recipe)

Wash and dry the vegetables. Slice off the tops

of the eggplants. Scoop out inside to within 1/2-inch of skin and poke into few places with a fork. Finely chop and reserve eggplant pulp. Sprinkle cavities with little salt and set aside. Slice off tops of tomatoes and reserve; scoop out pulp and sprinkle cavities with a little sugar if desired. Turn upside down to drain and set a side. Press pulp through food mill and reserve. Cut off tops of peppers and reserve; remove inner fibers and seeds, poke into few places with a fork. Trim ends from zucchini and with an apple corer, scoop out pulp, sprinkle with little salt and set aside. Finely chop and reserve zucchini pulp. Sauté onion with 2/3 cup of the oil until soft, add garlic and sauté few minutes longer. Add chopped eggplant and zucchini pulp, chopped tomatoes, salt and pepper, stir and cook slowly 5 minutes. Add 1 cup boiling water, rice and stir well, cover; and cook slowly 2 minutes. Remove from heat, add parsley, mint and dill and stir well to combine. Fill vegetables with rice mixture, cover with reserved covers and place in deep baking pan. Season potatoes with salt, pepper and garlic and toss well. Arrange potatoes between vegetables. Spoon remaining oil over tomatoes and sprinkle with breadcrumbs. Pour reserved pureed tomato, 1 tsp. sugar if desired and 1 cup water. Place pan on lower rack in over and bake in preheated 400 F 205 C) 90 minutes or until vegetables are tender. Serve hot or cold with feta cheese and fresh crusty bread. Serves 6-8.

※※※

ROASTED EGGPLANT
Melitzanes Psites

3 pounds large eggplants
Good quality olive oil for brushing
Salt

Remove stems of eggplants, rinse well. Peel if desired and cut into 1/3-inch slices crosswise. Lightly brush eggplant slices with olive oil and arrange in baking sheet lined with parchment, oiled side down. Brush top again with oil, bake in preheated 500 F (260 C) oven on second lower rack 20 minutes. Remove from oven and place

on serving platter. Repeat with remaining slices, using same parchment paper. Serve with Skorthalia sauce or Tzatziki dip (see index), and fresh crusty bread. Serves 6-8.

※※※

ROASTED SPICED POTATOES
Patates Myrothates to Fournou

5 pounds potatoes, peeled and cut into fourths
Salt and pepper to taste
1 Tbsp granulated garlic or more
1/2 tsp crushed Greek oregano
Juice of 2 lemons, more or less
1/2 cup or less olive oil
2 cups water

Place potatoes in large baking pan, sprinkle with salt, pepper, garlic and oregano, and toss well. Sprinkle with lemon juice and olive oil. Add water to pan. Bake in preheated 400 F. (205 C) oven 60 minutes or until golden brown. Serve as a side dish. Serves 6-8.

※※※

SPANAKORIZO
Spinach with Rice

4 pounds fresh spinach or 2 bags (16-ounces each)
frozen, cut leaf spinach (thawed), well drained
*   and chopped*
1/2 cup or less olive oil
1 bunch scallions, chopped
2 Tbsp finely chopped fresh dill
Salt and pepper to taste
1/4 cup tomato sauce or 3 medium ripe tomatoes,
*   peeled, seeded and finely chopped*
1 1/2 cups boiling water
1/2 cup long grain rice
Juice of 1 or more lemons

If spinach is fresh, remove roots and coarse leaves. Wash thoroughly. Drop spinach in 1 cup boiling water and bring to a boil. Boil 1 minute. Remove from heat and drain in a strainer. Drain moisture and chop. Let stand. Sauté scallions in oil until soft. Add spinach, stir well and sauté a few minutes more. Add the water, tomato sauce if desired, dill, salt and pepper. Stir, cover and cook 5 minutes. Sprinkle rice on top of spinach and push it down with a spoon until it is covered with the liquid, don't stir. Cover and simmer 20 minutes. Remove from heat, add lemon juice, and stir well to combine. Serve hot or cold, with feta cheese or meat and fresh crusty bread. Serves 4-6 as a main course or 8-10 as a first course.

❧❦❧

SPINACH CHEESE SOUFFLÈ
Spanaki ke Tyri Soufflé

1 large bunch of fresh spinach
2 scallions, finely sliced
1 Tbsp butter or margarine
1 Tbsp finely chopped flat leaf parsley
1 Tbsp finely chopped fresh dill
4 Tbsp all-purpose flour
4 Tbsp butter or margarine
1 cup scalding milk
Salt and pepper to taste
3 eggs, separated
1 cup pressed down coarsely grated Kaseri cheese
1/3 cup lightly pressed down grated Kefalotyri or Parmesan cheese

Remove stems and coarse leaves from plant and discard, keep only leaves and wash in several waters. Drain well and dry between kitchen towels. Chop into small pieces. Set aside. In a medium nonstick frying pan sauté scallions in hot butter if desired, until soft. Add spinach and sauté on high heat until spinach is wilted and liquid evaporates. Remove from heat. Spoon spinach mixture to a bowl, and add parsley, dill, salt and pepper. Prepare béchamel. In small saucepan, melt butter, over medium heat blend in flour until smooth using a whisk. Remove from heat and gradually add milk, stirring constantly until mixture is thick and smooth. Cook 3 minutes longer; add seasoning and blend. Spoon little by little of hot sauce into beaten egg yolks, stirring constantly. Gradually add egg mixture to sauce, and cook over very low heat 2 minutes, stirring constantly. Remove from heat, and let cool. Add spinach mixture and cheeses and mix well, and fold stiffly beaten egg whites. Grease a soufflé dish and spoon in the mixture. Bake in preheated 375 F (190 C) oven on middle rack for 30-45 minutes. Serve immediately.

❧❦❧

SPINACH GRATINEE
Spanaki Gratine

31/2 pounds fresh spinach
1/4 cup good quality olive oil
1 bunch scallions, finely chopped
Salt and pepper to taste
1/3 cup cream or milk
1/2 cup pressed down grated Parmesan or Pecorino cheese
4 ounces coarsely grated Kaseri or Swiss cheese

For the béchamel sauce:
6 Tbsp butter, margarine or olive oil
10 Tbsp all-purpose flour
4 cups scalding whole or 2% milk
3 extra large eggs, beaten

Clean spinach by removing roots and coarse leaves. Wash spinach several times in cold water, to get rid of the sand. Drain. Drop spinach in 1 cup of boiling water, and bring to boil, stirring and turning until it is wilted. Remove from heat and drain in strainer. With your hands, squeeze out excess water, and chop. Sauté scallions in 1/4 cup of oil until soft. Add spinach to scallions, salt and pepper and stir well, sauté 10 minutes or until liquid has evaporated. Add cream if desired and cook on low heat 3 minutes. Let stand. Prepare béchamel. In 3-quart saucepan melt butter if desired over medium heat, blend in flour until smooth using a wire whisk. Remove from heat and gradually add milk, stirring constantly. Return to heat and cook until it thickens, stirring constantly. Cook 3 minutes longer. Add seasoning and blend. Remove from heat and spoon little by little of hot sauce into beaten eggs, stirring constantly. Add egg mixture to sauce and continue stirring. Return to heat and cook 2 minutes longer. Remove from heat and let cool. Mix Parmesan and Kaseri cheese together. Add cheese except 1 cup to sauce and stir well to combine. *Assembling the dish:* Add 2 cups of sauce to spinach and stir well. In greased 9x13x2-inch baking casserole spread spinach evenly. Spoon remaining sauce over spinach and spread evenly. Sprinkle remaining cheese over sauce. Bake gratinee in preheated 375 F (190 C) oven on middle rack 30 minutes or until bubbling hot and sauce has browned nicely. Let stand 20 minutes. Serve as side dish with any kind of meat. Serves 6-12.

✻⊱✿⊰✻

SPINACH MOUSAKA
Spanaki Mousaka

21/2 pounds fresh spinach or 2 bags (16-ounces)
        each frozen, cut leaf spinach (thawed), well
        drained and chopped
4 Tbsp olive oil or butter
1/2 cup minced onion
1 pound lean ground beef
1/3 cup dry white wine or Vermouth
1/2 cup tomato sauce
Salt and pepper to taste
3 cups medium white sauce (see index for recipe)
3 large well-beaten eggs
1/2 cup grated Parmesan cheese
White pepper to taste

If spinach is fresh, remove roots and coarse leaves. Wash thoroughly. Drop spinach in 1 cup boiling water, and bring to a boil. Boil 1 minute. Remove from heat and drain in strainer. Drain all moisture and chop. Let stand. Sauté onion in 2 Tbsp. oil if desired until soft. Add ground meat and brown breaking up clumps as it browns. Add wine and sauté a few minutes longer. Add tomato sauce, 1/2 cup water, salt and pepper, stir, cover and cook slowly 45 minutes or until all liquid has absorbed. Remove from heat. Let stand. While meat sauce simmers, prepare white sauce as directed. Spoon hot saucelittle by little into beaten eggs, stirring constantly. Slowly add egg mixture to sauce and cook over very low heat 2 minutes stirring constantly, (don't let sauce boil). Add 1/3 cup grated cheese, salt and white pepper to sauce and stir well. Sauté spinach in oil if desired for few minutes. Spoon spinach in 12x11x3-inch greased baking dish. Cover spinach with meat sauce. Spoon white sauce to cover meat and spread evenly. Sprinkle with remaining grated cheese over sauce. Bake in a preheated 350 F (180 C) oven for 45 minutes or until golden brown. Let stand 15 minutes to cool. Cut into squares to serve. Serves 4-6 as a main course or 8-10 as a first course.

✻⊱✿⊰✻

SPINACH SOUFFLÈ
Spanaki Soufflé

2 pounds fresh spinach or 2 pounds frozen, cut leaf
        spinach (thawed), well drained and chopped
1/4 cup finely chopped onion
1 Tbsp butter or margarine
2 cups thick béchamel sauce (see index for recipe)
6 egg yolks, beaten until very light
6 egg whites, stiffly beaten
Salt and pepper to taste
1 cup grated Kaseri, Kefalotyri or Parmesan cheese

If spinach is fresh, remove roots and coarse leaves. Wash spinach in several waters, to get rid of the sand. Place spinach in 1 cup boiling water, and bring to boil. Boil 1 minute. Remove from heat and drain in a strainer. Cool spinach enough to handle and with your hands squeeze out excess water, and chop. Sauté onion in butter if desired until soft. Let stand. Prepare thick béchamel sauce as directed. When sauce is cool add beaten egg yolks, and stir to combine. Add spinach, cheese and onion to sauce, and stir well. Add egg whites and fold. Spoon soufflé into non-greased soufflé dish and bake in preheated 325 F (165 C) oven 60 minutes. Serve at once to prevent falling. Serves 8.

✻⊱✿⊰✻

SQUASH AND MEAT CASSEROLE
Kolokythi ke Kymas sto Fourno

4 pounds zucchini and yellow squash, mixed
Salt and pepper to taste
4 Tbsp good quality olive oil
1 pound lean ground beef
1/2 pound lean ground lamb
1 bunch scallions, finely sliced
1/4 cup lightly pressed down finely chopped
        flat leaf parsley
2 Tbsp finely chopped dill
7 extra large eggs, beaten
1/2 cup grated Kefalotyri, Pecorino Romano
        or Parmesan cheese

Wash squashes well, grate and sprinkle with salt and let drain in colander 60-90 minutes. While squash is draining, prepare meat. In large frying pan heat oil and sauté meat, breaking up clumps as it browns. Add scallions and sauté until soft. Season with pepper, add parsley, dill and grated squash, stir well to combine. Cook until liquid is absorbed. Season again if needed. Remove from heat and let cool 10 minutes. Add beaten eggs, little at a time, stirring constantly until you have finish with the eggs. Spoon mixture into greased casserole, and sprinkle with grated cheese. Bake in preheated 350 F (180 C) oven on middle rack 30 minutes or until golden brown. Serve hot with a salad and fresh crusty bread. Serves 6-8.

❧❀❧

STRING BEANS WITH MUSHROOMS
Fasolakia me Manitaria

2 pound string beans
1 pound fresh mushrooms, sliced
1 medium onion, thinly sliced lengthwise
2 garlic cloves, sliced
1 (16-ounces can) whole tomatoes, chopped
2 Tbsp. chopped flat leaf parsley
1/2 cup or less good quality olive oil
Salt and pepper to taste
1 cup water

Wash beans, string and snap them. Cut into 1 1/2-inch long pieces. Place all the ingredients together in a saucepan. Stir well. Cover and cook slowly for 60 minutes or until vegetables are tender. Serve hot or cold with feta cheese and fresh crusty bread. Serves 4-6.

❧❀❧

STRING BEANS WITH POTATOES
Fasolakia me Patates Lathera

2 pounds sting beans
1 medium onion, thinly sliced lengthwise
2 or more garlic cloves, sliced
4 medium size ripe tomatoes, peeled, seeded
  and chopped
2 Tbsp. chopped flat leaf parsley
Salt and pepper to taste
1/2 cup or less olive oil
1 1/2 cups water
2-3 medium size potatoes, peeled and cut
  into quarters

Wash beans, string and snap them. Cut into 1 1/2-inch long pieces. Place all ingredients together except potatoes in 4-quart saucepan. Stir well to combine. Cover and cook slowly 30 minutes. Add potatoes and 1/2 cup boiling water, press

potatoes down with a spoon, to cover with liquid, cover; and cook slowly 45-60 minutes or until beans and potatoes are tender. Shake pan occasionally. Do not stir. Serve hot or cold with feta cheese and fresh crusty bread. Serves 4-6.

❧❀❧

STUFFED TOMATOES SURPRISE
Ghemistes Ntomates Surprise

12 medium ripe tomatoes
1/2 of the recipe Chicken or Turkey Rice gratinee
  (see index for recipe)

Wash and dry tomatoes. Cut off bottom of tomatoes and discard. Gently scoop out pulp of tomatoes and save for other use. Turn tomatoes upside down to drain. Follow recipe and preparation as directed in chicken or turkey rice gratinee. Fill tomatoes with chicken rice mixture. Sprinkle with grated cheese and bake in preheated 450 F (230 C) oven 15 minutes. Serve immediately as a first course, or as a lunch. Serves 6-12.

❧❀❧

VEGETABLES GRATINEE
Lachanika Gratinee

3/4 cup more or less good quality olive oil
2 pounds potatoes, peeled rinsed and thinly sliced
8 ounces carrots, peeled rinsed and thinly sliced
2 pounds large eggplant, rinsed and thinly sliced
5-6 medium size ripe tomatoes, rinsed and
  thinly sliced
2 large onions, peeled and thinly sliced
2 pounds small zucchini, rinse and thinly sliced
4 ounces of each coarsely grated Kaseri and
  Swiss cheese
10 Tbsp butter, margarine or 1/3 cup good
  quality olive oil
10 Tbsp all-purpose flour
4 cups scalding milk
3 extra large eggs, beaten
1/4 cup grated Parmesan cheese
Salt and pepper to taste

In a greased 14x11 1/2 x3-inch baking dish, first arrange potatoes slices, season with salt and pepper and lightly sprinkle with olive oil and 1/4 cup of Kaseri and Swiss cheese mixture. Second the carrots with the same order. Repeat

Nougat Torte

Loukoumathes

Kataifi

Karythopit[a]

Koulourakia and
Paxithakia

Galaktobouroko

Baklava

Greek Coffee

Pasta Flora

until you have finish layering. Top with remaining tomatoes slices, season with salt, pepper and olive oil, and no cheese. Bake in preheated 350 F (180 C) oven on middle rack 45 minutes or until vegetables are almost tender when pierced with a fork. While vegetables are baking, prepare white sauce. Melt butter if desired over medium heat, blend in flour until smooth using wire whisk. Cook 2 minutes longer, stirring constantly. Remove from heat and gradually add milk, stirring constantly, return to heat and cook until mixture is thick and smooth, stirring continuously. Cook 3 minutes longer. Remove from heat. Spoon little by little of hot sauce into eggs, stirring continuously. Add egg mixture to sauce and cook over very low heat (do not let sauce boil), 2 minutes. Remove from heat and add seasoning and the grated Parmesan, and mix well to combine. Remove dish from oven and spoon béchamel over vegetables, and spread evenly. Sprinkle remaining grated Kaseri and Swiss cheese. Return to oven, raise temperature to 375 F (190 C) and bake 20 minutes longer or until golden brown. Remove from oven and let rest 20-30 minutes. Serve with a large spoon as a main coarse or as a side dish.

❧❀❧

VEGETABLE CHEESE STUFFED TOMATOES
Tomates Ghemistes me Lachanika

12 red ripped medium tomatoes
1 large eggplant (about 1 1/2-2 pounds)
1 small shallot, minced
1 large garlic clove, minced
Good quality olive oil
1 cup cooked rice
1 cup dried breadcrumbs
3/4 cup crumbled feta cheese
2 Tbsp finely chopped flat leaf parsley
1 Tbsp finely chopped dill
Salt and pepper to taste

Wash and dry tomatoes. Cut off tops of tomatoes and reserve. Scoop out pulp and reserve, sprinkle cavity with a little of sugar if desired. Turn them upside down to drain and let them stand. Wash eggplant and cut into 1/4-inch thin slices. Place eggplant slices into baking sheet lined with parchment. Brush slices with olive oil, turn them upside down and brush again. Sprinkle with a little salt and bake in preheated 450 F (230 C) oven 15-20 minutes or until soft and golden brown. Remove from oven, transfer to plate and chop into small pieces. While eggplant is baking, sauté shallot with 2 Tbsp olive oil until soft. Add garlic and sauté few minutes longer. Chop tomato pulp into small pieces. In large bowl add eggplant, shallot mixture, rice, 1/3 cup of breadcrumbs, feta, parsley, dill, salt, pepper and one half the tomato pulp. Mix well. Fill tomatoes with eggplant mixture, place them in a baking pan, and covre with reserved tops. Add to pan remaining tomato pulp, 1/4 cup of olive oil, salt and pepper. Brush tops of tomato with olive oil and sprinkle with remaining dried breadcrumbs. Serve hot or at room temperature. Serves 6-12.

❧❀❧

BOILED ZUCCHINI
Kolokythakia Brasta

12 small thin zucchini (4-5-inches long)
1 Tbsp salt
1/2 cup or less good quality extra virgin olive oil
Juice of 1 lemon

Trim off and discard zucchini stems . Rinse well. Leave whole. Drop zucchini in boiling salted water. Bring to boil. Reduce heat to medium and boil partially covered 20 minutes or until tender. Gently drain well. Slice and place in serving bowl. In small bowl beat oil with the lemon. Pour olive oil mixture over zucchini slices. Serve hot or cold. Serves 6-8.

❧❀❧

FRIED ZUCCHINI
Kolokythakia Tighanita

*2 pounds medium zucchini (4-6-inches long and
        1-1 1/2-inches thick)*
Salt
1 1/2 cups all-purpose flour
Olive or salad oil for frying
Garlic or Tzatziki sauce (see index for recipe)

Trim ends from the zucchini and wash and dry well. Cut into 1/4-inch slices. Sprinkle with salt.

Let stand for 30 minutes or longer. Dredge zucchini slices into the flour. Shake off excess flour. Dip fry in 375 F (190 C) hot oil on both sides, until golden brown. Drain on paper towels. Serve hot with garlic sauce or tzatziki if desired. Serves 4-6.

❦❦❦❦

ZUCCHINI AND CHEESE PATTIES
Kolokythakia me Tyri Tighanites

2 pounds zucchini
1 large garlic clove, minced
1 small onion, grated
2 Tbsp finely chopped flat leaf parsley
2 extra large eggs
1/2 cup grated Parmesan cheese
Salt and pepper to taste
1 cup or more all-purpose flour
Good quality olive oil for frying

Wash and trim zucchini. Grate them with onion-grater. Combine 7 first ingredients and mix well. Add enough flour to make a thick batter. Spoon the zucchini mixture in hot oil and fry on both sides until golden brown. Serve hot or cold plain or with Skorthalia or Tzatziki sauce (see index).

❦❦❦❦

ZUCCHINI PATTIES
Kolokithokeftethes

3 pounds small zucchini
3 Tbsp good quality olive oil
1 cup finely chopped onion
1 cup grated Parmesan, Kefalotyri, Romano
    cheese or mixed
1 1/2 cups dried breadcrumbs (see index for recipe)
3 large eggs, lightly beaten
1/4 cup finely chopped flat leaf parsley
1/4 cup finely chopped dill
Salt and pepper to taste
Pinch of Cayenne pepper
Flour for dredging
Good quality olive oil for frying

Trim ends from zucchini and wash well. Boil zucchini in 2 cups boiling salted water and boil 20 minutes or until soft. Drain well. Arrange zucchini on paper towels to absorb extra moisture. Sauté onion in oil until soft. Place zucchini in large bowl, and mash well with fork.

Combine all ingredients except flour and olive oil, and mix well with your hand. If mixture is not thick enough add more breadcrumbs. Chill 1-2 hours or longer if desired. Shape mixture into balls, and dredge them in flour. Shake well with hands to remove excess flour. Fry balls in frying pan with hot oil, and brown on both sides. Serve hot or cold with Tzatziki or Scorthalia (see index for recipes), and fresh crusty bread. Serves 8-12.

❦❦❦❦

ZUCCHINI LITTLE SHOES
Kolokythakia Papoutsakia

1 pound lean ground lamb or beef (or half of each)
1/4 cup minced shallots
1 Tbsp good quality olive oil
1/2 cup dry white wine or Vermouth
1/3 tomato sauce
Salt and pepper to taste
1 Tbsp minced flat leaf parsley
2 Tbsp minced fresh dill
1 Tbsp dried breadcrumbs (see index for recipe)
1 extra large beaten egg (optional)
1 cup medium béchamel sauce (see index for recipe)
1 extra large beaten egg
1/2 cup grated Parmesan cheese
6-8 medium zucchini (5-inches long)
1 cup fresh beef or chicken stock or low sodium
    100% fat free chicken broth

Sauté onion in butter if desired until soft. Add ground meat and brown, breaking up clumps as you go. Add wine and sauté a few minutes longer. Add tomato, salt, pepper, parsley, dill and 1/2 cup water to meat and stir. Cover and cook slowly 45 minutes or until liquid evaporates. Remove from heat. Add breadcrumbs, 2 Tbsp. grated cheese, and 1 beaten egg if desired, stir well. Let stand. While meat sauce is simmering, prepare zucchini. Trim ends from zucchini and wash well. Drop zucchini in boiling salted water, and boil 10 minutes. Drain well, and cut in half lengthwise. Remove pulp from zucchini being careful to keep little shoes intact. In greased baking dish place zucchini, stuff with meat mixture and smooth surface. Prepare white sauce as directed. Spoon little by little of hot sauce into beaten egg, whisking constantly. Add egg mixture to sauce and cook over very low heat 2 minutes whisking constantly (don't let sauce to boil). Remove from heat. Add 5 Tbsp. grated cheese and stir well. Place 1 Tbsp. sauce on each little shoe to cover meat. Sprinkle with remaining grated cheese, add stock to pan and bake in preheated 350 F (180 C) oven 1 hour. Serve hot.

ZUCCHINI-MUSHROOM GRATINEE
Kolokythi ke Manitaria Gratine

2 pounds zucchini
1 pound mushrooms
2 Tbsp minced shallots
Salt and pepper to taste
1/4 cup butter, margarine or good quality olive oil
Pinch of pepper Cayenne
1/4 cup pine nuts, toasted
5 Tbsp butter, margarine or olive oil
6 Tbsp all-purpose flour
3 cups scalding milk
5 beaten eggs
2 cups lightly pressed down, coarsely grated Swiss,
    Kaseri cheese mixed
1/4 cup lightly pressed down grated Parmesan cheese

Trim and wash zucchini. Dry with paper towels, and shred. Place zucchini in a strainer and sprinkle lightly with salt, let stay for an hour or more. Trim mushrooms, wash rapidly under cold running water, dry with paper towels, and cut into thin slices. Place zucchini in cheesecloth and squeeze dry. In non-stick frying pan sauté in 2 Tbsp butter if desired over high heat 5-6 minutes or until all liquid evaporates. Season to taste with salt and peppers. Remove from heat and pan. In same pan sauté mushrooms in remaining butter over high heat 5-6 minutes or until all liquid evaporates. Then stir in shallots and sauté 1 to 2 minutes. Season to taste with salt and peppers. Remove from heat. Prepare béchamel. Melt butter if desired over medium heat, blend in flour until smooth using a whisk. Remove from heat and gradually add milk, stirring constantly. Return to heat and simmer until mixture is thick

and smooth, stirring constantly. Cook 3 minutes longer; add salt and pepper to taste. Remove from heat. Spoon little by little of hot sauce into eggs, stirring constantly. Gradually add egg mixture to sauce and cook over very low heat 2-3 minutes (do not let sauce boil), stirring constantly Remove from heat. In large bowl combine zucchini, mushrooms, pine nuts, shredded cheeses, and sauce and mix well. Spoon mixture in well greased 9x13x2 1/2 -inch rectangular dish and spread evenly. Sprinkle with Parmesan. Bake in preheated 375 F (190 C) oven 30 minutes or until golden brown. Serve immediately. Serve 8-10 as a first course or 6 as a main course.

ZUCCHINI SOUFFLÈ
Kolosythakia Soufflé

1/2 cup minced onion
1/4 cup butter, margarine or good quality olive oil
3 pounds small zucchini
 2 cups thick béchamel sauce (see index for recipe)
5 extra large egg-yolks, well beaten
5 egg whites, stiffly beaten with pinch of salt
Salt and pepper to taste
2 Tbsp finely minced fresh dill
1 cup grated Parmesan and Romano cheese mixed

Trim ends from zucchini and wash well. Dry, and shred zucchini. Place zucchini in colander and sprinkle lightly with salt, toss well. Let stand 30 minutes. With your hand take one handfull at a time, and squeeze out excess liquid. Sauté onion in butter if desired, until soft. Add prepared zucchini and sauté until soft and dry, add dill, and let cool. Prepare white sauce as directed. When sauce is cool, add beaten egg-yolks and stir well. Add onion zucchini mixture, cheese, and pepper to sauce, stir well. Gently fold in beaten egg whites. Spoon mixture into non-greased soufflé dish and bake in preheated 325 F (165 C) oven 60 minutes. Serve at once to prevent falling. Serves 8-10.

CHEESE & EGGS

CHEESE TART
Tarta Myzithras

For the crust:
2 cups all-purpose flour
1 tsp baking powder
1/4 tsp cinnamon
1/8 tsp salt
1/2 cup sugar
2/3 cup unsalted butter
1 egg, beaten
2 Tbsp of cold water

For the cheese filling:
4 eggs
3/4 cup sugar
1 pound unsalted mysithra (Greek cheese)
8 ounces cream cheese, at room temperature
1 cup milk
2 Tbsp all-purpose flour
1/8 tsp salt
1 tsp vanilla
1/2 tsp cinnamon
1/3 cup toasted chopped or slivered blanched almonds
1/4 cup sugar

Sift dry ingredients together. Cut in butter with a pastry blender until the mixture resembles coarse meal. Add beaten egg, water using 1 Tbsp at a time and toss to blend. Gather pastry together and form into a ball. Roll out the pastry on parchment paper from center to edges. Use short light strokes. Roll the pastry about 1-inch larger all around to a 10-11-inch tart pan. (I prefer glass or ceramic tart pan lined with parchment paper). Place your hand under and in the middle of the parchment paper and pastry and carefully invert and fit loosely in the bottom and sides of pan; press lightly to fit snug. Gently remove the parchment paper. Trim pastry around the edges. Chill while you prepare the filling. Beat eggs with sugar until light. Add cheeses, milk, flour, salt, vanilla and cinnamon to the egg mixture and beat well to combine. Press mixture through a food mill. Pour into prepared chill pastry shell. Bake in a preheated 350 F (180 C) oven on the middle rack for 30 minutes. Remove from the oven, sprinkle with the almonds and the sugar. Return to oven and bake for 30-40 minutes longer or until center is firm. Remove from oven and cool. Gently remove from pan and paper to a round serving platter. Serve chill or at room temperature.

~ · ~ · ~

CHEESE SOUFFLÈ
Soufflé me Tyri

6 Tbsp butter or margarine
5 Tbsp all-purpose flour
1 1/2 cups milk
Salt and pepper to taste
1 1/2 cups shredded Swiss cheese
6 eggs, separated
2 Tbsp grated Parmesan cheese

Melt the 5 Tbsp. of the butter if desired over medium heat, blend in flour until smooth using a whisk. Remove from heat and add the milk gradually, stirring constantly until mixture is thick and smooth. Return to heat and cook 3 minutes longer; add seasoning and blend. Remove from heat. Beat egg yolks, and spoon little by little of the hot sauce, stirring constantly. Gradually add egg mixture to the sauce stirring constantly. Add cheese and mix well. Beat egg whites until stiff but not dry, and fold in the cheese mixture. Grease a soufflé dish with the remaining of 1Tbsp butter, sprinkle with the grated cheese, and pour the mixture in. Bake in a preheated 375 F (190 C) oven for 40-45 minutes or until golden. Remove from over and serve immediately.

EGGS WITH TOMATOES PEPPERS AND CHEESE
Avga with Ntomates Piperies and Tyri

1 small onion, finely chopped
1/4 cup or less olive oil or butter
1 large bell pepper, seeded and chopped (optional)
4 large ripe tomatoes, peeled, seeded and chopped
Salt and pepper to taste
6 large well-beaten eggs
1/4 cup grated Parmesan cheese

Sauté onion in oil if desired until soft. Add chopped pepper if desired and sauté a few minutes longer. Add chopped tomatoes, salt and pepper. Simmer for 30 minutes. Add beaten eggs and cheese and cook slowly stirring constantly, until the eggs thicken. Serve immediately, for breakfast or lunch. Serves 3.

KATAIFI-CHEESE SOUFFLÈ
Kataifi me Tyria Soufflé

1 1/2 cups crumbled feta cheese
1 1/2 cups lightly pressed down coarsely grated Kaseri cheese
1 cup lightly pressed down coarsely grated Swiss cheese
1/2 cup crumbled blue cheese
1/2 tsp white pepper
1 pound Kataifi shredded pastry (thawed)
1 cup melted clarified unsalted butter or margarine
7 extra large eggs, lightly beaten
31/2 cups milk

Mix cheeses with the pepper, and set aside. Divide the Kataifi pastry into three parts. In a greased 13x11x3-inch baking dish, lay one part of the Kataifi pasty. Sprinkle evenly with half of the cheese mixture. Lay the second part of the Kataifi over cheese mixture. Then sprinkle evenly with the remaining cheese mixture. Cover with the remaining Kataifi. Sprinkle with the melted butter. Cut cheese soufflé with a sharp serrated knife into 2 1/2x2 1/2-inch squares. Mix the eggs with the milk and beat well. Pour over cheese soufflé. Chill 2-3 hours, or until all the liquid has absorbed. Bake in a preheated 300 F (150 C) oven for 70-90 minutes or until golden brown. Serve immediately. Serves 8-20.

MUSHROOM AND SPINACH OMELET
Omeletta me Manitaria ke Spanaki

1/2 pound mushrooms
10 leaves of spinach
4 slices bacon, cut into fourths
6 eggs
2 Tbsp good quality olive oil
1 Tbsp all-purpose flour
2 Tbsp. milk
2 Tbsp grated Parmesan cheese
Salt and pepper to taste
Pinch pepper Cayenne (optional)
1 Tbsp toasted sesame seeds

Trim mushrooms and rinse under cold running water, dry and slice. Set aside. Wash the spinach in several waters. Dry and set aside. In a large frying pan sauté the bacon until crispy, remove from the pan. In the same pan add the mushrooms and sauté until all liquid evaporates. While the mushrooms are cooking, prepare the eggs. In a bow beat 3 whole eggs, 3 egg yolks, the oil, the flour, the cheese, the milk, season with salt and peppers, and beat well. Beat egg whites until stiff but not dry. Fold into the egg mixture. Add spinach to the mushrooms and pour the egg mixture over. Cook slowly until eggs are set. Sprinkle with the sesame seeds and the bacon and serve immediately. Serves 2-3.

BREADS, CAKES & COOKIES

BOBOTA

3/4 cup butter, margarine or good quality
    light olive oil
4 extra large eggs, beaten
1 1/2 cups milk
1/2 cup orange or apricot marmalade
1/2 cup sugar
2 cups fine yellow cornmeal
2 1/2 cups all-purpose flour
6 tsp baking powder
1 cup seedless golden raisins
1 cup chopped walnuts or almonds

Sift cornmeal, flour and baking powder together. Add milk, eggs, butter if desired, marmalade and sugar to cornmeal mixture and mix well to combine. Add raisins and walnuts if desired and mix well. Pour into greased 9x13x3-inch baking pan and bake in a preheated 350 F (180 C) oven for 45 minutes or until cake tester inserted in center comes out clean. Cut and serve hot with butter or plain.

❦❦❦

BREADCRUMBS

Dried Breadcrumbs:

1 loaf sliced butter top white bread or homemade. Layer bread slices into baking sheets. Place baking sheets on the middle rack of the oven. Toast the bread in a preheated 325 F (165 C) oven 15 minutes or until slightly golden. Turn the other side and toast again. Remove from oven and cool completely. The next day cut toasted bread slices into small pieces and grind in blender or food processor until very fine. Spoon into jars and store in the refrigerator.

Soft Breadcrumbs:

Use one day-old firm Italian or French white bread. Remove the crust. Tear into chunks. Place the bread in a blender or food processor and make breadcrumbs. Use as directed in the recipe. Freeze any leftovers in a Ziploc bag.

❦❦❦

BREAD FOR ARTOCLASIA

Psomi Yia Artoklasia

2 Tbsp active dry yeast
6 cups warm water
1 cup fine quality light olive oil
1 cup sugar
4 tsp salt
1/2 tsp crushed masticha or anise seeds
20-22 cups unbleached flour, sifted
Religious seal (sphraghitha)
Melted clarified butter for brushing

Dissolve yeast in 1/2 cup of the water. Cover; let stand for 5 minutes. Add oil, sugar and salt to the remaining water and stir well to combine. Place 6 cups flour in a large mixing bowl, add the water mixture and the yeast. Beat well. Add enough flour to make soft dough. Turn out dough on floured board and knead until smooth and elastic. Place in a greased bowl, turning to greased top. Cover, let rise in warm place free from draft until doubled in bulk, about 75-90 minutes. Punch down dough and knead for few minutes. Divide dough into five round balls, cover and let rest for 10 minutes. Shape into round loaves and place in greased 8-9-inch round cake pans. Make an impression with the seal (sphraghitha), dip seal in flour and place on top of the bread, press well and then remove it. Cover, let rise in warm place until doubled in bulk, about 50-60 minutes. Brush with melted butter. Place the bread on the middle rack of the oven. Bake the bread in a preheated 350 F (180 C) oven for approximately 45 minutes or until done. Remove from the oven and let rest for 10 minutes, then remove from the pans and place on wire racks. When they are completely cold brush with rose water and sift on generously confectioner's sugar. Makes 5 artous.

❧✺❧

BREAD ROLLS
Phomakia

1 recipe of white or rich white bread
(see index for recipe)

Follow recipe and preparation as d
irected. Punch down dough. Divide dough into half and shape as plain rolls, crescent rolls or lucky clovers.

Plain Rolls:
Cut one third of the dough into pieces about the size of a large walnut. Fold sides under until top of roll is perfectly smooth. Place in greased baking sheets. Cover and let rise in warm place until doubled in bulk. Brush with beaten egg wash and sprinkle with sesame seeds if desired. Let stand for 5 minutes to allow the egg to dry. Bake the rolls in a preheated 425.F (220 C) oven for 12-15 minutes. Remove from the baking sheet and cool on wire racks. Makes 20 rolls about.

Crescent Rolls:
Roll out one third of the dough on a floured surface 1/4-inch thick and cut into triangles. Brush with melted butter or margarine. Roll each triangle beginning at the base. Place in greased baking sheets, with point underneath curving ends toward each other. Let rise and bake as for plain rolls. Makes 20 crescent rolls about.

Lucky Clovers:
Prepare the lucky clovers as the plain rolls. Places the rolls into greased muffin pan. With scissor cut each roll in half, then into quarters, cutting

through almost to bottom of rolls. Let rise and bake as with plain rolls. Makes 20 lucky clovers.

❧✺❧

CHRISTMAS BREAD
Christopsomo

1/2 cup warm water
1 Tbsp active dry yeast
31/2 cups scalding milk
3/4 cup sugar
1 tsp salt
3/4 cup butter, margarine or good quality
*   light olive oil*
1/4 tsp crushed masticha (optional)
12 cups unbleached flour (about), sifted
1 egg, beaten with 1 tsp water
2 Tbsp sesame seeds
10 whole walnuts

Dissolve yeast in warm water. Cover; let stand for 5 minutes. Add sugar, butter if desired and salt to the milk and cool to warm. Place dissolve yeast, milk mixture and 4 cups of flour in a large mixing bowl or a mixer bowl and beat well. Add masticha if desired and enough flour to make a soft dough. Turn out dough on floured board and knead until smooth and elastic. Place in greased bowl turning to greased top. Cover; let rise in warm place free from draft until doubled in bulk, about 60-70 minutes. Punch down dough and knead for a minute. Divide the dough into two large pieces and one small the size of an orange, cover and let rest for 10 minutes. Shape into rounds and place in greased 10-inch baking round pans. With the small pieces shape strips and make a cross on top of each loaf. Press a walnut in the middle of the cross and on each of the ends. Cover, let rise in warm place until doubled in bulk, about 50-60 minutes. Gently brush with egg wash and sprinkle with the sesame seeds. Let stand for 5 minutes to allow the egg to dry. Bake in a preheated 325 F (165 C) oven for approximately 45-55 minutes. Remove from the oven. Let stand for 10 minutes. Remove from pans and cool on wire racks. Makes 2 Christopsoma.

❧✺❧

DOUGH FOR BRIOCHE
Zymi for Brioche

1/2 cup lukewarm water
2 Tbsp dry active yeast
1/4 cup sugar
1/2 cup scalding milk
1 cup butter, cut into small pieces
1 tsp salt
6 extra large eggs at room temperature, well beaten
61/2 cups unbleached flour (about), sifted

Dissolve yeast in lukewarm water. Melt butter in a saucepan with the milk and add salt and sugar. When milk mixture is lukewarm slowly add the eggs and the dissolved yeast and mix well to combine. In a large mixer bowl add 4 1/2 cups of the flour, add the milk mixture and beat with the hook to blend. Beat in moderate speed for 4 minutes, and gradually start adding the rest of the four. Continue beating until the dough is elastic and smooth about 4 minutes. Add more flour if needed. The dough will be soft and smooth. Place the dough in lightly greased large bowl, and cover with a plastic wrap. Allow the dough to rise on the counter far from the sun for 2 1/2 hours or until tripled in bulk. Remove the dough from the bowl and need for a minute. Place the dough into the bowl, cover, and let rise again for 1-1 1/2 hours or until doubled in bulk. Chill over night or until ready to use if desired. Let the dough rest for 15-20 minutes. Form into a loaf and place into a sandwich bread pan with cover if possible and press down to a rectangular. The loaf should be less than in the middle of the pan. Generously brush top of dough with melted butter, cover, let rise until dough is lest than double in bulk. Brush the cover with butter, if the cover is possible. Bake in a preheated 375 F (190 C) oven for 45 minutes. Remove cover and bake for 10 minutes longer, or until golden brown. Remove from pan and place on wire rack to cool. With the rest of the dough you can make.

For Small Brioche:
Chill overnight or until ready to use. Let rest for 15-20 minutes. Form quickly into small balls and place in greased muffin pans. Let rise until doubled in bulk. Brush with egg wash. Let the small brioche to stay for 5 minutes to allow the egg to dry. Bake in a preheated 400 F (205 C) oven for 15-20 minutes or until golden brow. Remove from pans and place on wire racks to cool.

For Twists:
Roll the dough lightly to a rectangular sheet 1/2-inch thick. Brush with softened butter and fold lengthwise into thirds. Cut into 1-inch slices, place on greased baking sheets and let rest for 10 minutes. Lift each roll by the ends and twist one end. Return to the baking sheet. Rise and bake the twists as the Small Brioche.

For Bowknots:
Twist strips of dough lightly and tie in a bowknot. Bring the ends down and press to the pan. Rise and bake as the Small Brioche.

❧❦❧

LAGHANA
Flat Bread

1 recipe of white bread or rich white bread (see the index for the recipes)

Follow recipe and preparation as directed. Punch down dough and knead for few minutes. Divide dough into four or five round balls, cover and let rest for 10 minutes. Using a rolling pin, roll out one ball at a time on a floured board into an oval shape 1/2-inch thick. Place on greased baking sheet. Repeat with rest of the balls. Brush with beaten egg white and generously sprinkle with sesame seeds and press with the rolling pin to adhere. Then with your fingertips poke dough starting from the top to the bottom. Cover, let rise in warm place until doubled in bulk. Place baking sheet on the middle rack of the oven and bake in a preheated 400 F (205 C) oven for 15-20 minutes. Tear in pieces by hand and serve hot. Makes 4 laghanes.

❧❦❧

PITA BREAD
Pita for Souvlaki

1 Tbsp active dry yeast
4 cups warm water
1/4 cup olive oil
1 Tbsp wine vinegar
13 cups unbleached flour (about) sifted
4 tsp salt

Dissolve the yeast in 1/2 cup of the warm water. Add oil, vinegar, and the yeast into the remaining water. Stir together flour and salt. In a large mixer bowl add 4 cups flour and the yeast mixture. Beat well with the hook for 10 minutes. Add enough flour to make a soft dough. Turn out dough on floured board and knead until smooth and elastic. Place in greased bowl turning to grease top. Cover, let rise in warm place free from draft until doubled in bulk, about 45 minutes. Punch down dough and kneed for few minutes. Divide dough into 24 pieces. With your hands work pieces into very smooth balls. Place on a floured surface: cover and let rest for 20 minutes. Using a rolling pin, roll out one at a time on a generously floured surface into a disk 8-inches in diameter. Place rounds on a none greased baking sheet. Bake pita rounds in a preheated 450 F (230 C) oven for 5-6 minutes or until dough is puffed and set. Repeat with remaining dough, baking one batch before rolling and baking the next. Cool on wire racks. Stack together, pressing out air, and store in plastic bags in the refrigerator for 5 days or you can freeze them. Makes 24 pitas.

Note: Use pita bread for Lamb Shishkebab, gyro (see index for the recipe), or toasted and cut into wedges and serve with spreads, or you can eat it plain toasted with a piece of cheese. Pita bread makes delicious pizza too. Before baking the pita, spread some pizza sauce and sprinkle with cheese. Bake in a preheated 450 F (230 C) oven for 10 minutes. Serve hot.

PROSPHORON
Offering Bread

1/2 Tbsp active dry yeast
13/4 cups warm water
1/2 tsp salt

6 cups unbleached flour (about), sifted
Religious seal (sphraghitha)

Dissolve yeast in warm water. Cover, let stand for 5 minutes. In a large mixing bowl add 4 cups of the flour, salt and the yeast. Beat well. Add enough flour to make a soft dough. Turn out dough on floured board and knead until smooth and elastic. Place in a lightly greased bowl, turning to greased top. Cover, let rise in warm place free from draft until doubled in bulk, about 60-75 minutes. Punch down dough and knead for few minutes. Shape into 1 round loaf. Place in a lightly greased 9-10-inch round cake pan. Make an impression with the sphraghitha, dip seal in flour and place on top of the bread, press well and then remove it. Cover, let rise in warm place until doubled in bulk, about 45-55 minutes. Place the pan on the middle rack of the oven, and bake in a preheated 350 F (180 C) for 45 minutes or until done. Remove from oven and let rest for 10 minutes. Remove from pan and place on a wire rack to cool. Makes 1 prosphoron.

RICH WHITE BREAD
Psomi Polytelias

1/2 cup warm water
1 Tbsp active dry yeast
3 1/2 cups scalding milk
1/2 cup sugar
2 tsp salt
3/4 cup butter, margarine or 1/2 good quality
    light olive oil
1/4 cup crushed masticha (optional)
12 cups all-purpose flour, sifted
1 egg, beaten with 1 tsp. water
2 Tbsp. sesame seeds (optional)

Dissolve yeast in the water, cover; let stand 5 minutes. Add sugar, butter if desired and salt to the milk and cool to warm. Place milk mixture in a large mixer bowl and add dissolved yeast and 4 cups flour. Beat well. Add masticha if desired and enough flour to make a soft dough. Turn out dough on lightly floured board and knead until smooth and elastic. Place in a greased bowl turning to greased top. Cover; let rise in warm place free from draft until doubled in bulk, about 60-70 minutes. Punch down dough, cover and let rise again until almost double, about 30 minutes. Divide dough into three round balls, cover and let rest for 10-15 minutes. Shape balls into loaves and place in greased 9x5x3-inch bread pans. Cover; let rise in warm place until doubled in bulk, about 50-60 minutes. Brush with the beaten egg and sprinkle with the sesame seeds if desired. Let the loaves stay for 5 minutes to allow the egg to dry. Place the loaves in center of oven not touching each other or sides of oven. Bake in a preheated 350 F (180 C) for 30-35 minutes or until deep golden brown. To test the loaf, tap the crust. Loaf should sound hollow when done. If it doesn't, bake for few minutes longer. Immediately remove bread from pans. Place on wire rack to cool. When cool enough, place in plastic bags to store or to freeze. Makes 3 loaves.

❦❦❦

WHEAT FOR MEMORIAL SERVICE
Kollyva

1 pound whole wheat kernels for kollyva
1/2 tsp salt
1/3 cup toasted sesame seeds, crushed
1/2 cup chopped walnuts
2/3 cup golden raisins
1 1/4 tsp cinnamon
1/2 cup toasted blanched slivered almonds
Pomegranate seeds
1 Tbsp finely chopped flat leaf parsley
2/3-1 cup finely ground zwieback
1 1/2 cups confectioner sugar, sifted
White candied Jordan almonds or whole
*   blanched almonds*
1 silver tray or a large round platter
Paper doilies

Pick over wheat, three times. Rinse well. Place into a large pot and fill with warm water. Let stand overnight. In the morning drain and fill again with warm water; let stand for 8 hours longer. Drain. Cover with warm water, bring to a boil, reduce heat and simmer for 2-4 hours or until wheat is tender. Add water as needed and the salt. Stir often to prevent for sticking. Drain and rinse well with warm water. Spread on white

cloth rowel to absorb excess moisture and cover with another towel. Let stand overnight. The next-morning the day you will take it to church prepare the tray with the wheat. Combine wheat, sesame seed, walnuts, raisins, cinnamon toasted almonds, pomegranate seeds and parsley and mix well to combine. Line the edges of the tray with paper doilies; let overhang. Gently fill the whole tray with the wheat mixture, shaping it with the palms of your hands into a mound so there will be a rise in the center. Cover wheat with zwieback crumbs, pressing down, using a piece of waxed paper the size of the tray. Sift confectioner's sugar over the crumbs. Gently press down with clean waxed paper the size of the tray to form a smooth compact top. Make a cross in the center and the border around of the tray with the Jordan almond or the whole blanched almonds.

❦❦❦

WHITE BREAD
Psomi Aspro

21/2 cups warm water
1 Tbsp active dry yeast
1 cup scalding milk
2 Tbsp sugar
1/4 cup butter, margarine or light olive oil
4 tsp salt
2 Tbsp wine vinegar
12 cups all-purpose flour, sifted
1 egg white, beaten with 1 tsp. water (optional)
3 tsp sesame seeds (optional)

Dissolve yeast in 1/2 cup warm water, cover; let stand 5 minutes. Add sugar, butter if desired and salt to milk and cool to warm. Place milk mixture, the dissolve yeast and 4 cups of the flour in a large mixer bowl and beat well. Add enough flour to make soft dough. Turn out dough on floured board and knead until smooth and elastic. Place in a greased bowl, turning to greased top. Cove with a plastic wrap; and let rise in warm place free from draft until doubled in bulk, 60-70 minutes. Punch down dough, cover and let rise again until almost double, about 30 minutes. Divide dough into three round balls, cover and let rest for 10-15 minutes. Shape balls into loaves and place in greased 9x5x3-inch bread pans. Cover; let rise in warm place until doubled in bulk, about 50-60 minutes. Brush with egg white and sprinkle with sesame seeds if desired. Let stay 5 minutes to allow the egg to dry. Place the loaves in center of oven not touching each other or sides of oven. Bake in a preheated 425 F (220 C) oven for 30-35 minutes or until deep golden brown. To test the loaf, tap the crust. Loaf should sound hollow when done. If it doesn't, bake for few minutes longer. Immediately remove bread from pans. Place on wire rack to cool. When cool enough, place in plastic bags to store or to freeze. Makes 3 loaves.

❦❦❦

ATHENIAN RICH EASTER BRAIDS
Athenaika Tsourekia Paschalina

5 Tbsp active dry yeast
10 extra large eggs, at room temperature
1 1/2 cups scalding milk
3 cups sugar
1/4 tsp salt
1 1/2 Tbsp finely ground machlepi
2 cups melted clarified unsalted butter
  (see index for recipe)
14 cups unbleached flour (about), sifted
1 egg beaten with 1 tsp water
Slivered blanched almonds
6-8 red eggs

Dissolve yeast in warm milk. Cover; let stand for 5 minutes. In a large mixing bowl or in a large mixer bowl beat eggs, sugar and salt until eggs are thick and creamy. Add dissolve yeast, ground machlepi and 1 cup of the warm butter and beat with a whisk or with the mixer. Gradually stir in flour until dough is soft and smooth. Add more flour if needed. Add warm butter little by little greasing hands and bowl; knead until all the warm butter is used and dough is smooth. Cover and let rise in warm place free from draft until doubled in bulk, about 3 hours. Punch down dough and knead for a minute. Divide dough into 8 parts and round into balls. Cover, and let rest for 10 minutes. Divide each ball evenly into three parts. Roll each into a rope 20inches long. Press

one end together and braid loosely, press ends together and tuck under loaf. Place in baking sheets lined with parchment paper. In the center or in one end of each loaf place a red-dyed egg and press down. Cover and let rise in warm place until doubled in bulk. Gently brush with egg wash and sprinkle with almonds. Let stand for 10 minutes to allow the egg to dry. Bake in a preheated 350 F (180 C) oven for 15 minutes. Reduce heat to 325 F (165 C) and bake for 15 minutes. Check the tsourekia if the color is darkening too quickly, cover them loosely with foil. Remove from oven. Let stand for 10 minutes. Gently remove from pans and cool on wire racks. Makes 8 tsourekia.

❦❦❦

CHRISTMAS FRUIT NUT BREAD
Christougeniatiko Psomi Froutou

2 cups scalding milk
1 cup sugar
1/2 cup warm water
1 1/2 Tbsp dried yeast
11 cups all-purpose flour, sifted
6 eggs, lightly beaten
1 1/2 cups, melted unsalted butter
Grated fresh rind of 2 lemons and 2 oranges
1/2 cup cognac or brandy
1 1/2 cups dark raisins
1 1/2 cups golden raisins
2 cups dried fruits cut into very small pieces
1 cup chopped blanched almonds
1 cup chopped walnuts
1 egg white, beaten with 1/2 Tbsp of water
Confectioner's sugar for dusting

Add the sugar to the milk and stir, to dissolve the sugar. Dissolve the yeast in the warm water for 5 minutes. In a large mixer bowl add the yeast, the lukewarm milk mixture and 21/2 cups of the flour. Beat the batter until smooth, cover and let rise in warm place, free from draft until double in bulk. While the batter is rising soak the raisins and fruits with the cognac if desired 30 minutes. Add the beaten eggs, butter and the rinds to the yeast batter and mix well with the mixer. Gradually add enough flour to make soft dough. The dough must be very soft. Add the nuts, fruits with the cognac and kneed well to combine. Turn out dough on floured board and kneed until is smooth and elastic. Place dough in greased large bowl, grease the top of the dough, cover with plastic wrap and let rise in warm place, free from draft until doubled in bulk, about 60-70 minutes. Punch down. Divide dough into 4 parts and round into balls. Cover and let rest for 10 minutes. Shape into loaves and place in greased 9x5x3-inch bread pans, cover; let rise in warm place until double in bulk, about 50-60 minutes. Brush with the egg wash, let stand for 5 minutes to allow egg to dry. Bake in a preheated 350 F (180 C) oven for approximately 35 minutes. Let stand 5 minutes. Gently remove from pans and cool on wire racks. When they are completely cool, dusted with confectioner's sugar. Makes 4 loaves.

EASTER BRAIDS
Tsourekia Paschalina

1 cup scalding milk
21/2 Tbsp active dry yeast
8 eggs, at room temperature
13/4 cups sugar
1/4 tsp salt
1 Tbsp finely ground machlepi, 1/4 tsp crushed masticha or grated rind of one orange
1 1/4 cups melted clarified unsalted butter
(see index for recipe)
12 cups unbleached flour (about) sifted
1 egg, beaten with 1 tsp water
1/2 cup slivered or whole blanched almonds
5-6 red eggs

Dissolve yeast in warm milk. Cover; let stand for 5 minutes. In a large mixing bowl or mixer bowl beat eggs, sugar and salt until thick and creamy. Add dissolved yeast, machlepi if desired and half of the butter and beat to combine. Gradually stir in flour until dough is soft and smooth. Add more or less flour if needed. Add warm butter little by little greasing hands and bowl; knead until all the butter is used and dough is smooth. Cover; let rise in warm place free from draft until doubled in bulk, about 3 hours. Punch down dough and knead. Divide dough into 5-6

parts and round into balls. Cover and let rest for 10 minutes. Divide every ball into three parts. Roll each into a rope 20-inches long. Press one end together and braid loosely, press ends together and tuck under loaf. Place in baking sheets lined with parchment paper. In the center of each loaf place a red-dyed egg and press down. Cover and let rise in warm place until doubled in bulk. Gently brush with egg wash and sprinkle with almonds or decorate with the whole almonds. Let stand for 10 minutes to allow the egg to dry. Bake in a preheated 350 F (180 C) oven for 15 minutes. Reduce heat to 325 F (165 C) and bake for 15 minutes longer. Check the tsourekia if the color is darkening too quickly, cover them loosely with foil. Remove from oven and let stand for 10 minutes. Gently remove from baking sheets and cool on wire racks. Makes 5-6 tsourekia.

EASTER FRUIT NUT BREAD
Tsoureki Froutou

1 cup scalding milk
5 Tbsp active dry yeast
1 1/2 cups sugar
1/2 tsp salt
9 eggs, at room temperature
Grated rind of 1 orange and 1 lemon
1/4 cup cognac or brandy
1 1/2 cups melted clarified unsalted butter
(see index for recipe)
10 cups unbleached flour (about), sifted
2 cups chopped mixed dried fruit
1/2 cup golden seedless raisins
1 1/2 cups chopped blanched almonds
1 egg, beaten with 1 tsp water

Dissolve yeast in warm milk. Cover; let stand for 5 minutes. In a large mixing bowl or mixer bowl beat eggs, sugar and salt until eggs are light and creamy. Add dissolve yeast, grated rind and 1/2 cup of the butter to the egg mixture and mix well. Gradually stir in flour until dough is soft and sticky. Add more flour if needed. Add warm butter little by little greasing hands and bowl; knead until all the butter is used and dough is smooth. Soak fruits and raisins with the cognac if desired for 1-2 hours. Sprinkle with little flour and shake excess. Add fruits and 1 cup of the almonds to the dough and knead well to combine. Cover, let rise in warm place free from draft until doubled in bulk, about 3 hours. Punch down dough and knead for one minute. Divide dough into 6 parts and round into balls. Cover and let rest for 10 minutes. Shape into loaves and place in greased bread pans lined bottom with parchment paper, grease the paper. Cover, let rise in warm place until doubled in bulk. Gently brush with egg wash and sprinkle with the remaining almonds. Let stand for 10 minutes to allow the egg to dry. Bake in a preheated 350 F (180 C) oven for 15 minutes. Reduce heat to 325 F (165 C) and bake for 15 minutes longer. Check the color and if is darkening too quickly, cover with foil. Makes 6 Tsourekia Froutou.

❦❦❦

FRUIT NUT BREAD

Stafidopsomo

1 cup scalding milk
2 Tbsp active dry yeast
1 cup sugar
6 eggs, at room temperature
13/4 cups melted unsalted butter
Grated rind of 2 oranges or lemons or one of each
12 cups unbleached flour (about), sifted
1 cup finely chopped blanched almonds
1/3 cup cognac or brandy
1 1/2 cups chopped mixed dry fruit
2 cups golden seedless raisins
1 cup finely chopped walnuts
1 egg, beaten with 1 tsp water

Add sugar to milk, stir until it dissolves. Let cool to warm. Dissolve yeast in milk. Cover; let stand for 5 minutes. Beat eggs well, add milk mixture, butter, orange rind if desired and beat well. Gradually stir in flour until dough is soft and sticky. Soak fruits and raisins in cognac if desired for 1-2 hours. Add fruits, raisins, almonds and walnuts. Mix well to combine. Turn out dough on floured board and knead until smooth and elastic. Place dough in greased bowl turning to grease top. Cover; let rise in warm place free from

draft until doubled in bulk, about 60 minutes. Punch down dough and knead for 1 minute. Divide into four round balls, cover and let rest for 10 minutes. Shape into loaves and place in greased 9x5x3-inch bread pans lined with parchment paper. Cover; let rise in warm place until doubled in bulk, about 60 minutes. Gently brush the bread with egg wash. Let stand for 5 minutes to allow the egg to dry. Bake in a preheated 325 F (165 C) oven for approximately 45-55 minutes. Remove from oven and gently remove from pans immediately and cool on wire racks. Makes 4 Stafidopsoma.

❦❦❦

NEW YEAR'S BREAD

Vasilopita

1 recipe of Christmas Bread (see index for recipe)

Follow recipe and preparation as directed in Christmas Bread. Shape into rounds and place in greased 10-inch round baking pans. With the small piece of dough shape strips and design the numbers to devote the New Year, brush some egg wash in the middle of the bread (that will be your glue). Now place your numbers on top of the egg washed bread. Cover and let rise in warm place until doubled in bulk, about 60 minutes. Brush with egg wash. Let seat for 5 minutes to allow the egg to dry. Bake in preheated 325 F (165 C) oven for approximately 45-55 minutes. Remove from the oven. Let sit 10 minutes. Gently remove from pans and cool on wire racks. Makes 2 Vasilopites. After baking, a clean coin (wrapped in plastic wrap) is inserted through a slit in the base. Cut and serve the Vasilopita, first to the family starting from the Virgin Mary, the father, the mother, the rest of the family and the quests. The person who finds the coin will have luck in the New Year.

❦❦❦

RAISIN BREAD

Stafidopsomo

1 1/2 Tbsp active dry yeast
1 1/4 cups warm water

2 cups scalding milk
1/2 cup melted butter or good quality light olive oil
1/2 tsp salt
1 cup sugar
12 cups unbleached flour, sifted
2 cups golden seedless raisins
1 egg, beaten with 1 tsp water

Dissolve yeast in warm water. Cover; let stand 5 minutes. Add butter if desired, salt and sugar to milk and cool to warm. Place dissolve yeast, milk and 4 cups flour in a large mixing bowl or mixer bowl and beat well. Add enough flour to make a soft dough. Add raisins and mix well. Turn out dough on floured board and knead until smooth and elastic. Place in greased bowl turning to greased top. Cover; let rise in warm place free from draft until doubled in bulk, about 60-70 minutes. Punch down dough and knead 1 minute. Divide into 3 round balls, cover and let rest 10 minutes. Shape into loaves and place in greased 9x5x3-inch bread pans lined with parchment. Cover; let rise in warm place until doubled in bulk, about 45-60 minutes. Gently brush with egg wash, let stand 5 minutes to allow egg to dry. Bake in preheated 350 F (180 C) oven 30-40 minutes. Remove from oven and gently remove from pans immediately and cool on wire racks. Makes 3 stafodopsoma.

❦❀❦

RICH NEW YEAR'S BREAD
Vasilopita Polutelias

1/2 cup warm water
5 Tbsp active dry yeast
1 cup scalding milk
10 eggs, at room temperature
3 cups sugar
1/4 tsp salt
1 1/2 Tbsp finely ground machlepi, masticha or 1 Tbsp grated rind of 1-2 oranges
2 cups melted clarified unsalted butter
        (see index for recipe)
5 pounds unbleached flour (about), sifted
1 egg, beaten with 1 tsp water
Whole blanched almonds

Dissolve yeast in warm water, cover and let stand 5 minutes. In a large mixing bowl or mixer bowl

beat eggs, sugar and salt until eggs are thick and creamy. Add dissolved yeast, milk, ground machlepi if desired and 1/2 cup of the warm butter, beat well to combine. Gradually stir in enough flour to make a-soft and sticky dough. Add warm butter, little by little greasing hands and bowl; knead until all the warm butter is used and dough is smooth. Cover and let rise in warm place free from draft until doubled in bulk, about 3-5 hours. Punch down dough and knead for one minute. Divide dough into 3 parts and round into balls. Cover and let rest for 10 minutes. Shape into rounds and place in greased 10-inch round baking pans lined with parchment paper. Cover, let rise in warm place until doubled in bulk. Gently brush with egg wash and decorate with the whole almonds in numbers to devote the New Year, pressing lightly. Let stand for 5 minutes to allow the egg to dry. Bake in a preheated 325 F (165 C) oven for approximately 45-55 minutes. Check the color of the Vasilopita and if is darkening too quickly, cover loosely with foil. Remove from oven. Let stand for 10 minutes. Gently remove from pans and cool on wire racks. Makes 3 Vasilopites. After baking, a clean coin (wrapped with plastic wrap) is inserted through a slit in the base. Cut and serve the Vasilopita, first to the family starting from the Virgin Mary, the father, the mother, the rest of the family and the guests. The person who finds the coin will have luck in the New Year.

❦❀❦

RICH RAISIN BREAD
Stafidopsomo Polytelias

1/2 cup scalding milk
1/2 Tbsp active dry yeast
4 eggs, at room temperature
3/4 cup sugar
Grated rind of 1 orange
5 cups unbleached flour, sifted
1/3 cup melted unsalted butter or margarine
1 cup golden seedless raisins
1 egg, beaten with 1 tsp water

Cool milk to warm. Dissolve yeast in milk, cover; let stand 5 minutes. In a large mixing bowl or mixer bowl, beat eggs, sugar and orange rind until sugar has dissolved. Add milk mixture and beat. Gradually stir in flour until dough is soft and sticky. Add raisins and mix well. Add butter little by little greasing hands and bowl and knead until all the butter is used and dough is smooth. Cover; let rise in warm place free from draft until doubled in bulk, about 2 hours. Divide dough into two parts and round into balls. Cover; let rest for 10 minutes. Shape into loaves and place into greased 5x9x3-inch bread pans lined with parchment paper. Cover; let rise in warm place until doubled in bulk. Gently brush with egg wash. Let stand for 5 minutes to allow the egg to dry. Bake in a preheated 325 F (165 C) oven for approximately 45-55 minutes. Remove from oven and let stand for 5 minutes. Gently remove from pan and cool on wire racks. Makes 2 loaves.

SWEET CRESCENTS
Kruasan

For the dough:
*1 recipe of the Athenian Rich Easter Braids
        (see index for recipe)*
For the filling:
*1 1/3 cups sugar
2 cups coarsely chopped walnuts
1 tsp cinnamon
1/2 cup melted unsalted butter or margarine
1 egg, beaten with 1 tsp water
For the topping:
2 cups confectioner's sugar, sifted
2 Tbsp water
1/2 tsp vanilla extract*

Follow recipe and preparation for the dough as directed. Divide dough into 4 parts and round into balls. Cove; let rest for 10 minutes. While dough is resting, combine sugar, walnuts and cinnamon, mix well. Set aside. Using a rolling pin, roll out one part at a time on a floured surface into 1/4-inch thick. Cut into triangles. Brush with hot melted butter if desired and sprinkle with the walnut mixture. Roll each triangle beginning at the base. Place the crescents on a baking sheets lined with greased parchment paper, curving ends

toward each other. Cover; let rise in warm place until doubled in bulk. Brush with beaten egg. Let the crescents stay for 5 minutes to allow the egg to dry. Place sheets one at a time on the middle rack and bake in a preheated 350 F (180 C) oven for approximately 15 minutes or until they are golden brown. While crescents are baking prepare the frosting. In a small bowl combine confectioner's sugar, water and vanilla, mix well until smooth. Glaze crescent rolls when they are still hot.

Note: After crescents are baked, cool on racks with out the glaze. Store in plastic bags and freeze. When you are ready to use, place crescents in baking sheet, cover with foil and bake in a preheat oven 450 F (230 C) oven for 20 minutes or until soft to the touch. Glaze and serve hot.

WALNUT BREAD
Psomi me Karythia

*1 pkg. active dry yeast
1 cup warm milk
2 extra large eggs
1/2 cup sugar
1 tsp pure vanilla extract
Grated rind of 1/2 orange
1/2 cup melted unsalted butter or margarine
1/2 tsp salt
4 cups all-purpose unbleached flour (about), sifted
1/2 cup chopped walnuts
1 egg white, beaten with 2 Tbsp sugar*

Dissolve yeast in warm milk. Cover, let stand 5 minutes. In a large mixer bowl beat eggs with sugar until thick and creamy. Add the dissolve yeast, vanilla, orange rind, butter and salt, and stir well to combine. Gradually stir in flour until dough is soft and smooth. Add more flour if needed. Place the dough in greased bowl turning to greased top. Cover; let rise in warm place free from draft until double in bulk, about 1 to 2 hours. Punch down dough and add the walnuts and kneed gently. Cover; let rest for 10 minutes. Shape the dough into one loaf and place in greased 9x5x3-inch bread pan. Cover; let rise in warm place until double in bulk, about 45 to 55 minutes. Brush with beaten egg-sugar mixture.

Let the bread stay 5 minutes to allow egg to dry. Bake in preheated 350 F (180 C) oven and set rack in lower-middle level for 60 minutes. Remove bread from pan and let cool on a rack. Makes one loaf of walnut bread.

WALNUT STUFFED CROISSANT
Krouasan me Karythia

2 pkgs. Puff pastry
2 cups finely chopped walnuts
3/4 cup sugar
1/4 cup honey
2 Tbsp breadcrumbs
2 Tbsp melted butter
1 tsp baking powder
1/2 tsp cinnamon
3 eggs, beaten
1 egg, beaten with 1 tsp water
Sugar for sprinkling

Thaw the puff pastry as directed. Mix the first 8 ingredients together. Unfold the pastry and cut into triangles. Place on each triangle on the wide side 2 Tbsp of the filling and start rolling to the other end of the pastry, and curving ends toward each other. Place croissants in a baking pan lined with parchment paper. Brush croissants with beaten egg and sprinkle with sugar. Chill for 15 minutes. Bake in a preheated 400 F (22 C) oven on the middle rack for 20-30 minutes, or until golden. Serve hot or at room temperature.

ALMOND CAKE
Keik Amygthalou

5 eggs, separated
3/4 cup plus 2 Tbsp sugar
3 Tbsp cognac or brandy
1/2 tsp vanilla
1/4 tsp almond extract
3/4 cup cake flour, sifted with
1 tsp baking powder
6 ounces finely ground almonds
6 Tbsp melted unsalted butter or margarine
2 Tbsp finely chopped almonds
Confectioner sugar, sifted

Beat egg yolks with sugar until creamy. Add cognac, vanilla and almond extract and beat well.

Fold in stiffly beaten egg whites alternately with flour and ground almonds. Add butter and fold well to combine. Grease a tube pan and sprinkle with chopped almonds. Pour mixture and bake in a preheated 350 F (180 C) oven for approximately 45 minutes or until cake tester inserted in center comes out clean. Remove from oven and let stand for 5 minutes. Gently remove from pan and cool on wire rack. Dust with confectioner's sugar or serve with whipped cream if desired.

ALMOND CINNAMON CAKE
Amygthalopita

5 eggs, separated
1 1/2 cups sugar
1/4 tsp almond extract
2 tsp baking powder
10 ounces finely ground almonds
1/2 cup finely ground zwieback toast
1 tsp cinnamon
2 cups whipping cream, whipped

Beat egg yolks with sugar until thick and creamy. Add almond extract. Mix ground almonds, ground toast, baking powder and cinnamon together. Gradually add almond mixture to egg mixture and mix well. Fold in stiffly beaten egg whites. Pour into greased and floured tube pan and bake in a preheated 350 F (180 C) oven for approximately 40 minutes or until cake tester inserted in center comes out clean. Remove from oven and let stand for 5 minutes. Remove from pan and cool in wire rack. Slice and serve with whipped cream.

ALMOND FRESH FRUIT CAKE
Keik me Freska Frouta Amygthalou

For the crust:
1 1/2 cups all-purpose flour
2 tsp baking powder
1/4 tsp salt
1 cup unsalted butter, chilled and cut into small cubes
1/2 cup firmly packed brown sugar
1/2 cup ground almonds

For the fruit:
4 large apricots, pitted and coarsely chopped
2 large peaches, peeled, pitted and coarsely chopped
For the cake:
1 cup unsalted butter, at room temperature
1 1/2 cups sugar
4 extra large eggs, lightly beaten
1 tsp pure almond extract
1 1/2 cups plus 1Tbsp all-purpose flour
2 tsp baking powder
Pinch of salt
1/4 cup milk
1/4 cup finely chopped blanched almonds
Confectioner's sugar for dusting, sifted
Whipped cream

1) Prepare crust: In mixing bowl sift flour, baking powder and salt. Cut in butter until mixture resembles coarse crumbs. Add brown sugar and almonds and mix well to combine, divide dough into two parts. Place one part of the dough in greased 11-inch spring form pan lined and greased with parchment paper. Press with back of spoon to cover bottom of pan. 2) Divide fruit into two parts. Arrange one part of the fruit over the prepare pan, and let stand. 3) Prepare the cake. Beat butter and sugar together until creamy and fluffy. Add eggs one at a time, beating thoroughly after each addition. Add almond extract. Sift flour, baking powder and salt together. Gradually add flour to the butter mixture, alternately with the milk, and stir well to combine. Spoon the mixture over the fruit and spread evenly. Arrange the remaining fruit over the cake. And cover with the remaining crust dough, and press with the back of a spoon to cover the fruit. Bake in a preheated 350 F (180 C) oven on the middle rack for 60 minutes. Remove from the oven and sprinkle the almonds over the cake. Return the cake to the oven and bake for 15 minutes longer or until golden brown. Remove from oven and let stand for 10 minutes. Remove from pan and place on a round serving platter. Cool cake completely. Sprinkle the cake with confectioner's sugar. Cut and serve cake with whipped cream.

❧❀❧

ALMOND ORANGE CAKE
Amygthalopita Portokaliou

4 eggs, separated
1 1/2 cups sugar
1 cup finely ground almonds
1 cup finely ground zwieback toast
1/4 cup cognac or brandy
1/4 tsp almond extract
Grated rind of 1/2 orange or lemon
2 tsp baking powder
2 Tbsp finely chopped almonds
2 cups whipping cream, whipped

Beat egg yolks with sugar until thick and creamy. Add almond extract. Combine ground almonds, ground zwieback and baking powder and mix well. Gradually add almond mixture alternately with cognac. Add orange rind if desired and mix well. Fold in stiffly beaten egg whites. Grease a tube pan and sprinkle with chopped almonds, and pour cake mixture. Bake in a preheated 350 F (180 C) oven for approximately 45 minutes or until cake tester inserted in center comes out clean. Remove from oven and let stand for 5 minutes. Gently remove from pan and cool on wire rack. Slice and serve with whipped cream.

❧❀❧

ALMOND VANILLA CAKE
Cake Amygthalou me Vanillia

1 cup unsalted butter or margarine, at room temperature
2 cups sugar
5 extra large eggs, separated
1 tsp pure vanilla
1/2 tsp almond extract
31/2 cups all-purpose flour
5 tsp baking powder
3/4 cup milk
1 cup chopped blanched almonds or with skin on

Cream butter and sugar until light and fluffy. Add egg yolks one at a time beating thoroughly after each is added. Add vanilla and almond extract. Sift flour and baking powder together; add alternately with milk to creamed mixture beating until smooth after each addition. Add almonds and fold in stiffly beaten egg whites. Pour into well greased and floured 9-inch tube pan. Bake in preheated 300 F (150 C) oven 60 minutes or until cake tester inserted in center comes out clean. Remove from oven and cool 10 minutes. Gently remove from pan and cool on wire rack. Dust with confectioner's sugar if desired or serve with can fruit and syrup, ice cream or plain

❦❦❦

APPLE-APRICOT CAKE
Keik me Mila ke Verikoka

3/4 cup good quality olive oil
1 1/2 cups sugar
4 extra large-egg, beaten
21/2 cups all-purpose flour
3 tsp baking powder
1 tsp baking soda
1 tsp cinnamon
1/4 tsp ground cloves
1/2 tsp nutmeg
6 ounces coarsely chopped apricots
2 pounds coarsely grated apples
1/3 cup honey
1 1/4 cups shredded unsweetened coconut

Sift flour, baking powder, soda, cinnamon, cloves and nutmeg together. Set aside. In a mixing bowl beat oil, sugar and eggs until light and fluffy. Fold in flour mixture. Then add apricots, grated apples and 3/4 cup of the coconut, and mix well to combine. Spoon cake mixture into greased and floured 9x13x3-inch baking pan and spread evenly. Bake in a preheated 350 F. (180 C) oven for 60 minutes or until cake tester inserted in center comes out clean. Remove from oven and immediately spread honey over the cake and sprinkle with the remaining coconut. Let cool completely before you cut it.

❦❦❦

CHOCOLATE CAKE
Keik me Kakao

1/2 cup unsalted butter or margarine, at
    room temperature
2 cups sugar
6 large eggs, separated
Pinch of salt
1 cup plain yogurt
1 tsp pure vanilla extract
13/4 cups all-purpose flour

4 tsp baking powder
1/4 tsp salt
1/2 cup cocoa
Confectioner sugar, sifted

Cream butter and sugar in a mixer bowl until light and fluffy. Add egg yolks one at a time beating thoroughly after each is added. Add yogurt and vanilla, beat well. Sift dry ingredients together. Gradually add flour and beat until smooth. Beat egg whites with pinch of salt until holds soft pick. Gently fold in egg whites to batter. Spoon batter into greased tube pan. Bake in preheated 350 F (180 C) oven on middle rack 45 to 55 minutes or until cake tester inserted in center comes out clean. Cool 10 minutes. Remove cake from pan and cool on wire rack. When completely cool, dusted with confectioner's sugar, and place on a round serving dish.

❦❦❦

CHRISTMAS FRUIT NUT CAKE
Keik Christougeniatiko

1 cup unsalted butter or margarine, at
    room temperature
2 cups sugar
5 extra large eggs
Grated rind of 1 orange
21/2 cups unbleached flour
1 tsp baking soda
2 tsp baking powder
1 tsp cinnamon
1/2 tsp nutmeg
1/2 cup cognac or brandy
1/2 cup fresh orange juice
1/2 cup chopped walnuts
3/4 cup seedless golden raisins
3/4 dried mixed fruits, chopped
1/2 cup chopped almonds

Cream butter if desired and sugar until light and fluffy. Add eggs one at a time beating thoroughly after each is added. Add orange rind. Sift dry ingredients together and mix with raisins and fruits. Add flour-fruit mixture alternately with orange juice and cognac if desired and beat well. Add walnuts and almonds and mix well to combine. Pour into well-greased and floured tube pan and bake in a preheated 325 F (165 C) oven approximately 60 minutes or until cake tester inserted in center comes out clean. Remove from oven and cool on wire rack 10 minutes. Remove from pan and place on wire rack to cool. When completely cool, place on a round serving platter.

DATE-NUT CAKE (L.CHOL L.FAT)
Keik me Hourmathes ke Karythia

1 1/2 cups all-purpose flour
1 cup whole wheat flour
3 tsp baking powder
1/2 tsp baking soda
1/2 tsp ground cinnamon
3 egg whites
Grated rind of 1 orange
1 cup orange juice
1 1/2 cups finely chopped dates
1/2 cup finely chopped dry cranberries
1 cup finely chopped walnuts
Confectioner's sugar for dusting (sifted)

Sift dry ingredients together. In a medium mixing bowl beat the egg whites with a wire whisk, until frothy. Add the orange rind and juice and beat well to combine. Gradually add the flour mixture and beat well. Add the dates, cranberries and walnuts and mix well to combine. Pour into a greased bread loaf pan lined with a greased parchment paper, and spread evenly. Bake in a preheated 350 F (180 C) oven on the middle rack for 45 minutes or until cake tester inserted in center comes out clean. Remove from oven, and cool for 10 minutes. Gently remove from the pan, and let cool on a rack. When completely cool dusted with the confectioner's sugar. Slice and serve with a cup of Greek coffee or tea.

FRUIT CAKE
Keik Froutou

1 cup unsalted butter or margarine, at room temperature
1 cup sugar
5 extra large eggs
1 tsp vanilla
1/4 cup brandy or cognac
3 cups unbleached flour
5 tsp baking powder

1 tsp cinnamon
1/2 tsp nutmeg
3/4 cup milk
1 cup chopped walnuts
1 cup chopped dried fruits
1 cup seedless golden raisins

Cream butter if desired with sugar until light and fluffy. Add eggs one at a time beating thoroughly after each one is added. Add vanilla and brandy if desired. Sift dry ingredients together and mix with the fruits. Gradually add flour mixture alternately with milk and beating until smooth after each addition. Add walnuts and stir well to combine. Pour into well-greased and floured tube pan and bake in a preheated 350 F (180 C) oven for approximately 60 minutes or until cake tester inserted in center comes out clean. Remove from oven and cool for 10 minutes on a wire rack. Remove from pan and cool completely on a wire rack.

LENTEN COCONUT CAKE
Keik Nistisimo me Karytha

3/4 cup fine semolina
1 cup all-purpose flour
6 tsp baking powder
1 tsp cinnamon
1 1/4 cups sugar
1 cup good quality light olive oil or salad oil
1 1/3 cups water
Grated rind of 1 orange
3/4 cup chopped almonds
1 cup chopped walnuts
1 1/4 cups unsweetened coconut
Confectioner sugar for dusting

Sift dry ingredients together. Add sugar, oil, water and rind; stir until well blended. Add chopped nuts and coconut, mix well to combine. Pour into greased and floured 8-inch tube pan. Bake in a preheated 350 F (180 C) oven for approximately 60 minutes or until cake tester inserted in center comes out clean. Remove from oven and let stand for 10 minutes. Remove from pan and dust with confectioner's sugar.

LENTEN SPICE CAKE
Keik Nistisimo Myrothato

3 3/4 cups all-purpose flour
1 1/2 tsp baking soda
1 tsp cinnamon
1/4 tsp ground cloves
1/2 tsp ground nutmeg
1 1/2 cups sugar
3/4 cup good quality light olive or salad oil
1/2 cup cognac or brandy
3/4 cup water
1/2 cup fresh orange juice
Grated rind of 1 orange
1 cup seedless golden raisins
1 cup chopped walnuts
Confectioner's sugar for dusting

Sift dry ingredients together in a mixing bowl. Add the rest of the ingredients and stir until well blended. Pour into greased and floured 8-inch tube pan. Bake in a preheated 350 F (180 C) oven for approximately 60 minutes or until cake tester inserted in center comes out clean. Remove from oven and let stand for 10 minutes. Remove from pan and dust with confectioner's sugar.

❧✻❧

NEW YEAR'S CAKE
Vasilopita

1 cup unsalted butter or margarine, at room temperature
2 cups sugar
4 extra large eggs
41/2 cups all-purpose flour
6 tsp baking powder
1 1/3 cups milk
1/4 tsp ground masticha or 1 tsp pure vanilla extract

Cream butter if desired with sugar until light and fluffy. Add eggs one at a time beating thoroughly after each one is added. Sift dry ingredients together; add alternately with milk and vanilla if desired to creamed mixture, beating until smooth after each addition. Pour into well-greased 10-inch baking pan or spring form pan and bake in a preheated 350 F (180 C) oven approximately 60 minutes or until cake tester inserted in center comes out clean. Remove from oven and let stand 10 minutes. Remove from pan and let cool completely on wire rack. After baking a coin is inserted through a slit in the base. Cut and serve Vasilopita, first to the family starting from the Virgin Mary, the father, the mother, and the rest of the family and them the quests. The person who finds the coin will have luck in the New Year. Makes one Vasilopita.

❧✻❧

TAHINI CAKE (L. CHOL. L. FAT)
Tahini Keik Horis Lypara ke Holisterini

10 ounces tahini (sesame paste)
1 cup water
2 Tbsp cognac or brandy
1/2 cup fresh orange juice
2 Tbsp fresh lemon juice
21/2 cups sugar
Grated rind of 1 orange
21/2 cups all-purpose flour
1 tsp baking soda
2 tsp baking powder
1 2/3 cups fine semolina
1 tsp cinnamon
1/4 tsp ground cloves
3/4 cup finely chopped walnuts
1 cup seedless golden raisins
Confectioner's sugar for dusting

In a mixing bowl combine first six ingredients. Beat until sugar is dissolved, add orange rind and stir well. Sift dry ingredients together and mix with raisins and walnuts. Gradually add flour mixture to the tahini mixture and stir until well blended. Pour into a 9x13x3-inch baking pan lined with greased parchment paper. Bake in a preheated 350 F (180 C) oven on the middle rack for approximately 60 minutes or until cake tester inserted in center comes out clean. Remove from oven and let stand for 10 minutes. Dust with confectioner's sugar. Cut into squares when the cake is completely cold.

❧✻❧

YOGURT ALMOND CAKE
Yiaourtopita me Amygdala

1 cup unsalted butter or margarine, at room temperature
21/2 cups sugar
5 extra large eggs, separated
1 tsp vanilla

32/3 cups all-purpose flour
5 tsp baking powder
1 1/2 cups plain yogurt
1 cup finely chopped almonds
Confectioner's sugar for dusting

Cream butter if desired with sugar until light and fluffy. Add egg yolks one at a time, beating thoroughly after each one is added. Add vanilla. Sift flour and baking powder together. Add alternately with yogurt to creamed mixture, beating until smooth after each addition. Add almonds and mix well. Fold in stiffly beaten egg whites. Pour into a well-greased and floured 8-inch baking tube pan. Bake in a preheated 350 F (180 C) oven for approximately 60 minutes or until cake tester inserted in center comes out clean. Remove from oven and let stand for 10 minutes. Remove from pan and dust with confectioner's sugar. Cut when completely cold.

ALMOND BUTTER CHRISTMAS COOKIES A

Kourabiedes Amygthalou

21/2 cups unsalted butter or margarine, at room temperature
1 cup confectioner's sugar, sifted
3 egg yolks
3 Tbsp cognac or brandy (optional)
1 cup finely chopped toasted blanched almonds (optional)
6 cups all-purpose flour
1/2 cup cornstarch
4 tsp baking powder
Rosewater
Confectioner sugar, sifted

Cream butter if desired with electric beater, 30 minutes. Add sifted sugar and beat well. Add egg yolks one at a time, beating thoroughly; add cognac if desired and almonds if desired and beat well. Sift dry ingredients together. Gradually add flour mixture and mix well with hands until a soft dough. Add more flour if needed. Break off pieces of dough the size of a walnut and shape into half-moon or roll into balls and pinch tops twice making 4 indentions. Place on baking sheets lined with parchment. Bake kourabiedes

in preheated 350 F (180 C) oven on middle rack approximately 20 minutes or until lightly golden. Cool for 10 minutes and sprinkle with rosewater. Gently dip the kourabieder one at a time, in the confectioner's sugar, to cover all sides and place on a large container in layers and tightly covered. When ready to serve sift more sugar on top until they are generously covered. Place each one in a paper cup and arrange on serving platter to serve.

ALMOND BUTTER CHRISTMAS COOKIES B

Kourabiedes Amygthalou

2 cups unsalted butter or margarine, at room temperature
2/3 cup confectioner's sugar, sifted
2 egg yolks
1/4 cup fresh orange juice
2 Tbsp cognac or brandy (optional)
1 tsp vanilla
1/2 tsp almond extract
1 cup finely chopped toasted blanched almonds (optional)
41/2 cups all-purpose flour
5 Tbsp cornstarch
4 tsp baking powder
Rosewater
Confectioner's sugar, sifted

Cream butter if desired with electric beater 30 minutes. Add sifted sugar and beat well. Add egg yolks one at a time, beating thoroughly; add cognac if desired and almonds if desired and beat well. Sift dry ingredients together. Gradually add flour and mix well with hands until a soft dough. Add more flour if needed. Break off pieces of dough the size of a walnut and shape into half-moon or roll into balls and pinch tops twice making 4 indentions. Place on baking sheets lined with parchment paper. Bake the kourabiedes in a preheated 350 F (180 C) oven on the middle rack 20 minutes or until golden. Cool 10 minutes and sprinkle with rosewater. Gently dip the kourabiedes one at a time, in the confectioner's sugar, to cover all sides and place on a large container in layers and tightly covered. When ready to serve sift more sugar on top until they are generously covered. Place each one in a paper cup and arrange on a serving platter to serve.

ALMOND COOKIES
Amugthalota

10 ounces blanched almonds
2 cups sugar
3 egg whites
1/2 tsp cream of tartar
1 tsp vanilla
1/2 tsp almond extract
Whole blanched almonds split lengthwise into halves

In a blender of food processor grind almonds and sugar together, a little at a time. Beat egg whites with cream of tartar until soft peaks. Gently fold in the rest of the ingredients until mixture becomes thick but nut stiff, if stiff add some egg white. Spoon mixture into a pastry bag use tip 6 or 8 and pipe onto cooking sheets lined with parchment paper forming rosettes. Press a almond in the center on each rosette. Bake the cookies in a preheated 300 F (150 C) oven for approximately 20 minutes or until lightly golden.

ALMOND JAM BARS
Ravdi Amygthalou me Marmelada

3/4 cup unsalted butter or margarine, at
         room temperature
3/4 cup sugar
2 eggs
1 1/2 cups all-purpose flour, sifted with
1 1/2 Tbsp cornstarch
1 cup apricot jam
4 eggs
1 cup sugar
1/3 cup all-purpose flour, sifted with
1/2 Tbsp cornstarch and
1 tsp baking powder
1/2 tsp almond extract
2 cups chopped blanched almonds
4 tsp melted unsalted butter or margarine
1/2 cups pine nuts
1 Tbsp of rosewater

Cream butter if desired and sugar until light. Add one egg at a time beating thoroughly. Gradually add flour beating until smooth after each addition. Spoon batter in 10 1/2 x 15 x 2-inch greased baking pan in a very thin layer. Spread jam over crust. In a medium bowl beat the eggs with sugar until thick and light. Beat in almond extract. Add chopped almonds, flour mixture and butter to egg mixture and blend well to combine. Spoon mixture over the jam, spread evenly and sprinkle with the pine nuts. Bake in a preheated 350 F (180 C) oven for approximately 45-55 minutes. Remove from oven and sprinkle with rosewater. Cool and cut into bars.

ALMOND MACAROONS
Amygthalota

2 cups sugar
2 cups whole blanched almonds
2 pkgs (3.5 ounces each) almond paste
1/2 tsp almond extract
5 egg whites, slightly beaten
1/3 cup sifted cake flour

In a blender or food processor grind almonds and sugar together, a little at a time. Beat egg whites with cream of tartar until soft peaks. In a large mixer bowl beat almond paste until smooth. Add beaten egg whites and blend thoroughly. Add ground almonds, almond extract and flour, to the almond paste and mix well. Spoon mixture into a pastry bag with 3/4-inch star tip, and pipe onto baking sheets lined with parchment paper. Bake the macaroons in a preheated 300 F (150 C) oven for approximately 20-30 minutes or until golden. Gently remove from paper while still warm. If the macaroons stick to the paper, pour some water in the pan under the parchment paper, let stand for few minutes to moisten it on the underside. Makes 6-dozen.

BUTTER COOKIES
Koulourakia Voutyrou

1 cup unsalted butter or margarine, at room
temperature
1 1/4 cups sugar
2 eggs

1 tsp vanilla
31/2 cups all-purpose flour (about), sifted with
4 tsp baking powder
1 egg, beaten with 1 tsp water

Cream butter if desired with sugar until light and fluffy. Add eggs one at a time beating thoroughly as each is added. Add half the flour at a time, beating until smooth after each addition to make soft dough. Add flour if needed. Break off pieces of dough the size of a walnut, roll into long cord and shape into twists or rings. Arrange on baking sheets lined with parchment. Brush lightly with egg wash. Let stay 5 minutes to allow the egg to dry. Bake in a preheated 375 F (190 C) oven on middle rack, approx. 15 minutes or until golden.

COCONUT COOKIES
Biskota Karythas

1 cup unsalted butter, at room temperature
2 cups sugar
2 extra large eggs
1 tsp pure vanilla extract
31/4 cups all-purpose flour
4 tsp baking powder
1/4 cup milk
1 1/2 cups unsweetened coconut

Cream butter and sugar until light and fluffy. Add eggs one at a time, beating thoroughly after each is added. Add vanilla. Sift dry ingredients together. Gradually add flour alternately with milk, beating until smooth. Add coconut and mix well to combine. Divide dough into four portions. Shape each piece of dough into a roll, and roll it onto a piece of parchment. Chill for 2 to 4 hours. When the dough is firm enough, cut into very thin slices. Bake in preheated 375 F (190 C) oven on the middle rack approx. 12 minutes or until golden. Make about 5 dozens.

COCONUT JAM BARS
Ravdi Karydas me Marmelada

3/4 cup unsalted butter or margarine, at
*   room temperature*
3/4 cup sugar
2 egg whites, stiffly beaten

1 1/2 cups all-purpose flour, sifted with
1 1/2 Tbsp cornstarch
1 cup apricot jam
4 eggs plus 2 egg yolks
1 1/4 cups sugar
1/4 cup all-purpose flour, sifted with
1 tsp cornstarch and
1 tsp baking powder
1 Tbsp of rosewater
1/2 tsp almond extract
2 cups unsweetened coconut
1/4 cup melted unsalted butter or margarine
1 cup chopped blanched almonds

Cream butter if desired and sugar until light and fluffy. Gradually add flour mixture. Fold in stiffly beaten egg whites. Spoon batter in 10 1/2 x 15 x 2-inch grease baking pan and spread in very thin layer. Bake in a preheated 350 F (180 C) oven for approximately 10 minutes. Cool for 5 minutes. Spoon the jam over the baked crust and spread evenly. While the crust is baking prepare the topping. In a medium bowl beat the eggs and egg yolks with sugar until light. Beat in rosewater and almond extract. Add coconut, flour mixture and melted butter if desired and blend well. Spoon over jam and spread evenly. Sprinkle with chopped almonds. Return to oven and bake for 25 minutes longer. Cool and cut into bars.

COCONUT MACAROONS WITH MILK
Makarouns Karydas me Gala

4 cups unsweetened coconut (about)
1 can sweetened condensed milk
1 tsp pure vanilla extract
Whole blanched almonds

Combine all ingredients except whole almonds, mix well to make a soft dough. Add more coconut if needed. Break off pieces of dough the size of a walnut and shape onto balls. Lightly press down with palm and place a whole almond into the center of each ball of coconut. Arrange onto baking sheets lined with parchment. Bake macaroons in preheated 375 F (180 C) oven approx. 10 minutes or until lightly golden. Remove from paper while still warm. If macaroons stick to paper, pour some water in the pan under the parchment, let stand for few minutes to moisten it on underside.

※◆※◆※

COCONUT MACAROONS
Makaroons Karythas

1 1/2 cups sugar
1 tsp vanilla
4 1/2 cups unsweetened coconut (about)
1/4 cup cornstarch
5 egg whites
Whole blanched almonds for decoration

In a large mixing bowl place the coconut, sugar cornstarch. Add egg whites and vanilla, mix well to combine. Add more egg white or coconut if needed. Break off pieces of dough the size of a walnut and shape onto balls. Lightly press down with your palm and place a whole almond into the center of each macaroon. Arrange onto baking sheets lined with parchment paper. Bake the macaroons in a preheated 300 F (150 C) oven for approximately 20-30 minutes or until lightly golden. Gently remove from paper while still warm. If the macaroons stick to the paper, pour some water in the pan under the parchment paper, let stand for few minutes to moisten it on the underside.

※◆※◆※

FRUIT NUT BARS
Ravdi Froutou

3/4 cup unsalted butter or margarine, at room temperature
1 cup sugar
5 eggs, separated
1 tsp vanilla
1/2 tsp almond extract
1/4 cup milk
2 cups plus 2 Tbsp all-purpose flour, sifted with
2 Tbsp cornstarch and
3 tsp baking powder
3/4 cup chopped mixed dried fruit or dates
1 cup seedless golden raisins
1 cup chopped almonds
1 cup chopped walnuts
Confectioner's sugar for dusting

Cream butter if desired and sugar until light and fluffy. Add egg yolks one at a time beating

thoroughly after each one is added. Beat in vanilla and almond extract. Gradually add flour mixture alternately with milk to creamed mixture beating until smooth after each addition. Add fruits and nuts and mix thoroughly. Fold in stiffly beaten egg whites. Spoon into well greased and floured 13x9x2-inch baking pan and spread evenly. Bake in a preheated 350 F (180 C) oven for approximately 25 minutes or until cake tester inserted in center comes out clean. Cool thoroughly, dust with confectioner's sugar and cut into bars.

※◆※◆※

HONEY CHRISTMAS COOKIES A
Melomakarona or Fenekia

2 cups fine quality light olive oil
1 cup unsalted butter, at room temperature
3/4 cup fresh orange juice
1 cup sugar
1/2 cup cognac or brandy
21/2 tsp ground cinnamon
2 eggs
10 cups all-purpose flour (about)
1 1/4 tsp baking soda
5 tsp baking powder
For the syrup:
3 cups honey
2 cups sugar
21/2 cups water
2 cups or more finely chopped walnuts

In a large mixer bowl combine first 6 ingredients; cover with a kitchen towel, and beat for 10-15 minutes or until light and creamy. Add eggs and beat well. Change the beater to a petal. Sift dry ingredients together. Gradually add the flour mixture to the butter oil mixture and mix into a-soft dough. Add more flour if needed. Break off pieces of dough the size of a large walnut. Shape into ovals 2-inches long and press them lightly with the tips of your fingers on a cheese grinder. Place onto baking sheets lined with parchment paper. Bake in a preheated 375 F (190 C) oven on the middle rack for approximately 20 minutes or until golden brown. Remove from heat and let stand overnight. Combine syrup ingredients except the walnuts in four-quart saucepan. Bring to a boil. Reduce heat to medium and boil 5 minutes, being carefully not to over boil syrup. Skim off froth and discard. Fill large baking pan with melomakarona in one layer, close to each other, and pour boiling syrup over them. Cover with larger baking pan or piece of foil. Let soak 20-30 minutes, then gently turn them over with 2 forks. Cover again and let stay 20-30 minutes longer. Gently remove melomakarona to one side of pan and lift pan to drain them. Gently place in large container into layers and sprinkle with chopped walnuts and cover tightly. When ready to serve, place each one in a paper cup and sprinkle with more nuts if needed and arrange on a serving platter to serve.

Note: Substitute olive oil for the butter if desire.

HONEY CHRISTMAS COOKIES B
Melomakarona or Fenekia

3 cups good quality light olive oil
1 cup sugar
3/4 cup cognac or brandy (optional)
1 cup fresh orange juice
2 1/2 tsp cinnamon
1 cup finely chopped walnuts (optional)
9 cups all-purpose flour (about)
1 1/2 cups fine semolina
2 tsp baking soda
5 tsp baking powder
For the syrup:
3 cups plain honey
2 cups sugar
3 cups water
2 cups or more finely chopped walnuts

In a large mixer bowl combine first 5 ingredients; cover with a kitchen towel, and beat for 10-15 minutes or until light and creamy. Beat in the walnuts if desired. Change the beater to a petal. Sift dry ingredients together. Gradually add the flour mixture to the oil mixture and mix into a soft dough. Add more flour if needed. Shape into ovals 2-inches long and press them lightly with the tips of your fingers on a cheese grinder. Place onto baking sheets lined with parchment paper. Bake in a preheated 375 F (190 C) oven on the middle rack for approximately 20 minutes or until

golden brown. Cool for 60 minutes. Combine syrup ingredients except the walnuts in four-quart saucepan. Bring to a boil. Reduce heat to medium and boil for 5 minutes, being carefully not to over boiled. Skim the froth. Fill a large baking pan with the melomakarona in one layer and pour boiling syrup over them. Cover with a larger baking pan or with a piece of foil. Let them soak for 20-30 minutes and then gently turn them over with two forks. Cover again and let stay for 20-30 minutes longer. Gently remove the melomakarona to one side of the pan and lift the pan to drain them. Gently place in a large container into layers and sprinkle with chopped walnuts and cover tightly. When ready to serve, place each one in a paper cup and sprinkle with more nuts if needed and arrange on a serving platter to serve.

HONEY CHRISTMAS COOKIES C
Melomakarona or Fenekia

1 cup good quality light olive oil
1 cup unsalted butter, at room temperature
1 cup fresh orange juice
3/4 cup sugar
1/3 cup cognac or brandy (optional)
2 tsp cinnamon
2 Tbsp plain honey
1 egg
6 cups all-purpose flour (about)
1 tsp baking soda
4 tsp baking powder
For the syrup:
3 cups plain honey
2 cups sugar
21/2 cups water
2 cups or more finely chopped walnuts

Follow preparation as directed in Honey Christmas Cookies A (see index for the recipe).
Note: Substitute the olive oil for the butter if desire.

JAM FILLED ALMOND CHOCOLATE COOKIES
Biskota Amygdalou Sokolatas Gemista

10 ounces almonds, finely ground with
1 1/3 cups sugar

5 eggs, beaten
5 Tbsp sifted cocoa
2 Tbsp cognac or brandy
1 tsp vanilla
1 cup more or less apricot jam
Sliced almonds

Combine first six ingredients and mix until mixture becomes thick but not stiff. Mold with a cookie press into 2-inch long cookies onto cookie sheets lined with greased parchment paper. Top the cookies with the sliced almonds. Bake in a preheated 400 F (205 C) oven for approximately 10 minutes. Cool. Spread with apricot jam one cookie and top with another.

❦❦❦

JAM FILLED ALMOND MACAROONS
Amygdalota Gemista

20 ounces blanched almonds
1 1/2 cups sugar
8 egg whites
1 tsp cream of tartar
1 1/2 tsp vanilla
1 tsp almond extract
1 cup more or less apricot jam or your desire

In a blender or food processor grind almonds and sugar together, a little at a time. Beat eggs whites with cream of tartar until soft peak. Fold in ground almonds and the rest of the ingredients except the jam. Drop heaping teaspoonfuls of the mixture spaced apart on cooking sheets lined with parchment paper and spread evenly. Bake the macaroons in a preheated 300 F (150 C) oven for approximately 25-30 minutes or until lightly golden. Cool. Spread with apricot jam on one macaroon and top with another.

❦❦❦

JAM FILLED COGNAC BISCUITS
Biskota me Koniak Yemista

1 cup unsalted butter or margarine, at
        room temperature
2 cups or less sugar
3 eggs
1 1/2 tsp vanilla
1/4 cup cognac or brandy
4 cups all-purpose flour, sifted with
4 tsp baking powder

1 cup jam or marmalade to your taste

Cream butter if desired and sugar until light and fluffy. Add eggs one at a time beating thoroughly after each is added. Add vanilla and cognac, mix well. Gradually add flour mixture beating until smooth after each addition to make a soft dough. Roll out a portion of dough about 1/8-inch thick on parchment and cut into rounds or squares. Place on baking sheets lined with parchment and bake in preheated 350 F (180 C) oven approx. 12 minutes or until golden. Cool. Spread with jam if desired on one biscuit and top with another.

❦❦❦

JAM FILLED ORANGE ALMOND BISCUITS
Biskota Amygdalou Yemista

3 cups all-purpose flour, sifted with
3 tsp baking powder
1 1/4 cups sugar
Grated rind of 1 orange
1 1/2 cups finely ground almonds
3/4 cup unsalted butter or margarine, cut
        into small cubes
2 eggs, beaten
1/2 cup orange marmalade
1 egg, beaten with 1 tsp water

Combine first six ingredients in food processor (steel blade). Blend until crumbly. Add eggs and blend until dough forms a ball. If dough seems too soft add 1 Tbsp or more flour and mix until incorporated. Roll out half the dough about 1/8-inch thick on parchment and cut into rounds with doughnut cutter. Place rounds on baking sheets lined with parchment. Spread a little marmalade; set aside. Roll out the other half of dough and cut with doughnut cutter with hole in the middle and place on top of the orange marmalade. Brush with beaten egg wash. Let stay 5 minutes to allow the egg to dry. Bake in a preheated 350 F (380 C) oven for approximately 12-15 minutes.

❦❦❦

JAM FILLED BUTTER COOKIES
Biskota Voutyrou Gemista

1 1/2 cups butter or margarine, at room
temperature
1 1/2 cups sugar

1 tsp vanilla
4 extra large eggs
4 cups all-purpose flour
1/4 cup cornstarch
4 tsp baking powder
Jam to your desire (optional)

Cream butter if desired and sugar until light and fluffy. Add vanilla and eggs one at a time, beating thoroughly after each is added. Sift flour, cornstarch and baking powder together. Gradually add flour, beating until smooth after each addition. Mold with cookie press onto baking sheets lined with parchment. Bake cookies in preheated 400 F (205 C) oven 10 minutes or until golden brown. Cool. Spread with jam on one cookie and top with another if desired.

MUST COOKIES
Moustokouloura

1 cup good quality light olive oil
1 cup must or molasses
1 cup sugar
1/4 cup cognac or brandy
4 eggs
1/4 cup warm water
8 cups all-purpose flour about
1 1/4 tsp cinnamon
1/2 tsp nutmeg
1/8 tsp ground cloves
1 1/2 tsp baking soda
4 tsp baking powder

Combine first 6 ingredients in large bowl and beat well. Sift dry ingredients together. Gradually add flour mixture and mix thoroughly. Add more flour if needed to make a soft dough. Break off pieces of dough the size of a walnut, roll into a long cord and shape into twists or rings. Place on baking sheets lined with parchment. Bake in preheated 375 F (180 C) oven 15-20 minutes.

NUT FRUIT ROCK DROPS
Vrahakia

1 cup unsalted butter or margarine, at
*   room temperature or*
3/4 cup good quality light olive or salad oil
1 1/3 cups sugar

3 eggs, separated
1 tsp vanilla
21/2 cups all-purpose flour
1 tsp baking soda
1 tsp cinnamon
1/4 tsp ground cloves
1/2 cup milk
3/4 cup seedless golden raisins
3/4 cup chopped walnuts or almonds
1/2 cup chopped candied fruit (any kind)

Cream butter if desired and sugar until light and fluffy. Add egg yolks one at a time, beating thoroughly after each is added. Add vanilla. Sift dry ingredients together. Gradually add flour mixture alternately with milk, beating until smooth after each addition. Add raisins, walnuts if desired and fruit and stir well to combine. Fold in stiffly beaten egg whites. Drop from teaspoon onto cooking sheets lined with parchment, spacing apart as they will spread while baking. Bake in preheated 400 F (205 C) oven -15 minutes. Remove from oven and remove from cooking sheets. Serve hot or cool.

Note: Substitute nuts with 1/4 cup raisins and 1/2 cup candied fruit.

NUT RAISIN TURNOVERS
Skaltsounia

For the crust:
3 cups all-purpose flour, sifted with
2 tsp baking powder and
1/3 tsp cinnamon
2 Tbsp sugar
1 1/4 cups sesame tahini
1 Tbsp sesame oil or good quality olive oil
1/4 cup lukewarm water
For the filling:
1/2 cup finely chopped almonds
1/2 cup finely chopped walnuts
1/2 cup chopped seedless golden raisins
3/4 cup apricot jam or your desire
For the topping:
1/4 cup rosewater
Confectioner sugar, sifted

Combine filling ingredients and mix well. Set aside. Combine dough ingredients except water and cut with pastry cutter until mixture resembles coarse crumbs. Add water and gently toss with fingers. Form dough into 2 balls. Roll out one ball at a time to 1/8-inch thick sheet. Cut dough into rounds 3-inches in diameter. Place 1 tsp of filling on each circle of dough. Dampen edge of each circle lightly with water. Fold dough over filling to form a half-moon. Place skaltsounia on non-greased baking sheets. Bake in preheated 350 F (180 C) oven approximately 30 minutes. Remove from oven and sprinkle with rosewater. Sift confectioner's sugar on a piece of parchment, place skaltsounia on sugar. Sift more sugar on top and sides. When cool place on serving platter.

❧⊱✠⊰❧

PLAIN KOULOURAKIA
Koulourakia Apla

1 cup unsalted butter or margarine, at
      room temperature
13/4 cups sugar
5 eggs
Grated rind of 1 orange
5 cups all-purpose flour (about), sifted with
1 tsp baking soda and
3 tsp baking powder
1 egg, beaten with 1 tsp water

Cream butter if desired and sugar until light and fluffy. Add eggs one at a time beating thoroughly after each is added. Add grated rind and gradually add flour mixture beating until smooth after each addition to make a soft dough. Add more flour if needed. Break off pieces of dough the size of a walnut, roll into a long cord and shape into twists or wreaths. Arrange on baking sheets lined with parchment. Brush lightly with egg wash. Let stay 5 minutes for egg to dry. Bake in preheated 375 F (190 C) oven 18 minutes or until golden brown.

❧⊱✠⊰❧

SESAME COOKIES
Koulourakia Sousamiou

1 cup unsalted butter or margarine, at
      room temperature
13/4 cups sugar
3 eggs
1/4 tsp salt
1 tsp pure vanilla extract
5 cups all-purpose flour (about)

1 tsp baking soda
3 tsp baking powder
1 egg, beaten with 1 Tbsp of water
Sesame seeds

Cream butter and sugar together, until light and fluffy. Add eggs one at a time, beating thoroughly after each is added. Add salt and vanilla. Sift dry ingredients together. Gradually add flour mixture, beating until smooth after each addition to make soft dough. Add more flour if needed. Break off pieces of dough the size of a walnut, roll into a long cord and shape into twists. Arrange on baking sheets lined with parchment. Brush lightly with beaten egg wash and sprinkle with sesame seeds. Let stay 5 minutes to allow egg to dry. Bake in preheated 375 F (190 C) oven on middle rack 18 minutes or until golden brown.

❧⊱✠⊰❧

SESAME KOULOURAKIA
Koulourakia Sousamiou

2 cups sugar
1 cup milk
4 extra large eggs
1 cup melted unsalted butter or margarine
1 1/2 tsp vanilla
9 cups all-purpose flour (about), sifted with
2 tsp baking soda and
4 tsp baking powder
2 egg whites, beaten with 1 Tbsp of water
2 cups sesame seeds

Combine first 5 ingredients in large mixing bowl, beat well. Gradually add flour mixture beating until smooth after each addition to make soft dough. Add more flour if needed. Break off pieces of dough the size of a walnut and form into cylinders. Dip in beaten egg whites and roll lightly in sesame seeds. Arrange on baking sheets lined with parchment. Bake in preheated 375 F (190 C) oven 18 minutes or until golden brown.

❧⊱✠⊰❧

SLICED ALMOND COOKIES
Biskota Amygdalou

1 cup unsalted butter or margarine, at
      room temperature
1 1/3 cups sugar

1/4 cup whipping cream
1 tsp fresh lemon juice
2 egg yolks
1/4 tsp pure almond extract
1/2 cup finely ground blanched almonds
23/4 cups all-purpose flour
1/2 tsp baking soda
Finely chopped almonds

Cream butter if desired and sugar until light and fluffy. Add egg yolks one at a time, beating thoroughly. Add cream, lemon juice, almond extract and ground almonds; mix well. Sift flour and baking soda together. Gradually add flour, beating until smooth after each addition. Add more flour to make soft dough. Divide dough into four portions. Shape each piece of dough into a 1x8-inch roll. Wrap in plastic wrap and chill 60 minutes. When firm, slice very thin and arrange in baking sheets lined with parchment paper. Sprinkle cookies with finely chopped almonds. Bake in a preheated 375 F (190 C) oven for approximately 12 minutes or until golden.

❧❀❧

SMYRMA KOULOURAKIA A.
Koulourakia Smirneika

21/3 cups unsalted butter or margarine, at
    room temperature
2 cups sugar
2 extra large eggs
2 tsp pure vanilla extract
9 cups all-purpose flour (about)
2 Tbsp baking powder
1/2 tsp salt
3/4 cup fresh orange juice, mixed with
1/3 cup cognac or brandy
1 egg, beaten with 1 tsp water

Cream butter if desired and sugar in large mixing bowl until light and fluffy. Add eggs one at a time beating thoroughly as each is added. Beat in vanilla. Sift dry ingredients together. Gradually add flour alternately with orange juice mixture beating until smooth after each addition to make soft dough. Add flour if needed. Break off pieces of the dough the size of a walnut, roll into a long cord and shape into spirals. Arrange on baking sheets lined with parchment. Brush lightly with

egg wash and let stay 5 minutes to allow egg to dry. Bake in a preheated 375 F (190 C) oven for approximately 18 minutes or until golden brown.

❧❀❧

SMYRNA KOULOURAKIA B.
Koulourakia Smyrneika

5 cups all-purpose flour (about)
4 tsp baking powder
1 cup unsalted butter or margarine, at
    room temperature
1 1/4 cups sugar
1/3 cup milk
1 tsp pure vanilla extract
1/4 tsp salt
2 extra large eggs, slightly beaten
Grated rind of 1 orange
1/4 cup fresh orange juice, mixed with
3 Tbsp cognac or brandy
1 egg, beaten with 1 tsp water

Sift flour and baking powder together in a large mixing bowl. Add butter and cut with a pastry blender or with your palm of your hands. Form a hole in the center and add into it the rest 8 ingredients. Knead all the ingredients together into soft dough. Add more flour if needed. Break off pieces of the dough the size of a walnut, roll into a long cord and shape into spirals. Arrange koulourakia onto baking sheets lined with parchment paper. Brush lightly with egg wash and let stay for 5 minutes to allow the egg to dry. Bake in a preheated 375 F (190 C) oven for approximately 18 minutes or until golden brown.

❧❀❧

SPICED KOULOURAKIA
Koulourakia Myrothata

3/4 cup unsalted butter, at room temperature
3/4 cup good quality light olive oil
1 1/2 cups sugar
Grated rind of 1 orange and 1 lemon
5 cups all-purpose flour (about)
1 tsp baking soda
3 tsp baking powder
1 tsp cinnamon
1/4 tsp ground cloves or nutmeg
1/2 cup cognac or brandy, mixed with
1 cup fresh orange juice
2 egg whites, beaten with 1 tsp water

Sesame seeds

Cream butter, oil and sugar until light and creamy. Beat in the orange and lemon rind. Gradually add flour mixture alternately with cognac and orange juice mixture beating until smooth after each addition to make soft dough. Add more flour if needed. Break off pieces of dough the size of a walnut and shape into cylinders. Arrange onto baking sheets lined with parchment paper. Brush with egg wash and sprinkle with sesame seeds. Let stay 5 minutes to allow the egg to dry. Bake in a preheated 375 F (190 C) oven approximately 19 minutes or until golden brown.

Note: Substitute the butter with olive oil if desired. Follow recipe and preparation as directed.

❦❦❦

VANILLA COOKIES
Glosses

*1 cup unsalted butter or margarine, at
        room temperature*
1 cup sugar
4 egg whites, well beaten
1 tsp vanilla
1 1/2 cups all-purpose flour
1 1/2 Tbsp cornstarch
1 tsp baking powder

Cream butter if desired and sugar until light and fluffy. Add beaten egg whites and vanilla beating thoroughly. Sift flour, cornstarch and baking powder together. Gradually add flour to cream mixture, beating until smooth after each addition. Mold with cookie press onto baking sheets lined with parchment paper. Bake the cookies in a preheated 400 F (205 C) oven for approximately 7 minutes or lightly golden. Serve with ice cream.

❦❦❦

WINE KOULOURAKIA
Koulourakia Krasiou

1 1/2 cups good quality light olive oil
2 cups sugar
*1 1/2 cup Mavrodaphne (Greek wine) or
        Marsala sweet wine*
6 cups all-purpose flour (about)
3 Tbsp baking powder

1 tsp baking soda
2 egg whites, beaten with 1 tsp water
Sesame seeds

Into a blender container blend oil, sugar and wine, covered for 5 minutes. Sift dry ingredients together into a large mixing bowl. Form a hole in the center and pour into it the oil mixture. Knead all the ingredients together into soft dough. Add more flour if needed. Break off pieces of dough the size of a walnut and shape into cylinders. Arrange onto baking sheets lined with parchment paper. Brush with egg wash and sprinkle with sesame seeds. Let stay 5 minutes to allow the egg to dry. Bake in a preheated 375 F (190 C) oven for approximately 18 minutes or until golden brown.

❦❦❦

YOGURT SPICE COOKIE DROPS
Biskota Myrothata me Yiaourti

*1/2 cup unsalted butter or margarine, at
        room temperature*
13/4 cups sugar
2 eggs
1 tsp vanilla
3 cups all-purpose flour
1 tsp baking soda
1 tsp cinnamon
1/4 tsp ground cloves
1/2 tsp nutmeg
3/4 cup plain yogurt
1/2 cup finely chopped walnuts

Cream butter if desired and sugar until light and fluffy. Add eggs one at a time, beating thoroughly after each one is added. Add vanilla. Sift dry ingredients together. Gradually add flour mixture alternately with yogurt to creamed mixture, beating until smooth after each addition. Add walnuts and mix thoroughly. Drop from heaping teaspoonfuls of mixture spaced apart on cookie sheets lined with parchment paper and spread evenly. Bake in a preheated 350 F (180 C) oven on middle rack approximately 16-20 minutes or until golden. Makes 4 dozen cookies.

❦❦❦

ALMOND PAXIMATHAKIA
Paximathia Amygthalou

4 eggs, separated
1 1/4 cups sugar
1 tsp vanilla
1/2 tsp almond extract
Grated rind of 1/2 orange
1 1/4 cups all-purpose flour
1 1/2 tsp baking powder
1 1/2 cups whole blanched almonds

Beat egg yolks with sugar until thick and creamy. Add vanilla, almond extract and orange rind. Sift flour and baking powder together. Gradually add flour and whole almonds. Fold in stiffly beaten egg whites. Spread mixture into 10x15x2-inch baking pan lined with greased parchment paper. Bake in a preheated 350 F (180 C) oven for 15 minutes. Remove from oven. Turn the pan quickly up side down on a cutting board lined with parchment paper. Let stand for 10 minutes. Gently slice with serrated knife into 3/4-inch thick and 3-inch long bars. Place into a large baking sheet and return to oven for 10-15 minutes or until lightly golden brown. Remove from oven and cool. When completely cool, store in air-tight containers.

⋙—✠—⋘

ALMOND PAXIMATHAKIA
Paximathakia amygthalou

81/2 cups all-purpose flour (about)
2 tsp baking soda
6 tsp baking powder
1/4 tsp salt
21/2 cups melted unsalted butter
4 eggs, beaten
3 cups sugar
21/2 cups milk
2 tsp pure vanilla extract
1 tsp pure almond extract
1 1/2 cups coarsely chopped almonds
1 egg, beaten with 1 tsp water

Sift dry ingredients together in a large mixing bow. Add the melted butter, and mix well with your hands. Add the rest of the ingredients except the egg, and mix until the dough is smooth and soft. Add more flour if needed. Divide dough into 8 parts. Shape into long flat loaves about 2-inchs wide and 3/4 -inch thick. Place on baking sheets lined with parchment paper1 1/2-inches apart. Brush with beaten egg. Let stand for 5 minutes to allow the egg to dry. Bake in a preheated 375 F (190 C) oven on the middle rack for 20 minutes. Remove from the oven, cool for 10 minutes; cut diagonally into 3/4-inch slices, with sharp serrated knife. Place in the baking sheets and separate. Return to oven and bake for 10-15 minutes longer or until golden brown. Cool completely and store in airtight containers.

⋙—✠—⋘

CINNAMON-SUGAR LOW CHOL PAXIMATHAKIA
Paximathakia Kanellas

13/4 cups good quality light olive oil
1 1/4 cups sugar
1/4 cup cognac or brandy (optional)
8 extra large egg whites
1 cup finely chopped walnuts (optional)
7 cups all-purpose flour (about)
41/2 tsp baking powder
1 1/4 tsp baking soda
1 tsp cinnamon
1/4 tsp cloves
1/4 tsp salt
1 egg white, beaten with 1 Tbsp of water
1/2 cup sugar
1 tsp cinnamon
2 12x17-inches baking sheets
Parchment paper

In a large mixer bowl beat oil, sugar and cognac if desired on high speed for 7 minutes. Add egg whites and beat for 6 minutes longer. Add the walnuts if desired. Sift dry ingredients together. Turn the speed to stir and gradually add the flour mixture beating until smooth after each addition to make a-soft dough but not sticky. Add more flour if needed. Divide dough into 6 parts. Shape each part into a loaf 16-inches long. Gently lift the loaf and place on the baking sheet lined with parchment paper. Repeat with the remaining parts. Use your fingers to press down the loaves to make 2-inches wide and 1/2-inch thick. Brush with the beaten egg white mixture and generously sprinkle with cinnamon-sugar mixture. Let stay 5 minutes to allow the egg to dry. Bake in a preheated 375 F (190 C) oven on the middle rack for 20 minutes. Remove from oven and let cool for 5 minutes. With a serrated knife cut diagonally into 1/2-inch thick slices and separate. Return to oven and bake for 12-15 minutes or until golden brown. Remove from the oven and let the paximathakia to cool. When paximathakia are completely cool, store in air-tightly containers (preferably glass).

❧❦❧

CINNAMON-SUGAR PAXIMATHAKIA
Paximathakia Kanellas

1 cup unsalted butter, at room temperature
1 cup good quality olive oil
1 1/4 cups sugar
4 extra large eggs
1 cup finely chopped walnuts
7 cups all-purpose flour (about)
41/2 tsp baking powder
1 1/4 tsp baking soda
1 tsp cinnamon
1/4 tsp cloves
1/4 tsp salt
1 egg white, beaten with 1 Tbsp of water
1/2 cup sugar, mixed with
1 tsp cinnamon
2 12x17-inches baking sheets
Parchment paper

In a-large mixer bowl cream butter, oil and sugar until light and creamy. Add eggs one at a time, beating thoroughly after each one is added. Add walnuts. Sift dry ingredients together. Turn the speed to stir and gradually add flour mixture beating until smooth after each addition to make a-soft dough but not stick. Add more flour if needed. Divide dough into 6 parts. Shape each part into a loaf 16-inches long, Gently lift the loaf and place on the baking sheet lined with parchment paper. Repeat with the remaining parts. Use your fingers to press down the loaves to make 2-inches wide and 1/2-inch thick. Brush with the beaten egg white mixture and generously sprinkle with cinnamon-sugar mixture. Let stay 5 minutes to allow the egg to dry. Bake in a

preheated 375 F (190 C) oven on the middle rack for 20 minutes. Remove from oven and let cool for 5 minutes. With a serrated knife cut diagonally into 1/2-3/4-inch thick slices and separate. Return to oven and bake for 12-15 minutes or until golden brown. Remove from the oven and let the paximathakia to cool. When paximathakia are completely cool store in air-tightly containers (preferably glass).

❧❦❧

FRUIT NUT PAXIMATHAKIA
Paximathakia Froutou

1 1/2 cups unsalted butter or margarine, at
        room temperature
1 1/2 cups sugar
4 eggs
1 tsp vanilla
1 cup seedless golden raisins
1 cup finely chopped almonds or walnuts
5 cups all-purpose flour (about)
1/2 tsp baking soda
4 tsp baking powder
1 egg, beaten with 1 tsp water
2 12x17-inch baking sheets
Parchment paper

Cream butter if desired and sugar until light and fluffy. Add eggs one at a time, beating thoroughly after each is added. Add vanilla, raisins and almonds if desired, mix well. Sift dry ingredients together. Gradually add flour, beating until smooth after each addition to make soft dough. Add flour if needed. Divide dough into 5 parts. Shape into long loaves about 2-inches wide and 3/4-inch thick. Gently lift loaves and arrange on baking sheets lined with parchment, 1 1/2-inches apart. Brush with egg wash and let stay for 5 minutes to allow egg to dry. Bake in preheated 375 F (190 C) oven 20 minutes. Remove from oven and cool 10 minutes. Cut diagonally into 3/4-inch slices with serrated knife and separate. Return to oven and bake 10-15 minutes or until golden brown. Cool and store in tightly covered containers.

❧❦❧

PLAIN PAXIMATHAKIA
Paximathakia Apla

1 cup unsalted butter, at room temperature
2 Tbsp good quality light olive oil
1 1/2 cups sugar
3 extra large eggs
1 tsp vanilla
41/2 cups all-purpose flour (about)
1 tsp baking soda
1 Tbsp baking powder
1 egg, beaten with 1 tsp water
Sesame seeds
2 12x17-inches baking sheets
Parchment paper

In a-large mixer bow cream butter, oil and sugar until light and fluffy. Add eggs one at a time, beating thoroughly after each is added. Beat in vanilla. Sift dry ingredients together. Turn speed to stir and gradually add flour, beating until smooth after each addition to make a-soft dough but not sticky. Add flour if needed. Divide dough into 4 parts. Shape each part into a log 16-inches long. Gently lift the loaf and place on baking sheet lined with parchment. Repeat with remaining parts. Use fingers to press down loaves to make 2-inches wide and 1/2-inch thick. Gently lift loaves and arrange in baking sheets lined with parchment paper, 1 1/2-inches apart. Brush with beaten egg mixture and sprinkle with sesame seeds. Let stay 5 minutes to allow the egg to dry. Bake in a preheated 375 F (190 C) oven on the middle rack for 20 minutes. Remove from oven and let cool for 5 minutes. With a serrated knife cut diagonally into 1/2-3/4-inch thick slices and separate. Return to oven and bake for 12-15 minutes or until golden brown. Remove from the oven and let the paximathakia to cool. When paximathakia are completely cool store in tightly covered containers (preferably glass).

SPICED PAXIMATHAKIA
Paximathakia Myrodata

1 1/2 cups good quality olive oil
1/2 cup unsalted butter, at room temperature
1 cup fresh orange juice
13/4 cups sugar

1/2 cup cognac or brandy
Grated rind of 1 orange
Grated rind of 1 lemon
81/2 cups all-purpose flour (about)
2 tsp baking soda
4 tsp baking powder
1/2 tsp ground cloves
2 tsp cinnamon
2 egg whites, beaten with 1 tsp water
Sesame seeds
2 12x17-inches baking sheets
Parchment paper

Combine first five ingredients in large mixer bowl and beat well. Beat in grated rind. Sift dry ingredients together. Turn speed to stir and gradually add flour mixture, beating until smooth after each addition to make a-soft dough but not stick. Add flour if needed. Divide dough into 6 parts. Shape each part into a log 16-inches long. Gently lift loaf and place on baking sheet lined with parchment. Repeat with remaining parts. Use fingers to press down loaves to make 2-inches wide and 1/2-inch thick. Brush with egg wash and sprinkle with sesame seeds. Let stay 5 minutes to allow egg to dry. Bake in preheated 375 F (190 C) oven on middle rack 20 minutes. Remove from oven and let cool 5 minutes. With serrated knife cut diagonally into 1/2-3/4-inch thick slices and separate. Return to oven and bake 12-15 minutes or until golden brown. Remove from oven and let cool. When are completely cool store in tightly covered containers (glass).

HONEY FOLDS
Diples

8 eggs
1 tsp vanilla
2 Tbsp fresh lemon juice
6 cups unbleached all-purpose flour
1 1/2 tsp baking powder
3 Tbsp melted butter
6 cups fine quality oil for frying
3 cups honey
1/2 cup water
Cinnamon
1 cup finely ground walnuts (optional)

Beat eggs until thick and light. Add vanilla. Sift

flour with baking powder together. Gradually add flour to egg mixture alternately with lemon juice, beating until smooth. Add enough flour to make soft dough. Gradually add melted butter, knead until smooth and elastic. Divide dough into 3 parts. With hands work each part of dough at a time into a very smooth ball. Place on dish and cover with plastic wrap. Let stay 4 hours or longer at room temperature. On flour surface roll out each ball at a time into a 1/16-inch thin sheet (fillo dough). Cut into 6x2-inch strips. Keeping covered so they don't dry out, with a damp (not wet) towel. Pour oil into deep electric fryer. Heat oil on 350 F (180 C). Drop strips one at a time in hot oil, press down and turn immediately. Gently roll up in hot oil with big fork; fry until slightly golden on both sides. Drain into colander or lay on absorbent paper. You may dip them in the honey after you fry them, or when you need them. Keep in plastic container, before or after you dip in honey. Boil honey with water 2 minutes. Skim off foam. Dip folds in honey one at a time and remove immediately. Sprinkle with cinnamon and walnuts if desired. Serve cool.

❦❦❦

LOUKOUMATHES
Loukoumathes

1 Tbsp active dry yeast
21/2 cups lukewarm water
3/4 tsp salt
5 cups all-purpose flour, sifted
6 cups good quality oil for frying
For the syrup:
2 cups honey
1 cup sugar
3/4 cup water
Ground cinnamon

Dissolve yeast and salt in one cup of the lukewarm water and let stay for 5 minutes. Place the flour into a large mixing bowl and make a well in the center of the flour. Add the yeast and the lukewarm water and beat with a wire whisk to make a-very soft dough, not to thick or not to thin. Add more lukewarm water if needed. Beat well. Cover and let stay in a warm place for 2 hours or until the dough begins to bubble and is

doubled in bulk, the batter is ready. Heat oil into a deep electric fryer on 350 F (180 C). With your hand take a handful of dough. Close the hand, squeezing the dough until it comes in a round piece through the top of your closed hand. With a damp teaspoon, drop the dough in spoonfuls into the hot oil, 8 to 10 spoonfuls at a time. Puffs will swell and float to the surface, turn them up side down and fry until golden. Remove from the oil with a slotted spoon and lay on an absorbent paper to drain. Repeat the same procedure until you used all the dough. In a 3-quart saucepan combine syrup ingredients together. Bring to boil, reduce heat and boil for 5 minutes (being careful not to over boil the syrup). Serve immediately with warm honey and sprinkle with cinnamon.

Note: You can use as much of the dough as you needed, the rest you can refrigerate for the next day if you wish. Let the dough stay at room temperature before you use it.

❦❦❦

RUSTIC LOUKOUMATHES
Agrotiki Loukoumathes

3 extra large eggs
1/2 cup sugar
1/3 cup melted unsalted butter
1/3 cup milk
4 cups all-purpose flour (about)
5 tsp baking powder
Pinch of salt
4-6 cups good quality oil for frying
For the syrup:
1 cup sugar
1 cup honey
2/3 cup water
Ground cinnamon for dusting

Beat eggs in a large mixer bowl until frothy. Gradually add sugar and beat well. Add melted butter and milk, mix to combine. Sift dry ingredients together. Gradually add to egg mixture, knead until dough is thick and smooth. Add flour if needed. Roll out dough on a flour surface to 1/3-inch thick. Cut into rounds or other shape you desire. Drop a few loukoumathes at a time into 350 F (180 C) hot oil. The loukoumathes will float to surface and become golden-honey color. Turn the other side to fry. Remove from oil and place on absorbent paper. Prepare syrup. Combine sugar, honey and water in 2-quart saucepan and bring to boil, being careful not to over boil syrup. Reduce the heat to low and boil 5 minutes. Skim foam and discard. Serve hot with syrup and dust with cinnamon.

YOGURT LOUKOUMATHES
Loukoumathes me Yiaourt

1 1/2 cups whole milk or 2%
1 1/2 Tbsp fresh squeezed lemon juice
2 cups hot water
1/4 tsp salt
1/2 tsp sugar
1/2 Tbsp active dry yeast
6 cups all-purpose unbleached flour (about), sifted
Oil for frying
Honey
Cinnamon for dusting

Add lemon juice to milk, let stand for a minute to thicken (that is your yogurt). In a large deep bowl place milk mixture, the hot water, salt and sugar, and stir well. Add yeast and stir well to combine. Gradually add flour, stirring constantly until you make a thick batter (not too thick or running). Cover and let stay in cool oven 60-90 minutes or until doubled in bulk and looks full of bubbles. Place oil in a heavy deep saucepan over medium heat, until it reaches 350 F (180 C). With a damp teaspoon drop batter in teaspoonfuls into hot oil. The lookoumathes will float to surface, then turn them and fry until golden on all sides. Remove from oil with a straining spoon and lay on absorbent paper to drain. Serve hot with warm honey and sprinkle with cinnamon.

GREEK COFFEE
Kafes Ellinikos

Very sweet coffee:
Kafes varies glykos
1 demitasse cup water (1/2 cup)
2 tsp sugar
1 1/2 tsp Greek coffee

Medium sweet coffee:
Kafes metrios glykos
1 demitasse cup water
1 tsp sugar
1 1/2 tsp Greed coffee

Light sweet coffee:
Kafes elafris glykos
1 demitasse cup water
1/2 tsp sugar
1 1/2 tsp Greek coffee
1 briki (special small coffee pot needed
for Greek coffee)

Combine water and sugar in a small briki, let water get warm, stirring until sugar has dissolved. Add coffee and stir well to blend. Remove pot from heat before coffee boils and destroys foam. Gently pour into demitasse cup. Let coffee stand 30 seconds before sipping, so grounds may settle. Serve with a slice of cake, cookies or sheet preserve and a glass of ice water. Serves 1.

DESSERTS

ARGOLAVOUS
Almond Delights

4 1/2 cups blanched almonds
3 cups sugar
1 tsp vanilla extract or grated rind of 1 lemon
1 tsp almond extract
4 egg whites or more
2 cups chopped blanched almonds

In food processor grind almonds and sugar together one cup at a time until almonds are very fine. Return ground almond mixture back to food processor, add vanilla and almond extract, plus egg whites one at a time, blend until smooth and stiff. Add egg white if needed. Break off pieces of mixture the size of large walnut and shape into oval with palm of hand to a thick cookie and roll in chopped almonds if desired. Place on baking sheets lined with parchment. Bake in preheated 325 F (165 C) oven 20-30 minutes or until golden. Gently remove argolavous from paper while still warm. If argolavous stick to paper, pour some water in pan under parchment paper, let stand a few minutes to moisten underside. Makes about 4 dozen.

꿎꿎

ALMOND PRALINE
Pralina me Amygdala

1 cup sugar
1/3 cup water
3 Tbsp light corn syrup
1 cup lightly toasted whole almonds or cut in halves
1 Tbsp unsalted butter
1/4 tsp baking soda
Good quality light olive oil or butter for greasing
In small heavy saucepan combine sugar, corn syrup and water. Bring to boil, reduce heat to medium-high and boil until golden. Add almonds, stirring constantly and cook until golden brown. Add butter and baking soda, mix well and spread on generously greased baking sheet. When cool remove from sheet and break into small pieces or place large pieces of praline in a plastic bag, close it and lightly pound with a mallet. Store in a glass jar.

꿎꿎

HAZELNUT PRALINE
Pralínes me Foudoukia

1 1/2 cups sugar
1/3 water
2 Tbsp butter
1 tsp baking soda
1 1/2 cups hazelnuts blanched

Spread hazelnuts on baking sheet and bake in preheated 350 F (180 C) oven 10 minutes. Remove from oven and from pan into a kitchen towel and rub with your hands until all skin has removed. In medium heavy frying pan place sugar, water and butter. Stir until sugar has dissolved. Bring to boil, reduce heat to medium and cook until golden brown. Remove from heat, add hazelnuts and soda and stir well to combine. Spread on greased baking sheet and let cool. When completely cool break into pieces and store in glass jar.
Note: You can use pistachio nuts, peanuts, almonds or walnuts.

꿎꿎

ALMOND BAKLAVA
Baklavas Amygdalou

3 cups finely chopped blanched almonds
1/3 cup sugar
1/3 cup finely ground Zwieback toast or
*   dried breadcrumbs (see index for recipe)*
1 tsp cinnamon
1 cup melted clarified unsalted butter or margarine
*   (see index for recipe)*
1 pound Phyllo pastry, thawed
For the syrup:
4 cups sugar
2 cups water
1 Tbsp fresh lemon juice
1 tsp almond extract
1/2 cup pistachio nuts, chopped (optional)

Combine first 4 ingredients. Brush 10x15x3-inch baking pan with the melted butter. Lay two sheets of phyllo in the bottom of the pan, brush with hot melted butter, cover with two more sheets, brush again with hot melted butter, and repeat this process until you have used 8 sheets. Then sprinkle evenly with 1/3 cup the almond mixture, cover with two sheets brush with the hot melted butter and sprinkle evenly with almond mixture. Repeat this process until all almond mixture is used. Then cover with the remaining sheets, brushing every other one with the hot melted butter. With a sharp knife cut the baklava into square and then into triangle shape. Bake in a preheated 300 F (150 C) oven for 90 minutes. Cool. With the sharp knife cut again the baklava all the way down. Combine syrup ingredients except almond extract and pistachio nuts. Bring to a boil, reduce heat to medium and boil for 10 minutes add the almond extract. Pour hot syrup over cool baklava. Sprinkle with pistachio nuts if desired. Cover until cool. Drain if desired, to remove excess syrup. Place baklava on a serving platter and serve with Greek cup of coffee.

ALMOND-WALNUT BAKLAVA
Baklava me Amygdala ke Karythia

1 1/2 cups finely chopped blanched almonds
1 1/2 cups finely chopped walnuts
1/3 cup finely ground Zwieback toast or dried
bread crumbs (see index for recipe)

1 tsp cinnamon
1 1/2 cups melted clarified unsalted butter or
margarine (see index for recipe)
1 pound fillo pastry (thawed)
For the syrup:
4 cups sugar
2 cups water
1 Tbsp fresh lemon juice
1/2 tsp almond extract

Follow preparation as directed in Baklava with Almonds (see index for recipe).

PUMPKIN NUT BAKLAVA
Kolokytha Baklava

2 cups cooked and mashed fresh pumpkin
3 Tbsp unsalted butter or margarine
1/4 tsp salt
1/4 cup finely ground Zwieback toast or dried
breadcrumbs (see index for recipe)
Grated rind of 1/2 orange
1/2 tsp cinnamon
3/4 cups finely chopped walnuts
1/4 cup honey
1/2 cups sugar
1 pound fillo pastry (thawed)
1 cup melted clarified butter or margarine
1 cup finely chopped blanched almonds
1/4 cup sugar
1/4 cup finely ground Zwieback toast
1/4 tsp cinnamon
For the syrup:
3/4 cups sugar
1/3 cup honey
2/3 cup water

Prepare the pumpkin as directed in Butternut or Pumpkin Pita (see index for recipe). Melt butter if desired in a medium saucepan. Add 2 cups mashed pumpkin (save the rest for other use or freeze it) and sauté for few minutes, add salt, stirring constantly. Remove from heat; add ground toast, grated orange rind, cinnamon, honey, sugar, the walnuts and mix thoroughly to combine. Set aside. Mix almonds, ground toast, sugar and cinnamon together. Brush a 9x13x3-inch baking pan with hot melted butter if desired. Lay 6 fillo sheets on the bottom of the pan one on top the other brushing every other one with hot melted butter. Then sprinkle evenly with a hand full of the almond mixture, cover with 2 sheets of fillo, brush with hot butter and sprinkle again with a hand full of the almond mixture. Repeat this process until you have used 14 sheets all together. The sheets will extend up the sides of the pan. Pour in the pumpkin mixture and spread evenly. Fold one fillo sheet and place in the middle of the pan. Repeat with ones more fillo. Fold overhanging fillo sheets over the filling to enclose it and brush with hot butter. Lay the rest of the fillo sheets over the top, brushing every other one with hot butter and sprinkle with the almond mixture. Tuck in overhanging sheets inside the pan. Score top layers of fillo (over the filling) with a sharp serrated knife into diamond shapes. Bake in a preheated 350 F (180 C) oven for approximately 45 minutes or until golden brown. Cool to lukewarm. Combine syrup ingredients in a small saucepan. Bring to boil, reduce heat to medium and boil for 5 minutes. Pour hot syrup over the lukewarm pumpkin baklava. Let cool. Cut through the scored lines.

❦❦❦

WALNUT BAKLAVA
Baklavaa me Karythia

Substitute walnuts for the almonds. Follow recipe and preparation as directed in Baklava with Almonds (see index for recipe). Subtract almond extract from the syrup.

❦❦❦

SARAILI
Nut Pastry Rolls

31/2 cups finely chopped walnuts, blanched
      almonds or mixed
1/3 cup sugar
1 tsp cinnamon
1/3 cup finely ground zwieback toast or lightly toasted breadcrumbs (see index for recipe)
1 pound fillo pastry (thawed)
1 cup melted clarified unsalted butter or margarine
For the syrup:
3 cups sugar
13/4 cups water
1 Tbsp fresh lemon juice
1 tsp almond extract if you use almonds

Combine first four ingredients. Brush two fillo sheets with hot melted butter if desired and sprinkle with 1/3 cup of walnut mixture if desired. Lay two more sheets of fillo on top of walnuts, brush with hot butter and sprinkle with 1/3 cup walnut mixture. Gently roll up pastry in jelly roll fashion, starting with a wide end and not very tight. Place saraili into greased baking pan, seam side down. Repeat this process until all fillo sheets and walnut mixture are used. Generously brush with hot butter and cut each roll into 2-3-inches long pieces. Bake in preheated 350 F (180 C) oven approximately 20 minutes or until golden brown. Cool to lukewarm. Pierce each one with a fork. Combine sugar, water and lemon juice in a saucepan, bring to a boil, reduce heat and boil 10 minutes. Remove from heat and add almond extract if you used almonds. Spoon hot syrup over saraili. Cover and let cool completely before serving. Serve with a cup of Greek coffee.

❦❦❦

ALMOND CAKE IN FILLO PASTRY
Keik Amygthalou se Fillo

6 extra large eggs, at room temperature
1/2 cup sugar
1/2 cup cognac or brandy
1/4 cup water
2 cups ground almonds
3/4 cup fine semolina
1 Tbsp baking powder
1/4 tsp salt
1 tsp cinnamon
1 pound fillo pastry (thawed)
1 cup melted clarified unsalted butter or margarine
      (see index for recipe)
For the syrup:
41/2 cups sugar
3 cups water
2 Tbsp fresh lemon juice
1 tsp almond extract

Beat eggs until frothy, add sugar and beat until creamy and thick. Add cognac if desired and water; mix well. Mix dry ingredients together. Gradually add to egg mixture and mix well to combine. Brush 11x17x3-inch baking pan with hot melted butter if desired. Lay 10 fillo sheets on bottom of pan, one on top the other brushing every other one with hot butter. The sheets will extend up the sides of the pan. Spoon in egg-almond mixture and spread evenly. Butter and fold overhanging sides and ends of fillo sheets over filling to enclose it. Take one fillo sheet, fold it and place on top of the uncovered filling and brush with hot butter. Repeat two more times. Lay remaining fillo sheets over the top, brushing every other one with hot butter. Score with sharp serrated knife into 3-4 lines lengthwise. Bake in preheated 350 F (180 C) oven approximately 45 minutes or until golden brown. While pasty is baking prepare syrup. Combine sugar and water in a 4-quart saucepan, bring to a boil, reduce heat and boil for 5 minutes add the lemon juice and boil for 2 minutes longer. Remove from the heat add the almond extract. Cut pastry through the scored lines and into diamond shapes. Spoon the hot syrup over the hot pastry. Let cool completely. Serve pastry with a cup of Greek coffee if desired.

MILOPITA IN FILLO PASTRY
Milopita me Fillo

For the filling:
8 large apples, cored, pared and thinly sliced
2 Tbsp fresh lemon juice
1/2 cup finely ground Zwieback toast
1/2 tsp ground cinnamon
1 cup sugar
1 1/3 cups blanched toasted almonds or walnuts, chopped
3/4 cup seedless golden raisins
1 pound fillo pastry (thawed)
1 cup melted clarified butter, margarine, good quality light olive or salad oil

For the syrup:
1 1/2 cups sugar
3/4 cup water
1 Tbsp fresh lemon juice
1 1-inch long cinnamon stick

Mix dry ingredients together. Add sliced apples and lemon juice and mix well. Brush an 11x15-17x3-inch about baking pan with butter. Line the pan with one half of the fillo sheets, brushing

every other sheet with the hot butter if desired. The fillo sheets will extend up the sides of the pan. Spoon in the apple mixture and spread evenly. Take one fillo sheet and folded into half crosswise and cover the filling and brush with the hot butter. Repeat the same procedure with a second fillo sheet, and place over the first sheet and brush again with the butter. Fold overhanging fillo sheets over the filling to enclose it. Top with the rest of the fillo sheets brushing every other one with hot butter and tuck in overhanging sheets inside the pan. Generously brush top with hot butter. Score to layers of fillo sheets all the way to the filling with a sharp serrated knife into three lines lengthwise. Bake in a preheated 350 F (180 C) oven on the middle rack for 50-60 minutes or until golden brown. Cool to warm. While the milopita is cooling prepare the syrup. Combine syrup ingredients in a 1-quart saucepan. Bring to boil, reduce heat to medium-low and boil for 10 minutes. Pour warm syrup over warm apple pastry. Let cool. When you are ready to serve, cut through scored lines and them into 3x3-inch squares. Serve at room temperature.

MILOPITA WITH PUFF PASTRY
Milopita me Sfoliata

1 pkg puff pastry (thawed)
10 large apples any kind you desired, pared, cored, and cut into 12 slices
2 cups sugar
1 cup water
3 sticks of cinnamon
1/2 cup toasted pecans, chopped
1/2 cup golden raisins
1 egg, beaten, with 1 Tbsp of milk

In a large non-stick frying pan, add the apples, sugar, water and the cinnamon sticks. Bring to boil, reduce heat to medium, covered, and cook until the water has been absorbed and the sugar begin caramelized. Add the pecans and the raisins, and gently stir to combine. Let the mixture cook for few minutes longer, uncovered, been careful not to burn the caramel. Remove from the heat. Line one piece of the puff pastry on an 83/4x131/2x13/4-inch Pyrex pan or a baking dish. If the pastry is not long or wide enough, place on a working surface, and lightly dusted with flour, and roll out to the size you needed, and line the pan. Spoon the apple mixture, remove the cinnamon sticks, and spread evenly. Brush the edges of the bottom pastry with the beaten egg. Cover with the second piece of puff pastry to cover the apples. If needed to roll out the pastry, repeat the same procedure as above. Then with your fingers press firmly the two pastries together to seal them. Brush the top of the milopita with the beaten egg. Let stand for 5 minutes, to allow the egg to dry. Bake the milopita in a preheated 450 F (230 C) oven on the middle rack for 20 minutes. Reduce the oven temperature to 400 F (200 C), and bake for 20-25 minutes longer, or until golden brown. Watching the milopita does not brown too much, if does, reduce the oven temperature to 375 F (190 C), and cover loosely with a pieces of foil. Remove from the oven and let cool. Serve plain, with ice cream or whipped cream if desired.

APPLE NUT FILLED FLUTES
Flogheres Gemistes me Mila

8 medium apples, pared cored and chopped
2 Tbsp fresh lemon juice
2 Tbsp cognac (optional)
1/3 cup finely ground Zwieback toast
1/2 tsp cinnamon
1 1/2 cups sugar
1 cup chopped walnuts
1/2 cup golden raisins
1 pound fillo pastry (thawed)
1 cup melted clarified unsalted butter or margarine
Confectioner sugar for dusting

Mix dry ingredients together. Add chopped apples, lemon juice and cognac, and mix well. Cover fillo sheets with damp cloth, to keep them from drying while working. Take one fillo at a time. Brush each fillo with hot melted butter if desired, and fold in half crosswise. Place one 1/2 cup of the apple mixture, at the narrow end of the fillo strip. Turn sides in toward the middle to

enclose filling. Brush with the hot butter and roll up lengthwise to the other end into a flute shape. Place in greased baking sheet. Repeat filling and rolling process. Generously brush each one with the hot butter. With sharp serrated knife cut two steam slits 1/2-inch long, going down through the fillo to the apples. Bake in a preheated 350 F (180 C) oven on the middle rack for 30 minutes or until golden. Cool to lukewarm. Dust with confectioner sugar and serve. Makes 20-24.

COPENHAGEN PASTRY GREEK STYLE
Kopinhagen me Jymi Pastas Floras

For the crust:
1 1/2 cups all-purpose flour
1 tsp baking powder
Pinch of salt
3/4 cup unsalted butter, at room temperature
1/4 cup sugar
2 Tbsp cognac or brandy
1 extra large beaten egg
Grated rind of 1/2 orange
For the filling:
1/2 cup apricot jam
3/4 cup sugar
6 extra large eggs, separated
1/2 cup cognac or brandy
13/4 cups finely ground almonds
1 cup finely ground Zwieback toast
1 Tbsp baking powder
1 tsp cinnamon
6 sheets of fillo pastry (thawed)
1/3 cup melted clarified unsalted butter
        or margarine (see index for recipe)
For the syrup:
3 cups sugar
2 cups water
2 Tbsp fresh lemon juice
1/2 tsp almond extract

In a bowl sift dry ingredients together, and cut in butter. Add egg, cognac if desired and orange rind. Mix until mixture will hold together. Press dough in bottom of greased 13x9x3-inch baking pan and spread evenly. Bake in preheated 400 F (205 C) oven on middle rack 15 minutes. Spread jam over baked crust. Set aside. Beat egg yolks until frothy, add sugar and beat until thick and creamy. Add cognac if desired. Mix ground almonds, toast, baking powder and cinnamon together. Gradually add to egg mixture and mix well. Fold in stiffly beaten egg whites. Spread mixture over jam. Lay 6 fillo sheets over egg-almond mixture, brushing every other one with hot melted butter if desired. Score with sharp serrated knife into diamond shapes. Bake in preheated 350 F (180 C) oven on middle rack approximately 40 minutes or until golden brown. While the pastry is baking, prepare the syrup. Combine sugar and water in a 4-quart saucepan, bring to boil, reduce heat and boil for 5 minutes, add the lemon juice and boil for 2 minutes longer. Remove from heat, and add the almond extract. Cut pastry through the scored lines and spoon hot syrup over hot pastry. Let cool completely. Serve pastry with a cup of Greek coffee.

❧✦❧

CREAM PUFFS
Sou A La Cream

For the shells:
3 cups milk 1 recipe Puff Pastry B (see index
for recipe)
Vanilla cream filling:
1 cup sugar
1/4 tsp salt
4 Tbsp flour
3 Tbsp corn-starch
4 egg yolks
2 Tbsp unsalted butter
1 tsp vanilla
1 cup whipping cream, whipped
Caramel topping:
3/4 cup sugar
3 Tbsp water
1 Tbsp corn syrup
1/2 cup toasted chopped or sliced blanched
almonds or pistachio nuts

Prepare puff pastry as directed. Prepare cream filling. Scald 2 1/2 cups of milk. Combine sugar, salt, flour, cornstarch, egg yolks and 1/2 cup of remaining milk, and mix well using a wire whisk. Gradually stir in scalding milk and cook slowly on top of a double boiler, whisking constantly until mixture thickens. Cover and cook 5 minutes longer. Remove from heat. Add butter and vanilla and stir well to combine. Cover with a piece of

plastic wrap touching the cream to prevent a skin from forming. Chill. Fold in whipped cream. Spoon cream filling into a pastry bag with 1/2-inch round tip, and pipe filling into puffs to fill them. Prepare caramel topping. Place sugar and water into a small heavy pan, cook slowly moving pan occasionally until light brown, being careful not to scorch. Remove pan from heat, add corn syrup and stir well. Pour 1 Tbsp caramel on top of each puff and immediately sprinkle with chopped nuts. Makes 30 cream puffs.

For Chocolate Cream Puffs:
Add 3 ounces chopped bittersweet chocolate with the butter and vanilla to cream filling and stir well to melt. Cool. Add whipped cream and fill shells as above with cool chocolate cream filling. Lightly spread with a brush the outside of the shells with some of the chocolate cream filling and cover with chocolate sprinkles or decorate with caramel and nuts. Chill. Makes 30 chocolate cream puffs. Or divide the vanilla cream filling into two parts. Leave one part plain and the second part mix with the half of the chocolate. Makes 15 vanilla and 15 chocolate cream puffs.

❧✦❧

ÈCLAIR
Ekler

For the shells:
1 recipe for cream puffs A or B (see index
for recipe)
For the cream filling:
1 recipe vanilla cream filling (see index for
cream puffs)
For the chocolate frosting:
2 ounces bittersweet chocolate
2 Tbsp unsalted butter or margarine
1/2 cup confectioner's sugar, sifted
2 Tbsp water
1/2 tsp vanilla extract

Follow recipe and preparation as directed for cream puffs. Shape pastry into strips 3/4-inch wide and 3 1/2-inches long into greased baking sheet. Bake in a preheated 450 F (230 C) oven 20 minutes. Reduce heat to 350 F (180 C) and bake 10 minutes longer. When cool split éclairs ops. Prepare vanilla cream filling as directed. Fill the bottom of the éclairs with the vanilla filling. Cover with tops and chill. Prepare the chocolate frosting. Combine chocolate and butter in a double boiler over lightly simmering water, stirring continuously. Remove from heat. Add confectioner's sugar, water and vanilla, stirring until the mixture is smooth and glossy. Frost éclairs when chocolate is still hot.

❧❀❧

GALAKTOBOUREKO (L. CHOL)
Cream Filled Pastry

For the cream filling:
4 whole eggs, separated
1 cup sugar
1 cup fine semolina
8 cups scalding milk (2/100)
Rind of 1/2 lemon
2 Tbsp good quality light olive oil, unsalted
*   butter or margarine*
1 tsp pure vanilla extract
1 pound fillo pastry (thawed)
3/4 cup good quality light olive oil or half melted
*   clarified unsalted butter, margarine and*
*   half olive oil*

For the syrup:
3 cups sugar
1 1/2 cups water
2 Tbsp fresh lemon juice

Combine egg yolks and sugar in 4-quart saucepan, beat well using wire whisk. Add semolina and mix well. Gradually add milk stirring constantly, add lemon rind and cook slowly over medium-low heat, stirring constantly until it thickens. Remove from heat. Remove lemon rind, add vanilla and oil if desired, stir to mix well. Cover and let cool. Beat egg whites with a pinch of salt until soft peaks hold. Gently fold egg white into cream filling. Brush 11x17x3-inch baking pan with olive oil if desired. Lay 12 fillo sheets on bottom of pan, one on top the other brushing every other one with olive oil. The sheets will extend up the sides of pan. Spoon in cream filling and spread evenly. Butter and fold overhanging sides and ends of fillo sheets over the filling to enclose it. Take one fillo sheet,

folded in two and place on top of the filling and brush with olive oil. Repeat two more times. Lay the remaining fillo sheets over the top, brushing every other one with the olive oil. Score with a sharp serrated knife into 3-4 lines lengthwise. Bake in a preheated 350 F (180 C) oven 45 minutes or until golden brown. Cool to warm. While the galaktoboureko is cooling, prepare the syrup. Combine syrup ingredients in a three-quart saucepan. Bring to a boil, reduce heat to medium-low and boil 10 minutes partially covered. Spoon the warm syrup over warm galaktoboureko. Let cool. Cut through scored lines, then into squares or diamond shapes. Serve with Greek coffee.

❧❀❧

GALAKTOBOUREKO
Cream Filled Pastry

For the cream filling:
8 egg yolks
1 1/2 cups sugar
1 cup fine semolina
8 cups scalding milk
Rind of 1/2 lemon
2 Tbsp unsalted butter or margarine
1 tsp vanilla extract
3/4 cup finely chopped blanched almonds
*   (optional)*
1 pound fillo pastry (thawed)
1 cup melted clarified unsalted butter or margarine
*   (see index for recipe)*

For the syrup:
3 cups sugar
1 1/2 cups water
2 Tbsp fresh lemon juice

Combine egg yolks and sugar in 4-quart saucepan and beat well using wire whisk. Add semolina and mix well. Gradually add milk stirring constantly, add lemon rind and cook slowly over medium-low heat stirring constantly until it thickens. Remove from heat. Remove lemon rind. Add vanilla, butter and almonds if desired and stir to mix it well. Cover and let cool. Brush 11x17x3-inch baking pan with melted hot butter if desired. Lay 12 fillo sheets on bottom of pan, one on top the other brushing every other one with the hot butter. The sheets will extend up the sides of the pan. Spoon in cream filling and spread evenly. Butter and fold overhanging sides and ends of fillo sheets over filling to enclose it. Take one fillo sheet, fold it and place on top of the uncover filling and brush with hot butter. Repeat two more times. Lay remaining fillo sheets over the top, brushing every other one with hot butter. Score with sharp serrated knife into 3-4 lines lengthwise. Bake in a preheated 350 F (180 C) oven approximately 45 minutes or until golden brown. Cool to warm. While galaktoboureko is cooling prepare syrup. Combine syrup ingredients in 3-quart saucepan. Bring to a boil, reduce heat to medium-low and boil for 10 minutes partially covered. Spoon the warm syrup over warm galaktoboureko. Let cool. Cut through the scored lines and after into squares or diamond shapes and serve.

GALATOPITA WITH PUFF PASTRY
Galatopita me Sfoliata

1 cup plus 2 Tbsp sugar
4 eggs
4 cups milk
1/2 cup fine semolina
Pinch of salt
1 tsp pure vanilla extract
Grated rind of one half of lemon
1 tsp unsalted butter
1 pkg puff pastry (thawed)
Confectioner sugar, sifted

Beat 3 eggs with 3/4 cup plus 2 Tbsp sugar until creamy. Boil milk in 3-quart saucepan. Remove from heat and sprinkle the semolina, and salt over the milk, stirring continuously, return to heat and cook on low heat until thickens, stirring constantly. Slowly add beaten eggs to semolina mixture, stirring continuously (do not let mixture boil). Add vanilla, lemon rind, and butter, and stir well. Remove from heat. Cover with piece of plastic wrap, touching the cream, to prevent skin from forming. While cream cools, prepare puff pastry. Line puff pastry in greased 11-inch tart pan. Pour cream over pastry, and spread evenly. Beat remaining 2 eggs with remaining

sugar well. Pour over cream. Bake in preheated 370 F (190 C) oven on middle rack 45 minutes. Serve galaropita warm or cool, dusted with confectioner's sugar.

PASTRY FOR PUFFS A
Zymi yia Sou

1 cup boiling water
1/2 cup unsalted butter
1 cup all-purpose flour
4 eggs, at room temperature

Follow preparation as directed in Pastry For Puffs B (see index for recipe).
Makes 20 large cream puffs.

PASTRY FOR PUFFS B
Zymi Yia Sou

1 cup water
1/2 cup unsalted butter, at room temperature
1 1/2 cups all-purpose flour, sifted
6 eggs, at room temperature

In a 3-quart saucepan add water and bring to a boil. Reduce heat, and add the butter, bring to a boil again. Remove from the heat and add flour all at once and stir vigorously with a wooden spoon until the mixture forms a ball, leaving pan clean. Remove from heat. Spoon the pastry in the bowl of a mixer fitted with a paddle. Add the eggs one at a time, beating until dough is smooth and shiny. In this form it is ready to use it as you desired. For cream puffs follow the preparation. Spoon the mixture into a pastry bag, and pipe in 1-inch mounds using a #7 round tip, on a baking sheet lined with parchment paper 1-inch apart. Or drop with a teaspoon or tablespoon, (depending on the size you desire). Bake in a preheated 450 F (230 C) oven for 20 minutes. Reduce heat to 350 F (180 C) and bake for 5 minutes longer. Cool. Make slit on one side of each puff and fill with cool cream filling. Makes 30 large puffs.

QUINCE IN PUFF PASTRY ROLL UP
Kythonia se Sfoliata Rolo

1 box puff pastry (thawed)
3 pounds quinces, peeled, cored and thinly sliced
1 Tbsp fresh lemon juice
3 extra large eggs
1 1/4 cups sugar
1/2 cup finely chopped toasted blanched almonds
3 Tbsp fine semolina
1 tsp pure vanilla extract
1 egg, beaten with 1 tsp water
Confectioner's sugar

In a large mixing bowl beat eggs with sugar until light and fluffy. Add almonds, semolina and vanilla to the egg mixture and mix well. Add the prepared quinces and lemon juice to the egg mixture, and stir well to combine. Cover and chill for 2 hours or until all the liquids have absorbed. Place one piece of foil on a working surface, and lay the puff pastry one piece at a time. Spoon one half of the mixture on the puff pastry lengthwise, leaving 1-inch border all around the dough to prevent leakage of filling during baking. Brush border of dough with the beaten egg. Gently lift the pastry and start rolling lengthwise without the foil, place on a baking sheet seam side down. Repeat the same procedure with the remaining pastry and filling. Make few slits with the tip of a sharp knife on top of the pasty to release steam. Brush with beaten egg and bake in a preheated 450 F (230 C) oven and set the rack on the lower-middle level for 20 minutes or until has puffed and start to brown. Reduce the heat to 400 F (205 C) and bake for 20 to 30 minutes longer. Cover loosely with a piece of foil before it does brown too much. Remove from the oven and let cool before you slice it. Dust with confectioner's sugar and serve warm or at room temperature.

❧❀❧

CREAM FILLED KATAIFI
Kataifi me Krema

For the cream filling:
4 whole eggs, separated
1 cup sugar
1 cup fine semolina

8 cups scalding milk, you can use 2 %
Rind of 1/2 lemon
2 Tbsp unsalted butter or good quality light
    olive oil
1 tsp pure vanilla extract
3/4 cup finely chopped blanched almonds
    (optional)
1 pound kataifi shredded pastry (thawed)
1 cup melted clarified unsalted butter or 1/2 cup
    good quality light olive oil or half butter
    and half oil mixed

For the syrup:
3 cups sugar
1 1/2 cups water
2 Tbsp fresh lemon juice

Combine egg yolks and sugar in a four-quart saucepan, beat well using a wire whisk. Add semolina and mix well. Gradually add milk stirring constantly, add lemon rind and cook slowly over medium-low heat, stirring constantly until it thickens. Remove from heat. Remove the lemon rind, add the vanilla, butter if desired and almonds if desired, stir to mix well. Cover and let cool. Beat egg whites with a pinch of salt until soft pick. Gently fold egg whites into the cream filling. Gently separate kataifi pastry into two parts. Brush a 10x15x3-inch baking pan and lay one part of the kataifi pastry. Sprinkle with the half of the hot melted butter if desired. Spoon cream filling over the pastry and spread evenly. Lay the remaining kataifi pastry. Sprinkle with the remaining hot butter. Bake in a preheated 350 F (180 C) oven for approximately 45 minutes or until golden brown. Cool to lukewarm. Cut into square pieces. Combine syrup ingredients in a three-quart saucepan. Bring to a boil, reduce heat to medium-low and boil for 5 minutes. Spoon the hot syrup over kataifi pastry. Cover and let cool. Serve with a cup of Greek coffee.

❧❀❧

KATAIFI
Kataifi

21/2 cups finely chopped blanched almonds
1/3 cup sugar
1/3 cup finely ground toast or dried breadcrumbs
1 tsp ground cinnamon
4 Tbsp cognac or brandy

1 pound Kataifi shredded pastry (thawed)
1 cup melted clarified unsalted butter (see index)
For the syrup:
4 1/4 cups sugar
2 2/3 cups water
1 Tbsp. fresh lemon juice
1 tsp. pure almond extract (optional

Combine first 4 ingredients together. Add cognac if desired and mix well to combine. Gently separate kataife pastry into three parts. Lay one part of the kataifi pastry evenly in a 9x13x3-inch baking pan. Sprinkle evenly with one half of the almond mixture. Lay the second part of the kataifi pastry over the almond mixture. Sprinkle with the remaining almond mixture over the pastry. Lay with the remaining pasty evenly to cover the filling. Sprinkle with the hot melted butter. Bake in a preheated 350 F. oven for approximately 45 minutes or until golden. Cool to lukewarm. Combine syrup ingredients in a saucepan. Bring to boil, reduce heat to medium and boil for 5 minutes, add almond extract if desired. Pour hot syrup onto lukewarm kataifi. Cover and let cool. Cut into 2x2-inch squares or rectangles and serve with a cup of Greek coffee.

❧❀❧

CAKE WITH CHEESE AND PINEAPPLE
Keik me Tyri ke Anana

For the cake:
1/3 cup unsalted butter at room temperature
1 1/2 cups sugar
5 extra large eggs, separated
Rind of one lime or lemon, cut lengthwise and
    thinly sliced
1/2 tsp pure vanilla extract
2 cups all-purpose flour
Pinch of salt
3 tsp baking powder
1/2 cup milk
For the filling and topping:
2 pkgs cream cheese, or low fat, at
    room temperature
1/2 tsp pure vanilla extract
1/2 cup sugar
1 20-ounces can, pineapple chunks in light syrup
1 lime or lemon cut in half lengthwise and thinly sliced

Prepare the cake. Cream the butter until light and fluffy. Gradually add sugar, and beat well until creamy. Add eggs one at a time beating thoroughly after each one is added. Add lime rind and vanilla. Sift dry ingredients together add alternately with the milk to the cream mixture, beating until smooth. Pour into a greased 10-inch spring form pan, and spread evenly. Bake in a preheat 350 F (180 C) oven on the middle rack for approximately 50 minutes or until cake tester inserted in center comes out clean. Cool on wire rack for 10 minutes. Remove from pan and cool on wire rack. Prepare filling and topping. Beat cream cheese, sugar and vanilla until smooth and fluffy. Split the cake into two layers horizontally. Drain the pineapple and reserve the liquid. Brush the cake layers with the pineapple liquid. Coarsely chop the 3/4 of the pineapple chunks, and add to the cream mixture and mix well to combine. Place one cake layer on a round serving dish and spread one half of the cream pineapple mixture and spread evenly. Place the second cake layer over the cream. Spread the other half of the cream over the cake and spread evenly. Decorate the cake with the reserved pineapple chunks and lime slices. Serve at room temperature.

❧❀❧

UNBAKED CHEESECAKE WITH FRESH FRUIT
Apsito Keik Tyriou me Freska Frouta

For the crust:
1/3 cup unsalted butter
12 Coconut Cookies, crushed (see index for recipe)
For the filling:
3 ripped mangos
1 ripped papaya
1/4 cup fresh orange juice
2 envelops unflavored gelatin
2 pkgs cream cheese Philadelphia or low fat, at
room temperature
3/4 cup sugar
3 egg yolks
13/4 cups sour cream, or low fat, at
    room temperature
1/4 cup unsweetened coconut

Prepare crust. In small saucepan melt butter, remove from heat, let cool a few minutes, add crushed coconut cookies, mix well to combine. Spoon mixture on lightly greased with oil a 10-inch spring form pan, and press with top of your fingers or back of a spoon the bottom of pan until firm. Chill. Prepare filling. Peel two mangos and remove flesh, leave pit, chop and place in food processor. Peel and cut papaya in half lengthwise, with spoon remove seeds and discard. Chop and add to mangoes, add orange juice. Process fruit until smooth. Place fruit mixture in saucepan, sprinkle gelatin over, on low heat, stir mixture until gelatin dissolves. Remove from heat and let cool. Beat cheese with sugar until smooth and fluffy. Add egg yolks, one at a time, beating thoroughly after each is added. Add fruit-gelatin mixture and sour cream and beat well. Add more sugar if needed. Spoon mixture into prepared pan, and spread evenly. Cover with plastic wrap. Chill overnight. The next day, gently remove sides of pan. Place cheesecake in a round serving dish. Peel and cut remaining mango, remove pit. Cut into nice slices, and decorate cheesecake, sprinkle with coconut. Chill until ready to serve.

❧❦❧

ALMOND CAKE WITH SYRUP
Keik Amygthalou me Syropi

*3/4 cup unsalted butter or margarine, at
    room temperature*
3/4 cup sugar
4 eggs
1 tsp vanilla extract
3 cups all-purpose flour, sifted with
4 tsp baking powder
1 cup milk
1 cup finely chopped almonds
For the syrup:
21/2 cups sugar
1 1/4 cups water
1 Tbsp fresh lemon juice
1 tsp almond extract

Cream the butter if desired and sugar together until light and fluffy. Add eggs one at a time beating thoroughly after each one is added. Add

vanilla and flour mixture alternately with the milk to cream mixture beating until smooth. Add almonds and mix well to combine. Pour batter into greased and floured 9x13x3-inch baking pan. Bake in a preheated 350 F (180 C) oven for 45 minutes or until cake tester inserted in center comes out clean. Cool. Prepare the syrup. In a four-quart saucepan combine syrup ingredients except the almond extract. Bring to boil, reduce heat to medium and boil for 5 minutes. Pour hot syrup over cool cake. Let stay until completely cool. Cut and serve with whipped cream if desired.

❧❦❧

ALMOND-WALNUT CAKE WITH SYRUP
Keik me Amygthala ke Karythia

6 extra large eggs, separated
1/2 cup sugar
1 cup finely ground almonds
1 cup finely ground walnuts
1 1/2 cups finely ground Zwieback toast
3 tsp baking powder
1 1/2 tsp cinnamon
1/2 cup cognac or brandy
Whipped cream (optional)
For the syrup:
3 cups sugar
3 cups water
1 Tbsp fresh lemon juice

Beat the egg yolks with sugar until thick and creamy. Mix ground almonds, walnuts, toast, baking powder and cinnamon together. Gradually add almond mixture alternately with cognac if desired and mix well. Gently fold in stiffly beaten egg whites. Spoon the mixture into a greased 15x10x3-inch baking pan. Bake in a preheated 350 F (180 C) oven for approximately 45 minutes. Remove from oven and let cool. Combine syrup ingredients in a three-quart saucepan; bring to a boil, reduce heat to medium-low and boil for 5 minutes. Spoon hot syrup over the cool cake and cover with a larger baking sheet or a piece of foil. Let cool completely. Cut and serve with whipped cream or plain.

❧❦❧

CAKE WITH SYRUP
Keik me Siropi

For the cake:
4 extra large eggs, separated
1/2 cups sugar
1 tsp baking powder
1 tsp pure vanilla extract
Grated rind of 1/2 orange
1 cup all-purpose flour
1/3 cup melted unsalted butter or margarine
1/3 cup finely chopped blanched almonds

For the syrup:
2 cups sugar
1 cup water
1/3 cup Grand Marnier
8 ounces whipping cream, whipped
Chocolate curls

Beat egg-yolks until frothy. Add 1/4 cup of the sugar and beat until thick. Beat egg whites until frothy, gradually add the remaining 1/4 cup sugar and beat until holds stiff pick. Fold egg yolks and egg whites together. Add the vanilla and orange rind. Sift dry ingredients together. Gradually add the flour alternately with the melted butter to the egg mixture and fold. Add the almonds and mix well to combine. Pour the mixture in a 10-inch spring form pan, lined with parchment paper. Bake in a preheated 350 F (180 C) oven on the middle rack for approximately 30 minutes. Let stand for 10 minutes, remove from the pan. Let cool on ware rack. Prepare the syrup. In a 3-quart saucepan combine the sugar with the water, bring to boil, reduce heat to medium-low and boil for 5 minutes partially covered. Remove from heat and add the Grand Marnier. When the cake is completely cool, split into two layers horizontally. Place cake layers into two dishes, and with a skewer poke all over the cake. Spoon warm syrup into the layers evenly. Cover with plastic wrap, and let cool completely. Place one layer of the cake in a round serving dish. Spread one half of the whipped cream, and place the second layer over, and spread the remaining whipped cream. Decorate with chocolate curls. Serve at room temperature.

COCONUT CAKE WITH SYRUP
Keik Karythas me Siropi

For the cake:
1 cup unsalted butte or margarine, at
        room temperature
1 cup sugar
5 extra large eggs, at room temperature separated
1/2 tsp vanilla extract
1 1/2 cups all-purpose flour, sifted with
21/2 tsp baking powder
21/2 cups unsweetened coconut
1 cup milk

For the syrup:
2 cups sugar
2 cups water
1 Tbsp fresh lemon juice

Cream butter if desired with sugar until light and fluffy. Add egg yolks one at a time beating thoroughly after each one is added. Add vanilla and gradually add flour mixture alternately with the milk, beating until smooth after each addition. Add 2 cups coconut and mix well to combine. Gently fold in stiffly beaten egg whites. Spoon the mixture into a greased 13x9x3-inch baking pan and spread evenly. Bake in a preheated 350 F (180 C) oven for approximately 45 minutes. Let cool. Combine syrup ingredients in a two-quart saucepan, bring to a boil, reduce heat to medium-low and boil for 5 minutes. Spoon hot syrup over cool cake, and sprinkle with the remaining coconut. Let cool completely. Cut and serve with a cup of Greek coffee if desired.

KARYTHOPITA A
Walnut Cake with Syrup

For the cake:
1/2 cup unsalted butter or margarine, at
        room temperature
1/2 cup sugar
5 extra large eggs, separated
Grated rind of 1 orange
1 1/2 cups finely ground Zwieback
1 1/2 tsp baking powder
1 tsp ground cinnamon
1/4 tsp ground nutmeg
3 cups finely ground walnuts
1/2 cup cognac or brandy
Whipped cream (optional)

For the syrup:
2 1/2 cups sugar
2 1/2 cups water
1 Tbsp fresh lemon juice

Cream butter if desired and sugar until light and fluffy. Add egg yolks one at a time, beating thoroughly after each is added. Add orange rind. Combine dry ingredients. Gradually add alternately with cognac if desired to creamed mixture, beating until smooth after each addition. Add ground walnut and stir well. Gently fold in stiffly beaten egg whites. Spoon into well-greased 15x10x3-inch baking pan and spread evenly. Bake in preheated 350 F (180 C) oven approximately 45 minutes. Remove from oven and let cool. Combine syrup ingredients in 3-quart saucepan, bring to boil, reduce heat to medium-low and boil 5 minutes. Spoon hot syrup over karythopita, cover with a larger baking sheet or a piece of foil. Let cool completely. Cut and serve with whipped cream if desired or plain.

❧❀❧

KARYTHOPITA B
Walnut Cake with Syrup

For the cake:
1 cup unsalted butter or margarine, at
    room temperature
1/2 cup sugar
6 extra large eggs
2 1/2 cups all-purpose flour
4 tsp baking powder
1 1/4 tsp ground cinnamon
1/4 tsp freshly ground nutmeg
1/2 cup milk
1/4 cup cognac of brandy
1 1/2 cups finely chopped walnuts
For the syrup:
2 1/2 cups sugar
1 3/4 cups water
1 Tbsp fresh lemon juice
Whipped cream (optional)

Beat butter if desired and sugar until light and fluffy. Add eggs one at a time, beating thoroughly after each is added. Sift dry ingredients together. Gradually add alternately with milk and cognac if desired to creamed mixture, beating until smooth after each addition. Add chopped walnuts

and mix well to combine. Spoon mixture into well-greased 9x13x3-inch baking pan. Bake in preheated 350 F (180 C) oven approximately 45 minutes. Remove from oven and let cool. Combine syrup ingredients together in 3-quart saucepan, bring to a boil, reduce heat to medium-low and boil for 5 minutes. Spoon hot syrup over cool karythopita; cover with a larger baking sheet or a piece of foil. Let stay until completely cool. Cut and serve with whipped cream or plain if desired and with a cup of Greek coffee.

❧❀❧

KARYTHOPITA C
Walnut Cake with Syrup

For the cake:
5 extra large eggs
1/2 cup sugar
3/4 cup unsalted butter or margarine, at
    room temperature
1 1/4 cup fine semolina
1 1/4 cup all-purpose flour
5 tsp baking powder
1 tsp ground cinnamon
1/4 tsp ground cloves or nutmeg
1/4 tsp salt
1 cup milk
1/4 cup cognac, brandy
1 1/2 cups finely chopped walnuts
Whipped cream (optional)
For the syrup:
3 cups sugar
3 cups water
2 Tbsp fresh lemon juice

Beat eggs with sugar until thick and creamy. Add butter and beat well. Sift dry ingredients together. Gradually stir in flour alternately with milk and cognac if desired and stir thoroughly. Add chopped walnuts and stir well to combine. Spoon mixture into greased and floured 9x13x3-inch baking pan and spread evenly. Bake karythopita in preheated 350 F (180 C) oven on middle rack approximately 45 minutes or until golden brown. Prepare syrup. Combine syrup ingredients in 3-quart saucepan, bring to boil, reduce heat to medium and boil 5 minutes. Spoon hot syrup over hot karythopita. Cover with foil and let stay until all syrup has absorbed, about 60-90 minutes.

Then turn cake upside down in a larger baking pan and let stand 2 hours or more in order for syrup to penetrate the rest of the cake. Cut into square pieces and serve with a cup of Greek coffee if desired.

❧✦❧

YOGURT CAKE WITH SYRUP
Keik me Syropi

For the cake:
1 cup unsalted butter or margarine, at room temperature
1/2 cup sugar
4 extra large eggs, separated
1 tsp pure vanilla
3 cups all-purpose flour
1 tsp baking soda
1 tsp baking powder
1 cup plain yogurt
1 cup finely chopped almonds
For the syrup:
3 cups sugar
21/2 cups water
2 tbsp fresh lemon juice

Cream butter if desired with sugar until light and fluffy. Add egg yolks one at a time beating thoroughly after each one is added. Add vanilla. Sift flour, soda and baking powder together; add alternately with yogurt to creamed mixture beating until smooth each addition. Add almonds and stir well. Fold in stiffly beaten egg whites. Pour into well-greased 9x13x3-inch baking pan. Bake in a preheated 350 F (180 C) oven for approximately 45 minutes or until cake tester inserted in center comes out clean. Remove from oven and cool. Cut into square pieces. Combine syrup ingredients in a saucepan, bring to a boil, reduce heat and boil for 5 minutes. Spoon the syrup over the cool cake and cover with a piece of foil. Cool completely before you serve.

❧✦❧

BAKED ALMOND HALVA RINAS
Halvas tis Rinas Amygthalou

1 1/4 cup unsalted butter or margarine, at room temperature
1 cup sugar

7 extra large eggs, separated
21/2 cups fine semolina, sifted with
4 tsp baking powder and
1 tsp cinnamon
1/2 cup cognac or brandy
21/4 cups finely chopped almonds
For the syrup:
31/2 cups sugar
31/2 cups water
2 Tbsp fresh lemon juice
1 tsp almond extract

Cream butter if desired with sugar until light and fluffy. Add egg yolks one at a time beating thoroughly after each is added. Gradually add semolina mixture alternately with cognac if desired to a creamed mixture, beating until smooth after each addition. Add chopped almonds and mix thoroughly. Spoon into greased 15x10x3-inch baking pan and spread evenly. Bake in preheated 350 F (180 C) oven approximately 45 minutes. While halva is baking prepare syrup. Combine syrup ingredients except almond extract in 3-quart saucepan. Bring to a boil, reduce heat to medium-low and boil 5 minutes. Remove syrup from heat and add almond extract. Remove halva from oven and spoon hot syrup over it. Cover halva with a larger baking sheet or piece of foil and let stay until completely cool. Cut into pieces and serve.

❧✦❧

BAKED HALVA RINAS
Halvas tis Rinas

1 cup unsalted butter or margarine, at room temperature
1/2 cup sugar
4 extra large eggs
2 cups fine semolina
1/2 cup all-purpose flour
1 tsp cinnamon
1 cup milk
2 Tbsp cognac or brandy
1 1/4 cup chopped almonds or walnuts
For the syrup:
31/2 cups sugar
31/2 cups water
1 Tbsp fresh lemon juice
6 whole cloves
1 tsp almond extract if used almonds

Cream butter if desired with sugar until light and fluffy. Add eggs one at a time beating thoroughly after each is added. Sift dry ingredients together. Gradually add alternately with milk to creamed mixture, beating until smooth after each addition. Add cognac and chopped almonds if desired and mix thoroughly. Spoon mixture into well greased 9x13x3-inch baking pan and spread evenly. Bake in preheated 350 F (180 C) oven approximately 45 minutes. While halvas is baking prepare syrup. Combine syrup ingredients in 4-quart saucepan except almond extract. Bring to a boil, reduce heat to medium-low and boil 5 minutes, add almond extract. Remove halva from oven and spoon hot syrup over it. Cover halva with a larger baking sheet or piece of foil and let stay until completely cool. Remove clove, cut into pieces and serve.

BAKED HALVA RINAS WITH MILK SYRUP
Halvas tis Rinas me Siropi Galaktos

1 cup unsalted butter or margarine,
*   at room temperature*
1/2 cup sugar
5 extra large eggs
3 cups fine semolina
1 1/4 tsp cinnamon
5 tsp. baking powder
1 1/2 cups milk
1 1/2 cups finely chopped almonds
For the syrup:
4 cups sugar
41/2 cups scalding milk
6 whole cloves
1/2 tsp almond extract (optional))

Cream butter with sugar until light and fluffy. Add eggs one at a time beating thoroughly after each is added. Sift dry ingredients together, and gradually add alternately with milk to creamed mixture, beating until smooth after each addition. Add chopped almonds and mix thoroughly. Pour into well greased and floured 9x13x3-inch baking pan. Bake in preheated 350 F (180 C) oven 45 minutes. While halvas is baking prepare syrup. Combine sugar, milk and cloves, and stir well to

dissolve sugar, bring to a boil, reduce heat to medium-low and boil 5 minutes. Pour hot syrup over hot halva. Cover with larger baking sheet and let stay until completely cool. Remove cloves cut into pieces and serve.

HALVA FROM ISLAND SAMO
Halvas Samiotikos

1 cup good quality light olive oil
1 cup blanched whole almonds
1/2 cup finely chopped pistachio nuts
2 cups coarse semolina
1/2 cup sugar
For the syrup:
4 cups water
2 cups sugar
2 cinnamon sticks
3 whole cloves
Rind of 1/2 lemon
For the topping:
1/2 cup grated unsweetened coconut

Combine syrup ingredients in a three-quart saucepan, bring to boil, stir well and reduce heat to medium-low and simmer for 5 minutes partially covered. Remove from the heat and remove the cinnamon, cloves and lemon rind and discard. While the syrup is boiling sauté the semolina. In a four-quart saucepan sauté the almonds in oil for one minute in medium-low heat, stirring constantly with a wooden spoon. Add the semolina and one half of the pistachio nuts, stirring constantly until lightly golden. Add the sugar and stirring for one minute. Slowly and carefully add the syrup to the semolina mixture, stirring continuously over low heat until the halva becomes thick and has been absorbed all the syrup. Remove from the heat. Spoon the halva into a 10-cup tube pan, and spread evenly. Let stand for 15 minutes. Invert the halva onto a round serving dish. Sprinkle the halva with the coconut, and then sprinkle with the remaining pistachio nuts. Serve when the halva is completely cool. Cut and sever with a cup of Greed coffee if desired.

HALVAS WITH BUTTER OR OLIVE OIL
Halva me Boutyro or Elaiolatho

4 cups water
2 cups sugar
1 tsp cinnamon
1 cup unsalted butter or 3/4 cup quality olive oil
2 cups coarse semolina (farina)
2/3 cup slivered or chopped blanched almonds
        (optional)
1/4 cup pine nuts (optional)

In a 3-quart saucepan combine water, sugar and cinnamon; bring to a boil, reduce heat to medium-low and boil for 5 minutes partially covered. Set aside. Melt butter if desired in a 4-quart saucepan, add almonds and sauté for 2 minutes, on a medium-low heat, stirring continuously. Add semolina and pine nuts, stirring continuously with a wooden spoon for 5 minute or until the semolina turns to a golden color. Remove from heat. Slowly and carefully add the syrup to the hot semolina mixture. Stirring continuously over low heat until the halva becomes thick, and no longer sticks to the pan. Remove from heat, cover with a kitchen towel and let stand for 20 minutes. Stir frequently. Turn halva into 10-cups mold or individual molds. When is partially cool, invert into a platter. Sprinkle with sugar and cinnamon if desired. Cut into serving pieces and serve. Serve hot, room temperature or cold.

SAMALI (L. CHOL-L. FAT) CAKE
Samali Horis holisterini

3 cups fine semolina or (cream of wheat) regular
4 tsp baking powder
1 1/2 cups sugar
2 cups whole milk or 2% milk
Grated rind of one lemon or 1 tsp pure vanilla extract
1 1/2 cups finely chopped almonds
For the syrup:
31/2 cups sugar
31/2 cups water
Juice of 1/2 lemon
1/2 tsp almond extract

Sift semolina and baking powder together; add rest of ingredients except almonds. Mix

thoroughly. Add almonds and mix well to combine. Pour into generously greased 9x13x3-inch baking pan. Spread evenly with wet spatula or your hand. Bake in preheated 350 F (180 C) oven 30 minutes. Remove from oven; cut in square pieces. Return to oven and bake 30 minutes longer. While cake is baking prepare syrup. Combine syrup ingredients (except almond extract) in 3-quart saucepan; bring to boil, reduce heat and boil partially covered 5 minutes. Add almond extract and spoon hot syrup over hot cake. Cover with larger pan or a piece of foil, let stand until completely cool. After 3-4 hours turn cake upside down in larger baking pan and let stand 1 hour or more in order for syrup to penetrate the rest of the cake. Cut into square pieces and serve with Greek coffee if desired.

CHOCOLATE LOG
Kormos Sokolatas

5 extra large eggs
1 cup sugar
1 tsp pure vanilla extract
1/2 cup all-purpose flour
2 Tbsp cornstarch
2 tsp baking powder
1/3 cup unsweetened good quality cocoa powder
1 cup whipping cream
2 Tbsp confectioner sugar, sifted
1/2 tsp pure vanilla extract
2 Tbsp Grand Marnier
1/4 cup sugar
Confectioner sugar for dusting, sifted

Beat eggs with sugar until thick and has lemon color. Add vanilla. Sift dry ingredients together. Fold flour into egg mixture. Pour into jellyroll pan 13x17x1-inch lined with parchment. Bake in preheated 400 F (205 C) oven on middle rack 15 minutes. Dust a clean cloth kitchen towel with 1/4 cup sugar. Turn cake out onto prepared towel; remove parchment paper. Trim cake's edges. Starting with a long side, tightly roll up cake with towel. Transfer cake, seam side down, to wire rack to cool. While cake is cooling, prepare whipped cream. Beat cream until frothy. Add sugar and vanilla, and beat until holds soft peak. Add Grand Marnier and beat well to combine. Chill until ready to use. Unroll cake; remove towel. Spread prepared whipped cream over cake to within 1/2-inch of edges. Re-roll cake; place seam side down on platter. Dust with confectioner's sugar before serving, decorate with colorful berries and springs of mint. Cut log into 1-1 1/2-inch slices and serve.

Note: You may spread whipped cream on top of log if desired and lightly dust with cocoa powder. Or spread chocolate frosting and lightly dust with confectioner's sugar. Excellent for Christmas Holidays.

ALMOND RAVANI
Ravani Amygthalou

1 cup unsalted butter or margarine, at
    room temperature
1/2 cup sugar
5 extra large eggs, separated
Grated rind of 1 orange
1 cup fine semolina
1 cup all-purpose flour
4 tsp baking powder
1 tsp vanilla extract
2/3 cup milk
1 cup chopped almonds
For the syrup:
21/2 cups sugar
21/2 cups water
1 Tbsp fresh lemon juice
1 tsp almond extract
Whipped cream (optional)

Cream butter if desired with sugar until light and fluffy. Add egg yolks one at a time, beating thoroughly after each one is added. Add orange rind. Sift dry ingredients together. Gradually add flour mixture alternately with milk, beating until smooth after each addition. Add almonds and mix well. Gently fold in stiffly beaten egg whites. Spoon into well greased 13x9x3-inch baking pan. Bake in a preheated 350 F (180 C) oven for approximately 45 minutes. Combine syrup ingredients except the almond extract in a three-quart saucepan. Bring to a boil, reduce heat to medium-low and boil for 5 minutes. Spoon the

hot syrup over hot ravani. Cover the ravani with a larger baking sheet or a piece of foil. Let stay until completely cool. Cut and serve with whipped cream if desired or plain.

WALNUT RAVANI
Ravani me Karythia

1 cup unsalted butter or margarine, at
    room temperature
1/2 cup sugar
5 extra large eggs, separated
Grated rind of 1 orange
2 cups fine semolina
1 cup all-purpose flour
5 tsp baking powder
1 tsp cinnamon
1 1/2 cups milk
1 cup finely chopped walnuts
Whipped cream (optional)
For the syrup:
4 cups sugar
4 cups water
1 Tbsp fresh lemon juice

Cream butter if desired with sugar until light and fluffy. Add egg yolks one at a time, beating thoroughly after each one is added. Add orange rind. Sift dry ingredients together. Gradually add semolina mixture alternately with milk, beating until smooth after each addition. Add walnuts and mix well. Gently fold in stiffly beaten egg whites. Spoon mixture into well-greased 15x10x3-inch baking pan and spread evenly. Bake in a preheated 350 F (180 C) oven for approximately 45 minutes. Combine syrup ingredients together in a three-quart saucepan, bring to a boil, reduce heat to medium-low and boil for 5 minutes. Spoon the hot syrup over the hot ravani. Cover with a larger baking sheet or a piece of foil. Let stay until completely cool. Cut and serve with whipped cream if desired or plain.

APPLE MERINGUE TART
Tarta Milou me Marenga

2 Tbsp unsalted butter or margarine
5 large granny smith apples, cored and cut

into thin wedges
1/2 cup chopped walnuts or blanched almonds
1/4 cup golden seedless raisins
1 cup sugar
1/2 tsp ground cinnamon
3 extra large eggs, separated
Pinch of salt
1 tsp cornstarch
1 tsp all-purpose flour
1 1/2 cups milk
1 tsp unsalted butter or margarine
1/2 tsp pure vanilla extract

In a large frying pan melt the butter, add the prepared apples, walnuts if desired, raisins, half the sugar and the cinnamon, stirring constantly until the apples star to caramelize. Remove from the heat and spoon into a 10-11-inch tart dish. Prepare the cream filling. In a small bowl combine egg yolks, one half of the remaining sugar, cornstarch and flour, beat well using a wire whisk. Gradually stir in scalding milk, and cook slowly on top of a double boiler, whisking constantly until mixture thickens. Remove from heat. Add the butter and vanilla and mix well to combine. Spoon over the prepare apple mixture and spread evenly. In a large mixer bowl beat the egg whites with a pinch of salt until frothy. Gradually beat in the remaining sugar, a little at a time. Continue beating until stiff and glossy. Pile meringue onto hot cream filling. Pull up points for decorative top. Bake the tart in a preheated 400 F (205 C) oven for 8 to 10 minutes, or until lightly browned. Serve warm.

APPLE TART WITH FILLO PASTRY
Tarta Milou me Fillo

10 apples, peeled, core and cut into 1/2-inch slices
3 Tbsp butter or margarine
3 Tbsp honey
1 cup sugar
3/4 tsp cinnamon
3 Tbsp fresh lemon juice
1/2 cup of more toasted blanched slivered almonds
        or chopped walnuts
1/2 cup golden raisins
14 sheets or more of fillo pastry
1/2 cup of more clarified melted butter or margarine
7 Tbsp sugar

In a large heavy frying pan melt the three Tbsp butter if desired, add apples and sauté for few minutes. Add honey, sugar, cinnamon and lemon juice, and cook slowly until apples are tender but not too soft. Add almonds if desired and raisins, stir to combine. Remove from heat. Let stand. Grease a 9x13x1-inch baking pan with butter. Line prepared pan with 8 fillo sheets, brushing every other sheet with hot melted butter if desired and sprinkle with one Tbsp of the sugar. The sheets will extend up the sides of the pan. Spoon in the apple filling and spread evenly. Fold one fillo sheet and cover apple mixture and brush with the hot butter. Fold overhanging fillo over the filling to enclose it. Top with the rest of the fillo sheets brushing every other one with hot butter, and sprinkle with one Tbsp sugar and tuck in overhanging sheets inside the pan. Brush top with butter and sprinkle with sugar. Score top six layers of fillo with a sharp serrated knife into three layers lengthwise. Bake in a preheated 350 F (180 C) oven for 45 minutes or until golden brown. Remove from oven. When you are ready to serve, cut through scored lines into 3x3-inch squares or rectangles. Serve hot or at room temperature. Dusted with confectioner's sugar if desired.

APRICOT PASTRY
Glykisma me Verykoka

For the cake:
1/2 cup unsalted butter, at room temperature
1/2 cup sugar
3 extra large eggs
1 tsp pure vanilla extract
1 1/2 cups all-purpose flour
2 tsp baking powder
Pinch of salt
1/2 cup milk

For the topping:
1 29-ounces can halves or whole peaches, cut into halves
1/2 cup sugar
1/4 cup or more cognac or brandy
1 cup whipping cream, whipped with

1/2 tsp pure vanilla extract

Cream butter and sugar until light and fluffy. Add eggs one at a time, beating thoroughly after each one is added. Add vanilla. Sift dry ingredients together. Gradually add flour mixture alternately with the milk, to the cream mixture, beating lightly until smooth. Pour mixture into a greased 10-11-inch round baking pan, lined with greased parchment paper, and spread evenly. Bake in a preheated 350 F (180 C) oven on the middle rack, for 30 minutes or until cake tester inserted in center comes out clean. Remove from the oven, and let stand for 5 minutes. Remove the cake to a platter, cover and let cool completely. Piece the whole cake with a skewer. Drain the apricot liquid to a small saucepan, add the sugar, and bring to boil, boil for 2 minutes in medium-low heat. Remove from the heat and add the cognac. Slowly spoon hot syrup over the cake, cover and let the cake absorb the syrup. When cake is cool, arrange the apricot halves around the rim of the cake. Save one half for the center of the cake. Finely chop the rest of the apricots and fold into the whipped cream. Spoon the whipped cream over the cake, and leave the apricot halves uncovered. Place the reserved half apricot in the center of the cake. Chill.

❧❀❧

APRICOT TART WITH PUFF PASTRY
Tarta Verikoko me Sfoliata

3 cups scalding milk
4 extra large egg yolks
1/2 cup sugar
3 Tbsp all-purpose flour
Grated rind of 1 lemon
1 pkg frozen puff pastry (thawed)
1 can apricots in syrup, sliced or halved, drained
1/3 cup slivered toasted blanched almonds
1 10-11-inch tart pan

Combine egg yolks and sugar and beat with a wire whisk until frothy. Add the flour and beat well. Add the lemon rind and gradually stir in milk and cook slowly on top of a double boiler, whisking constantly until mixture thickens.

Remove from the heat, cover and set aside. Line the tart pan with the puff pastry. Spoon the cream in the prepare tart and spread evenly. Arrange the apricot slices or halves over the cream and sprinkle with the almonds. Bake in a preheated 350 F (180 C) oven on the second lower rack for approximately 25-30 minutes. Remove from the oven and let cool. Chill, cut and serve.

❧❀❧

APRICOT TART
Tarta me Verikoka

For the crust:
2 cups all-purpose flour
1/3 cup sugar
Pinch of salt
1 tsp baking powder
2/3 cup plus 1 Tbsp unsalted butter
2 large eggs beaten with
4 Tbsp cognac or brandy
For the filling:
1 1/2 pounds ripped firmed apricots, pitted and cut into fourths
1 1/4 cup sugar
3 Tbsp cognac or brandy
3 large egg yolks
1 Tbsp cornstarch
2 cups scalding milk
For the topping:
1/2 cup whipping cream
2 Tbsp confectioner's sugar, sifted
1/2 tsp pure vanilla extract
1/4 cup chopped toasted blanched almonds

Prepare the crust. Sift dry ingredients together. Cut in butter with a pastry blender. Add beaten eggs with cognac and mix until the pastry will hold together. Roll out on a piece of parchment paper for 10-11-inch tart pan. Line greased tart pan with the pastry. Line pastry shell with parchment paper and partially fill with beans. Bake in a preheated 450 F (230 C) oven on the middle rack for 10 minutes. Remove from the oven and remove the beans and the paper. Return to the oven and bake for approximately 15 minutes or until golden. Cool. While the crust is baking prepare the filling. In a large frying pan add the 2/3 of the apricots, 3/4 cup sugar, 1/2 cup water and 3 Tbsp of cognac, and stir well.

188

Bring to boil, reduce heat to medium and cook until they are caramelized. Remove from the heat and cool. While the apricots are cooling, prepare the cream filling. In a small bowl add the egg yolks with the remaining sugar and with a wire whisk beat well. Gradually stir in the scalding milk and slowly cook on top of a double boiler, whisking constantly until the mixture thickens. Remove from the heat. Cover with plastic wrap, the plastic will touch the cream, to prevent a skin from forming. Cool. When the prepared apricots are completely cool arrange on the baked tart. Spoon the cream filling over and spread evenly. Beat the whipping cream with the confectioner's sugar and the vanilla. Spread the whipped cream over the tart and decorate with the remaining apricot slices. Sprinkle with the almonds. Chill. Serves 8-10.

Note: Substitute the apricots with peaches, plums or cherries if desired.

FRESH FRUIT TART
Tourta me Freska Frouta

For the crust:
2 cups all-purpose flour
1/3 cup sugar
1/8 tsp salt
1 tsp baking powder
3/4 cup unsalted butter
1 large egg, beaten with
2 Tbsp cognac or brandy

For the filling:
4 large egg yolks
1/3 cup sugar
1/2 cup dry Marsala wine
1 envelope unflavored gelatin
1 cup whipping cream, whipped

For the topping:
1 pint strawberries, sliced
2 kiwifruit, peeled and sliced
1/3 cup apricot preserves or jam

Prepare the crust. Sift dry ingredients together. Cut in butter with a pastry blender. Add beaten egg mixture and mix well until pastry will hold together. Roll out on parchment paper to a 10-11-inch tart pan. Line greased tart pan with the

pastry. Line pastry shell with parchment paper or foil and partially fill with beans. Bake in a preheated 450 F (230 C) oven on the middle rack for 10 minutes. Remove the tart from the oven and remove the beans and the paper. Return to oven and bake for approximately 15 minutes or until golden. Remove from the oven and cool. Gently remove the tart from the pan and place on a flat serving platter. Prepare the filling. Beat egg yolks with the sugar and the wine in a small mixing bowl. Cook over very low heat on top of a double boiler, whisking constantly until mixture lightly thickens. Remove from the heat. Gradually add the gelatin, stirring constantly, until gelatin melts. Cover the cream with a piece of plastic wrap, the plastic will touch the cream, to prevent a skin from forming. Cool. Fold in the whipped cream. To assemble the tart, spread cream filling in cool tart shell. Arrange fruit slices decoratively on top in concentric circles. Melt apricot jam in a small saucepan; strain through fine sieve. Brush the fruit with the apricot glaze. Serves 8-10.

HONEY CHEESE TART
Melopita Sifnou

For the crust:
2 cups all-purpose flour
1 tsp baking powder
1/8 tsp salt
3 Tbsp sugar
2/3 cup unsalted butter
4-6 Tbsp of ice water

For the filling:
5 eggs
2/3 cup sugar
1 1/2 pound unsalted myzithra or ricotta cheese
1 cup honey
1/2 cup milk
4 Tbsp all-purpose flour
1 tsp cinnamon
1/8 tsp salt
Grated rind or 1/2 lemon
1 Tbsp fresh lemon juice
1/3 cup slivered blanched almonds or walnuts

Sift dry ingredients together. Cut in butter with a

pastry blender until the mixture resembles coarse meal. Add water using 1 Tbsp at a time until mixture will hold together. Gather pastry together and form into a ball. Roll out on parchment paper from center to edges. Use short light strokes. Roll the dough about 1-inch larger all around to a 10-11-inch tart pan. (I prefer glass or ceramic pan and lined with parchment paper. Place your hand under and in the middle of the parchment paper and pastry and carefully invert and fit loosely in the bottom and sides of pan; press lightly to fit snug. Gently remove the parchment paper. Trim pastry around the edges. Chill while you prepare the filling. Beat eggs with sugar until light. Add the rest of the ingredients except the almonds and mix well to combine. Press mixture through a food mill. Pour into prepared chill pastry shell. Sprinkle with almonds. Bake the tart in a preheated 350 F (180 C) oven on the middle rack for 60 minutes or until center is firm. Remove from oven and cool. Remove from the pan and paper and place on a round serving platter. Serve with a touch of cinnamon.

❦❦❦

PASTA FLORA

For the crust:
3 cups all-purpose flour
1/2 cup sugar
1/8 tsp salt
1 1/2 tsp baking powder
1 1/4 cups unsalted butter
2 egg yolks, beater with
1/4 cup cognac or brandy
For the filling:
1 1/2 cups apricot preserved or jam or your desire
1/3 cup toasted slivered blanched almonds

Sift dry ingredients together. Cut in butter with a pastry blender until the mixture resembles coarse meal. Gradually add beaten egg-cognac mixture and toss to blend. Gather dough together and form into a ball. Roll out 3/4 of the pastry on parchment paper from center to edges. Use short light stokes. Roll the pastry about 1-inch larger all around to a 10-11-inch tart pan. (I prefer glass or ceramic tart pan and lined with parchment

paper). Place your hand under in the middle of the parchment paper and carefully invert and fit loosely in the bottom and sides of the pan; press lightly to fit snug. Gently remove the parchment paper. Trim outer edge of pan. Cover with the preserved and sprinkle with almonds. Let stand. Roll out the remaining pastry and trims into1/8-inch thick on parchment paper. Cut strips 1/2-inch wide, 12-inches long, with a sharp knife or a pizza cutter. Lay strips horizontally on filling 1-inch apart. Do the same for the vertical strips to a lattice design. Trim even with outer edge of tart pan. Moisten edge. Lay a strip all around the edge of pan to cover the strips. Bake in a preheated 350 F (180 C) oven on the middle rack for approximately 45 minutes or until golden brown. Cool. Gently remove from the pan and the paper place on a round serving platter. Cut and serve with a cup of Greek coffee.

❦❦❦

STRAWBERRY-CREAM TART
Tarta Fraoulas me Crema

For the crust:
Follow recipe and preparation as directed in Strawberry Tart (see index for recipe)
For the cream filling:
1/2 of the recipe from Cream Filling for Tortes (see index for recipe)
Follow recipe and preparation as directed
For the topping:
1 pound or more small fresh strawberries, washed and well drained
1/2 cup strawberry jam
1 Tbsp rum
1 Tbsp confectioner's sugar, sifted

Prepare the crust and cream filling as directed. When tart is completely cool, spoon in the cream filling and spread evenly. Arrange the strawberries over the cream filling. Mix the jam and rum in a small frying pan and bring to boil on a low heat. Remove from the heat.
Cool the jam and brush the strawberries to give a nice shine. Sprinkle the confectioner's sugar over the strawberries. Chill.

❦❦❦

STRAWBERRY TART WITH PUFF PASTRY
Tarta Fraoulas me Sfoliata

1 pkg puff pasty (thawed)
1 small box strawberry gelatin
1 cup water
1/4 cup maraschino liqueur
1/2 cup brandy
1 pound small strawberries, washed and well dried
1 8-ounces cool whip
1/2 cup chopped toasted unsalted pistachio nuts
1 Tbsp confectioner's sugar, sifted

Line a greased 10-11-inch tart pan with the puff pastry. Pierce the bottom of the pastry with a fork. Bake in a preheated 400 F (205 C) oven on the middle rack for approximately 20 minutes or until golden brown. Remove from the oven and let cool. Gently remove from the pan to a serving dish. While the tart is cooling prepare the gelatin. In a small saucepan add 1 cup of water and the gelatin, stirring constantly over very low heat, until the gelatin dissolves. Remove from the heat, let cool completely. Add the maraschino and the brandy, and stir well to combine. Coarsely chop 1 1/2 cups of the strawberries, and add to the gelatin, add the 3/4 of the cool whip, and the pistachio nuts, and fold gently. Spoon over the prepare tart and spread evenly. Decorate the tart with the whole strawberries, and between them make rosettes with the remaining cream, and lightly dust the strawberries with the confectioner's sugar. Chill.

❧❀❧

STRAWBERRY TART
Tarta Fraoulas

For the crust:
2 cups all-purpose flour
1/3 cup sugar
1 tsp. baking powder
3/4 cup unsalted butter
2 egg yolks, beaten with
3 Tbsp cognac or brandy
For the filling:
3/4 cup strawberry jam
3/4 cup water
4 tsp. cornstarch
1 1/2 cups whipped cream
1 pound or more mall fresh strawberries,

washed and well drained
1/3 cup chopped pistachio nuts

Sift dry ingredients together. Cut in butter with pastry blender until the mixture resembles coarse meal. Gradually add beaten egg-cognac mixture and toss to blend. Gather pastry together and form into a ball. Roll out on parchment paper from center to edges. Use short light strokes. Roll pastry about 1-inch larger all around to a 10-inch tart pan. (I prefer glass or ceramic tart pan and lined with parchment paper). Place your hand under and in the middle of parchment paper and pastry and carefully invert and fit loosely in the bottom and sides of the pan; press lightly to fit snug. Gently remove parchment. Trim outer edge of pan. Line pastry shell with parchment and partially fill with beans. Bake in a preheated 450 F (230 C) oven on the middle rack for 10 minutes. Remove beans and paper and return back to the oven for 5 minutes longer or until golden. Cool. Carefully remove from tart pan and the paper. Place on a flat serving platter. Mix jam with 1/2 cup water, bring to boil on low heat; mix 1/4 cup water with 4 tsp. cornstarch to a paste. Slowly add to jam mixture stirring constantly until it thickens. Remove from heat. Cool. Spread on baked tart and chill for 2 hours or longer. Spread whipped cream over jam mixture and cover with fresh strawberries. Sprinkle with chopped pistachio nuts. Gently remove from the pan and paper to a round serving platter.

❧❀❧

APRICOT TARTLETS
Tartaletes me Berukoko

1 pkg. puff pastry (thawed)
3 Tbsp melted unsalted butter
1/4 cup sugar
6 large apricots or beaches, halved and
*   pit removed*
3/4 cup apricot jam (about)
3 Tbsp cognac or brandy
Whipped cream (optional)

On lightly floured surface, role out puff pastry. Cut out 12 rounds tartlets 3-inches in diameter.

Place tartlets on baking sheets lined with parchment paper. Chill about 30 minutes or longer. Prick each tartlet with fork. Brush each with butter and sprinkle with 1/2 tsp sugar, and place a half apricot if desired on the middle of each tartlet. Brush with butter again and sprinkle with sugar. Make small flutes around the edge of the tartlets. Bake in preheated 400 F (205 C) oven on middle rack 20 minutes or until golden brown. While tartlets are baking, prepare glace. In a small frying pan add apricot jam and cognac if desired and bring to boil, reduce heat and boil 1 minute. Remove from heat and generously brush the tartlets. Serve warm with whipped cream if desired. Serves 12.

FRUIT TARTLETS
Tartaletes Froutou

For the crust:
Follow recipe and preparation as directed in Honey Cheese Tart (see index for recipe)
For the filling:
Any fresh fruit, any sweet preserved well drained, any compote well drained
1 1/2 cups whipped cream
1/2 cup or more unsalted and toasted chopped pistachio nuts or toasted chopped blanched almonds

Line 12 or more well greased tart pans with the pastry. Prick and bake in a preheated 450 F (230 C) oven on the middle rack for 8 minutes or until golden. Gently remove from tart pans and cool. Fill baked tartlets with the fruit you desired. Spoon whipped cream on top and sprinkle with the pistachio nuts. Chill and serve.

NOUGAT CHOCOLATE TARTLETS
Tartaletes Nougatina me Socolata

For the crust:
4 extra large egg whites
Pinch of salt
1/2 cups sugar
1 cup finely ground almonds, skins on
21/2 Tbsp flour

1/2 tsp ground cinnamon
12 or more tartlet pans
For the cream filling:
1/2 recipe cream filling for tortes (see indexrecipe)
4 bittersweet chocolate, finely chopped
1 cup whipped cream
Raspberries for decoration
Confectioner's sugar for dusting

Mix ground almonds, flour and cinnamon together. Beat the egg whites with the salt in a large mixer bowl at high speed until foamy. Gradually add sugar, beating until holds stiff pick. Gradually fold in almond mixture. Divide egg white mixture into 12 about tartlet pans lined with parchment paper, and spread evenly using the back of a spoon. Place the prepare tartlets in a large baking pan. Bake them in a preheated 350 F (180 C) oven in the middle rack for approximately 20 minutes or until lightly golden. Gently remove the nougat crust from the pans and cool. Follow recipe and preparation as directed in cream filling. Add the chopped chocolate, stirring until smooth. Cover with a piece of plastic wrap, touching the cream, to prevent a skin from forming. Cool. Spoon the cream mixture into the nougat crust. Chill for overnight. The next day decorate with the whipped cream and raspberries. Dust the raspberries lightly with confection's sugar. Chill until ready to serve. Serves 12 or more.

RASPBERRY TARTLETS
Tartaletes me Raspberries

For the crust:
2 cups all-purpose flour
1 tsp baking powder
1/3 cup sugar
3/4 cup unsalted butter or margarine
2 large egg yolks, beaten with
3 Tbsp cognac or brandy
For the cream filling:
4 Tbsp all-purpose flour
2 Tbsp cornstarch
1/4 cup sugar
3 extra large egg yolks
1/2 cup milk
2 cups scalding milk

1 tsp pure vanilla extract
1 Tbsp unsalted butter
For the topping:
4-6 ounces bittersweet chocolate
1 pkg. raspberries
1 pkg. blackberries
1/2 cup raspberry jam
3 Tbsp Grand Marnier
12 or more, small tart pans

In a medium size bowl sift dry ingredients together. Cut in butter with a pastry blender. Add beaten egg with the cognac and mix until pastry will hold together. Roll out on parchment paper to a 10x12-inch. Cut rounds and line 12 or more greased small tart pans with the pastry. Prick tarts and place in a large baking sheet. Line each pastry shell with small piece of parchment paper and partially fill with beans. Bake in a preheated 450 F (230 C) oven on the second bottom rack for 8-10 minutes or until golden. Remove the bean and paper and gently remove the shells from the tart pans and cool. While the tarts are baking prepare the filling. Combine dry ingredients together, and add the egg yolks and 1/2 cup milk, and mix well using a wire whisk. Gradually stir in scalding milk and cook slowly on top of a double boiler, whisking constantly, until the mixture thickens. Cover and cook for 5 minutes longer. Remove from heat. Add vanilla and butter and stir well to combine. Cover with plastic wrap, the plastic will touch the cream, to prevent a skin from forming. Cool. Melt the chocolate and generously brush each tart. Let cool. You can brush again with the chocolate if you have any extra and cool again. Spoon cream filling over the chocolate and decorate with the berries. In a small frying pan place the raspberry jam and the Grand Marnier and bring to boil in medium-low heat, reduce heat to low and simmer for 30 seconds. Press through a sieve and brush the fruit with the mixture. Chill. Serves 12 or more.

❦❦❦

ALMOND PRALINE ICE CREAM TORTE
Tourta Pagoto me Amygthala Pralina

For the cake:

1/2 recipe Cake for Tortes (see index for recipe)
For the syrup:
1/2 cup sugar, dissolve in
1/2 cup warm milk (if you use ladyfingers
        increase the milk to 1 cup)
For the praline:
1 recipe Almond Praline (see index for recipe)
For the filling:
4 extra large eggs, separated
1/2 cup confectioner's sugar, sifted
1/2 cup cream, chilled
1 16-ounces whipped topping (partially thawed)
8 ounces bittersweet chocolate, melted with
        6 Tbsp water
1 tsp pure vanilla extract
1 cup whipping cream, whipped with
1/4 cup confectioner's sugar, sifted and
1/2 tsp pure vanilla extract

Follow recipe and preparation as directed in cake for tortes. Pour batter into a 10-11-inch spring form pan lined with parchment. Bake as directed only reduce baking time from 30 minutes to 20. Let cool 10 minutes. Remove from pan and remove parchment. Let cool. Place back into clean pan. Spoon hot syrup over cake. Set aside. If you used ladyfingers, deep them fast in and out in the syrup. Prepare the praline as directed. Prepare the filling. In a small mixing bowl beat egg yolks with 1/4 cup of the confectioner's sugar with a wire whisk over double boiler, over very low heat until thick and creamy and has a yellow color, whisking constantly. Remove from the heat and beat until cool. Add chilled cream and beat well. In a large mixing bowl beat egg whites with a pinch of salt with a wire whisk over double boiler, over very low heat until the mixture lightly thickens. Gradually add the remaining confection's sugar and beat until holds soft peaks, whisking constantly. Remove from the heat and beat until cool. Gently fold the egg yolks in beaten egg whites and then fold in whipped topping. Divide the cream mixture into two parts. Divide praline into three parts. In one part of the cream mixture add the vanilla and one part of the praline, mix well and spoon over the prepare cake and spread evenly. Freeze for 60 minutes. In the second part of the cream mixture add the cool melted chocolate and the second part of the praline and mix well to combine. Remove torte from the freezer and spoon the chocolate mixture over the vanilla mixture and spread evenly. Cover and freeze again for overnight or longer. Gently remove the sides of the pan and place torte on a serving dish. Decorate sides and top as you desired with whipped cream. Sprinkle with remaining praline. Keep the torte in the freezer. Remove from freezer when you are ready to serve. Cut and serve.

❦❦❦

ALMOND TORTE
Tourta Amygdalou

For the cake:
5 eggs, at room temperature
1 cup sugar
1 tsp vanilla
1/3 cup cognac or brandy
3/4 cup all-purpose flour, sifted with
3/4 cup fine semolina and
2 tsp baking powder
1 1/2 cups finely ground almonds
For the syrup:
1 1/3 cups sugar
1 1/3 cups water
1/2 tsp almond extract
For the filling:
1 recipe of Cream Filling for Tortes (see index
     for recipe and preparation)
For the frosting:
1 1/2 cups whipping cream, whipped with
1/4 cup confectioner's sugar, sifted and
1/2 tsp vanilla
2/3 cup sliced or chopped toasted
     blanched almonds
Maraschino cherries

Beat eggs with sugar until thick and creamy. Add vanilla and gradually add flour mixture alternately with cognac to egg mixture. Add ground almonds and mix well to combine. Pour into 10-11-inch spring form pan lined with parchment paper. Bake in a preheated 350 F (180 C) oven on the middle rack for approximately 45 minutes. Cool. Remove cake from pan, and turn cake up side down on a flat dish, cover and let stay overnight. Remove the parchment paper and split cake into three layers with a long serrated knife horizontally. Combine syrup ingredients in a small saucepan, bring to a boil reduce heat to medium and boil for 5 minutes. Place each cake layer in separated large plate and spoon the hot syrup over cool cake layers. Cover and let cool. While cake is cooling prepare the filling. Follow recipe and preparation as directed. Place one cake layer in the spring form pan and spread 1/3 of the cream filling. Place the second cake layer over cream. Repeat layers. Cover with a piece of plastic wrap and chill over night. Gently remove the sides of the pan and place the torte on a serving round dish. Frost the sides and top of the torte with the whipped cream, as desired. Sprinkle with chopped almonds and arrange cherries on top. Chill.

❦❦❦

APPLE CHARLOTTE TORTE
Tourta Sarlot Milou

1/3 cup sparkling cider
1 cup sugar
1 pound apples, peeled, cored and sliced
Juice and rind of one lemon
1/2 cup milk
2 egg yolks
5 Tbsp all-purpose flour
1 tsp. vanilla
1 cup whipping cream
3 ounces ground almonds
9 ounces butter or margarine at room temperature
Slices of whole wheat bread, crust removed
1/4 cup crystallized sugar
Raspberries for decoration

In small saucepan dissolve 1/4 cup sugar in sparkling cider on a low heat, stirring constantly. Add sliced apples, lemon juice and rind. Bring to a boil, cover, reduce heat, simmer 5 minutes. Drain apples, set aside, and reserve liquid. In double boiler combine milk, egg yolks, remaining sugar and beat well with whisk. Blend in flour, stirring constantly. Add the reserved liquid and cook slowly over lightly boiling water, stirring constantly until mixture is thick and smooth. Remove from heat. Fold in the cream, almonds and reserved apples. Prepare bread slices by spreading on both sides with butter. Stand bread slices around sides of a greased 10-inch spring form pan. Line bottom with more prepared slices of bread. Pour the cream mixture into prepared pan. Cover cream with prepared bread. Cover top of pan with a buttered parchment paper, the sizes of the pan. Bake in a preheated 375 F (190 C) oven for 50 minutes. Remove from oven and remove the parchment paper. Invert the Charlotte on a serving platter, sprinkle with the crystallized sugar and decorate with raspberries. Serve warm or chilled.

❧❀❧

ATHENIAN TORTE
Athinaiki Tourta

2 1/2 cups whipping cream
1 2/3 envelopes unflavored gelatin
4 extra large egg yolks
7 ounces confectioner's sugar, sifted
1 pound plus 2 ounces anthotyro or mascarpone
1/2 cup finely ground blanched almonds
3/4 cup Grand Marnier liqueur
8 ounces or more ladyfingers
1/2 cup finely chopped toasted blanched almonds

Dissolve the gelatin in 1/2 cup warm cream. Beat egg yolks with confectioner's sugar until light and creamy. Add the anthoryro if desired, ground almonds, gelatin and 1/4 cup of the liqueur, and mix well to combine. Beat the whipping cream, and add to the egg mixture, except for 1 cup and fold. Mix the remaining liqueur with 1/3 cup of water, and dip the ladyfingers fast. Stand ladyfingers around sides of a 10-inch spring form pan. Line bottom with more ladyfingers. Pour the cream mixture into prepared pan, and spread evenly. Cover and chill for overnight. Remove the sides of the pan leaving the bottom. Gently place the torte on a serving dish. Decorate with the remaining whipped cream and sprinkle with the chopped almonds. Chill.

❧❀❧

BUTTER CHOCOLATE FILLING
Krema Boutyrou Sokolatas

2 egg whites, at room temperature
1/2 cup sugar
1 cup unsalted butter, at room temperature
1 1/2 cups confectioner sugar, sifted
1/4 cup cocoa powder, sifted
1 tsp pure vanilla extract

Beat egg whites and sugar over a double boiler, on low simmering water, beating constantly with a wire whisk until the mixture is frothy and the sugar has dissolved, and it is hot when you tasted with your finger. Remove from the heat. Beat with an electric mixer until soft peak, and the mixture is completely cool. While you beating the egg whites, prepare the butter. Cream butter and sugar until light and fluffy. Add cocoa and vanilla, and beat well to combine. Gently fold the egg whites into the butter mixture. The mixture is ready to use as directed in your recipe.

❧❀❧

CAKE FOR TORTES
Keik for Tourtes

6 eggs
1 1/4 cups sugar
1 tsp pure vanilla extract
1 1/2 cups all-purpose flour, sifted with
1 1/2 tsp baking powder

Beat eggs until frothy, add sugar and beat until thick. Add vanilla and fold in flour. Pour into 10-11-inch spring form pan lined with parchment. Bake in preheated 350 F (180 C) oven on middle rack approximately 30 minutes. Cool. Remove from pan. Turn cake up side down on a flat dish, cover. The next day remove paper and split cake first into two horizontally, then each one into two horizontally again. Use as directed.

❧❀❧

CHEESE CAKE GREEK STYLE
Keik Tyriou

18-ounces cream cheese
1 3/4 cups sugar
1 1/2 cups sour cream
6 eggs, separated
3 Tbsp flour, sifted
1/3 cup fresh lemon juice
1 tsp vanilla

Beat cream cheese and sugar until creamy. Add sour cream and blend well until light. Beat egg yolks until cream color; add to the cheese mixture and mix well. Add flour, lemon juice and vanilla and mix well to combine. Fold in stiffly beaten egg whites. Pour into 10-11-inch spring form and spread evenly. Bake in a preheated 325 F (165 C) oven for 60 minutes. Turn off heat, open the oven door and let stand for 60 minutes longer. Remove from oven and cool on wire rack. Gently remove the spring form and place the cake on a round serving platter.

※◦✖◦※

CHOCOLATE CAKE FOR TORTES
Keik Sokolatas for Tourtes

6 eggs
1 1/4 cups sugar
1 tsp pure vanilla extract
1 1/2 cups all-purpose flour
3/4 cup cocoa
1 1/2 tsp baking powder

Beat eggs until frothy, add sugar and beat until thick. Add vanilla. Sift dry ingredients together. Fold in flour. Pour into 11-inch spring form pan lined with parchment paper. Bake in a preheated 350 F (180 C) oven on the middle rack for approximately 30 minutes or until cake tester inserted in center comes out clean. Cool. Remove from pan. Turn cake up side down on a flat dish, cover with plastic wrap. The next day split the cake into three or four layers horizontally. Use as directed.

※◦✖◦※

CHOCOLATE FROSTING
Glaso Sokolatas

1 cup whipping cream
1 Tbsp cocoa powder, sifted
10 ounces semisweet chocolate, coarsely grated
1 Tbsp unsalted butter, at room temperature

In a small saucepan place the cream and the cocoa, stirring constantly to dissolve. Bring to boil. Remove from the heat and add the grated chocolate, stirring constantly with a wire whisk

until smooth. Add the butter and blend well to combine. The mixture is ready to use as directed in your recipe.

※◦✖◦※

CHOCOLATE SWEET HEARTS
Glykes Karthoules Sokolatas

For the cake:
1 cup unsalted butter at room temperature
1 1/2 cups sugar
6 eggs separated
1 tsp pure vanilla extract
3 cups all-purpose flour
3/4 cup unsweetened cocoa
5 tsp baking powder
3/4 cup milk
Pinch of salt
For the syrup:
2/3 cup hot water
1/2 cup sugar
1/4 cup coffee liqueur
For the topping:
13/4 cups whipping cream
2 Tbsp unsweetened cocoa, sifted
14 ounces bittersweet chocolate, finely chopped
2 Tbsp butter, at room temperature

Cream butter and sugar until light and fluffy. Add egg yolks one at a time, beating thoroughly after each one is added. Add vanilla. Sift dry ingredients together, add alternately with the milk to creamed mixture, beating until smooth. Beat egg whites with the pinch of salt until reach soft peak. Gently fold egg whites into the cake mixture. Pour mixture into a greased 16x11x2-inch baking pan lined with parchment paper. Bake in a preheated 350 F (180 C) over for approximately 20-25 minutes or until cake tester inserted in center comes out clean. Cool completely, then cover with plastic wrap. The next day, turn cake up side down on a piece of parchment paper. Remove the paper and split cake into two layers horizontally. Place the two layers together again, and with a heart cutter, cut into small hearts, and set aside. Prepare the syrup, add the sugar in the hot water and stir well until the sugar has dissolved. Add the coffee liqueur and stir well.

Brush one half of the syrup mixture evenly over the bottom layer of the hearts, and let aside. Prepare the filling. In a small saucepan place the cream and cocoa, stirring constantly over medium heat. Bring to boil. Remove from the heat and stir until cocoa has dissolve. Add the chopped chocolate, stirring constantly with a wire whisk until smooth. Add the butter and blend well to combine. Beat the mixture until cool. Spread a small amount of the chocolate mixture over the bottom layer of the hearts, and place the second layer over the chocolate filling. Brush the top of the hearts with the syrup evenly. Place a wire rack in a baking pan, and arrange the hearts on the rack, not to close to each other. Pour chocolate frosting over the each heart, to cover the top and sides. Chill. Remove from the refrigerator 60 minutes before serving. Serves 12-14 hearts.

CHOCOLATE TORTE
Tourta Sokolatas

*1 recipe Cake for Tortes (see index for recipe) add
1/4 cup sugar and 1/2 cup cocoa*
For the chocolate cream filling:
1 cup unsalted butter, at room temperature
2/3 cup confectioner's sugar, sifted
6 eggs, separated
8 ounces semi sweet chocolate, melted with
6 Tbsp of warm water
*2 Tbsp Maraschino, cognac or dark rum liqueur
     (optional)*
1 cup whipping cream, whipped
For the syrup:
1/2 cup sugar, dissolve in
1/3 cup warm water and
*3 Tbsp Maraschino, cognac or dark rum liqueur
     (optional)*
For the chocolate glaze:
1/2 cup or more apple, pear or mixed jam
6 ounces semi sweet chocolate, chopped
2/3 cup scalding cream
1/2 tsp pure vanilla extract
5 raspberries
Confectioner sugar

In the recipe cake for tortes, add the sugar and cocoa into the ingredients then follow the

preparation as directed in cake for tortes. Prepare chocolate filling. Cream the butter until light and fluffy. In a mixing bowl beat egg yolks and 1/3 cup of the sugar with a wire whisk over double boiler, over very low heat until thick and creamy and has a yellow color, whisking constantly. Remove from heat and beat until cool. Add to the butter mixture and beat well to combine. Add the cool melted chocolate and maraschino if desired; mix well. Chill. In a mixing bowl beat egg whites with a pinch of salt with a wire whisk over double boiler, over very low heat until gets thick. Gradually add the remaining 1/3 cup of sugar to the egg whites and beat until holds soft peaks, whisking constantly. Remove from heat while continuing to whisk until cool. Fold in chocolate mixture. Add the whipped cream and fold. Place one cake layer in the spring form pan, brush with the syrup evenly and spread 1/3 of the chocolate filling. Place the second cake layer over the filling. Repeat layers; cover and chill over night. Gently remove sides of the pan and place the torte on a dish. Lightly spread top and sides of the torte evenly and smooth with the jam. Return to the refrigerator. Prepare the chocolate glaze. Add scalding cream to the chopped chocolate and vanilla and mix well with a whisk. Place a rack in a baking pan and place the torte on the rack with out the dish. Slowly pour hot chocolate glaze in the middle of the torte to cover top and sides. Chill. Place the torte on a round serving dish and arrange raspberries in the middle of the torte and dust them with a little of confectioner's sugar and chill until ready to serve.

COCONUT TORTE
Tourta Karythas

For the crust:
2 cups finely ground almonds, skins on
5 Tbsp all-purpose flour
8 egg whites
Pinch of salt
1 cup sugar
1 tsp pure vanilla extract or pure coconut extract
For the cream filling:

1 recipe cream filling for tortes (see the index)
For the frosting:
1 1/2 cups whipping cream, whipped with
1/4 cup confectioner's sugar, sifted and
1 tsp pure coconut extract
2-3 cups unsweetened coconut

Prepare meringue. Mix ground almonds and flour together. Beat egg whites with a pinch of salt until frothy. Gradually add sugar and beat until holds soft pick add vanilla and mix. Gently fold in almond mixture with a rubber spatula. Grease and line with parchment paper and grease again and floured three 9x13-inch baking sheets. Spoon the meringue onto the prepare pans and spread evenly with a blade spatula. Bake the meringues in a preheated 350 F (180 C) oven in the middle rack for approximately 15 minutes or until lightly golden. Gently remove from baking sheets leave the paper on and cool on racks. Prepare the cream filling as directed. Cool completely. Gently fold in the cream 1cup of the coconut and 1 cup of the whipped cream. Line with plastic wrap a 9x13-inch baking pan, let the plastic to extend up the sides of the pan (with the overhanging plastic will cover the torte). Assembling the torte. Remove the parchment paper from the meringues one at a time as you go. Place one meringue in the prepare pan, spoon 1/3 of the cream mixture and spread evenly. Place the second meringue over cream. Repeat layers. Cover well with the overhanging plastic wrap, to prevent of drying and chill overnight. Gently lift the plastic wrap from the torte and hold tight to lift the torte and place on a serving dish. Gently remove the plastic wrap from the torte. Lightly frost sides and top with the whipped cream. Generously sprinkle with the remaining coconut. Chill and serve with a cup of Greek coffee.

❧❦❧

CRANBERRY-ORANGE TORTE
Cranberry-Portokali Tourta

For the cake:
1 recipe cake for tortes (see index for recipe)
For the syrup:
1/2 cup warm water

1/2 cup sugar
1/4 cup dark rum
For the cream filling:
1 recipe for cream filling for tortes
For cranberry-orange marmalade:
1 1/2 cups cranberries
1/2 cup sugar
1/2 cup orange marmalade
For the topping:
1 1/2 cups whipping cream
2 Tbsp confectioner sugar, sifted
1 tsp pure vanilla extract

Prepare the cake as directed. Dissolve sugar in the warm water and add the rum, set aside. Prepare the cream filling as directed. While the cream filling is cooling, place cranberries and sugar in a 2-quart saucepan, bring to boil, reduce heat and cool slowly until thick. When cool add the orange marmalade and stir well to combine. Beat the whipping cream with the sugar and vanilla, and chill. When the cream filling is cool add one cup of the whipped cream and fold gently. Place one cake layer in the spring form pan, and brush with the prepared syrup. Spoon one half of the cream filling, and spread evenly. Place second cake layer, brush with the syrup, spoon one half of the cranberry orange mixture, and spread evenly. Place third cake layer, brush with the syrup, spoon the remaining cream filling over, and spread evenly. Place fourth cake layer, brush with the syrup, spoon the remaining cranberry orange mixture, and spread evenly. Cover and chill for overnight. Decorate top and base of torte with the remaining whipped cream. Chill until ready to serve.

❧❦❧

CREAM FILLING FOR TORTES
Krema yia Tourtes

3 cups scalding milk
1/2 cup sugar
5 Tbsp all-purpose flour
3 Tbsp cornstarch
5 egg yolks, beaten with
1 cup milk
2 Tbsp unsalted butter
1 tsp pure vanilla extract

Combine sugar, flour, cornstarch and beaten egg yolks, beat well using a wire whisk. Gradually stir in scalding milk and cook slowly on top of a double boiler, whisking constantly until mixture thickens. Cover and cook for 5 minutes longer. Remove from heat. Add butter and vanilla and mix well to combine. Cover with plastic wrap, the plastic will touch the cream, to prevent a skin from forming. Cool and use as directed.

HAZELNUT TORTE
Tourta Fountoukiou

For the cake:
3/4 cup unsalted butter
1 cup sugar
4 extra large eggs
1 tsp pure vanilla extract
1 3/4 cups all-purpose flour, sifted with
4 tsp baking powder, and
3/4 cup cornstarch
1/4 cup milk
1 cup unsalted blanched finely ground hazelnuts
For the syrup:
3/4 cup sugar, dissolved in
1 cup warm water and
2 Tbsp cognac, brandy or dark rum liqueur (optional)
For the filling:
1 recipe Cream filling for tortes (see index)
For the frosting:
1 1/2 cups whipping cream, whipped with
1/4 cup confectioner sugar, sifted and
3/4 tsp pure vanilla extract
3/4 cup chopped unsalted blanched
*   toasted hazelnuts*
Maraschino cherries

Cream butter and sugar until light and fluffy. Add eggs one at a time, beating thoroughly after each one is added. Add vanilla. Gradually add flour mixture alternately with the milk, beating until smooth after each addition. Add ground hazelnuts and mix thoroughly. Pour mixture into well greased and floured 10-11-inch spring form pan. Bake in a preheated 350 F (180 C) oven on the middle rack for approximately 45 minutes. Cool. Remove from the pan. Turn upside down on a flat dish. Cover. The next day split cake into four layers horizontally. Prepare cream filling. Follow recipe and preparation as directed. Place one cake layer in the spring form pan. Brush with the syrup evenly and spread with 1/3 of the filling. Place the second cake layer over the filling. Repeat layers; cover and chill over night. Gently remove the sides of the pan and place the torte on a serving dish, adjusting strips of parchment paper to fit just under its edges. Frost sides and top of torte with whipped cream. Sprinkle top with chopped hazelnuts. Decorate with maraschino cherries. Gently remove the paper strips and chill.

KATAIFI TORTE
Kataifi Serai

For the crust:
1 pound kataifi shredded pastry (thawed)
1 cup melted clarified unsalted butter or margarine
For the syrup:
21/2 cups sugar
1 2/3 cups water
1 Tbsp fresh lemon juice
1/2 tsp vanilla
For the cream filling:
3 cups scalding milk
1/2 cup sugar
5 Tbsp all-purpose flour
3 Tbsp cornstarch
5 egg yolks, from extra large eggs, beaten with
1 cup milk
1 Tbsp unsalted butter
1 tsp pure vanilla extract
21/2 cups whipped cream
Maraschino cherries

Gently separate kataifi pastry. Lay kataifi evenly in a 9x13x3-inch baking pan. Sprinkle with the hot melted butter if desired. Bake in a preheated 350 F (180 C) oven for approximately 30 minutes or until golden brown. Cool to lukewarm. While kataifi is cooling prepare the syrup. Combine syrup ingredients in a four-quart saucepan. Bring to a boil stirring constantly to dissolve the sugar, reduce heat to medium and boil for 5 minutes. Spoon hot syrup over kataifi, cover with plastic wrap, let stand until cool. Prepare the cream filling. Combine sugar, flour, cornstarch and beaten egg yolk mixture, beat well using a wire whisk. Gradually stir in scalding milk and cook slowly on top of double boiler, whisking constantly until mixture thickens. Cover and cook for 5 minutes longer. Remove from heat. Add butter and vanilla, mix well to combine. Cover with a piece of plastic wrap, touching the cream, to prevent a skim from forming. Chill. Gently remove crust from pan and place on a serving dish. Spoon cream filling over the crust and spread evenly. Cover top with whipped cream. Chill over night. Cut into squares and place one cherry on each square. Chill and serve.

KOK PASTRY

For the cake:
6 eggs, separated
1/8 tsp salt
2/3 cup sugar
1 cup plus 2 Tbsp flour, sifted with
1 tsp baking powder
1 tsp pure vanilla extract

For the filling:
1 recipe cream for tortes (see index for recipe)
Follow recipe and preparation as directed
1 cup whipped cream
For the topping:
4 ounces bittersweet chocolate

Prepare cake. Beat egg yolks with 1/3 cup sugar until thick and creamy, add vanilla and stir well. Beat egg whites until frothy, gradually add remaining 1/3 cup sugar and beat until holds stiff peak. Gently fold egg whites alternately with flour to egg yolk mixture. Fill a pastry bag and #9 tip with the pastry and make 24 about 4-inch rounds, on a baking sheets lined with parchment, 1 1/2-inch apart, then fill inside of the rounds. Bake in preheated 400 F (205 C) oven on middle rack 8 minutes or until golden. Remove from oven and cool. Prepare filling as directed in recipe. Fold in whipped cream and chill 1 hour. Fill a pastry bag and #7 tip with cream filling and cover half of the rounds. Gently top with remaining rounds without pressing down. Chill

60 minutes before serving, melt the chocolate and gently dip only the top of the pastry, and chill. Arrange in serving dish and serve with a cup of Greek coffee. Make 12 koks.

LEMON-ORANGE TORTE
Tourta me Lemoni ke Portokali

For the cake:
1 recipe cake for tortes (see index), and add
Grated rind of 2 oranges
Grand Marnier
For the filling:
1/2 cup fresh lemon juice
1 cup fresh orange juice
3 Tbsp all-purpose flour
1/2 cup sugar
2 Tbsp unsalted butter or margarine
1 tsp pure vanilla extract
Confectioner's sugar, sifted

Follow recipe and preparation as directed in cake for tortes and add the orange rind. The next day remove the paper and split the cake into three layers horizontally. Prepare the filling. In a 3-quart saucepan add the juices, flour and sugar and whisk well to combine. Cook slowly until thickens, whisking constantly. Remove from the heat and add the butter and vanilla and mix well to combine. Cover with a piece of plastic wrap, the plastic with tough the cream, to prevent a skin from forming. Cool. Place one cake layer in the same spring form pan you have baked the cake. Generously brush with the Grand Marnier and spoon one half of the lemon-orange filling and spread evenly. Repeat layers. Cover the torte with a piece of plastic wrap, to prevent of drying, and chill overnight. Remove the sides of the spring form pan and gently lift the torte. Place the torte on a round serving dish. Sprinkle sides and top with confectioner's sugar. Chill.

MILFEY PASTRY
Pasta Milfey

*1 box (171/4-ounces) frozen puff pastry sheets
(thawed)*

For the filling:
3 cups scalding milk
6 Tbsp all-purpose flour
3 Tbsp cornstarch
3/4 cup sugar
Pinch of salt
4-5 egg yolks, beaten with
1/2 cup milk
1 Tbsp unsalted butter
1 tsp pure vanilla extract
1 cup whipped cream (optional)
Confectioner sugar for dusting

Combine sugar, flour, cornstarch and beaten egg mixture, beat well using whisk. Gradually whisk in scalding milk, and cook slowly on top of a double boiler, whisking constantly until mixture thickens. Cover and cook 5 minutes longer. Remove from heat. Add butter and vanilla, mix well. Cover with plastic wrap. Plastic will touch cream to prevent skin from forming. Let cream stay until cool. Place cream if you wish on a bed of ice. Thaw pastry sheets in box at room temperature 30 minutes, or overnight in refrigerator. Unfold pastry on lightly floured surface, one at a time. Roll out each into 9x15-inch rectangle, and cut into 3 strips, each strip 3x15-inch. Place strips in baking sheet and poke with a fork on the surface. Repeat with second sheet of pastry. Chill 60 minutes or more. Bake pastry in preheated 400 F (205 C) oven 15 minutes or until is golden. Remove from oven and let cool. On a rectangle-serving platter, place one pastry sheet, and spread with 1/4 of the cream filling. Place second pastry sheet over cream, and cover with 1/4 of the filling, and top with third pastry sheet. Repeat with other 3 strips. Makes two pastries. Chill uncovered a few hours or overnight. Sift top of pastry with confectioner's sugar. Slice each pastry into 6-8 pieces with serrated knife and serve. Serves 12-16.

❧❧❧

MILK CHOCOLATE TORTE
Tourta Serano

For the cake:
1 recipe Cake for Tortes (see index for recipe)

For the chocolate cream filling:
2 cups heavy cream or whipping cream,
    whipped with
1/4 cup confectioner's sugar, sifted and
1 tsp pure vanilla extract
5 extra large eggs, separated
1/2 cup confectioner's sugar, sifted
8 ounces semi sweet chocolate, melted with
4 Tbsp warm water
2 Tbsp maraschino, cognac or dark rum (optional)
For the syrup:
1 cup milk
1/4 cup sugar
4 Tbsp maraschino, cognac or dark rum (optional)
Pistachio nuts and maraschino cherries

Follow recipe and preparation as directed in cake for tortes. Prepare chocolate cream filling. In a mixing bowl beat egg yolks and sugar with a wire whisk over double boiler, over very low heat until thick and creamy and has a yellow color, whisking constantly. Remove from the heat and beat until cool. Add cool melted chocolate, vanilla and liqueur if desired. Beat well to combine. In a mixing bowl, beat egg whites with a wire whisk over double boiler, over very low heat until the mixture gets thick and holds soft peaks, whisking constantly. Remove from the heat while continuing to whisk until cool. Fold the beaten egg whites in the egg chocolate mixture and whipped cream (keep 2/3 of a cup for decoration). Stir milk, sugar and liqueur until sugar has dissolve to make the syrup. Place one cake layer in a 9x13x3-inch baking dish. Brush with the syrup and spread 1/4 of the cream filling. Place the second cake layer over the cream. Repeat layers; finish with cream filling. Cover and chill overnight. Use whipped cream to decorate with lattice design. Arrange cherries and pistachio nuts on top the torte. Chill.

❧❧❧

MOSAIC TORTE
Tourta Mosaiko

1 cup unsalted butter, at room temperature
1 1/2 cups confectioner's sugar, sifted
4 extra large eggs, separated
Pinch of salt
1 tsp pure vanilla extract

2 Tbsp cognac or dark rum
1/4 cup good quality cocoa, sifted
1 cup chopped toasted blanched almonds
2 pkg. (7-ounces each) Pettit Beurre Biscuits
1 1/2 cups whipping cream, whipped with
1/4 cup confectioner sugar, sifted and
1 tsp pure vanilla extract
1 cup sliced toasted blanched almonds

Place biscuits in a large plastic bag close it and pound until all the biscuits are about 1/3-inch pieces (don't over pounded). Cream the butter until light and fluffy. In a mixing bowl beat egg yolks and 1/2 cup of the sugar with a wire whisk over double boiler, over very low heat until thick and creamy and has a yellow color, whisking constantly. Remove from the heat and beat until cool. Add egg yolk mixture, the vanilla and the cognac to the butter and mix well. Gradually add cocoa, chopped almonds and biscuits and mix well to combine. In a mixing bowl, beat egg whites with a pinch of salt with a wire whisk over double boiler, over very low heat until the mixture gets thick. Gradually add the remaining 1/2 cup of sugar and beat until holds soft peaks, whisking constantly. Remove from the heat while continuing to whisk until cool. Fold in chocolate mixture. Add 1 1/4 cups whipped cream and fold. Place the mixture into a 10-inch spring form pan. Cover and chill over night. Gently remove the sides of the pan. Place a large piece of parchment paper on the counter and place the sliced almonds. Place one hand under the cake to hold it and with the other hand sprinkle all around the sides of the cake with the sliced almonds. Place the cake on a round serving dish and decorate the top with rosettes or any other design you desired. Chill.

※◦✕◦※

NOUGAT TORTE
Tourta Nougatina

For the crust:
2 cups finely ground almonds, skins on
5 Tbsp all-purpose flour
1 tsp cinnamon
8 egg whites

1 cup sugar
For the cream filling:
1 recipe Cream Filling for Tortes (see index)
For the frosting:
2 cups whipping cream, whipped with
1/3 cup confectioner's sugar, sifted and
1 tsp pure vanilla extract
1/2 cup chopped toasted blanched
      almonds for decoration and
Maraschino cherries

Prepare meringue. Mix ground almonds, flour and cinnamon. Beat egg whites with a pinch of salt until frothy. Gradually add sugar, and beat until holds soft pick. Gently fold in almond mixture with a rubber spatula. Grease and line with parchment paper and grease again and flour 2 baking sheets and trace 3 rounds on them 10-12-inch in diameter. Spoon the meringue onto the traced rounds and spread evenly with a blade spatula. Bake the meringues in a preheated 350 F (180 C), on the middle rack of the oven, for approximately 15 minutes or until lightly golden. Gently remove from baking sheets and leave the paper on and cool on racks. Prepare the cream filling as directed. Assembling the torte. Remove the parchment paper from the meringues one at a time as you go. Place one meringue in a 10-12-inch spring form pan and spread 1/3 of the cream mixture. Place the second meringue over the cream. Repeat layers. Cover the torte with plastic wrap, to prevent drying, and chill overnight. Remove the sides of the spring form pan, and gently lift the torte. Place the torte on a serving dish. Frost the sides and the top of the torte with the whipped cream. Sprinkle the top of the torte with chopped almonds, and decorate the base and the top of the torte with whipped cream and cherries. Chill and serve with a cup of Greek coffee.

※◦✕◦※

ORANGE TORTE
Tourta Portokaliou

For the cake:
1 recipe Cake for Tortes (see the index for recipe)
For the cream filling:

1 recipe Cream Filling for Tortes (see the index for recipe)

For the syrup:
1/2 cup orange marmalade, mixed with
1/2 cup frozen concentrated orange juice (thawed) and
1/4 cup Grand Marnier (liqueur)

For the frosting:
1 1/2 cups whipping cream, whipped with
2/3 cup confectioner's sugar, sifted with
3 Tbsp cocoa, and
1 tsp pure vanilla extract, and
1 Tbsp water
1/2 cup chopped unsalted and toasted pistachio nuts or blanched toasted almonds

Follow recipe and preparation as directed in cake for tortes. Follow recipe and preparation as directed in cream filling for tortes. Prepare syrup; combine syrup ingredients together. Assembling the torte. Place one crust in the spring form pan; generously brush with the orange mixture and spread evenly 1/3 of the cream filling. Place the second crust over the cream and brush again with the orange mixture. Repeat layers. Cover the torte with a piece of plastic wrap, to prevent of drying, and chill overnight. Prepare the frosting. Gently remove the sides of the spring form pan, and gently lift the torte. Place the torte on a serving dish. Frost the sides and the top of the torte with the whipped cream mixture. Sprinkle the top and sides of the torte with the pistachio nuts if desired. Chill and serve with a cup of Greek coffee.

❧❀❧

ORANGE-PISTACHIO NUT TORTE
Tourta me Portokali ke Fistikia Eginis

6 extra large eggs, at room temperature
3/4 cup sugar
Grated ring of 1 orange
1 1/4 cups all-purpose flour, sifted with
1 Tbsp cornstarch and
1 Tbsp baking powder
4 Tbsp melted butter, at room temperature

For the syrup:
1/3 cup sugar
1/3 cup water
1/4 cup Grand Marnier

For the filling:
1 cup or more orange marmalade

1 cup toasted unsalted pistachio nuts, chopped

For the topping:
1 cup heavy cream, whipped with
2 Tbsp confectioner sugar, sifted and
1/2 tsp pure vanilla extract

In a large mixing bowl beat eggs with sugar with a wire whisk over simmering water (double boiler) until the mixture has the temperature of 115 F (46 C). Remove from the heat and beat with an electric mixer until thick and has lemon color. Gradually fold orange rind and flour mixture into egg mixture then add the butter and fold well to combine. Pour into a 13x17x1-inch baking pan lined with greased parchment paper and spread evenly. Bake in a preheated 400 F (205 C) oven for 15 minutes or until golden. Cool completely. Cover with plastic wrap. When ready to use, release the sides of the cake with a knife and turn quickly onto parchment paper, remove the paper from the cake and trim sides. Cut into three or four strips (layers) crosswise. Dissolve sugar in water and Grand Marnier. In a rectangular serving platter, place one cake layer, brush with 1/4 of the sugar mixture. Spread 1/3 of the orange marmalade if you have four layers and sprinkle with 1/4 of the chopped pistachio nuts. Top with second cake layer. Repeat layers. Cover with plastic wrap and chill for few hours. Spread sides and top with whipped cream and sprinkle with the remaining pistachio nuts. Chill. Cut into slices and serve with a cup of Greek coffee.

❧❀❧

PINEAPPLE-STRAWBERRY PRESERVES
Anana ke Fraoule Marmelatha

3 pounds ripe firm strawberries
1 pound peeled fresh pineapple, cut into cubes
1 1/2 cups water
5 1/2 cups sugar
1 tsp pure vanilla extract

Select ripe, firm, juicy strawberries. Wash the berries and drain well. Then pick them over. Remove the stems and hulls. Halve large strawberries. Set aside. In a large pot combine the water and sugar. Bring mixture to boil, reduce heat to medium and cook for 3 minutes. Add the pineapple cubes to the syrup, bring to a boil, and reduce heat to medium and cook for 10 minutes. Add the vanilla and stir well. Add strawberries, stir well, bring to a boil, reduce heat and cook for about 20 minutes or until syrup thickens. Remove from heat and spoon hot preserve immediately into sterilized hot pint jars. Screw on hot lids. Let cool completely. Store in a cool dry place. Makes 4-5 pints.

PUMPKIN TORTE
Tourta Kolokythas

For the crust:
1 recipe cake for tortes (see the index for recipe)
For the pumpkin filling:
2 cups scalding milk
1 cup sugar
4 Tbsp all-purpose flour
4 Tbsp cornstarch
5 extra large egg yolks, beaten with
1/2 cup cream or milk
2 cups fresh cooked, well drained mashed pumpkin
Pinch of salt
1/2 tsp cinnamon
1/2 tsp pumpkin pie spice
3 Tbsp unsalted butter
For the syrup:
1/4 cup sugar, dissolved in
1 cup milk
For the frosting:
1 1/2 cups whipping cream, beaten with
1/3 cup confectioner's sugar, sifted and
1/2 tsp pure vanilla extract
1 1/4 cups or more finely chopped walnuts

Follow recipe and preparation for the cake as directed. Prepare cream filling as directed. Combine sugar, flour, cornstarch and beaten egg yolks, beat well using a wire whisk. Gradually stir in scalding milk and cook slowly on top of a double boiler, whisking constantly until mixture thickens. Add the mashed pumpkin, salt, cinnamon and pumpkin pie spice to the cream and whisk well to combine. Cover and cook for 5 minutes longer. Remove from heat. Add butter, and mix well. Cover with a piece of plastic wrap,

the plastic will touch the cream, to prevent a skin from forming. Cool. Add 1/2 cup of the walnuts and mix well. Assembling the torte. Place one crust in the spring form pan, brush with syrup and spread evenly with 1/3 of the cream filling. Place the second crust over the cream. Repeat layers. Cover the torte with a piece of plastic wrap, to prevent of drying and chill overnight. Gently remove the sides of the spring form pan, and gently lift the torte. Place the torte on a serving dish. Frost the sides and the top of the torte with the whipped cream and sprinkle the top and sides with the walnuts. Decorate base and top of torte with whipped cream if desired. Chill, and serve with a cup of Greek coffee.

STRAWBERRY CHARLOTTE TORTE
Tourta Charlotte me Fraoula

41/2 cups scalding milk
1 cup sugar
1 Tbsp. cornstarch
7 egg yolks, beaten with
1/2 cup milk
3 envelopes unflavored gelatin
1 1/2 cups whipping cream, whipped with
1/3 cup confectioner's sugar, sifted
1 Tsp. vanilla
2/3 cup strawberry jam
5 Tbsp rum
2 pkgs. Ladyfingers

Combine sugar, cornstarch and beaten egg yolks with milk and beat well using a whisk. Gradually stir in scalding milk and cook slowly on top of a double boiler, whisking constantly until mixture lightly thickens. Gradually add gelatin into hot cream, stirring constantly. When the gelatin has dissolved, remove from heat. Cool completely. Fold in whipped cream. Stand ladyfingers around the sides of a 10-inch spring form pan. Line bottom with more ladyfingers. Mix 1/3 cup jam with 3 Tbsp of the rum and brush the ladyfingers. Pour the cream mixture into prepared pan. Arrange some of the ladyfingers on top of the cream as you desired. Cover and chill overnight. Remove the sides of the pan leaving the bottom.

Place the torte on a serving plate. Boil 1/3 cup of the remaining jam with 2 Tbsp. of the remaining rum for 3 minutes. Spread top evenly with jam mixture and chill again 1 hour or longer.

❀❀❀

STRAWBERRY TORTE
Tourta Fraoulas

For the cake:
1 recipe Cake for Tortes (see the index for recipe)
For the cream filling:
1 recipe cream filling for tortes (see the index for recipe)
For the syrup:
1 1/2 cups chopped fresh strawberries, mixed with
1/2 cup sugar and
1/3 cup rum and chill
For the frosting:
1 1/2 cups whipping cream, whipped with
1/3 cup confectioner's sugar, sifted and
1 tsp pure vanilla extract
Whole strawberries (pick the strawberries the same size)

Prepare the cake as directed. Prepare the cream filling as directed. Assembling the torte. Place one cake layer in the spring form pan. Brush with the strawberry-sugar liquid and sprinkle with 1/3 of the chopped strawberries. Spoon 1/3 of the cream filling and spread evenly. Place the second cake layer over the cream filling. Repeat layers. Cover the torte with a piece of plastic wrap, to prevent of drying, and chill overnight. Remove the sides of the spring form pan and gently lift the torte. Place the torte on a serving dish. Frost sides and top of the torte with the whipped cream and decorate the base and top with decorating tip, as you desired. Arrange whole strawberries or cut into half. Chill.

❀❀❀

STRAWBERRY WHIPPED CREAM CHARLOTTE TORTE
Sarlot Fraoulas me Cream Santigi

2 envelopes unflavored gelatin
1 cup sugar
4 extra large eggs, separated
Pinch of salt
1/2 cup water
1 pound or more small fresh strawberries, washed and well drained
1/3 cup fresh lemon juice
2 cups whipping cream, whipped with
1/2 cup confectioner's sugar, sifted and
1 tsp pure vanilla extract
1/2 cup strawberry jam
3 Tbsp rum
8 ounces ladyfingers (about)

In a double boiler add the gelatin, 1/2 cup of the sugar, egg yolks, salt and water, and mix well to combine. Stirring the mixture constantly over lightly simmering water, until the gelatin dissolved. Remove from the heat, cover and let cool completely. While the gelatin mixture is cooling, prepare the strawberries. Slice one half of the strawberries and sprinkle with the lemon juice. Add the sliced strawberries with the lemon to the gelatin mixture, and stir well. Beat the egg whites with a pinch of salt until hold a soft pick. Add the remaining 1/2 cup sugar and beat until hold stiff pick. Fold in the egg whites and 3/4 of the whipped cream to the cool gelatin mixture. Stand ladyfingers around sides of a 10-inch spring form pan. Line bottom with more of the ladyfingers. Mix the jam with the rum, and brush the ladyfingers. Pour the gelatin mixture into the prepare pan. Cover, and chill overnight. Remove the sides of the pan leaving the bottom. Place the torte on a serving dish. Spread to of the torte with the remaining whipped cream and decorate with the whole strawberries. Chill again.

❀❀❀

TIRAMISU GREEK STYLE

For the cake:
2 extra large eggs
1/2 cup sugar
1/2 tsp pure vanilla extract
1/2 cup all-purpose flour, sifted with
1/2 tsp baking powder
For the syrup:
3/4 cup evaporated milk
1/4 cup coffee liqueur
For the filling:
6 ounces Philadelphia cream cheese, at room temperature
1 cup whipping cream

1 small envelope instant vanilla pudding
1 1/4 cups milk
Cocoa powder for dusting

Prepare cake. Beat eggs until frothy, gradually add sugar and beat until thick. Add vanilla. Fold in flour. Pour into 10-inch baking pan, lined with parchment paper. Bake in a preheated 350 F (180 C) oven on the middle rack for approximately 15 minutes or until golden brown. Cool for 10 minutes, remove from the pan and cool completely on ware rack. When the cake is completely cool, remove the paper, and spoon the syrup over until is soaked. Prepare the topping. In a blender combine the cream cheese, whipping cream, instant vanilla cream, milk and the remaining of the syrup if any. Beat until thick. Spread over the prepare cake and spread evenly. Dust the surface of the tiramisu with cocoa powder. Chill until ready to serve.

❧❀❧

TRIPLE CHOCOLATE TORTE
Tourta Sokolatas

For the cake:
1 recipe Chocolate Cake for Tortes (see index)
For the chocolate filling:
3/4 cup scalding whipping cream
12 ounces bittersweet chocolate
2 Tbsp unsalted butter, at room temperature
1 tsp pure vanilla extract
3/4 cup sugar
41/2 Tbsp water
3 Tbsp light corn syrup
3 egg whites, at room temperature
For the syrup:
1/3 cup hot water
1/2 cup sugar
3 Tbsp brandy or cognac
1/2 cup whipping cream, whipped
Maraschino cherries

Prepare the cake as directed. Prepare the syrup to brush the cake and let cool. Cut the chocolate with a sharp serrated knife into very thin slices. Add the chocolate into the scalding milk and stir until is melted. Add butter and stir well to combine. Set aside. In a small saucepan, add the sugar and the water, bring to boil, reduce heat

and simmer until is thick syrup. To tasted, drop a drop of syrup in cold water, lifted with your finger and if it is hart is ready. Add the corn syrup and cook for 1 minute. Remove from the heat. While the syrup is simmering, beat the egg whites until very stiff. Gradually add the hot syrup while you are beating the egg whites. Keep beating until is cool. Fold in egg whites in to chocolate mixture. Assembling the torte. Place one cake layer in the spring form pan, and generously brush with the syrup. Divide the chocolate mixture into four parts. Spread 1 part of the chocolate mixture. Place second cake layer, repeat layers. Finish with the third cake layer. Remove the parchment paper and brush with the remaining syrup. Cover and chill for 3 hours. Gently remove sides of the pan and place on a rack with a larger pan under it. Pour the remaining chocolate in the middle of the cake and spread top and sides evenly. Chill for few hours. Gently remove the torte from the rack and place on a serving platter. Decorate with whipped cream and maraschino cherries.

❧❀❧

WALNUT TORTE
Tourta me Karythia

6 extra large eggs, separated
9 Tbsp sugar
1 tsp vanilla extract
12 Tbsp finely ground walnuts
9 Tbsp finely ground Zwieback toast
2 tsp baking powder
1/2 cup cognac or brandy
For the syrup:
2 cups sugar
2 cups water
1 Tbsp fresh lemon juice
For the frosting:
2 cups heavy cream, whipped with
1/4 cup confectioner sugar, sifted and
1/2 tsp pure vanilla extract
2 cups finely chopped walnuts, lightly toasted

Beat egg yolks with sugar until thick and creamy. Add vanilla. Combine dry ingredients together. Gradually add alternately with cognac to the egg mixture and mix well. Gently fold in stiffly beaten egg whites. Spoon into 10-11-inch spring form pan lined with parchment paper. Bake in a preheated 350 F (180 C) oven for approximately 45 minutes. Let cool. Remove from pan turn cake up side down on a flat dish and cover with plastic wrap, let stay overnight. Split cake into three layers horizontally. Combine syrup ingredients together in a two-quart saucepan, bring to a boil, reduce heat to medium-low and boil for 5 minutes. Generously brush the cake layers with the hot syrup until you have used it all. Cover and let cool completely. Place layers of parchment paper strips on a round serving platter in such a way that they can be slipped out from sides and ends of cake after frosting the cake. Set one cake layer on the prepare platter, spoon the 1/4 of the whipped cream and spread evenly. Set the second cake layer on top the whipped cream. Repeat layers. Spread the remaining whipped cream all around the sides of the cake. Then, with the palm of one hand, brush the toasted walnuts all around the torte. Scatter walnuts also on top. Gently cover and chill over night or for a day or two.

WALNUT-ORANGE TORTE
Tourta me Karythia ke Portokali

6 extra large eggs, separated
3/4 cup sugar
Grated rind of 1 orange
1 cup finely ground walnuts
1 cup finely ground Zwieback toast
1 tsp cinnamon
2 tsp baking powder
1/2 cup cognac or brandy

For the syrup:
2 cups sugar
2 cups water
1 Tbsp fresh lemon juice

For the frosting:
2 cups heavy cream, whipped with
1/4 cup confectioner's sugar, sifted and
1/2 tsp pure vanilla extract
2 cups finely chopped walnuts, lightly toasted

Beat egg yolks with sugar until thick and creamy. Add orange rind. Combine dry ingredients together. Gradually add walnut mixture to egg

mixture alternately with cognac if desired and mix well. Beat egg whites with a pinch of salt until stiff but nut dry. Gently fold the beaten egg white into the egg-walnut mixture. Spoon into 10-11-inch spring form pan lined with parchment paper. Bake in a preheated 350 F (190 C) oven for approximately 45 minutes. Let cool. Remove from pan turn cake up side down on a flat dish and cover with plastic wrap, let stay overnight. Split cake into three layers horizontally. Combine syrup ingredients together in a two-quart saucepan, bring to a boil, reduce heat to medium-low and boil for 5 minutes. Generously brush the cake layers with the hot syrup until you have used it all. Cover and let cool completely. Place layers of parchment paper strips on a round serving platter in such a fashion that they can be slipped out from sides and ends of cake after frosting the cake. Set one cake layer on the prepare platter, spoon the 1/4 of the whipped cream and spread evenly. Set the second cake layer on top the whipped cream. Repeat layers. Spread the remaining whipped cream all around the sides of the cake. Then, with the palm of one hand, brush the toasted walnuts all around the torte. Scatter walnuts also on top. Gently cover and chill over night or for a day or two.

BREAD PUDDING WITH MUSCAT SAUCE
Poudinga Psomiou me Saltsa Moscatou

3 medium ripe pears, pared, halved, cored, and chopped
1/4 cup currants
1/3 cup Muscat wine (Greek sweet wine from island Samos)
6 slices white bread, cubed
2 cups scalding milk
4 well-beaten eggs
1/2 cup sugar

For the sauce:
5 egg yolks
1/2 cup sugar
2 tsp cornstarch
1 1/4 cups milk
1 1/4 cups cream
1 strip lemon zest
1/3 cup Muscat wine

In small bowl, combine pears, currants and wine. Let stand 40 minutes. In large bowl place bread cubes, pour milk over and let stand 15 minutes. Add pear mixture, sugar and eggs, to bread mixture, and stir well. Divide between 8 well-greased individual ramekins, or in one large gratin dish. Place ramekins in deep roasting pan; pour boiling water into pan to come halfway up sides of ramekins. Bake in preheated 350 F (180 C) oven 40 minutes, or until cake tester inserted in center of pudding comes out clean. Remove from oven, let stand until cool. Chill. Serve in ramekins or unmold if desired. Serve with Muscat sauce. Serves 8. While the pudding is chilling, prepare sauce. In small bowl, beat egg yolks, sugar and cornstarch until well blended. While egg yolks are blending prepare milk mixture. In small saucepan, combine milk, cream and lemon zest and bring to boil. Turn off heat and let stand 6 minutes. Remove zest from milk and discard. Gradually pour milk mixture into egg mixture, stirring constantly with wire whisk. Return mixture to saucepan. Cook slowly on top of double boiler, whisking constantly until mixture thickens enough to coat spoon. Do not boil sauce. Remove from heat; let cool. Stir in Muscat wine. Serve immediately over pudding or place plastic wrap directly on surface and chill.

※◦※◦※

CHOCOLATE MOUSSE
Mous Sokolatas

2 cups scalding milk
5 extra large egg yolks
1/2 cup sugar
Pinch of salt
1 tsp pure vanilla extract
10 ounces bittersweet chocolate, coarsely grated
1/4 cup cognac or brandy
1 1/2 cups whipping cream, whipped
1 (7-ounces) Pettit Beurre biscuits, chopped into
    very small pieces
1/2 cup milk

Combine eggs, sugar, salt and vanilla, mix well using wire whisk. Gradually stir in scalding milk and cool slowly on top of a double boiler, whisking constantly until mixture lightly

thickens. Remove from heat, add chocolate and 2 Tbsp cognac if desired, stirring until chocolate is melted. Cover with plastic wrap, touching cream to prevent skin from forming. Chill 3 hours or until set. Beat chocolate mixture with electric mixer until creamy and fluffy. Fold in 1 1/2 cups whipped cream. Add remaining cognac to milk, stir well. Divide chopped biscuits into wide champagne or wine glasses, sprinkle with milk mixture, and cover with chocolate mixture. Cover each with plastic wrap as before. Chill. When ready to serve mousse, decorate with whipped cream, and place maraschino cherry on top.

※◦※◦※

CHOCOLATE SOUFFLÈ WITH CREAM SAUCE
Socolata Soufflé me Crema

8 Tbsp unsalted butter
3/4 cup all-purpose flour, sifted
2 1/2 cups scalding milk
1 1/4 cups sugar
3 extra large eggs, separated, plus 2 egg yolks
Pinch of salt
1/2 cup cocoa powder, sifted
1 tsp pure vanilla extract
3 Tbsp cognac or brandy (optional)
For the cream topping:
1 extra large egg yolk
1/3 cup sugar
1/2 tsp pure vanilla extract
1 Tbsp cognac or brandy (optional)
1 1/4 cups scalding milk
8 small individual soufflé cups
Unsalted butter for brushing
Sugar for sprinkling

In 2-quart saucepan melt butter, and blend in flour, using wire whisk, until smooth. Remove from heat, gradually add milk, whisking continuously, add 3/4 cup sugar and pinch of salt. Bring to boil, cook 3 minutes, stirring continuously. Remove from heat. Lightly beat 5 egg yolks, with cocoa, vanilla, and cognac if desired until smooth. Gradually add to flour the milk mixture, stirring continuously until combined. Cover mixture with plastic wrap, touching cream to prevent skin from forming. Let cool. Beat egg white with pinch of salt, until holds soft peak. Gradually add 1/2 cup sugar and beat until holds stiff peak. Gently fold egg whites in cream mixture. Spoon mixture in prepared soufflé cups. Arrange cups in baking pan. Bake in preheated 350 F (180 C) oven on middle rack 30 minutes. Remove from oven. While soufflé is baking, prepare cream topping. Combine egg yolk, sugar, vanilla and cognac if desired and mix well using wire whisk. Gradually stir in scalding milk, and cook slowly on top of a double boiler, whisking constantly until mixture lightly thickens or covers back of a spoon. Make a dip slit with a spoon in middle of each soufflé, and spoon some of cream on top. Serve immediately. Serves 8.

CHOCOLATE SOUFFLÈ
Soufflé Sokolatas

4 Tbsp unsalted butter
4 Tbsp all-purpose flour
1/2 cup sugar, dissolved in
1 1/2 cups scalding milk
4 ounces bittersweet chocolate, cut into
    small pieces
5 extra large eggs, separated
1 tsp pure vanilla extract
Pinch of salt
Butter to grease
Sugar to sprinkle

Melt butter over medium heat blend in flour until smooth using whisk. Gradually add milk whisking constantly until mixture is thick and smooth. Add chocolate, stir until melted. Remove from heat. Gradually add egg yolks and vanilla, beat well to combine. Cool. Beat egg whites with pinch of salt until holds soft peak. Fold egg whites into he chocolate mixture. Spoon mixture in greased and sprinkled with sugar a 6-7-cup soufflé dish. Bake in preheated 350 F (180 C) oven on middle rack 40-45 minutes or until firm to touch and well risen. Serve immediately with creme fresh or whipped cream if desired.

CREAM CARAMEL
Krema Karamele

3/4 cup sugar

3 Tbsp water
8 extra large eggs
1/8 tsp salt
3/4 cup sugar
1 tsp pure vanilla extract
5 cups scalding whole or 2 % milk

In heavy small frying pan combine 3/4 cup sugar and 3 Tbsp water. Bring to boil, reduce heat to medium-high, cook until golden brown shaking pan frequently. Pour immediately into an 11-cup bundt pan and before it hardens move pan about so the caramel will coat sides and bottom of pan. Let caramel harden while you prepare cream. Beat eggs with salt and sugar until frothy. Add vanilla and beat well to combine. Gradually add milk beating constantly. Pour egg mixture into prepared caramelized pan. Set in pan of hot water and bake in preheated 300 F (165 C) oven on middle rack 60 minutes or a knife blade inserted in center come out clean. Cool completely. Chill overnight. The next day, remove from refrigerator and gently invert cream caramel into a round serving dish. Cut and serve with caramel syrup.

CREAM CARAMEL IN INDIVIDUAL RAMEKINS
Krema Karamele se Atomika Formakia

6 extra large eggs
Pinch of salt
3/4 cup sugar
3/4 tsp pure vanilla extract
1 cup heavy cream, mixed with
23/4 cups scalding milk
8 small ramekins
1/2 cup sugar

Beat eggs with salt until frothy. Add sugar and vanilla and beat until thick and light. Gradually add milk, stirring lightly. Spoon mixture into 8 ramekins. Set in pan of hot water and bake in preheated 300 F (165 C) oven on middle rack 45 minutes or until firm. A knife blade run into the center of cream comes out clean. Cool completely. Chill overnight. The next day cover surface of cream with sugar. Place prepared ramekins under grill in preheated oven 3 to 5 minutes until sugar is caramelized. Remove from oven, cool completely. Chill until ready to serve. Serves 8.

CREAMY RICE PUDDING

Rizogalo

3/4 cup boiling water
1/2 cup sort or long grain rice
1/4 tsp salt
71/2 cups milk
4 Tbsp cornstarch
3/4 cup more or less sugar
Ground cinnamon for sprinkle

Pick over rice, wash thoroughly. Add rice and salt to boiling water, stir, cover and cook slowly until water evaporates. Add 7 cups milk, stirring well, bring to boil and cook slowly 30 minutes, stirring occasionally. Dissolve cornstarch in remaining milk and gradually add to rice mixture, add sugar, stirring constantly; bring to boil, cook in low heat 5 minutes. Remove from heat, spoon in bowls, sprinkle with cinnamon. Chill.

PUMPKIN MOUSSE

Kolokytha Mous

4 cups cooked, mashed pumpkin (1 small pumpkin)
1/3 cup unsalted butter
1/4 tsp salt
1/2 cup finely ground Zwieback toast
Grated rind of 1/2 orange
1/2 tsp cinnamon
1/2 cup honey
1 1/2 cups finely chopped walnuts
1 cup or less sugar
1 1/2-2 cups whipping cream, whipped with
1/4 cup confectioner sugar, sifted and
1 tsp pure vanilla extract
Fresh mint leaves for decoration (optional)

Prepare pumpkin as directed in Butternut or Pumpkin Pita (see index). Melt butter in medium saucepan. Add 4 cups mashed pumpkin, sauté a few minutes, add salt, stirring constantly. Remove from heat; add ground toast, grated rind, cinnamon, honey, sugar, 1 cup walnuts, mix thoroughly. Set aside until cool. When ready to serve fold in whipped cream except 1 cup. Serve in glass bowls, dollop with remaining whipped cream, sprinkle with remaining walnuts, decorate with mint. Serves 10-14.

STRAWBERRIES IN CUSTARD

Fraoules se Crema

2 pounds strawberries, hulled, washed, cut in fourths
3 Tbsp sugar
Juice of one lemon
For the custard:
5 cups scalding milk
5 extra large egg yolks
1/4 cup sugar
1 tsp baking powder
1 tsp pure vanilla extract
1 cup cream
6 Tbsp sugar

In bowl place strawberries, sugar and sprinkle with lemon juice, stir well and chill. Prepare custard. In bowl beat egg yolks with sugar using whisk until thick and creamy. Add baking powder, vanilla and gradually stir in scalding milk, cook slowly on top of double boiler, whisking constantly until lightly thickens. Remove from heat, gradually add cream, stirring constantly. Cover with plastic wrap touching cream to prevent skin from forming. Cool. Divide strawberries in 6 to 8 small ramekins. Spoon custard over strawberries, cover and chill. When ready to serve, sprinkle sugar over custard to cover surface. Place under broiler until sugar melts and caramelizes. Serve immediately.

STRAWBERRY MOUSSE

Mous Fraoula

1 1/2 pounds hulled and rinsed strawberries
1/4 cup fresh lemon juice
3/4 cup sugar
2 envelopes unflavored gelatin
8 ounces whipping cream
1 8 ounces plain yogurt

Place strawberries in food processor and process until they are mashed. In 4-quart saucepan pour strawberries, lemon juice and sugar. Sprinkle gelatin over strawberry mixture, stir and let stand 5 minutes. Stir over low heat until gelatin completely dissolves, about 2-5 minutes. Cool completely. Beat whipping cream, add yogurt and beat 6 seconds. Fold whipped cream mixture with strawberry mixture. Spoon strawberry mousse into lightly greased tub pan and chill 8 hours or overnight. Invert mousse in round serving dish and garnish with small strawberries.

HONEYDEW MELON GRANITA
Granita Peponi

4 cups water
1 1/4 cups honeydew melon, mashed into a
    food processor or in a food mill
1/3 cup fresh lemon juice
1 cup fresh orange juice

Combine water and sugar in 4-quart saucepan, bring to boil, stir to dissolve the sugar; boil 5 minutes. Cool completely. Add mashed melon, lemon juice and orange juice to syrup and mix well to combine. Pour into a 9x1x3-inch stainless baking pan. Freeze 3-4 hours. Remove from freezer and with a spoon cut into small pieces and process in food processor until looks like shaved ice. Place granita into plastic container, cover and freeze again. When ready to serve, scrape granita with spoon and serve in wide champagne glasses.

MANGO GRANITA
Granita Mango

4 cups water
1 1/4 cups sugar
4 cups ripped mangos, mashed in a
    food processor or in a food mill
1/3 cup fresh lemon juice
1 cup fresh orange juice

Combine water and sugar in 4-quart saucepan, bring to boil, stir to dissolve sugar; boil 5 minutes. Cool completely. Add mashed mangos, lemon juice and orange juice to syrup and mix well. Pour into a 9x13x3-inch stainless baking pan. Freeze 3-4 hours. Remove from freezer and with a spoon cut into small pieces and process in food

processor until looks like shaved ice. Place granita in plastic container, cover and freeze again. When ready to serve, scrape granita with a spoon and serve in wide champagne glasses.

PEACH GRANITA
Granita Yiarma

4 cups water
2 cups sugar
4 cups ripped peaches peeled and mashed in
    a food processor or in a food mill
1/3 cup fresh lemon juice
1 cup fresh orange juice
1 tsp pure almond extract

Combine water and sugar, bring to boil, stir to dissolve sugar; boil 5 minutes. Cool completely. Add mashed peaches, lemon juice, orange juice and almond extract to syrup and stir well. Pour into 9x13x3-inch stainless baking pan. Freeze 3-4 hours. Remove from freezer and with a spoon cut into small pieces and process in a food processor until looks like shaved ice. Place granita in plastic container, cover and freeze again. When ready to serve, scrape granita with a spoon and serve in wide champagne glasses.

STRAWBERRY GRANITA
Granita Fraoulas

4 cups water
2 cups sugar
4 cups strawberries, mashed in a food processor
2 Tbsp fresh lemon juice

Combine water and sugar in 4-quart saucepan, bring to boil and stir well to dissolve sugar. Cool completely. Add mashed strawberries and lemon juice to syrup and mix well. Pour into 9x13x3-inch stainless baking pan. Freeze 3-4 hours. Remove from freezer and with spoon cut into small pieces and process in a food processor until looks like shaved ice. Place granita in plastic container, cover and freeze again. When ready to serve, scrape granita with spoon and serve in wide champagne glasses.

POPI'S HANDY TIPS

Adding Liquid to Pot:
1-When pot needs water added (after it reduces), put water into hot lid to warm before adding to pot.
2-Condensation from pot lid should be returned to pot only if additional liquid is needed, otherwise throw into sink.

Béchamel Sauce:
Remove pot with butter and flour mixture from heat before adding milk. Return to heat until sauce is ready. This way you never have lumps in your sauces.

Cakes:
1-After you pour cake mixture in pan, bounce pan on counter top to pop bubbles.
2-Don't over beat cake and cookie batter, or your cakes and cookies will not be crispy.Custard

Custard Cream:
Put a piece of plastic wrap on top of cooked cream and press all the way down to touch top of cream. This prevents a skin from forming.

Eggs:
1-Add salt to the water when you boil eggs, and they peel easily.
2-Beat egg whites with a pinch of salt or tsp of sugar, whip starting slowly.

Frying:
When frying with a lid, remove frying pan from heat for about a minute or two before lifting top to turn or remove the food; this prevents spattering, which can burn you.

Herbs:
Cut springs of herbs (such as parsley, dill, or mint). Wash well several times in cold water, then dry. Spread on towel and roll it. Place in refrigerator overnight. The next day, fill a plastic bag very tightly, and roll the bag with the herbs. Secure with a rubber band. Place bags in a Ziploc and freeze. To use, just take out of the bag and slice herbs as needed.

Smoking Butter:
When frying with butter: if it starts smoking, add a little olive oil to cool the butter.

Tomatoes:
1-Wash and core tomatoes, then freeze them. When ready to use, run under warm water to peel easily.
2-Wash and core tomatoes, cut in half crosswise. Squeeze one tomato half at a time with your hand to remove seeds. Place cut side of tomato on wide side of grater and coarsely grate until all tomato is grated and only skin is left. Discard skin and repeat same procedure with remaining tomatoes.

Tomato Sauce:
When you are cooking tomato sauce, remove the saucepan from the heat for about a minute or two before lifting top to stir the sauce, or to serve, to prevent spattering, which can burn you.

Liquid Measurements:
If you want only 1 cup of water or any other liquid but are usinga 2-cup measure: spill out liquid until bottom rim (when tilted) meets bottom edge.

INDEX

TRAHANA SOUP 26
TURKEY AVGOLEMONO SOUP 26
VEGETABLE SOUP 26

SALADS
ARTICHOKES SALAD 27
BEET APPLE WALNUT SALAD 27
BEET SALAD 27
BOILED BEEF SALAD 27
CABBAGE APPLE SALAD 28
CABBAGE SALAD 28
CHICKEN OR TURKEY CABBAGE APPLE SALAD 28
MACARONI SALAD W/ FETA CHEESE 28
MACARONI SALAD 28
MEAT SALAD IN A MOLD 29
POTATO SALAD 29
RICE SALAD W/ FETA CHEESE 29
RUSSIAN SALAD GREEK STYLE 30
SHRIMP OR LOBSTER SALAD 30
SHRIMP SALAD 30
SPRING SALAD 30
SPRING SALMON SALAD 31
SUMMER COUNTRY STYLE SALAD 31
SUMMER RICE SALAD 31
TOMATO SALAD 31
TOMATO SURPRISE SALAD 32
VEGETABLE SALAD 32
WALNUT-YOGURT AND FRUIT SALAD 32

SEAFOOD
BAKED FISH FILLETS W/ LEEKS 33
BAKED FISH W/ LEMON 33
BAKED FISH W/ ONIONS AND TOMATOES 33
BRAISED SHRIMP IN GARLIC SAUCE 34
BREADED FLOUNDER 34
CODFISH CROQUETTES 34
CODFISH PATTIES 34
COD FISH AU-GRATIN 35
COD FISH GRATINEE 35
CODFISH RAGOUT 36
FILLET OF FLOUNDER ROLLS W/
    AVGOLEMONO SAUCE 36
FILLET OF SOLE W/ FETA CHEESE 36
FISH AND SHELL FISH AU-GRATIN 37
FISH BALLS AVGOLEMONO 37
FISH SHISH KEBOB 38
FRIED CODFISH W/ GARLIC SAUCE 38
FRIED SHRIMP W/ TOMATO SAUCE 38
FRIED SHRIMP 39
FRIED SQUID 39
GRILLED RED SNAPPER OR PORGY 39

HOW TO BOIL AND CLEAN A LOBSTER 39
LOBSTER AU-GRATIN 40
MUSSELS RICE PILAF 40
MUSSELS W/ SPAGHETTI 40
OCTOPUS IN WINE 41
SALMON W/ LINGUINI 41
SEAFOOD W/ RICE PILAF 41
SEAFOOD W/ SPAGHETTI 41
SEAFOOD W/ SPINACH AU GRATIN 42
SHRIMP CROQUETTES 43
SHRIMP RAGOUT W/ RICE PILAF 43
SHRIMP W/ LINGUINE 43
SHRIMP W/ MUSHROOM AND RICE 44
SHRIMP W/ PIQUANT SAUCE ON RICE 44
SHRIMP W/ RICE 44
SQUID IN WINE 45
STEAMED FISH 45

MEATS

BEEF
BAKED MEATBALLS W/ CUMIN 46
BEEF CUTLETS IN PUFF PASTRY 46
BEEF ESCALOP W/ MARSALA SAUCE 47
BEEF KAPAMA W/ RICE 47
BEEF KAPAMA W/ SPAGHETTI 47
BEEF RAGOUT W/ EGGPLANT 48
BEEF RAGOUT W/ PEAS 48
BEEF SOFRITO 48
BEEF TENDERLOIN W/ MUSHROOMS 48
BEEF STIFATHO 49
BEEF W/ OREGANO 49
BEEF W/ WINE 49
FILLET MIGNON ATHENIAN 50
FILLET MIGNON GRATINEE 50
FILLET MIGNON IN FILLO PASTRY 50
FILLET MIGNON IN MADERA SAUCE 51
FILLET MIGNON IN VERMOUTH SAUCE 51
FRIED MEATBALLS 51
HAMBURGERS 52
HAMBURGERS W/ BEEF AND LAMB 52
LAYERED BEEF MEDALLIONS GRATINEE 52
LEMON ROAST BEEF SUPREME 53
MEATBALLS AVGOLEMONO 53
MEATBALLS W/ SPINACH 53
MEAT PATTIES IN MARSALA SAUCE 56
MEAT STUFFED CREPES 56
SMALL MEATBALLS W/ PILAF 55
STUFFED FLANK STEAK ROLL UP 55
STUFFED GROUND MEAT ROLLUP 55
STUFFED MEAT ROLL 56
TAS KEBOB 56

LAMB

ATZEM PILAF 57
BAKED CHEESE STUFFED LEG OF LAMB 57
BAKED LAMB COUNTRY STYLE IN FILLO PASTRY 58
BAKED LAMB SHANK W/ KRITHARAKI YOUVETSI 58
BAKED LAMB W/ KRITHARAKI 58
BAKED SPINACH STUFFED LEG OF LAMB 59
BAKED STUFFED BREAST OF LAMB 59
BAKED STUFFED EASTER LEG OF LAMB 60
EASTER BAKED STUFFED SUCKLING LAMB 60
EASTER BAKED SUCKLING LAMB 61
FRIED LAMB LIVER W/ SAUCE PIQUANT 61
GRILLED LAMB CHOPS 61
GYROS 61
LAMB AND MUSHROOMS W/ KRITHARAKI 62
LAMB CHOPS CUTLETS 62
LAMB CHOPS IN PUFF PASTRY 62
LAMB FRICASSEE 63
LAMB KAPAMA W/ RICE 63
LAMB KAPAMA W/ SPAGHETTI 63
LAMB RAGOUT W/ EGGPLANT 63
LAMB RAGOUT W/ PEAS 64
LAMB ROLL UPS IN FILLO PASTRY 64
LAMB SOUVLAKIA 64
LAMB W/ ARTICHOKES AVGOLEMONO 65
LAMB W/ PEAS AVGOLEMONO 65
LAMB YOUVETSI W/ KRITHARAKI 65
LEG OF LAMB COUNTRY STYLE 66
ROASTED LEG OF LAMB W/ POTATOES 66
SUCKLING LAMB ON A SPIT 66

PORK

HOMEMADE FRESH SAUSAGES 67
ROAST PORK LOIN 67

VEAL

VEAL CUTLETS 68
VEAL CUTLETS AU GRATIN 68
VEAL CUTLETS W/ CHEESE 69

GAME

DEER STIFATHO 69
GRILLED DEER STEAKS 69
HARE OR RABBIT KAPAMA W/ PASTA 69
HARE OR RABBIT STIFATHO 70
ROASTED LEG OF DEER 70

POULTRY

BAKED LEMON CHICKEN 71
BRAISED CHICKEN IN WINE 71
BREAST OF CHICKEN CUTLETS W/ CHEESE 71
CHICKEN BREAST W/ WINE (L.CH. L.FAT) 72
CHICKEN AND CHEESE STUFFED PEPPERS 72
CHICKEN AND PEPPERS W/ RICE PILAF 72
CHICKEN OR TURKEY CROQUETTES 73
CHICKEN OR TURKEY FILLETS IN WINE SAUCE 73
CHICKEN OR TURKEY RICE GRATINEE 74
CHICKEN OR TURKEY W/ MUSHROOM-
      PEA GRATINEE 74
CHICKEN RICE PILAF IN MUSHROOM
      MARSALA SAUCE 74
CHICKEN ROLL-UPS 75
CHICKEN STIFATHO 75
CHICKEN W/ EGG CREAM SAUCE 75
CHICKEN W/ GARLIC 76
CHICKEN W/ OKRA 76
QUAILS W/ RICE PILAF 76
ROASTED SPICED CHICKEN AND POTATOES 77
ROASTED STUFFED TURKEY 77
STUFFED BREAST OF CHICKEN 77
TURKEY BREAST CUTLETS ROLL UPS 78
TURKEY BREAST CUTLETS 78
TURKEY MEATBALLS W/ CUMIN (L.CH. L.FAT) 79
TURKEY MOSAIC IN FILLO PASTRY 79
TURKEY OR CHICKEN SOUFFLÈ 79
TURKEY W/ EGG-CREAM SAUCE GRATINEE 80

HOMEMADE PASTRY & PITA

BUTTERNUT-PUMPKIN SQUASH CHEESE PITA 81
BUTTERNUT OR PUMPKIN SQUASH PITA 81
CHICKEN OR TURKEY AND HAM PITA 82
CHICKEN OR TURKEY AND SPINACH PITA 83
CHICKEN OR TURKEY PITA 83
CHICKEN PITA IN PUFF PASTRY 84
CLARIFIED BUTTER OR MARGARINE 84
HOMEMADE PASTRY FOR TYROPITAKIA 84
HOMEMADE PASTRY FOR PITA 85
KREATOPITA W/ HOMEMADE PASTRY 85
LAMB PITA 86
LEEK AND RICE PITA 86
LEEK CHEESE PITA 87
MIXED VEGETABLES PITA 87
MUSHROOM-HAM AND CHEESE PITA 88
MUSHROOM AND LEEK IN FILLO PASTRY 88
PUMPKIN CHEESE PITA W/ HOMEMADE PASTRY 89
RUSTIC SPINACH PITA 89
SCALLIONS CHEESE PITA 90
SPANAKOPITA A 90
SPANAKOPITA W/ PUFF PASTRY 91
SPINACH TART W/ PUFF PASTRY 92
SUMMER YELLOW SQUASH PITA 92
TYROPITA A 92
TYROPITA B 93

217

218

CHEESE & EGGS

BREADS, CAKES & COOKIES

DESSERTS